Occupation: Prizefighter

Occupation: Prizefighter

Andrew Gallimore

seren

Seren is the book imprint of
Poetry Wales Press Ltd
Nolton Street, Bridgend, CF31 3AE
www.seren-books.com

ISBN 978-1-85411-395-5

The publisher works with the support of the Welsh Books Council

Printed in Plantin by CPD (Wales), Ebbw Vale

Contents

Acknowledgements

Thanks go as always to Lydia for pretty much everything; my mum and dad for all their support and hospitality; Nanette and John for the 'office'; Peter and Paul for motivation and Bernie for inspiration. I'd also like to thank Patricia Meola and Robert Hageman from the Summit Historical Society, Sue Moore from the Chatham Township Historical Society, Shelby Coffey III, Thomas Staley, Steven Isenberg, Matthew J. Bruccoli and James Lardner. The following establishments also deserve a special mention: the New York Public Library, the Newark Free Library, the National Archives and Records Administration in Washington DC, the New York Municipal Archives and Patrick Kavanagh's at 33rd & Third.

Prologue

Broadway the Invincible

The previous night's thunderstorm finally offered some respite from the heat, but it was to bring only temporary relief. As the morning sun broke through the clouds the humidity was so great that the dirty white streets of Hell's Kitchen were more oppressive than ever. Along West 52nd Street dozens of people clustered on the steps of ice-cooled theatres, basking in the chill emanating from lobbies they couldn't afford to enter. Outside Edward Devlin's funeral parlour a solitary man shuffled around on the shadeless sidewalk. He'd been there, weeping, since the sun first rose over the East River in the early hours. Through the window Devlin recognized him as Young Griffo, an old-time boxer no longer fit for fighting, but a familiar figure on Broadway. Back in the days when Young Griffo really was young, he was so fast that his party piece was catching a fly in mid-flight between thumb and forefinger before setting the unharmed insect free. The undertaker stepped out into the blazing heat, put his arm around the bulky frame of the old fighter and sent him to Eighth Avenue. "Go around to the Boyertown Chapel this afternoon," he told the old man. "He'll be laid out there."

The next visitors to Devlin's were a bunch of 'palookas', small-time fighters from Lou Stillman's gym, boxing togs under their arms, stopping to see the body of a champion. There followed a trickle of shabby men whose cauliflower ears and twisted noses betrayed their profession. At the corner where West 52nd meets the Great White Way, a newspaper hoarding informed the neighbourhood that it had lost one of its own. Under the headline 'Ex-Champ Worn Out By Low Punches Of Broadway' that morning's *New York Daily News* reported:

> Broadway the invincible, the champion double crosser of all time, which no man ever licked and which no man ever will, erased another name yesterday from the roster of celebrities who helped build up its reputation.
> Freddie Welsh, former light-weight champion of the world, and as game a scrapper as ever bowed before a cheering populace from the centre of a squared circle, was its victim.

By mid-afternoon the mercury had hit the mid-nineties. Outside the St. Paul Hotel on 60th Street children had opened so many fire hydrants that a policeman, armed with a wrench, was sent to patrol

the block. Inside the hotel the live-in housekeeper was telling
newspapermen how the "big fellows" of boxing, who had been her
estranged husband's friends, had neglected him in his time of
trouble. Brahna Weinstein, formerly Brahna Welsh, was forced to take
a menial job after her husband became depressed and started to
drink. When Freddie was world champion, the family had a home in
the best apartments at the St Paul, overlooking Central Park and
complete with its own library. Now Brahna changed the linen and
cleaned the bathrooms. She'd not lived with Freddie for several
months, but she visited frequently. Indeed she called at his cheap
hotel room just off Broadway a few days before he died. She'd been
told of Freddie's death within minutes of the maid finding his body.
Her husband was just forty-one years old. "This is a hard boiled age.
When you're up you're way up, but when you're down you are sure
down," Brahna told the reporters. "Freddie knew them all when he
was on top, but none of them knew him when he was down and out."
She said that when Freddie had money any friend could get it from
him; but when he lost it none of them "gave him a tumble". They
didn't even invite him to the big fights any more: Freddie Welsh, who
was a champion and fought the best of them in his day. Bitterly, she
told the assembled pack how Freddie had asked New York State
Athletic Commissioner William Muldoon for a job, any job, but the
official wrote back to say there was no place for him. Freddie had
repeatedly tried to raise money to meet mortgages due on a health
farm he owned in New Jersey and even his championship belt had
been pawned for $100. She was particularly angry with Jack
Dempsey, who Freddie had supported when he was accused by the
press of being a 'slacker' following the United States' entry into the
Great War. Brahna said that Freddie had written newspaper articles
to disprove the allegations made against Dempsey just before he won
the world heavyweight championship from Jess Willard in 1919. She
claimed to have telegrammed Dempsey on the day of his recent fight
with Jack Sharkey to ask him to visit Freddie. She got no reply. "He
wouldn't even come to see Freddie last week when he was sick," said
Brahna. "Freddie wrote and asked Jack to stop in and say hello, and
Dempsey didn't even answer the letter. My man was proud, and
when the men he had lavished money and attention on, turned away
from him, it just broke his heart, that is all."

   They may not have visited him in his time of trouble, but the great
and the good of the boxing world turned up to say farewell to the
former lightweight champion. The day after he died over five
thousand people visited the chapel to pay their last respects. A

procession of sporting celebrities, actors and fight fans belied talk about a hero forgotten. One of the New York papers described how "the men whom she [Brahna] had denounced when the boxer's death became known, as having deserted him when he was in financial straits, did their inarticulate best to show their affection for him as he lay on his bier". He may have spent his last days alone and penniless, but in death, Freddie Welsh regained the trappings and standing of the rich man he once was. "All day long the body of the erstwhile champion and captain of the United States Army, clad in the uniform he earned during the World War, lay in state, with candles flickering and sheaves of expensive flowers filling the air with heavy fragrances," reported the *New York Herald Tribune*, "and to this opulent corner came the citizens of fistians, great and little, paying tribute to a fallen hero".

The more prosperous element of the boxing fraternity told of their surprise at Freddie's demise. The former champion hadn't asked them for help, because he had been too proud to do so they said. Joe Lynch, the former bantamweight champion, went to visit the body at Devlin's and said that he'd met with Freddie just before his death, and that he'd made no mention of any financial problems. "He seemed in good spirits when I saw him a few weeks ago. I asked him how he was getting on and he said, 'fine'. He didn't tell me he needed money. He could have had it from me," Lynch claimed.

Pride was a family trait. Freddie's brother Stanley was also living in the United States, working in the automobile business in New Jersey. On the day of the funeral, Stanley took particular offence at reports of Freddie's financial predicament at the time of his death. "I cannot imagine why she [Brahna] would give the impression that he was penniless," said Stanley, who did everything in his power to change the impression that his brother died poor. Stanley told reporters that Freddie's one great ambition in life was to make his family independent and that he succeeded. Freddie had no living relatives besides his brother and an uncle and aunt in Wales "who would be broken-hearted if they heard the story of his poverty," said Stanley. He also claimed to be "perfectly sure" that Freddie still owned $129,000 in real estate, with property valued at $83,000 in California and $46,000 on lots around Bayside, Long Island. All of this was still drawing money according to Stanley. Others had a more realistic grasp of Freddie's finances. Edward Devlin, the undertaker who had charge of the funeral, dismissed Stanley's comments and told reporters that Freddie "died without a nickel". The boxing promoter Humbert Fugazy had arranged for Devlin to take over the

funeral arrangements, the services and the burial. Fugazy was generally credited for persuading Freddie to first don a pair of gloves. Dan
McKetterick, another old friend from the early days, helped with the
arrangements. Baron Long, who managed the Jefferies Arena near
Los Angeles where Freddie fought many of his biggest bouts, sent a
telegram offering to pay all the funeral expenses. Within days of
Freddie's death these men raised a trust fund for the dead boxer's
two children, Elizabeth who was thirteen at the time, and eleven-
year-old Freddie Jr.

Freddie Welsh was cremated on July 30th 1927. It was, according
to one scribe, "a perfect summer's day". The heat wave had finally
broken and a cool breeze swept through the streets and avenues of
Manhattan. The funeral service was held at Boyertown Chapel,
tucked away behind Times Square. The chapel smelled of lilies and
sweat. The wreaths were from many of those castigated by Brahna a
few days previously: Jack Dempsey, Philadelphia Jack O'Brien,
Benny Leonard and Tex Rickard. The first to bring flowers was
Robert Emmet Boyle, an old fighter who'd lost a leg. Boyle counted
Freddie as the best friend he ever had. The two met while Boyle was
begging on the streets of San Francisco in the days when Freddie was
at the height of his fame. Later, when Boyle killed a man in a street
brawl and was sent to serve a life sentence in San Quentin, Freddie
succeeded in getting him paroled into his custody at the Walter Reed
Hospital in Washington DC, where he was working in a rehabilitation
programme for wounded soldiers. Another caller was the Reverend
Elbert Kay of the Episcopal Monastic Order of St John the
Evangelist, who learned of Freddie's death while on a train from
Boston to Washington and decided to get off at New York to say a
prayer over the body. Among the pallbearers was Benny Leonard, the
man who'd taken the world title from Freddie ten years earlier.
Leonard had sent a wreath with one word, "Sympathy". Other
pallbearers included the former featherweight champion Johnny
Dundee, former light-heavyweight champion Mike McTigue and
former featherweight world titleholder Abe Attell.

Freddie was a Universalist. He believed that everyone eventually
reached heaven after death and that formal religion was irrelevant
and unnecessary. In line with his beliefs he did not want a public
funeral, but Brahna had consented to the wishes of his friends.
Freddie's two children were taken to a summer camp at Hope Farm
in Burbank, New York. Their mother stopped them attending the
funeral. Five hundred people showed up at the chapel while
hundreds more stood in the street. It was a brief ceremony; Reverend

Frank Cox read the service for the dead, but there was no singing or music. Freddie was, however, accorded a military funeral and was cremated in the uniform he wore as a captain in the United States Army. Eight soldiers, under Major Rowe from Governors Island, were sent by orders from the War Department in Washington. The Stars and Stripes was draped around the casket and the military rites simply consisted of the soldiers standing to attention. No rifles were fired. The soldiers later formed an aisle through which the flag-draped coffin was carried into the street. Freddie was still a captain in the reserve corps and had hoped to be commissioned a major in fall of that year. "He had plenty of friends yesterday," said Brahna on the day after the funeral.

After the ceremony his body was cremated at Fresh Pond, Queens, New York State. A few weeks later a tribute in *The Ring* magazine read:

> Such is the way of the world! One day a hero, with millions of hero worshippers at your door; the next, a down-and-outer with none to offer succor!
>
> Poor Freddy Welsh! Nothing but his ashes as the only visible remains of a champion who fought the greatest men of his time, a wizard of boxing, a teacher of ring art, and a soldier!
>
> Captain Freddy Welsh, we salute your memory. May your soul rest in Peace!

One

A Rebel by Birth and Nature

Morgan Thomas' face was stained walnut brown by pickling solution. The vinegar toughened the skin and made it more resistant to cuts. His fists had been hardened by curing in brine. Morgan Thomas was a champion mountain fighter, a peculiarly Welsh strain of the Sweet Science. He plied his trade on the 'bloody spots' scattered across the bare moorlands of the South Wales coalfield, away from the prying eyes of the authorities. Thomas and his backers, followed by large crowds, trudged up mountain tracks where the valleys narrow steadily as they bite deeper into the hills. A ring would be rigged up using railway sleepers for corner posts and coiled wire stolen from colliery workings for the ropes that slashed open a lattice of scars across the fighters' backs. These men fought bare-knuckled brawls, often fuelled by personal animosity, for stake money and side bets. Rounds ended only when one of the combatants fell to the ground and if the stricken fighter was able to recover in thirty seconds and come up to scratch, the fight would go on. A bout would often last thirty, forty or even fifty rounds or more until one of the combatants, occasionally dead or dying, could fight no more.

Morgan Thomas' son, John, became a respected and successful auctioneer. John's son, Frederick, became Freddie Welsh, lightweight champion of the world. "I suppose that I take after my grandfather more than my father," Freddie once wrote. "He never spoke a word of English in his life, and he was generally content to take life as he found it. My father, on the other hand, was a very particular person about his clothes, appearance, and mode of life generally. He was a strict observer of the conventions, and I have never been able to cultivate a liking for any of them."

Frederick Hall Thomas was born at 17 Morgan Street, Pontypridd, on Friday, March 5th 1886. The town is compressed into a cluster of hillsides at the point where the Taff and Rhondda valleys meet. At the end of the nineteenth century Morgan Street was a stretch of blue-grey houses, squeezed in between the black river and the black railway, and home to the new town's new professional classes. Nearly everything in Pontypridd was new at this time. Just a generation earlier it had been a small village at a convenient crossing point on the river, but as industrialization spread across the valleys, a town emerged to cater for the needs of the iron and coal settlements upstream. After he became world champion Freddie wrote of his hometown: "As my friend Mr. Elbert Hubbard has said, 'God made the country, man made the cities, but the Devil made the small towns,' and though it is my birthplace I have to confess that Pontypridd was one of his Satanic Majesty's pet edifices. We were a tough collection, and had little to do but fight, at least that is about the only occupation we boys could find, or, rather, the one we preferred to all others."

Satan's edifice was a work in progress when Freddie was growing up. It was a time when the population of Wales was increasing at a rate only exceeded, in percentage terms, by the United States. This was the last surge of the industrial revolution and it created a society that was vibrant, edgy and dangerous. Freddie's home on the corner of Morgan Street shuddered to the sound of endless wagons rolling up and down the valleys, emblazoned with names like the Ocean Coal Company, Marine and Naval, Navigation and Victoria Coal.

Before she married, Freddie's mother was Elizabeth Hall, the daughter of an hotelier from Merthyr. Freddie's father, John Thomas, was a well-liked, very ambitious local man made good. He was always very busy and frequently away from home on business. "He always went for big deals and made good money – and spent it. That trait, by the way, has been my chief inheritance from him," Freddie wrote. Elizabeth Hall Thomas persuaded her often absent husband to buy the Bridge House Hotel in Pontypridd when the boy was a few months old. She ran the business and within a few years Freddie had been joined by a sister, Kate, and a brother, Stanley. But even with two new babies to care for it was the health of her firstborn that concerned Elizabeth the most. The child who would grow to be a great athlete was a sickly, fragile infant. In later life his mother told Freddie that she would often count his ribs and wonder whether they would ever get properly covered with flesh, but that his father used to reassure her by patting his son's chest, and as a joke, predicted that the boy would be a champion one day. A well as being the leading auctioneer of the district John Thomas was one of the town's sportsmen, a particular breed of gentleman who patronised all kinds of athletic pursuits. His main passion was for foot running, which had its origins in the English public schools, but became very popular all over the valleys with races often being staged along the tramways. These road races were held over distances ranging from short sprints to staggered events over hundreds of miles, with big bets wagered on the outcome. Like all of the town's sportsmen and certainly its working men, John Thomas was also a follower of 'the noble art of self-defence', and he decided that a few boxing lessons would

1. The Hall Thomas family, 1891. Rear: Elizabeth and John; front: Kate, Stanley and Freddie

toughen-up young Frederick. These sessions took place behind the bar of the Bridge House Hotel, and when he was just about old enough the unfortunate Stanley was 'invited' to take part. The two toddlers were given a penny each to box in the bar with towels tied to their fists. Because he was taller Freddie had to kneel down in the sawdust for the contest. Fighting and drinking were a popular and often complementary part of everyday life in Pontypridd in the twilight years of the nineteenth century. Indeed if anything rivalled sport as the most popular activity and entertainment it was the pub. But this was a time when the whole land was in the grip of a religious revival that battled with secular pleasures for the soul of the nation. The rise of Methodism in Wales during the eighteenth century had transformed the country. When John Wesley's ideas and later John Wesley in person arrived, deacons combed the land denouncing sinners, and the chapel pulpits resounded to sermons of Sodom and Gomorrah. They preached a self-restrained, teetotal morality that scorned such trivial and worldly pursuits as sports, theatre, the music hall and dancing. The great century of the chapels succeeded in stifling many things, but prizefighting flourished. In August 1897 thousands of men packed the trains and horse-trams to see a big fight at Pandy Field near the square in Tonypandy. After eight rounds of brutal boxing the referee declared a winner, but cheered on by the crowd the loser insisted on fighting on for another four blood-soaked rounds. He died later that night. A few weeks later one of the valley's newspapers, the Rhondda Leader, asked:

> How come it is that in a country where Nonconformity is so strong and boasts of its strength, and the Church of England is also active, that so large a proportion of the colliers spend their leisure in such questionable forms? Is it because they prefer these brutal pastimes, or are they driven to it because there is a complete absence of any form of light and harmless amusement to be found in the village after the day's work is done?

From the time he was a young boy, "light and harmless amusement" held no attraction for Frederick Hall Thomas. One of his best friends as a child in Pontypridd was Tom Davies whose brother Jack was a heavyweight contender. Tom was from the poor side of the tracks and he often went round to the Bridge House and threw pebbles at Freddie's window just to get somewhere to sleep. Tom repaid the debt by teaching Freddie how to box. "We shared bed and money together," Freddie recalled. "It was my bed, and the money came from my mother. I guess I was born with a lucky spoon in my mouth, for looking back from to-day I can remember that it was always easier for me to get a pound from her than it was for Kate and Stanley to get pennies."

Freddie attended a nursery school run by a Miss Evans in Morgan Street and from there he went to Copermaen School. At the age of four he was sent to his first boarding school, Mr McClune's Grammar School, one of the dozens of such establishments that educated the children of Pontypridd's professional classes. Life at McClune's wasn't very different from being the centre of attention at the Bridge House to begin with. He was still a rather weak, unhealthy-looking child and was given extra allowances of milk and the special attention of Miss Mary McClune, the headmaster's daughter. Miss McClune not only dry-nursed the boy but she gave him the biggest dose of discipline he was to get from anyone in authority and even as a four-year-old he was caned several times. Mr McClune, however, spared the rod in Freddie's case but gave him his first lessons in dealing with the tension of waiting in the corner of a ring for a fight to start. Freddie would be sent up for punishment and told to wait in McClune's room, where he would be kept in "all the agonies of suspense and expectation" for about half an hour and then dismissed with a lecture. This was Freddie's introduction to authority and a world of strict rules governing every detail of his life at every moment of night and day, with ferocious punishments for actual or alleged infraction of these rules. He had to grovel to his superiors in order to obtain the slightest privilege or favour, which could, at any time, be removed on a whim. It was also the place where he was first exposed to the practice he despised more than anything – bullying. At McClune's Freddie had his first taste of 'fagging', an organised system of brutality and cruelty in which young boys were frequently kept up until the early hours of the morning, waiting on their seniors and suffering an array of abusive behaviour at their hands. Freddie resolved to be no-one's fag, so his fighting career started. "The bigger boys bullied us generally, as in all schools which I have ever known or of which I have ever heard," Freddie recalled. "I was a rebel by birth and nature, and I wouldn't stand it. I wanted to put a stop to the lecturings I was getting, and so I practised boxing whenever I could with other boys in the lower forms and always fought back whenever anyone started to hammer me." He bought and borrowed books on boxing and practised different punches and defensive movements in front of a mirror at home or at school. For a young boy growing up in a town like Pontypridd, learning to fight, or more importantly, learning to box, was somehow akin to receiving a 'sacred knowledge'.

The accepted wisdom in boxing circles is that Freddie Welsh learned his trade in America, and fought like the Americans fought. Frederick Hall Thomas learned to box in Pontypridd, and fought like a Welshman. "I have seen it repeatedly stated that I learnt all my boxing in America, but that isn't true. I taught myself, and I taught myself at school," Freddie wrote after he became champion. He worked out theories and diligently practised all the moves. Besides boxing with other boys he would give his brother Stanley a penny a time to let him try out a new punch he had thought out or read about. Stanley objected because Freddie hurt him so it was agreed that the younger brother could hold a pillow to protect himself. Stanley was Freddie's first paid sparring partner, but he was by no means the only one. Freddie would go down the street, find another boy, and bribe him with a penny for a few round's work. He eventually engaged scores of sparring partners that cost him a good deal more than the first ones did, but throughout his career Freddie doubted whether any of them were of greater utility.

Those childhood days in Pontypridd ended abruptly however. Freddie's father died and the family began to break apart. His mother, faced with running the hotel alone, sent the three children to live with relatives. Kate and Stanley went to an aunt in Merthyr, while Freddie was sent to Radyr in Cardiff to live with his non-prize-fighting grandfather. From here he attended the local board school but after a year Freddie was homesick and he returned to Pontypridd and his mother at the Bridge House. All the villages and towns in the mining valleys had a tremendous number of public houses and beer shops and Pontypridd boasted the highest number of convictions for drunkenness in the area. One of the town's busiest and most notorious pubs was kept by Freddie's aunt. Regulars at the Bunch Of Grapes made up a healthy proportion of the drunk and disorderly cases brought before local magistrates. Many a Salvationist, armed only with several copies of *The War Cry*, had to run for cover when the ale started to flow at the Bunch of Grapes. For a young boy rather keen on fighting, Pontypridd was a good place to be. On his return to the town Freddie was sent to Graig Board School where his fighting days began in earnest. The boys at the school and around the neighbourhood were a very tough lot. Pontypridd had its very own fight club at the time, with each street or district boasting its own gang. Freddie joined the 'Bridge gang' that patrolled the area looking for a scrap. Challenges were issued as rival factions 'raided' enemy territory, but there was nothing scientific or noble about these fights. Everything went. Sticks, stones and brickbats were used and the youths became the terror of the town.

The 'Gangs Of Pontypridd' took their inspiration from duelling societies at Austrian universities. In the late nineteenth century upper class Austrians and Germans considered fighting as a way to draw a strict line between men of honour and the rest of society. So the duelling scar or bragging scar signified inclusion in a social elite. The true winner was the man who walked away with a prominent scar to show that he'd stood the test. The point was not to punish your opponent, but to show that you could take it. Students too afraid to actually duel would cut themselves with razors and then repeatedly tear open the wound to irritate it, as well as applying salt, wine, and even sewing horsehair in the cut to ensure an angry scar. This was the upmarket tattoo of the day borne by a generation of doctors, jurists,

professors and officials, certifying the owner's claim to manly stature
and cultivated rank. The duelling scar was certain to attract pretty girls
because it signified virility and breeding. Freddie though, wasn't interested in bragging scars or social standing; he just enjoyed fighting.

Eventually the gang fighting became "rather a scandal" as Freddie
described it, so his mother decided to send him away again, this time
to the Higher Grade School in Porth, the next town up the Rhondda
Valley. It was during his spell at this school that Freddie made his first
appearance in the press and to the astonishment of all, especially his
mother, the boy was commended not condemned. In February 1899,
the *Glamorgan Free Press* reported how a twelve-year-old boy named
Frederick Hall Thomas jumped into the Berw Pool on the River Taff
to save a drowning man. The Royal Humane Society presented
Freddie with a scroll for his act of bravery and, for a short period of
time at least, he was a local hero. But his life-saving exploits were
soon forgotten as his enjoyment of fighting showed no sign of
waning. Mrs Thomas decided that Freddie needed greater discipline
than she was capable of issuing so he was sent to Long Ashton
School near Bristol, which numbered among its many famous schol-
ars both Lord Roberts and Dr W.G. Grace, as well as several
international rugby footballers. Her intention in sending him to a
public school was to set him on a journey through various grades of
academia so that the street fighter would become a minister or a
professor. But the English public school system did little to take the
fight out of Frederick Hall Thomas; in fact it just made him a better
practitioner. Freddie had known about Long Ashton's reputation for
producing fine athletes and it was for that reason that he asked his
mother to send him there when it became obvious he would have to
move away from Porth. But the school was celebrated for something
else as well, as Freddie was soon to discover.

In Victorian times the public schools of England gained a reputation for being violent and unspeakably cruel places with highly
organised and brutally disciplined regimes and Long Ashton had a
rich tradition of bullying and hazing. The school operated a house
system with a rigid and finely graded hierarchy among the boys, with
different powers and privileges designated by slight gradations in a
complicated system of uniforms. The power of older boys over
younger ones was formalised under the prefect and house captain
system and backed by the authority of the masters. For a boy from
Pontypridd, where bullying was regarded as the ultimate act of
cowardice, the regime of an English public school was distasteful. He
was used to violence, he enjoyed it, but for Freddie fighting was a

matter of honour and there was certainly no honour in beating boys who had neither the strength nor inclination to fight back.

In later life Freddie spoke of his astonishment at the latitude, and in many instances actual encouragement, accorded by the various head and other masters of English schools to the practice of bullying. The teachers pleaded ignorance and the very first principle of the schoolboy code of honour was that he 'must not sneak'. But the heads of the school and its various houses did not need Freddie to tell them about bullying or bullies. They were victims of the system first and very probably bullies themselves afterwards. Freddie launched a one-boy crusade against the Long Ashton regime as soon as he arrived. One of the school's celebrated traditions was the 'crowning' ceremony, whereby new boys would be initiated by liberal doses of hurt and humiliation. Even at the age of twelve, Freddie was used to receiving and inflicting physical pain. He often punched other boys; in fact he wasn't averse to wielding sticks, stones and even bricks. But this was different. Most of the initiation ceremonies with which a new boy was admitted to his dormitory were revolting as well as painful. Freddie saw no sense in them and no reason for them so he decided to challenge one of the most hallowed of the school's traditions and refused to undergo any initiation ceremony. There was some spirit of sportsmanship about the place however, and it had a tradition that any boy who refused to be crowned could undergo a 'trial by combat': a fistfight against 'the cock' of the dormitory. In practice this was the biggest boy in the house giving a small boy a battering, after which the loser would be crowned with due solemnity and then made to 'run the gauntlet'. This additional punishment involved the whole dormitory arming itself with knotted towels, the knots being as hard and as many as the towels could be made to hold, and then the culprit was stripped naked and thrashed around the room.

"I refused to be crowned, flatly refused, and would sooner have died than submitted. In some schools, I daresay in most, I should probably have been compelled to go through it, or whatever substitute there may have been locally, for in most of these places these ceremonies are held to be intimately associated with the honour of the school," Freddie recalled. So he accepted the challenge and was thrown in with one of the best "rough and tumble scrappers" at the school. The other boys gathered to watch this scruffy, brash boy from Wales get a sound, severe and well-deserved beating. The fight began with 'the cock' lunging at Freddie, who took half a pace back, lightly tapped his assailant on the nose and moved away. The fight continued on in much the same manner with the older boy charging

forward with wild, swinging punches while Freddie jabbed away with
increasing force, each punch clattering against his opponent's face.
His adversary was able to grab Freddie a few times but the young
Welshman allowed himself to be thrown easily whenever they
grappled so as to not waste any strength in struggling. The bigger
boy's eyes were nearly swollen closed and both his nose and mouth
were in sad need of repair before he owned that he had had enough.

Word of Freddie's performance quickly spread through the
school, and the matter of Hall Thomas' one boy rebellion was no
longer confined to the dormitory. It became a scandal and the
honour of Long Ashton was at stake. Here was a new boy who
refused to be induced in accordance with the best traditions of the
school but who'd also proved himself to be the best fighter in his
dormitory and was therefore entitled to be treated with grudging
respect. A 'monitorial conference' decided that another trial of
strength was needed. Two boys were deputed to bring Freddie to
reason, though it was agreed that he was not to be attacked from
behind. One of them was Freddie's former opponent who was still
sore both in mind and body, but imbued with a fair amount of
respect. The other was more ambitious, but neither particularly liked
his job. Two against one outraged the finest of all schoolboy principles; fair play. Freddie was rather badly punished but he still
managed to pull through. On the strength of this double victory he
was allowed to escape the crowning ceremony but instead yielded to
a performance that "had nothing objectionable about it" and the
matter was allowed to pass. "All I can say is that if the Long Ashton
crowning ceremony was calculated to do anything other than
degrade, coarsen, and quite probably ruin a boy's character irretriev-
ably, then all I can say is that I don't know anything of human
nature," Freddie wrote. "I will admit, of course, that the school has
turned out many fine men, who have made great names for
themselves in after life, but I maintain that this has been in spite of
its worst traditions and not because of them."

Later in his Long Ashton career, Freddie was forced to 'run the
gauntlet', an ordeal he later described as "one of the unpleasantest
experiences of my life". He received a particularly fierce beating for
leading a 'fag rebellion', a heinous crime in the eyes of the older boys.
These ceremonies were allowed to continue and even to flourish
unchecked simply and solely because they were the most hallowed
traditions of the school, and because every new boy had been forced
to undergo them since the school was first founded. It was inconceiv-
able to Freddie how any man who could recall his experiences of this

nature could rest quiescent on the matter. He didn't understand how the mere knowledge that a man's own sons may have to submit to the same disgusting ceremonies didn't force a person to revolt, to ventilate the scandal, and to demand its abolition. Yet many boys who passed through these ceremonies eventually became masters at the very school that was the scene of their torture and degradation, and, though then in a position to put an end to the practices, preferred to shut their eyes and consciences and to pretend that they knew nothing about them. The virtues that the public school tried to instill, the stiff upper lip and deference to the social hierarchy, were not qualities Freddie cared for. All his life Freddie had been a rebel, and a pretty fierce one. Rebellion against the customs of bullying at the school forced Freddie to learn to protect himself. It encouraged him to study the art of boxing and to practice sparring and fighting with anyone he could get into trouble with. "If I hadn't been blessed with those instincts, by the way, I don't suppose I should ever have been a professional boxer," Freddie later wrote. The public schools of England can certainly lay claim to producing a champion prizefighter.

By the time he was fourteen, and much to his mother's disappointment, Freddie showed no inclination for the ministry or academia but had decided instead to become an engineer. When he was back in Pontypridd on holiday, Freddie took a job at a local machine shop and vowed never to go back to Long Ashton. His mother eventually relented and he was apprenticed to Messrs Llewellyn & Cubitt at Pentre, a village some eight miles up the Rhondda Valley from Pontypridd. They agreed to pay him £50 a year for five years, but Freddie was soon bored with the life of a trainee engineer. Day after day he worked on the same drilling machine at a factory where promotion was unknown unless someone died. In fact Freddie only managed to tolerate Messrs Llewellyn & Cubitt for just over two years, or more likely Messrs Llewellyn & Cubitt only managed to tolerate Freddie for this time. He wasn't popular with the foreman due to an "old besetting weakness" for poor timekeeping. The only way he could find to catch the early train was to dispense with bed altogether, so he dispensed with Llewellyn & Cubitt instead.

Freddie wasn't that popular with his fellow workers either and his boxing skills were often called upon. The scraps in the engineering shop were fights to the finish and Freddie learned far more about punching than he did about operating a lathe. He did make one friend there however, the local stationmaster's son Ernie Hurford. Ernie had been right through the shop system and was a fully-fledged journeyman, but he'd decided that Pontypridd no longer

held anything for him. Ernie and Freddie read newspaper advertise-
ments placed by Canadian Pacific Railway telling ambitious young
men of a golden future in a new world. The Canadian government
believed that massive agricultural immigration was the key to
prosperity and that industry and commerce would follow in its wake.
Canadian exhibits were mounted at fairs and public displays, while
'editorial articles' were inserted in foreign newspapers as journalists
were wined and dined on guided tours across the new nation. The
Canadian Pacific Railway owned a fleet of ocean liners that it used to
help advance immigration and settlement in Western Canada. The
company offered potential immigrants a single price for shipping
and transport by train to inland destinations. Its agents promoted
direct passage to Canada, to ensure that Europeans didn't disembark
at American ports and remain in the United States. Ships often
carried a thousand passengers on each Atlantic crossing, which took
a week or more. By equipping its fleet with steerage, a section in a
ship allotted to passengers paying the lowest fares, the CPR was able
to increase the number of people it could accommodate. Most other
companies at that time provided their steerage passengers with only
the barest necessities, but the CPR advertised a bed, a pillow, a
blanket and a full set of cutlery free of charge. It also provided as
many third-class passengers as possible with cabins and china table-
ware. It was certainly enough to entice Frederick Hall Thomas and
Ernest Hurford of Pontypridd, and along with a mutual friend Joe
Rosser, they decided that Canada was where their future lay. They
broke the news to their respective parents and after all sorts of
trouble, persuaded them that they were "in the right". Freddie had
the most trouble of the three as the youngest. He was just sixteen,
and his mother consented to him going only because Ernie Hurford
was going as well. Freddie also assured her that he would make his
fortune and she eventually gave way. The three set out for Montreal
with a small amount of money, the breeches and gaiters bought
especially for the journey and no idea about what awaited them on
the other side of the ocean.

Two

The Returned Prodigal with a Vengeance

Frederick Hall Thomas, Ernest Hurford and Joe Rosser were going to 'make good' and on arrival in Montreal they found rooms in a boarding house that were better than they could afford. It was January 1903 and the city was chilled by a storm track that drew fierce squalls from the Atlantic seaboard. It would be several weeks before the mercury crawled its way up towards zero. Montreal sits on an island in the Saint Lawrence River at the spot where the waters become impassable for ships sailing upstream from the Atlantic. When the Lachine Canal was opened in 1825, the city was connected to the Great Lakes and suddenly Montreal was the gateway from the Atlantic to a vast area of North America. It completely changed the appearance and texture of the city, attracting heavy industry, immigrants and the rural population of Quebec. The canal was eventually widened to handle the expanding inland shipping traffic, and the hydraulic energy it provided attracted all kinds of factories along its banks. The area clattered with the sounds of huge machines run by turbines, steam and then electricity.

Freddie, Ernest and Joe donned their breeches and gaiters and set off into the New World to look for work. But the welcome that awaited a trio of machine shop workers from the valleys of South Wales dressed-up like English country squires was colder than the 'noreasters' that blew through the industrial monoliths of Montreal. Freddie was under the impression that it was the way everyone dressed in Canada. They found no work and in several factories they were pelted with lumps of cotton waste soaked in oil and coated with iron and brass filings. Most of the workmen in the Montreal machine shops were French Canadians, and Englishmen were not popular with them. The three were advertising their Britishness and didn't know it. All they could see was that no one seemed to want them. With their money about to run out the Welshmen found an advertisement in a local newspaper for two expert machinists at a foundry owned by a family of industrialists from Missouri. Joe Rosser didn't know enough about machining to even pretend he could do the job, so he was left behind as Freddie and Ernie went to apply. On their arrival at the foundry the two would-be engineers were given a series of aptitude tests. Ernie, who'd worked at the engineering shops in Pontypridd for many years, passed with ease. Then it was Freddie's turn. As an apprentice at Llewellyn & Cubitt's he'd spent as much time fighting as working and had "only been able to nibble at the trade". The foreman set him the task of cutting a square thread in a side block and Freddie knew it was a hopeless cause. "The lathe was a new Yankee pattern, with any number of dodges," Freddie recalled. "I had never seen anything of the kind before, and though he told me what the different handles were for, there were so many I forgot." He'd expected to be given a spindle to turn, which was an easy task, but Freddie went ahead with the thread cutting and hoped for the best. He coped well until the time came to stop the lathe. He touched one of the handles but it was an accelerator. Freddie tapped another – and that finished the business. "This was the chuck-clutch, I believe they called it, and the complications which ensued sent cold shivers down my spine," Freddie wrote. The strap came off the pulleys and the lathe fell apart. Freddie knew at once that the boarding house would be about the safest place for him. When the foreman saw what he had done he'd want Freddie to work for a year without pay to make good the damage, so Freddie slipped on his coat and got out of the factory as quickly as he could. But at least his exploits did not stop Ernie getting a job and the the lodging bills were paid. The other two managed to pick up the odd labouring job, shoveling snow or carrying bricks until one day they saw an advertisement placed by a hunt club looking to employ two men; one to look after the horses and the other to wash dishes. Joe Rosser actually knew something about horses so Freddie headed for the kitchens. They turned up at the club in their Sunday best with stiff collars and cuffs to impress the steward, but it was a wasted effort. Freddie took his place at the sink where a constant supply of dirty dishes arrived from a nearby chute. They kept coming for hours and Freddie was sweating into his starched collar when he heard a whistle at the window. Joe was outside and was working up as much love for his job as Freddie was for the washing up. Rosser was told to groom a dozen horses and to polish twenty-four harnesses, and he had got tired. They agreed to quit leaving the silver uncleaned and a pile of dishes unwashed.

Freddie then became a waiter in a restaurant but resigned because it was only a "cheap affair" and the tips didn't add up to much. Joe Rosser did better, getting a job as an accountant to a café proprietor who couldn't read or write. That left only Freddie unemployed and by this time badly in debt, primarily to the keeper of the boarding house who was threatening to throw him out on the street. His luck finally changed when he met a Welshman who kept a drapery store at Pointe St Charles, an area between the canal and the river that was home to immigrant workers, mainly from England, Scotland and

Ireland. The British influence was very strong in Pointe St Charles and many of its streets had terraced houses built on the model of industrial cities in England. The Welsh draper had connections with the Grand Trunk Railway and thanks to his countryman Freddie got a job working as an 'improver' on the lines: setting out the centre lines and limits of earthworks on the new track. He also managed to get a job for Rosser in the superintendent's office and for Ernie, who left the foundry to join the 'connecting-rod gang' on the railway. Finally all three were gainfully employed but the Welshmen did little to ingratiate themselves with their new workmates and according to Freddie, the French-Canadians resented the entrance of three 'Englishmen' and they began to make things 'warm' for them. Lumps of oily, spiky cotton waste came across the shops at Freddie at regular intervals.

To discover who was doing the throwing, Freddie placed a small mirror on his machine and after two days he spotted his tormentor. Freddie didn't know it at the time, and wouldn't have cared much if he had, but the missile thrower was the bully of the shops. Since arriving in Canada Freddie had been to several gymnasiums and had learned a lot about the form of fighting that was very popular there. Everything was fair in their style of brawling. They didn't punch much, but they kicked, and they were all good wrestlers. "Their great idea was to get you down and then jump upon you, and for that reason you will see any number of men walking around Montreal with heel scars on their foreheads," said Freddie. So on the morning he finally caught the cotton waste thrower in the act, Freddie dropped his tools, jumped across to his target and smashed his jaw. He went down but was up in a flash and jumped at the Welshman. Freddie dodged the first kick and punched his opponent once more. The Canadian lunged again and this time he caught Freddie. They rolled and pitched about the machines for a while and then Freddie managed to twist around and kick the bully headlong into a heap of slag and broken metal. He was badly cut, but he didn't have the chance to fight on, because the foreman had arrived. The Canadian was fired straight away and then the foreman approached Freddie, who thought the same fate awaited him. So Freddie determined to get in first, slipped on his coat and told the foreman he was going to quit. It transpired that the foreman had no intention of sacking Freddie. He'd been looking for an excuse to get rid of the factory bully for a while but hadn't been able to do so without a sound reason. The foreman was also quite elderly and was afraid for his own safety. So Freddie, after a long succession of failures, had finally found favour with a boss and was given his first promotion.

This relative success was not enough to content Frederick Hall
Thomas who started to dream about his own business empire. He
began buying one of the most controversial magazines of the day,
Physical Culture published by Bernarr Macfadden. The first edition
hit the newsstands in 1898 but the magazine came to prominence
with an article in 1907 called 'Growing to Manhood' written to
inform young men about the facts of life. The postal authorities ruled
that it transgressed the laws on decency and an indictment followed.
Macfadden won the case and the attendant publicity caused sales of
the magazine to boom. He used *Physical Culture* to express his
distrust of doctors and generally scorned any form of medical aid in
favour of exercise, health foods, fasting, sleeping on the floor and
walking barefoot "to absorb the earth's magnetism". Freddie became
a disciple, and was soon teaching several other people, at a dollar each
per lesson, the finer points of wrestling, boxing and physical culture.
He applied to Macfadden for an agency in Montreal and sold the
apparatus, exercisers, food and books on commission. For a short
while, in fact a very short while, Freddie was making some money but
his "besetting weakness of missing trains and appointments" threw
him out of work once more. Macfadden advertised for an assistant in
New York, so Freddie quit his job with the Grand Trunk Railway and
took the train to the big city. He got there late and the job had been
given to someone else. Freddie looked around New York for other
work, found nothing, and with his money disappearing fast returned
to Montreal. He was soon back in the engineering shops with
Hurford and Rosser and earning $60 a month. That was a reasonably
good wage but the way in which it was remunerated was a problem.
They were paid monthly and were therefore tempted to go "all out
for a night or two" whenever they had any money. By this time
Freddie had been in Canada for ten months and was still not eighteen years old. With Christmas fast approaching, and without a dollar
to his name Freddie got homesick. He told his landlady, Mrs Falle, his
troubles. She had been good to Freddie since his arrival in Canada.
He had stayed at her boarding house and though she hadn't too much
money to spare she lent him $10 to help him get home. After he was
crowned world champion Freddie wrote in the *Weekly Dispatch* that
he hoped Mrs Falle was reading his article and appealed to her to
contact him so he could repay the debt. He even employed detectives
to search for her, but was never able to find a trace anywhere.

The $10 loan wasn't enough for a passage across the Atlantic, so
he was forced to work his way back as a 'stiff' on a cattle-boat. The
stiffs were deadbeats who worked as little more than slaves for the

cattlemen who were, according to Freddie, the toughest men alive. They had to be to handle the gangs they got on board. The cattlemen kicked the stiffs first and ordered them about later, and they did their best to make their words as painful as their boots. Practically all the cattle-boat foremen hailed from Ireland and the one on Freddie's ship was easily the most brutal man he had met. There wasn't a single 'dead beat' on board who didn't long to murder him. In fact they planned his murder dozens of times. Whenever they were off duty a gang would get together and plan the way they were going to put him out of this life as soon as they got to Liverpool. The scheme they favoured most was to follow the cattleman until he went into some public house and then to rush him. One stiff was to fasten the door shut, while the others were to get him down and stamp him to pulp.

The cattle-boat was a terrible vessel, packed full of suffocating animals, many with broken limbs, being thrown around on the stormy North Atlantic. Most of the beasts were lame with foot rot through standing for weeks in the wet muck of pens only occasionally cleaned out. When an animal died below deck, it was an awful job to drag it out along the narrow alleyways and to heave it overboard. Sometimes the carcass had to be cut up below and thrown out bit by bit. The cattle herded onto the boat in which Freddie sailed were nearly wild and had to be tied by the head in their pens, but they could still toss their heads a little and prod the careless or inexperienced passer-by. It was pitch black when Freddie first stepped on her deck. He was leading the file of stiffs, and was ordered to "get along sharp", an order which the foreman emphasized with his boot. But still Freddie hesitated and backed up. "That gangway looked so much like the road to the nether regions to me that I reckoned the foreman's boots less objectionable than the horns," Freddie recalled. But just as the foreman was about to launch a kick at Freddie an old-timer, who had made the voyage that way before, came to his rescue. "Let me go first kid," he said, and Freddie gladly yielded. He knew the ropes. The trick was to kick each of the beasts as you came up to it to make them draw back and then to nip along. Despite some fancy footwork Freddie received several prods in the back before getting below.

Nineteen stiffs were penned into a single, small cabin. The portholes were closed to keep the sea out, and the stench and heat were overwhelming. They didn't have the cabin to themselves either; rats kept them constant company throughout the voyage. The old-timer who'd helped Freddie cross the gangplank advised him to tuck his boots under his head before settling down for the night. They were about the only thing of value Freddie owned and any decent pair of footwear was fair game down below on a cattle-boat. If any man dropped out of his berth during the night every other occupant of the cabin would be awake and clutching at his shoes, if he had any worth stealing. Freddie escaped that worry about his clothes; no farmer would have accepted what he was wearing for a scarecrow.

That first night was a foretaste of the misery Freddie was to undergo for the next fortnight. The cabin was like an oven and the stench made him feel sick. He had been unable to touch the food and sleep was impossible. On the second night on board Freddie decided to sleep on deck, but was turned back and had to toss and turn until about 3.30 am when he was awoken by the foreman, armed with a cotton-bale stick and was sent to water and feed the cattle. The foreman was very fond of the bale stick and rarely hesitated to use it to attract someone's attention. It was thicker than his thumb and bound round with copper wire: a tough weapon which he used with particular regularity against a Jewish boy from Manchester who moved to Canada and became a lumberjack. He was sent to work at the same pens as Freddie and one day a bull swept his horns round and brought the Mancunian down. The animal promptly lashed out sideways with his hoofs and kicked his stricken prey twice in the solar plexus. Freddie got hold of his workmate's ankles and pulled him out. The stricken stiff was desperately trying to get his wind back when Freddie had a bright idea. He advised his friend to feign illness, which he did so well as to earn two blissful days in bed, until a doctor, suspecting foul play, decided that any food would be bad for the patient, and so starved him back to work.

Freddie was fortunate in being made to tend to the cattle that were kept amidships. The front of a ship lurches on the waves far more than the middle, so there was far less chance of Freddie being pitched over into the pens than there was for the men who tended the beasts in the forecastle. But one day, after a spate of accidents among the men in the bows he was ordered there for duty. This happened to be the day when hunger had driven him to eat some meat and he'd been taken sick. The meat was rank, green and rotten, and Freddie had only managed to eat it this once. Those who were driven by hunger to bite into it were always sick afterwards. The biscuits were full of weevils, and the stiffs practically lived on potatoes. Freddie laid his head on the rail and wished he was dead. The foreman yelled at him to get on with his work but as Freddie was too ill to pay any attention he came running at the prostrate Welshman. Freddie concluded that it was time to postpone his sickness and grab a pitch-fork. He dealt the foreman a glancing blow to the thigh that sent him to the floor. At that moment the ship plunged and Freddie went down too. They rose up together and the foreman rushed at Freddie. "He took a mighty kick at me, but I managed to dodge that and to grab him by the lapel of his coat," Freddie wrote. "Twisting round quickly and getting all the help I could from his rush, I managed to throw him right over my hip into one of the pens, and then to dodge away before he could get up. I guess that the beast in that pen was startled, for he didn't lash out, or if he did he must have missed."

The foreman rushed off to the captain to demand that Freddie be put in irons. Fortunately for the Welshman the captain disapproved of the foreman's sudden interruption and his gruff manner and was disgusted with his appearance. So when the captain heard that the boy to be put in irons was "that kid Thomas", he turned on the foreman and gave him a rare dressing down. The cattleman was not about to let his latest humiliation go un-avenged however. His chance came as the ship was tossing around the Devil's Hole, just off the Irish coast. The biggest beast on board was a huge black bull and by the time the cattle boat was within sight of Ireland, the animal was so sick and fierce that it managed to wrench its head from the rail. Free to move, it lashed out with its hooves until it kicked out the back partition of the pen. The situation was made worse because the pen from which it escaped was just over an open hatchway into the hold. It was 2 am, and one of the men whose duty it was to get up an hour before the rest in order to pitch the hay was in the hold when the bull fell in almost on top of him. The animal went for the unfortunate stiff with a bellow that aroused all on board. A crowd gathered at the edge of the hatchway holding lanterns and shouting contradictory advice, until one yelled to the trapped man to clamber up the hay bales. But it was a temporary refuge, as the bull began to tear the hay down. The foreman, meanwhile, was more concerned for the wellbeing of the bull that was smashing its head against the stanchions in its wild chase of the stiff. It was a valuable beast and the consequences for him if it was injured were grave. Someone would have to get into the hold and lasso the animal, and unsurprisingly the foreman chose Freddie to undertake the task. Freddie agreed; but with conditions attached. It was a fiver for the job and the bull had to be exhausted before he plunged into the hold. A deal was struck and in order to tire the beast lanterns were lowered for the bull to chase before pulling them up suddenly. Then they planned to lower a bucket of water before the worn out, thirsty bull and throw the noose over its head while it was drinking. Unfortunately for Freddie his plan worked too well. After the hapless bull had chased the disappearing light for over an hour the foreman himself went down and neglected to pay Freddie for his idea. The noose went over the bull's horns at the first attempt and when it was hauled off its fore feet, the crew had little trouble in slipping another rope around its middle and return- ing it to the pen. The stiffs went back to their duties full of regret that the foreman had not made a blunder of the lassoing, and been gored.

The cattle-ship had been trailed by rough weather for much of the voyage and the journey lasted four or five days longer than usual. Freddie's relief at finally arriving in Liverpool outweighed any notion of getting even with the cattleman. "I did it and survived; but I think if I had to do it again today that I would rather take my chance as a stowaway," said Freddie. "There may be worse jobs in this world than that of a stiff in a cattle-boat, but if there are I have yet to come across one."

The cattlemen were well paid but the stiffs were given just five shillings and a return ticket that was nearly always traded off at the landing stage. Freddie and the others crawled ashore, sick, hungry and bruised. They were met by an enterprising crowd, all anxious to purchase the return tickets to America for consideration either in cash or kind. One very zealous individual took Freddie to one side and tendered his overcoat. He explained that he had only a few shillings, which he needed about as badly as anyone could need anything and having looked at Freddie's clothes, he judged that the Welshman's most urgent need must be an overcoat which would hide them from the public gaze. So Freddie exchanged his return ticket for the overcoat, drew his five shillings pay and added it to the ten dollars that Mrs Falle had lent him. Freddie was going home broke, after having assured his mother he would make his fortune in Canada. There were another six weeks before Christmas, time enough to earn the money he needed to make a splash on his return to Pontypridd. He borrowed a map and saw that the town of Brecon, where he had a few friends, looked about halfway between Liverpool and home. He reckoned that ten shillings would be enough for the fare, and the rest of his money would be useful in providing some compensation for the troubles and trials of the voyage. Freddie later wrote that it would be best to draw a veil over the next twenty-four hours.

His period of rest and recuperation came to an abrupt halt when he arrived at the railway ticket office the following morning only to find out that he was four shillings short of the fare and there were also cloakroom charges. Freddie told the booking clerk of his misfor- tunes on the high seas who on hearing the tale "melted like a snowball in an oven". The clerk gave Freddie the balance on the ticket and another shilling to pay the cloakroom charges and the cost of the ferry out of the port. Freddie took the name and address of his latest benefactor and left him with the promise that the money would be repaid. Once again he lost the piece of paper but after he became world champion Freddie made a public appeal through the press for the clerk to come forward so the debt could be settled.

Such was his desperation to leave Liverpool that he jumped on the first ferry he saw, but it was the wrong one. Freddie realized that the journey was taking much longer than he'd anticipated so he asked when the ferry docked in Birkenhead. "Not on this trip" he was told, so Freddie calculated that he would be landed even further down the coast and he didn't even have a single penny to pay the cost of getting back. The only thing he had left to sell was a pocketknife, for which he'd paid six shillings, so he walked up and down deck offering to sell it for six pennies. Everyone steered clear of the scruffy youth and things were beginning to look bleak until one of the crew assured him that the Brecon train would pass through the station the ferry was headed for and that he could catch it there. His change of fortune did not last long. He had written to his mother, informing her of his return home for Christmas, and hinting of great success in Montreal. Freddie left six or seven letters with Ernie Hurford to post at weekly intervals from Canada to avoid letting her know that he was already back in Wales, a pronounced failure and without the price of a meal. Freddie fancied that he had arranged the whole thing most beautifully, but he had underestimated the news-carrying capabilities of small Welsh towns. He learned that everyone knew everybody else's business in such places as Brecon, and his mother soon heard he was back in Wales. Freddie had been in Brecon just a few days when an aunt swooped down on him and marched him home to Pontypridd. The reception wasn't as bad as he'd feared. "It was now a case of the returned prodigal with a vengeance. I don't know why it is, but one has to admit that the black sheep of the family invariably receive the softest and fattest times. I was an open and confessed failure, but in spite of this I had the run of the house and all the money I asked for," Freddie wrote. But then he ran into trouble. He was still only a boy, but the other boys and young men of Pontypridd looked on him as a hero. He had been across the Atlantic, had had adventures, and they wanted Freddie to lead them against a group of touring actors who had filched all the girls away from the local boys. The Pontypridd girls and boys had grown up together, and would have continued relations if the touring companies had not arrived to spoil the boys' market. There were several fights and the police decided that

Frederick Hall Thomas needed to be curbed. He managed to dodge
them for a while but eventually a constable famed for his sprinting
powers, and specially imported from Newport, caught him. Freddie
was charged with creating a disturbance, but he escaped with a
moderate fine. Nevertheless the experience forced him to give some
thought to his future prospects.

Freddie had come back from Canada in worse circumstances than
he had left. Since returning to Pontypridd all he'd done was fight, run
from the police and write letters of application for various jobs and
read the refusals. He helped his mother wind up her affairs at the
Bridge House Hotel after seventeen years and they moved back to 17
Morgan Street, the house in which Freddie was born and where his
mother wanted him to stay. But Freddie was getting restless again. He
believed he had gained both in maturity and independence, despite
his most recent capers. The more Freddie thought things over the
more convinced he became that Canada or America would be the
best country for him. He would probably have returned there sooner
but for the "warmth, length, depth, and breadth" of his leave taking.
Weeks and then months went by and the lure of the New World
became stronger with each job rejection. By the summer of 1904, his
mother finally relented to Freddie's second emigration in as many
years. He had no small difficulty in convincing her that he was doing
the right thing and she raised every argument possible against the
idea. "It was hard to insist, because I could feel that I was hurting her,
but I could also feel that it was far wiser and better to go and also that,
unless I did go, I might quite possibly be the cause of other and worse
pain to her in the future," Freddie wrote. Eventually, after several
weeks of persuasion, Freddie got his wish and he left with his
mother's reluctant blessing, a new outfit that she paid for and twenty
pounds in his pocket. He was convinced the twenty pounds was more
than sufficient for his needs. Freddie was going away at this time,
perhaps for many years, and he had fully resolved that he would not
return until he could "more or less do so in state". Freddie went
around the town to say goodbye to friends and family and found that
the ceremony was a somewhat expensive one:

> I may as well confess that I have never been a great economist. I may
> have a knack of getting hold of money, and it is just as well that I have,
> or my gift of getting rid of it would surely cause me very considerable
> inconvenience. In the end I found I had broken that twenty pounds
> down to three and that I had not yet bought my passage. Things looked
> awkward, and it was indeed fortunate for me that there was a rate war
> on at the time and that I was thus enabled to get away. I was off again

on what was to prove my real career in life, though I was far from expecting this at the time. Before I came home again I had fairly launched out my journey towards the world's championship, despite the often very rough passages I was to traverse before I had even formulated my ambitions in that direction.

Three

Striking the Long Trail

Among the throng making its way into the depths of the *S.S. Baltic* were German and Norwegian wrestling teams, a large group of Russian emigrants and Frederick Hall Thomas. It was the morning of June 29th 1904, and the steamship, in the red and black colours of the White Star Line, was being readied for her maiden voyage. She would sail from Liverpool to New York in just nine days to take her passengers to a new life in a new world. There was accommodation for 425 people in first class, 450 in second class and another 2,000 down below in steerage. If it wasn't for such a large allocation of lower class tickets Freddie wouldn't have made the crossing. The £3 left over after the farewell party was enough to get on board ship, but he still had to go through American Customs and this required proof of financial health or a pre-existing job offer in the United States. Before setting off Freddie had to go back to his mother to "separate her from a few more of her hard earned sovereigns". Elizabeth Hall Thomas gave her son another £10 and the train fare to Liverpool.

Faced with several days of sitting around in third class accommodation, Freddie decided to seek out a companion for the journey. He found one on the very first day, Percy Bowen, commonly known as Pat. They were destined to be fellow adventurers for several months to come. Pat was an Australian, born to Welsh parents who had left Swansea for Adelaide on their marriage. He was only twenty-two years old when he met Freddie on the *Baltic* but Pat had already seen more of the world than most men twice his age. He had struck the long trail when still a boy, with eastern Australia in the grip of a severe economic depression. Pat made for the newly discovered goldfields in the west, but by the time he got there the alluvial gold deposits were largely worked out and the age of the independent digger was over. When the Boer War broke out in 1899 Pat heard the call. He tacked three or four years onto his age, fooled the authorities, and was enlisted in the Australian Bushmen, with whom he put in a spell of active service. He eventually left with excellent discharges and later returned to South Africa with a repatriation party and the intention of settling down to work as a blacksmith and gold prospector. The business failed and Pat set off for Wales to seek out his parents' families in Swansea. He spent all his money on a futile search and then decided to give America a try. And so the paths taken by Frederick Hall Thomas and Percy Bowen crossed in steerage on the

Baltic on a summer's day in 1904. "He was feeling quite as lonesome as I was," Freddie wrote. "We met face to face in the midst of a horde of Russians and Germans, took a look at each other, simultaneously burst out with the question: "Are you a Britisher?" and shook hands with an extra squeeze by way of answer." There started a wandering partnership destined to last several months, and a friendship which remained firm and close despite a continuing series of hardships.

The life of a steerage passenger was generally uncomfortable and always tedious, and conditions on the *S.S. Baltic* were no exception. American immigration law required that all emigrant ships landing passengers in the United States restrict the placement and movements of those in third class. The owners and master of an emigrant ship had by law to ensure that steerage passengers were kept to specifically allotted decks for the duration of the voyage. Congress had made this law for the stated purpose of ensuring decent conditions in steerage. But the other, more implied than stated, reason was to control the spread of disease often carried by the poorer elements of society. Any ship heading for New York not fitted with barriers around steerage, or found not to be using them correctly, risked being held at the Quarantine Station and unable to discharge any passengers until health officers completed the protracted process of checking each person. In practice they only checked those in steerage but in extreme cases passengers would be dumped on Ellis Island to be held in quarantine for forty days before completing the journey to New York.

Freddie was penned-in and bored so he decided to indulge in his favourite pastime, fighting. Pat was big and strong and had a great deal of experience as a bar-room brawler, but Freddie thought him lacking in the scientific side of boxing and wrestling and so took it upon himself to teach his new friend. Freddie's motives for under-taking the task were not altogether philanthropic. He'd taken a dislike to the biggest of the German wrestlers, who had been to America before and could speak English. Suddenly Freddie was back in public school fighting those "who believed that they had a prescrip-tive right to behave in any way they saw fit and to tyrannize over their meeker and weaker companions to their hearts' content".

To pass the time the professional wrestlers held tournaments every evening before dinner. Most of the team were too heavy for Freddie to handle but Pat was able to hold his own even with some of the best and heaviest of the Germans. Freddie challenged the wrestlers to a bout or two of boxing instead, and took great pleasure in giving them a painful introduction to the finer points of the noble art. Life on board was becoming tolerable, if not enjoyable, until the

big English-speaking German wrestler got drunk. He filled himself
with beer and began to hurl insults at the Russian emigrants. They
were too afraid to respond so he threw biscuits and hard rolls of
bread at them. One of these missiles struck Freddie full in the face.
He demanded an apology, but the German refused saying that he
had never started anything in his life that he could not finish, and
defied any 'Britisher' to force him to do something he didn't want to
do. Before Freddie even had time to get to his feet, Pat leapt over the
table and punched the German in the face. The blow sent the bully
to the deck and instantly two of the other wrestlers came to his assistance and soon "there was as pretty a rough-and-tumble battle as
anyone could wish to see in full swing". More Germans joined in the
fray as Freddie reached Pat's side and then one or two of the
Russians picked up the courage to seize the opportunity for revenge.
The Welsh-Russian alliance was badly outnumbered, but Freddie
"enjoyed the fun thoroughly". Everything went, the Germans used
their feet and any bottle they could grab, but Pat was knocking them
down like ninepins while Freddie was able to get in and out in a fairly
sprightly fashion to do his share towards damaging both the feelings
and bodies of the enemy. The stewards eventually broke up the brawl
but only after Freddie had secured the apology.

When they arrived in New York Pat and Freddie set off to see the
sights and find work. But jobs were none too plentiful in a city of
which neither man had any knowledge, so after a week they decided
to go further afield. Freddie thought they should find his old friends
Rosser and Hurford in Montreal. They headed north, but with no
money for the journey Pat and Freddie joined 'the noble army' of
hoboes. They pooled their remaining dollars and cents and bought
blankets, a rubber sheet, knives, forks, spoons, a frying pan, a kettle
and a couple of tin cups. They also bought some machinist and
blacksmith's tools, which they packed in an old Gladstone bag and
set off with the intention of working their way to Canada.

There were two distinct varieties of American hobo. The smaller
section, to which Pat and Freddie belonged, was known to the rest of
the fraternity as 'bindle-stiffs'. These wanderers made their way
around and through the States, impelled by the lure of the road, but
always willing to work whenever there was work to be had. They took
their name from the bindle carried on the back, which consisted of a
roll of blankets, containing a few belongings such as working tools.
The bindle-stiffs were regarded with contempt by the other brand, the
true hoboes, who never worked and had no intention of doing so. Pat
and Freddie were setting out on a hard road. It is just over three

hundred miles from New York to Montreal and the two had "but the haziest notion of the way to make it". They did know that the first step was to tramp out of the city as far as Yonkers, the first town on the River Hudson outside New York. From here they planned to 'jump a train' in true hobo fashion.

Pat had already been a 'sundowner' in Australia as he 'humped his swag' (carried his roll of blankets, billy, flour and tea) across much of the country. But he had no experience of jumping trains and the only ones Freddie had boarded were safely parked at a platform. "We were two of the biggest 'greenhorns' ever at the art of train-boarding," Freddie later admitted. They had been told that for the novice it was always wiser to try to jump a cattle-train that had open box cars rather than the other alternatives of riding the decks (the roofs) of passenger cars, or 'going underneath' which involved scrambling under a car and clinging on to the rods and break beams. Box cars are big barn-like trucks, boarded up the sides with roofs which make them look like windowless wooden houses. Their big sliding doors at the side led to their being known, in hobo jargon, as 'side-door Pullmans'. Pat and Freddie had been told the best places to jump a ride were by the water tanks placed at regular ten-mile intervals along the railroad. They hung around the first water tank out of Yonkers, hoping that a freight train with an open box car would either stop for water or pass so slowly as to afford them a chance of boarding it. The experienced hobo selects the dark hours as the best time to start out on a journey. Pat and Freddie were in hourly dread of being seen by a railway bull (policeman) who would have run them in. Neither had any prison experience and they had no desire to start an apprenticeship in any American pen. That day they drew a blank and the night was blank as well. Both men were afraid to sleep for fear of the bulls and they had not yet learnt to keep watch 'turn and turn' while the other slept. Trains pulled up at the tank, but none had an open box car on it and it was not until daylight once again they noticed that most of the trains which were pulling out of Yonkers were carrying men and boys all stealing rides. Pat and Freddie watched train after train go by, every one of them carrying several hoboes, yet neither man could summon up the courage to jump one. They were going too fast for their taste, but they had to do something. The pair had lingered there for nearly twenty-four hours and the railway bulls were getting suspicious. So they started to tramp along the railroad, stepping from sleeper to sleeper for ten miles, until they arrived at the next water tank where a bull came along and chased them off. Eventually they walked nearly two hundred miles out of New York, tramping over the sleepers and clinkers. Then, somewhere about the twentieth tank, they met up with an experienced hobo who went by the name of 'Frisco George. He was mostly Irish, with some Greek blood, had taken to the road when he was fourteen and expected one day to die on it. He had been in every state in the Union and had tramped across Canada four or five times. 'Frisco George was also on his way to Montreal. He told Pat and Freddie to hang around some forty or fifty yards in front of the water tank and to board the train as it was moving away because that's when the 'shacks', the railway guards employed to fend off hoboes from trains, would be back in their cars and wouldn't be watching out for them. Every shack carried a club which few hesitated to use any more than they hesitated to hurl a hobo on to the track. Huge numbers of hoboes were killed after being ditched from a speeding train.

When the first freight train eventually came by, Freddie, Pat and 'Frisco George all got hold with the first grab at the rail on the steps and swung aboard. Later on in his hobo life Freddie got used to the process, and didn't hesitate even to board and 'deck' a fast-moving overland mail train. But jumping that first freight nearly scared him to death. They managed to reach a platform at the end of a car, but 'Frisco George decided that it wasn't safe to stay there because a shack might come along at any moment. So the old hobo took them up to the roof. The roofs of American railway cars sloped down and projected out at the ends, and by standing up and reaching out 'Frisco George showed them how to grasp the protruding caves and to gradually muscle up. He went up first to show how it was done, but came down to give the two novices a lift when he saw they were having trouble. Despite his assistance, Pat and Freddie had a tough time of it before landing on the deck of the car. They were fairly safe, for although the shacks occasionally made a tour of the roofs, on which there was a twelve-foot plank for them to walk, they didn't promenade too frequently on freight trains. From then on it was "a simply glorious ride", and Pat was in ecstasies of delight. They were able to enjoy a delicious night's sleep without fear of danger, because George showed them how to tie themselves to the plank on the top of the car, and then, when morning broke, they awoke to feast their eyes on the glories of the Adirondacks and the Catskill Mountains, which Pat declared to be the finest country he had ever seen.

Freddie's first ride as a hobo went without incident until they crossed the St Lawrence River and were spotted by a shack who mounted the roof and came at them with a club. Freddie, Pat and George ran across the roofs of the moving carriages with nothing to hold them. The roof was more slippery than they cared to think about. They all sloped, or rather curved, down at the end and Pat, Freddie and George had to run along them and jump across the space on to the next car with the shack in pursuit. Even the fireman on the engine took a hand in the game and began to pelt them with coal. So the three hoboes dropped down over the end of a car, waited until the shack began to dangle his legs over to follow them, then jumped off the train. Pat and Freddie took a tumble, but fortunately the freight had not been travelling very fast, and they were soon up and running as fast as they could for the Canadian Pacific Railway depot at the end of the bridge. 'Frisco George parted from Pat and Freddie there, and went off to 'throw his feet'. He asked the other two to join fortunes with him but they did not like the idea of begging. George kindly consented to drink their health in beer and left.

They made the rest of the journey on foot, and after several days they finally arrived at the foot of Mount Royal, the tree-covered mountain in the heart of Montreal. Freddie was confident they would get work. They looked for Hurford and Rosser as well as other acquaintances Freddie had made during his first stint in the city but found nobody. This wasn't the flourishing town Freddie had left behind the previous year and work was hard to come by. Without a cent and nearly starving, the pair were finally taken on as part of a stripping gang in a Canadian Pacific Railway workshop; Pat as a blacksmith and Freddie as a labourer. Their new workmates were largely French-Canadian or Greek and it was only a short while before Freddie found himself in a fistfight with a few members of the stripping gang. It actually worked to his advantage because his opponent had intimidated the foreman who promoted Freddie to be his assistant. In essence Freddie was his bodyguard, for which he was paid $100 a month. For the first time since he had landed in New York Freddie began to feel sure that he was really going to carry out his ambition and 'make good'.

The good times didn't last long and after only a few weeks Freddie and Pat were fired, allegedly because work was slack in Montreal at the time and things were getting worse. But at least they'd made some money. Pat had always been keen to see the Niagara Falls and they were on the road again. Even though they had the means to pay for travel, the pair had been initiated into the trick of travelling without payment, and so they 'pulled out' on a freight train, and despite having to 'hit the grit' once or twice when the shacks spotted them they reached the town of St Thomas without incident. At this time the only way to cross the canyon at St Thomas was by train over a temporary bridge. Whenever it approached the bridge a train would pull up and cross very slowly so the shacks and the train crew kept a sharp look out for hoboes. Freddie and Pat decided to wait for darkness before jumping a ride across the bridge and spent the day fishing and swimming. They returned to the bridgehead by nightfall, only to discover that on every train the shacks and the conductor were riding the 'blinds', the platforms at the end of every carriage, with lighted lanterns and were "generally in the most suspicious frame of mind".

They waited all night but gave up the idea of jumping a train and decided to risk tramping across instead. It was the only alternative to giving up, and so they started their precarious walk. Freddie was as frightened as he had ever been in his life. There were just the cross beams to step on, and these were about a stride apart and looked like matches to Pat and Freddie. It was night and pretty dark, and they had to step from cross beam to cross beam, knowing that if either of them made a false step he would go straight down into the river beneath. It would have been a very long drop. The bridge was more than a quarter of a mile long and as they got halfway it began to rumble and shake. There was a train coming, so Pat and Freddie crouched back against the parapet to let it pass. But before the train reached them Pat had an idea: they should jump it. Freddie did not fancy it, but Pat, always pretty reckless, broke into a run along the cross beams and made one of the front cars on the train. He caught the side ladder of the second blind carriage and swung himself on board. There was no drawing back for Freddie now, and he reached out for the next side ladder as it came past. But his nerve failed him and he let it go. Freddie touched the side ladder of the next car and let it go. The train seemed an endless one. Freddie would have probably given up on the venture and trudged ahead in the hope of picking Pat up further along the road if it had not been so long, and even then he might not have made the attempt had he not noticed something white on an approaching car. He knew it was a cattle board. So he grabbed it when it came along, was able to get a firm hold and to swing himself up, bruised and shaken, and with badly scraped shins. Once on board he wanted to get to Pat, far down the train. The cattle cart was closed and there was only a most precarious foothold so Freddie clambered along the couplings to the next car, and from there by the couplings again to the next, and so on until he made it to Pat. He made the walk because his fear of falling was outweighed by his fear of being alone.

The shacks never suspected anyone would venture to jump the train on the bridge and made no further tours of inspection, so

Freddie and Pat 'held her down' all the way to Toronto. They got off in the city because Pat wanted to see City Hall but they didn't stay long. There was no prospect of work and Pat still wanted to see the Falls. So they rode a freight train out of Toronto to Hamilton and then tramped the forty-five miles to Niagara. The Falls held a particular fascination for hoboes in the States and Canada and the area was full of hobo 'jungles', eating-places or camps where crowds gathered to light fires and cook the food that had been begged in the neighbouring townships. The hand-outs were pooled and eaten in an al fresco banquet. When a freight train went by many of the hoboes jumped it as another crowd of hungry, shivering hoboes got off to feast on the remains. After he'd made his fortune Freddie wrote: "Many a time when I have felt that my backbone was pushing its way through my waistcoat, have I dropped off a freight at a welcome sight of a 'jungle' fire to find a luscious lump of steak, frying in a pan, with a liberal supply of bread lying around."

Such was the popularity of the Falls with hoboes the towns in the vicinity of the Falls, Hamilton and Niagara, became hostile places for them to visit. Hand-outs were rare and the bulls were very active. Pat and Freddie were able to beg some food from an old lady in a large house in Hamilton and they returned to the jungle with bacon, eggs and bread. After finishing the meal the two settled-in for some sleep when a rain of kicks to the ribs woke them both. The kicker was a bull who handcuffed the pair and marched them off to the station. He'd seen Pat and Freddie around the old lady's house that afternoon and suspected them of stealing the food. Both the Canadian and American police treated hoboes fairly brutally at this time. Pat and Freddie were charged with burglary and the policeman claimed he had caught them with the goods. They weren't worried about the burglary charges because the alleged victim, the old lady, would surely speak up for them. Freddie's main concern was the diary he'd kept since arriving in New York. It was by now full of his escapades living as a hobo and as it was certain that they would be searched and would consequently be charged for vagrancy. So while Pat was talking to the bull, Freddie tore out the offending pages from the diary, chewed and swallowed them. The two tried to explain that they were mechanics looking for a job, a tale that seemed more plausible because of their ineptitude at leading the life of a hobo and a couple of alien accents. "I suppose we had not yet shed our greenhorn skins, while I had my 'English with a big tail' sticking out of me, our stories somewhat impressed the bull," Freddie wrote.

They were questioned in separate rooms, but in the weeks and

months on the road Pat and Freddie had often discussed the chances
of being pinched and had agreed on the most likely tale to pitch in
such an event. They had fairly recent discharges (references) from
the Canadian Pacific Railway in Montreal, so both told a story of
journeying to Chicago in search of work before being tempted to
turn aside in order to see the Falls. When they compared notes afterwards they discovered that they'd escaped without contradicting
each other, but the story was not convincing enough to avoid a night
in the cells. They had stone slabs to sleep on and the walls were a
regular hobo directory, on which the names and directions of its
various occupants had been scratched. They learned that such and
such a town was good; that there was no profit in 'battering the main
stem' (begging on the main street) of another; that the Northern
Pacific was now a bad road; and that the bulls in yet another town
were terribly hostile.

The following morning they appeared in front of the magistrate
who seemed to be satisfied with their story and their discharges from
the CPR. They walked out of the town, and with no wish to be taken
back and recharged before the same magistrate, they didn't jump any
freight trains until several miles down the line. Pat and Freddie set off
for Port Sarnia, one of Ontario's principal gateways to the United
States, just across the St Clair River from Port Huron and the state of
Michigan. At the port Pat managed to bluff his way past the customs
officer but Freddie was not so fortunate. They were trying to cross
back into the United States from Canada so Freddie was once again
faced with the problem of having to show that he had enough money
on which to live in America. He first tried to persuade the officer that
he'd paid the steamship company his head tax, but the bluff didn't
work. Freddie was turned back although the officer hinted that he'd let
him through for a dollar. "I might have been willing to let him have
the bribe if he had not been a fellow Welshman," Freddie recalled. "I
had detected this at once, and had appealed to him on the score of our
joint nationality. But he wouldn't weaken. His terms were one dollar
cash or no passage, and I was so disgusted that I turned back."

By now Pat was on board ship. They had arranged that if they lost
each other they would meet at the General Post Office in Port Huron.
They were to go there between nine and ten every morning for three
days before giving each other up as hopelessly separated. Freddie
decided to take another route across the river. Where the Grand
Trunk ferryboats cross the distance is only three hundred yards. It
was a quick and easy passage, unobstructed throughout the year and
it was well known in the town that a group of Native Americans

operated a people-smuggling operation by canoe at the cost of a bottle of whiskey per passenger. It was illegal to give the Native Americans alcohol but that's exactly what Freddie did. He was landed clear of the Customs station in Port Huron but also a long way downstream from the town and he was late for his first rendezvous at the post office. Pat had their scant supply of money and Freddie was faced with the prospect of walking the streets of the town for twenty-four hours without a cent. That day he was pulled over four times by policemen suspecting him of vagrancy. Freddie had a story prepared for such an occurrence however. He had heard of a farmer named Jenkins who was looking for workers on his land just outside the town. Every time he was pulled over he said he was on his way to work at Jenkins' farm, with no intention of ever going there.

He met up with Pat on the second day and they headed for Chicago. It was not a good time to be heading for the Windy City with violent clashes between police and anarchists and work in short supply. The two managed to jump a freight out of Chicago and headed for Minneapolis. But their luck did not improve. They were spotted by shacks and jumped off the train before they were thrown off. They made a mail train into Milwaukee. Again they were spotted and were ditched before the first stop. This was a hostile road so they proceeded across country and at Jamesville they jumped a freight train taking in water. They hid among the coals and were not spotted by the fireman until they were within fifty miles of Madison City. They expected to be thrown off at once, but the fireman had a soft corner in his heart for hoboes. He told them to lie low and stay quiet, and Pat and Freddie were able to sleep. They were awoken several hours later by a stream of water. The fireman had turned the hose on them and was shouting "bulls, bulls". The train had stopped and there were a dozen police officers searching for hoboes. Pat and Freddie jumped off the coal wagon and ran into the darkness. After a journey that had taken them over the Atlantic and across a conti-nent, a distance of over three thousand miles, they finally lost each other. They had tramped and starved together. They had roughed it with the roughest and had been closer than brothers. Then they jumped off a coal tender in the night and never met again.

Freddie ran straight into a policeman so he "threw him on to his head" and darted off down the road. After about a mile Freddie laid down in the grass and waited for the train to overtake him, but when it did it was travelling too fast to risk jumping. Freddie had to walk the whole of the twenty-two miles into Madison. He did most of the journey that night, striding the sleepers and avoiding the carcasses of the animals killed by passing trains. Freddie headed for the post office as usual, fully expecting to see his partner waiting for him. Pat still had the money. But his old friend didn't show and for the first time Freddie was all alone and begging to survive.

First he had to beg for a pair of boots, and was lucky enough to be given a fairly serviceable pair. That was his best achievement as a professional beggar and he was never a success at it. He tried for food and a little money as well, but failed lamentably and had to climb an apple tree to get something to eat. The following day Freddie scribbled a note for the delivery window of the post office in case Pat eventually got there and then left Madison City to walk towards Minneapolis. Now that he was alone he could barely summon the courage to jump a freight. But Minneapolis was not a good town for a hobo to stop with at least twenty thousand men out of work there. Freddie just added to the number. He'd also arrived just after a cyclone hit the town. Scores of people had been killed, telegraph wires were all down and most of the town's trees had been uprooted. He had to sell his pocketknife just to get a meal, but at least there was a message from Pat in the post office window:

Hullo Fred, where did you get to? Only hope you were not pinched. I fell out among the corn. The bulls were thrashing all around and I judged it unsafe to show myself. So following my soldier's instincts, I rolled myself up in my blanket and slept like a baby. Beat my way to Minneapolis next day on the mail, have waited here three days for you and have gone on to Dakota for the thrashing. If you fail to grab a train will look for you daily at 10 am at the Salvation Army Barracks. But may get shipped out. Follow on.

By the time Freddie got to the barracks Pat had gone and so he limped back into the town, hungry and tired. In the days that followed he got work clearing away storm debris. He was paid $3 a day and kept the job for a week until misfortune struck again and an accident cut the skin on his right hand and arm so badly that he was hospitalized for a week. By the time Freddie was out of hospital his job had been taken, he was down to his last $2 and Pat's trail had gone cold. But at least the prospects of work were improving. It was harvest time and the farmers were clamouring for thrashers. With anything between $2 and $5 a day offered as well as free food and shelter, things were looking up, though at first Freddie wasn't particularly taken by his workmates. They were fifteen to twenty men in a tent so Freddie decided to sleep outside but the rain upset his plans and he had to crawl under a wagon to get some shelter before being reluctantly driven back inside. "We were savages, and if I was not one when I joined that thrashing camp I speedily became one," Freddie wrote. "It was not a case of a word and a blow with us. The blow usually came first."

Freddie was a rookie and was told to stand between two wagons and stack the bales that were pitched down towards him. But the bales were pitched not to Freddie but at him. They were also thrown at the same time, a bale from each side. The first bale and then the second knocked him over. At first Freddie thought it was his clumsiness and inexperience. But when a third heavy bale sent him flat to the ground amid a roar of laughter, he decided to make a stand, so he grabbed a pitchfork, dodged round to the other side of the wagon, and struck the bale thrower in his calf. While the injured 'joker' was on the floor of the wagon, cursing and nursing his leg, his three workmates jumped down and went after Freddie. The Welshman knocked out the first two but the third came at him with a pitchfork. By the usual custom of harvest field fighting he would have finished off his prey, so Freddie challenged him to throw his fork down and fight him with his fists. The bare knuckled contest lasted five minutes before Freddie's opponent gave in. Both his eyes had been closed in the pummelling but he took his defeat with good grace and became, in essence, Freddie's first fight promoter. He offered to back Freddie against anyone on the field that might fancy himself. So Freddie's prizefighting career began in a hayfield in St Paul, South Dakota. Over the following two nights, Freddie fought three bouts under whatever parts of the Queensbury rules the scrappers could recollect. Kicking was prohibited and it was also forbidden to jump on a downed fighter but everything else was permitted.

The fights allowed Freddie to earn a few dollars and the respect of the entire field. He started to enjoy the harvest but after a few weeks the dreadful conditions beat him and he was back on the road. Harvesters who quit the field traditionally stole a ride out of town. Even though they had money, they would never dream of giving a cent of it to the railway company. There was an occupational hazard however. A gang of thugs waited around the trains returning from harvest fields and lumber camps. These men pretended to be regular hoboes, but they stood in with the train crews, who let them ply their trade for a share of the spoils. Both the shacks and the thugs knew that returning harvesters and lumbermen had earned good money and had not had the chance to spend it. They chummed up with returning workers, both with those who paid their fares and with those who were stealing a ride, and picked their pockets or attacked them. Freddie was riding a box car with three other harvesters when they were trapped by a couple of shacks. They each paid up a dollar and were left alone once more. Then they heard a clanking sound and went for the doors but they had been closed and fastened. They were prisoners and didn't know whether the shacks were going to come back in force and take all their money or whether they would be handed over to the police at the next stop. Freddie and the others were locked in for an entire night without food or water. The following morning the train stopped and six shacks appeared. No train carried more than a couple of shacks in addition to the conductor and engine crew, so it was evident that at least four of the gang, if not all six, were thugs and "as bad and brutal a gang of men you could meet anywhere". They were all armed with iron bars, and they meant business. Right away they ordered the captives to hand over all their money. The thugs stood in the doorway while Freddie and the other three were bunched together in a corner. Suddenly one of the harvesters gave a yell and went for the gang with his head down. He met the first full in the stomach and sent him flying through the doorway. The other three came after him with a rush, and the thugs were all sent out backwards with Freddie and his fellow harvesters on top of them. They rose and scattered without waiting to read the casualty list. Freddie never saw any of that bunch again. He walked for many miles until he reached a jungle fire with a dozen hoboes clustered around it. They had water, coffee and plenty of food. He was nearly out of South Dakota by now and was told that there was a Welsh 'colony' called Spain that was close to the nearby town of Aberdeen. Freddie decided to go there trusting that he'd be given work on the strength of kinship, but these were hard times. There wasn't any work in Spain, Welsh blood or not, and hoboes were not popular there. By now Freddie's clothes were in rags and he was filthy. He washed in a stream and used some of his money to buy a decent pair of boots.

Freddie jumped a slow freight out of town, but this was a dangerous line. He saw a big man riding the couplings under the train and called him to climb into the box car, but the man was too scared to move. He was from Sweden originally, had been in Dakota for the harvesting and had made $60. He jumped the freight and found a Pullman but had been trapped by thugs and shacks. They beat him and took all his money, but somehow overlooked a lady's gold watch in his pocket. It was his mother's and was now the only thing of any value the Swede owned. He was still too afraid to leave the couplings even though he knew that if he fell asleep he would certainly be killed.

The Swede warned Freddie that there were thugs around and before they got to the next stop they heard them. Freddie looked through the end hole of the carriage and saw seven or eight men armed with clubs and iron bars had discovered the Swede. Freddie sank down inside the car and listened to the scuffle. He never knew if the Swede survived. There had been an attempted getaway, because he heard the gang run off shouting in pursuit of someone. Luckily for him it took the thugs' attention and they did not attempt to molest him until the next stop. Freddie had dozed off by now and didn't hear the train braking, but he woke up in enough time to hear someone trying to slide open the doors which he had wedged closed. Then there was some whispering, and presently, just as the train began to move on again, a head appeared at the end loophole. A man was trying to crawl in.

"Lend me a hand, bo," he whispered.

"How many of you are there?" Freddie asked.

"Only me," he answered, at which Freddie knew he was a thug because he could hear two or three moving on the platform at the end of the car. The train was gathering speed so Freddie moved towards the end loophole as if he was going to let in the thug. He picked up a pump handle from the floor of the carriage and hit his tormentor as hard as he could. "I don't know where he went, and I am afraid I don't care," Freddie recalled. "All I do know is that I was left to finish that ride all the way into Minneapolis undisturbed."

Minneapolis had been a difficult town on his first visit but things were much worse on his return. For many days he walked the streets looking for work, but at least he had the money for a room to sleep the night. Cheap lodging houses were charging just 10 cents for a bed. Many a hobo had warned Freddie about these beds and he made a point to strip them and sleep on the iron bars. He finally got work carrying great baulks of timber at a sawmill but the money was only just about enough to stave away starvation. He decided to walk the ten miles back to the neighbouring town of St Paul but he tramped into a rainstorm. He was wet through in about five minutes and failing to find any other shelter Freddie went to the police station. They took him in and packed him into a cell with about a dozen more homeless, penniless tramps, and there at last, after taking care to pull all the bedding off, Freddie lay down hungry and soaking to sleep on the wire mattress of a bed. After a cold and hungry night in the cells Freddie took to the streets of St Paul with a plan to get to Chicago. He was told that the best way was through the town of Midways, unsurprisingly half way between St Paul and Minneapolis, where the stock cattle trains to Chicago stopped. He managed to jump a train there that carried him some fifty miles before he was discovered by a brakeman who made him 'hit the grit'. This happened close to a village where he got some work shoveling sand and later picking gherkins for a pickle factory. This was piecework and Freddie made about half as much as the locals who were expert at it. With no prospect of making a fortune by picking gherkins it was time to move on again. He jumped a stock train bound for Chicago and settled down in comfort on the hay bales in the cattle trucks.

Freddie arrived in Chicago at the time of the great meatpacker's strike. On July 12th 1904, nearly twenty thousand skilled and unskilled workers walked out of the city's meat packing plants. The strikers were fighting against low wages and the excessive pace of work demanded by the big firms. The typical labourer at the time was foreign, unskilled, worked long, hard hours, and was paid less than twenty cents an hour. All the regular packing house workers were out and it was a particularly violent strike as the big firms drafted in strikebreakers from the southern states. Many were African Americans, but there were others from every nationality drafted in directly from Ellis Island. To keep them from the baiting hands of the strikers, the firms housed the blacklegs in improvised barracks on the packing-yards. These areas were defended by armed men hired from Pinkerton's, with cordons of armed police surrounding the factories. The pickets stood outside the cordon looking for any opportunity to rush the line and get at the strikebreakers. The strikers were more furious with the 'scabs' and the police than they were with the masters. There were bomb explosions, several murders and counter rushes by the police.

Freddie soon realized that Chicago was no place for him. The only question remaining was how to get out and he decided his best option was to find an employee of the stock trains. Railway regulations required at least one cattleman to every two trucks on a stock train to ensure the animals were properly fed and watered and the railroads were obliged to issue free tickets for the cattlemen on whose presence they insisted. But the stockowners believed the cattle could more or less look after themselves and the cost of paying extra men was unnecessary. So the free tickets were given away to anyone with sufficient influence with a superintendent to secure one. Freddie resolved to benefit from this system if possible. His problem was that the men with the tickets worked inside the cordon. So Freddie mixed with the strikers and asked about the superintendents and discovered one of them was a Welshman named Thomas. Freddie had a plan. He went up to a police officer and told him that he wanted to see a relation of his called Mr Thomas who worked as a superintendent in the packing yard. After making a few enquiries the police officer returned and led Freddie to his 'relation'. Putting on as strong a Welsh accent as he could muster Freddie found the unsuspecting Mr Thomas and claimed him as an uncle. Freddie was not able to establish this fact, but he did succeed in enlisting Thomas' patriotic sympathy and was offered a job as a strikebreaker. It was $4 a day but Freddie refused on the basis that he'd never been a blackleg in his life. Thomas raised the offer to $5 a day, and for this Freddie was to swing a club and boss the other strikebreakers. "I don't blame you, my boy, for hesitating," Thomas said. "I hate this job myself. I have no use for scabs either, but I have got my wife and children to consider, and the foremen have always to side with the bosses. Don't be foolish, take this job and crack the skulls of a few of the brutes. They are all vermin anyway. I will get you away in a stock train as soon as I can, but we shan't be making one up for a few days, and for that time you will have to live and eat with the others, and so you may as well earn good money and boss them while you are doing it."

It seemed to be the only way out of Chicago. Freddie was sent to the packing factory, which normally would have been a busy place, but the strike had reduced output and the big shed was now used to house two thousand strikebreakers who slept in bunks of five or six tiers. The strikebreakers were getting more money than they had ever handled before in their lives. They were being paid two or three times the regular wage for the job and no-one seemed to care much as the supply of meat to the outside was sufficient to stop any public protest against the strike. It wasn't really a strike at all, it was a lock-out. The bosses had no objection to paying extra money to blacklegs because they got it back from the public by raising the price of meat and they had the prospect of cutting the ordinary wages after the strike was broken. After a few days Freddie's train ticket arrived and his career as a blackleg came to an end. It was also the end of his career as a hobo. Frederick Hall Thomas was on the train to New York and his life on the road was over. At least it was nearly over. The journey from Chicago to New York took him through the state of Pennsylvania and Freddie knew that he'd be passing near to the town of Scranton, which he knew to be home to the largest Welsh community in America. Miners from Wales had flocked to the burgeoning coal industry there, so Freddie got off the train and went to look for work, but once again he failed to find any. He did, however, have the money he made as a strikebreaker in Chicago so he bought a new outfit and a "bath or two" and then jumped a stock train to New York. This was definitely the end of the line.

They used to tell me it was possible to quit the road after one or two months' life on it, but that after three the lure of it got into a man's bones, and he could never go back but must be a hobo until the end of his days. I suppose I never had the real hobo instinct. For though I followed the road for nearly six months, not counting in my spells of regular work, I was always planning how I could settle down. I could never force myself to beg, and never did I really feel the lure of the road in its fullest strength. My hobo life certainly filled me with the desire to see as much of the world as I could, and has not been without its influence in sending me across Canada on trip after trip and from end to end of the States. But then I have always gone with business occupying a big place in my mind and plans. It has helped me make more money in my profession than, I guess, I should have done otherwise. But best of all perhaps, by the time I commenced my ring career, that hobo life hardened me and brought me to full strength, with almost unlimited powers of endurance.

Four

Making Good

Every morning, just before nine o'clock, 1,554 men ambled down the wide marble stairs of Mills House Number One on West Bleecker Street, New York City. Exactly 1,554 men, one from each of the 1,554 small rooms packed into a vast grey box built by Darius Ogden Mills; gold prospector, banking magnate and philanthropist for the homeless of the East Side. For fifty cents all told a man could get a bed, breakfast and dinner at Mills House. There were smoking and writing rooms, a library, baths and a laundry. It was said that the same man who made the springs for the beds at the Waldorf Astoria made the springs for the beds at Mills House. But unlike his Waldorf Astoria counterpart, the Mills House guest did not have the option of whiling away the sunlit hours in his bed. The rooms were cleared out every morning and their occupants expected to trawl the city streets looking for gainful employment. The hotel opened its doors again at five o'clock in the afternoon, and one sweltering late summer's evening in 1905 Frederick Hall Thomas was in the queue waiting to get in. Many years later Freddie told a journalist that his first job on arriving in New York was that of a porter at Mills House, but the men who paid loose change for room and board had no bags to carry. Freddie almost certainly heard of the hotel from the strike-breakers in the meatpacking yard in Chicago. The massive unemployment of the early twentieth century gave rise in many large American cities to the 'fink market' where the out-of-work were recruited for strikebreaking. Men congregated at street corners or hotels recognized as recruiting points for large bands of replacement workers that could be assembled at very short notice. Mills House Number One on West Bleecker Street was a fink market and a good place for a new boy in town to sleep the night.

It was just over a year since Freddie stepped off the *S.S. Baltic* onto the dockside in New York and all his efforts to 'make good' had taken him to a hostel for the unemployed back in the city where he started. But he wasn't about to settle for life among the blacklegs and bums and his salvation came in the form of a flamboyant millionaire publisher and campaigner against pill-pushers, processed foods and prudery. Throughout his travels and whenever he had a spare nickel Freddie bought a copy of Bernarr Macfadden's *Physical Culture* magazine. Back in New York Freddie noticed the most recent edition carried an advertisement for a wrestling and boxing instructor. One of the many controversial ideas advocated by Macfadden was his belief that women should be physically fit. He went against the standards of the time by encouraging women to exercise, to participate in outdoor sports such as tennis and swimming and even to get tanned by the sun. Freddie told the manager of the Institute he'd be making a grave mistake in employing a professional boxer for the post because they were not the type he would want to have associate with the fair sex. Freddie explained that he was a college man and knew how to take care of himself in the presence of ladies. His sales pitch worked and Freddie got the job for which he was given a wrestling mat to sleep on in the gymnasium, all his meals and $1 a day. He was also admitted free of charge to all the anatomical and physical culture courses at the Institute.

Young ladies were encouraged to enroll at the Institute and one of the first female students became Mrs Freddie Welsh. She was Brahna Weinstein of Jewish Russian extraction who anglicized her name to Fanny Weston when the family moved to New York's East Side. Fanny took Freddie's boxing course and he was attracted to her clean living and athletic ability. "Physical development does the same thing for women as it does for men," Freddie wrote. "It steadies their nerves. Besides, it makes them much more attractive, unless they carry it to extremes. I don't think women realize the value of health and beauty of a well-developed figure. I don't like to see women laced in, or tipped forward on high heels. I don't like to see them wear clothes that in any way interfere with the movement or comfort or well being of the body. It is painful to me." After a week at the Institute Freddie collected his $7 and plucked up the courage to ask Miss Weston to the theatre. She agreed and they went to Daly's where William Gillette was playing Sherlock Homes. With Fanny on his arm Freddie proudly made his way towards the theatre but as they neared Daly's they saw a queue of people three blocks long waiting to get in. Fanny checked with Freddie that he'd bought the tickets beforehand. He lied and told her that he'd go and collect them from the box office. After an altercation with the man at the head of the queue Freddie was ordered out of the lobby but on the steps outside the theatre he was approached by a 'scalper' who offered him a pair of one-dollar seats for $6. "Still I was game," Freddie recalled. "I wanted to make a hit with this little lady, and I was bound that my first $7 would assist." With the tickets and his last dollar in his pocket Freddie took his date next door to Hatche's candy store and haughtily ordered a box of chocolates. He'd been used to buying such a box for about a quarter so when he handed over the dollar bill he held out his hand for the change. The girl behind the counter just smiled and told him that there was no change; the chocolates cost $1. "I felt my knees knock together, but I wasn't dismayed," Freddie recalled. "I took the little girl on my arm and pried my way into the show, happy, but dead broke. I didn't have a loose suspender button in my jeans."

They watched the show and then started for home. Fanny lived in Brooklyn and without thinking about his finances Freddie hailed a surface car. She was about to step into the carriage when according to Freddie "my poverty flashed on me like a bolt of lightning". He pulled her off the vehicle and said that as a pair of physical culturists they should walk the journey. So off they started down Broadway to the Brooklyn Bridge and across to North 60th Street. After walking for about an hour Freddie bid Fanny good night and started his way back to his wrestling mat at Macfadden's. By the time he got there the building was locked up and there was nothing to do but wait until the janitor came at seven o'clock the following morning. He had to spend the night on frozen steps and had blown his $7 but he had won a wife. In a very short time Freddie fell in love, proposed and eloped with Fanny. After he became a famous boxer, an old sparring partner of Freddie's, Eugene Lutz, told a different story that suggests that Fanny was instrumental in the Welshman's change of fortunes. According to Lutz, Freddie told him that the first job he got when he arrived in New York was a waiter in a restaurant and that it was while working there that he met Fanny. She saw him "playfully wallop several youngsters" who were causing trouble and advised him to apply for the boxing instructors job at the Institute where she was a pupil. Whichever way he got there, he stayed on at Macfadden's until he'd finished all the courses and got a job as physical director at Dr Knipe's Institute of Physical Training on Franklin Street in New York. However, his departure from Macfadden's may have been hastened by scandal. On October 5th 1905 Anthony Comstock of the Society for the Suppression of Vice, accompanied by officers of the New York Police Department, raided Macfadden's offices and charged him with spreading pornography. Posters for a *Mammoth Physical Culture Exhibition* to be held at Madison Square Garden had been displayed around the city. The offending items showed the winners of the previous year's physique competitions: ten or twelve young women in white union suits with sashes around their waists and Al Treloar, the men's winner, wearing a pair of sandals and a leopard's skin as a breechcloth. Comstock considered the posters pornographic and Macfadden was given a suspended jail sentence for a lewd display of carnality. The ensuing publicity ensured that special police units had to be called out on the show's opening night to handle the 20,000 spectators, 5,000 of whom had to be turned away. But anyone who bought a ticket to see a display of female flesh was disappointed. All the participants were modestly attired in union suits.

Whether Freddie left because of the scandal or simply because his courses had ended there's no doubt that his next job was as a trainer at Knipe's Institute, a move that had a profound effect on his life. Dr Joseph R. Knipe was an amateur heavyweight champion boxer and it was while watching him sparring that Freddie conceived of the idea of being a prizefighter. The Institute routinely staged public boxing exhibitions that were actually fully-fledged professional contests with the fighters being paid by collections from the crowd. On one occasion a boxer failed to show and Freddie was asked to step in. As an employee of the Institute he couldn't really refuse the fight. When the matchmaker heard that Freddie was 'English', he decided to put him on first to bring a little international flavour to the $2 match. Freddie didn't keep any note of the affair, and he forgot his opponent's name, but he remembered that he was a "pretty good boxer of some small repute as a preliminary fighter". It was only a three round affair and Freddie had the best of matters and left the ring feeling pretty sure his display had been a good advertisement for the gym. No one had taken the hat around for Freddie because he was working for the Institute, so a Mr Lunt, a New York fight-fan, intervened. He was so impressed with the boxing on show that along with two of his brothers and a couple of friends he collected $5 and presented it to Freddie as he left the dressing room. Freddie didn't see Lunt again until he was sailing back to the United States from the United Kingdom on board the *Imperator* ten years later as world lightweight champion. They met in the ship's swimming pool. Freddie recognized Lunt at once and he accosted his old benefactor and asked him if he remembered the incident. Lunt remembered the collection he took at the gymnasium for a novice English boxer but he hadn't realized that Fred Thomas of Knipe's was now Freddie Welsh.

To supplement his income at the Institute, Freddie worked as health director and boxing instructor at Brown's Gymnasium in New York. He helped the fighters prepare for bouts by fixing up their punching bags, tying on their gloves and washing their sweaters. Once in a while he'd put on the gloves himself to fill in when a sparring partner failed to show. The professionals who trained there enjoyed sparring with Freddie because he boxed like an Englishman and he fought differently to anybody else in the city. But when winter arrived in New York many of Dr Knipe's clients headed for warmer climates and Freddie was put to work on a part time basis. The financial impact of his reduced hours became apparent to Freddie at the end of his first week under the new arrangements. When his final shift ended on Saturday evening the doctor handed him $3.

"How in heaven's name am I to exist on this?" asked Freddie.

Dr Knipe suggested there would be a lot of money to be had shoveling snow in a New York winter and that he would even lend Freddie a shovel. He took up the doctor's offer and Freddie joined a snow-tossing brigade in Harlem at $2 a day. But as the cold began to bite into his blistered hands he packed up the shovel and became virtually destitute. He lived in a 2-cent coffee house on Bleecker Street. That is, when he had the 2 cents. He also joined the legions in New York City for whom the free lunch counter at the local saloon was practically the entire basis of their food supply. For the price of a nickel of beer they could help themselves to a counter generally laden with bread, cheese and pickles. When Freddie didn't have a nickel he would go without food for a few days at a time. One day he tottered into a saloon that furnished an especially enticing array of pickles and cheese. Freddie was cleaning up the counter when a few men who had known him at Brown's gymnasium came in and asked if he was "up against it". The question answered itself. Freddie just grinned and scooped up more small blocks of cheese from the free board. His old friends asked why he didn't go upstairs where a fighting club held nightly private bouts and get a match. Freddie refused. But the next day it was cold and snowy and he walked all day without finding a job or a meal. He was back at the lunch counter when his acquaintances from the gym came in again. They told him that a man called Billy Elmer would give him $2 to fight upstairs that night.

Freddie was too hungry to resist any longer. Two dollars meant a thick steak and some browned potatoes and a piece of pie and a cup of real coffee. He was ushered up into a little loft above the saloon; the matchmaker looked him over and offered Freddie a fight against the 'Knockout Kid'. His opponent's moniker was probably due to his ability to receive as opposed to deliver a knockout blow and Freddie duly flattened the 'Kid' in one round. Freddie collected his $2 and rushed for the nearest diner. From that night on he looked for boxing exhibitions that paid a fee. He was going day after day without food so to keep from starving he boxed at 'smokers and stags'. He'd turn up with his togs under his arm and take his place with all the boys lined up, waiting to get a chance in the ring. Even now, Freddie had no plan to forge a career in the ring and he kept no record or newspaper clippings of these fights. His ambition was to become a physical culture expert and he found a job in Philadelphia as an instructor at Herman's Institute. Fanny stayed in New York to finish her studies while Freddie set off to the City of Brotherly Love. But he lost the job within days and was out of work and out of money once more. He answered an advertisement for a salesman to sell punch balls at a big store in the city. Freddie turned up for an interview only to find a queue of hundreds of men waiting to fill one post. He dashed to the front, pretending to be a plumber, and told the proprietor, "Look here I want a job". He was offered the post because of his initiative but it would be ten days before the punch balls arrived and he was told to come back then. Freddie explained to the storeowner that he couldn't go that long without earning so he was paid to help around the store in the meantime. The ten-day delay proved a blessing as, embarrassingly for a future world's boxing champion, he had no idea how to use a punch ball. He could thump one all right but Freddie didn't know how to perform the fancy moves the proprietor wanted to see. When the store finally took delivery of the punch balls Freddie bought himself more time by saying that the demonstration platform wasn't good enough. It took another three days to build suitable staging but then Freddie found another problem with the bag itself. In all, Freddie managed to delay the inevitable by three or four weeks by which time he'd saved $30 in wages. Finally the owner called Freddie aside and told him to punch the bag or get out of the store. Freddie confessed that he had been bluffing but that he needed the money. The proprietor was furious and was going to have the Welshman thrown out. He maintained that he was a fighter by profession and so the storeowner decided to exact his revenge by summoning Freddie to his house for a challenge match.

When Freddie arrived the following morning he was taken down to the cellar where two experienced local boxers were stripped and ready to fight. With two clean right hooks Freddie won the forgiveness of his employer who agreed to retain him in his service at $10 a week instead of $15. However, by this time Freddie had managed to save a few dollars and he decided to go in for boxing as a business. One of the two men Freddie had knocked out in the cellar boxed at the Broadway Athletic Club in Philadelphia and he introduced the Welshman to its manager 'Diamond' Jim Bailey. Freddie was offered a bout but before the bill was publicized he told Diamond Jim that he didn't want to box under his own name. Freddie feared he might fail and that his mother might get to know about it, and might be hurt by it. At first he planned to call himself Fred Cymry, and he wrote to Fanny to ask her opinion on the subject. He explained that Cymry

Fighting for forgiveness in the store owner's basement.

meant Welsh, and it was Fanny who suggested that he should use
Welsh right out. "They'll get tied up in a knot over the other name,"
she wrote, and Freddie saw at once that she was right.

So it was that Freddie Welsh came to take his bow as a real professional. By this time he had been engaged by Jack Clancy as a boxing,
wrestling and physical culture expert at his gymnasium at South 13th
Street, Philadelphia. Clancy managed to get Freddie his first professional fight against a boxer known as Young Williams, a fairly
well-known preliminary boxer. The bout was staged at the Broadway
Athletic Club on December 21st 1905. Freddie knew he had to win
this contest if he was going to have any chance in the game and he
went for Williams for all he was worth and succeeded in putting him
away in the third round. He only received $3 for his services but as
Clancy pointed out, Freddie Welsh had made a start. He was back in
the ring a month later, against Johnny Kelly at the same club. One of
the local reporters wrote that the youngsters mixed it up merrily in
every round and that Welsh had the advantage at the finish. At this
time the law forbade Philadelphia referees to give any verdict in an
attempt to stop fixed fights. The idea was that a fix was less likely if the

only way to win was by knockout. Of course fight fans wanted a winner so the press took over rendering their own verdicts called 'newspaper decisions'. All Freddie's early fights were six-round no decision contests and he quickly became a favourite of the Broadway Athletic Club patrons. Freddie was rapidly promoted up the ranks of the 'semi-wind-up' fighters and after only a handful of fights he was usually second on the bill. He was matched against a trio of tough fighters in quick succession. Eddie Fay, Tommy Feltz and Tommy Love were the opponents and Freddie was given the newspaper decision in each case. Matching him with Tommy Feltz, a lightweight from Brooklyn with a good record, was particularly ambitious but according to one newspaper, "Welsh made a great impression both by his cleverness and hitting power, and was all over the Brooklynite during the six rounds, punishing him severely."

He boxed as a $5 a night fighter in ill-lit, smoke-laden halls that boomed to the rumble of male voices. The baying crowd sat on the same level and within touching distance of the bloodstained canvas ring. Uniformed policeman broke up the scuffles that routinely broke out among partisan spectators and swindled punters. And somewhere a few rows back, usually behind Freddie's corner, sat Fanny; the only woman in the house. "I know outside the ring Freddie looks like a heathen missionary out of a job, who's just yearning to be back 'mishing'," said Fanny. "He looks as if he might, if he saw a great, rude prizefighter with a thick neck and hairy chest approaching, sit down and pray. But wait till he gets in action! Those muscles slip along under his white skin like silver bands; his tread is the velvet tread of the panther; he fascinates his opponent like a cat does a canary bird – and those absurd dimples have elongated into stern creases! Oh, you ought to see him!"

Freddie's performances alerted other clubs in the city and he was offered a position with the National Athletic Club, which led to bigger fights and bigger purses. He made his debut at the National on March 24th 1906 in a match with Kid Stringer. He trained seriously for this one; Stringer had a good reputation and Freddie tasted the fear of defeat for the first time. His anxiety was misplaced and he "outclassed a game opponent". The club's matchmakers put together a strong card on the night of his fight with Stringer but Freddie had yet to rise to the 'percentage-privileged' class where he'd get a slice of the gate money, although he moved steadily towards it. His popularity with Philadelphia's boxing fraternity ensured that the clubs that hired him made good money and Freddie got plenty of work. He'd ask for and be given all the fights he wanted and was

Cartoon from the *New Orleans Item*, 28 December 1913

taking at least a bout a week during the winter of 1905/06. When he wasn't fighting, he was teaching boxing and wrestling at Clancy's gymnasium so he was constantly in training and always ready to take whatever ring engagements came his way. In fact, Freddie was probably doing too much training. On April 11th 1906 he boxed Billy Mahaig at Philadelphia's Tuxedo Club and disappointed for the first time. He won the newspaper decision but hadn't created much of an impression and looked stale. He was also saving himself a little for a forthcoming fight with Frank Carsey of Chicago at the National Athletic Club. Carsey had the best reputation of anybody he'd fought so far with a long list of knockouts on his record. Despite losing the last two rounds Freddie did manage to get the newspaper decision and according to one scribe, "Welsh, although giving away weight, put up a rattling good bout, and by his cleverness he had the crowd in a wild state of excitement in the last round."

Freddie took all of five days off after the Carsey fight before returning to the Broadway Club where he was matched with Jimmy Devine. Freddie remembered being very cautious to avoid his opponent's heavy right swings, and one journalist wrote that Devine failed to lay a glove on him in six rounds. Next up was a return match with Tommy Love. "Tommy had not been satisfied with his first beating, and so he got a worse one this time," Freddie recalled. But Tommy Love lost more than the decision. He was due to meet a well-known fighter, Matty Baldwin, on April 23rd at the Washington Athletic Club, but the club's management decided it would be better policy to secure Freddie's services for the fight instead. This was a big opportunity; Baldwin was considered to be the best 124-pound fighter in the eastern states at the time. Freddie had barely lost a round in his career to date, but Baldwin was fully 10lbs heavier, and it looked at the beginning that this disadvantage would lead to Freddie's first defeat. Baldwin had the better of the first three rounds after which time Freddie realized that his opponent wasn't "nearly such a terrible man-eater as he had been represented". According to one report:

> To the surprise of the crowd Welsh started to do a little on his own account in the fourth round and with clever left hand work had Baldwin up in the air. At the finish the Lowell man was bleeding from the mouth and nose, while Welsh was scarcely marked. It was a great finish, in which the Englishman won the cheers of the crowd.

Ten days later, on May 3rd 1906, Freddie was back at the Broadway to meet and beat Billy Willis in a wind-up bout, and was promptly rebooked to fight Jim Callahan, the man who became the first fighter to beat Freddie Welsh. Freddie nearly had Callahan out in the second round, in which he was saved only by the call of time. But in trying to finish matters off Freddie ran into a sharp left jab that shook him up and after that blow the Welshman lost his composure. The fourth round was a fierce affair, and though Callahan was shaken up badly he floored Freddie for a couple of seconds. Freddie recovered and was the stronger and the fresher at the close, but it could not disguise the fact that he had been out-pointed. Luckily, however, the opinions of the reporters were sufficiently divided for his reputation to remain undamaged. It was one of the defining fights in Freddie's early career. Callahan was a wily old fighter who gave him a beating over six rounds and after this bout Freddie trained obsessively to develop his left jab. He painted a white dot on a bag and practiced relentlessly so he could hit the spot with every punch. Two days after the scrap with Callahan he was back in action against another experienced fighter, Jack Reardon. When the two advanced to the middle of the ring Freddie put out his hand to touch gloves only to take a straight left on the jaw and was knocked down after just one second of the first round. Freddie was on the canvas for a count of nine but recovered and was given the newspaper verdict after six rounds. A week later he beat Kid Gleason at the National and after a few days' rest he scored his third knockout over Mike Laughlin, getting home a hard right to the jaw in the second round. On June 14th 1906 he was matched again with Frank Carsey who had been "thirsting to avenge" his previous defeat. Freddie learned in this fight that it does not pay to be over-confident. He under-rated Carsey after their previous meeting and some of the papers gave the American the verdict.

June was a busy month for Freddie. He wound up proceedings by giving Billy Glover "a fearful gruelling and a defeat" and then he got the contest that he'd been waiting for. Young Erne was "the daisy of the Philadelphia lightweight division" and could always be relied upon to draw a bumper house. Freddie was given a good percentage on the house receipts though Erne, as the main attraction, was able to stipulate better terms. Freddie had to give away 4lbs and was given a very hard fight. In the third round Erne thought the time to win quickly had come, and he rushed out to slug Freddie, who met him, and they battled all over the ring. Both punched without regard for the other's return. The crowd was screaming and to the astonishment of all present Freddie broke even in all the brawling. Then came the sensation. Erne, who was one of the cleverest lightweights in the East, was jabbed, hooked, and made to look a third-rater. Freddie stepped around and welted Erne until the blood trickled from his mouth and nose. The American became desperate at being beaten at his own game. He rushed, but Freddie was away, and then drove his opponent's head back with a left jab. In the last round both men slugged at each other without respite and the honours were certainly with Freddie by the final bell.

After that fight, and with only eight months of professional boxing, Freddie was essentially the champion of Philadelphia in his weight division. He was now a principal fighter at every club in the city and invitations were arriving from even further afield. He received word from the Gymnasium Club in Dayton, Ohio that it would like to stage a fight with Hock Keys, the lightweight champion of Australia. Freddie was only too pleased with the money on offer, though he knew that he was tackling a tough opponent. Keys had a big reputation and he was a fully blown lightweight into the bargain. Freddie was only a featherweight at the time and was giving Keys at least a seven-pound advantage on the night. The Australian was a short-priced favourite in the betting: he was a much bigger, more experienced fighter and the contest was to be held over a twenty-round course – a ring journey that Freddie had yet to travel. At least it was *scheduled* for twenty rounds. Freddie broke his right hand as he punched the top of Keys' head at the end of the sixth round. Many years later the veteran trainer Billy McCarney, who was in Freddie's corner that night, told the full story of the fight. According to McCarney Freddie was trying to get along using just his left, but after seventeen rounds the trainer thought his man was losing the fight and came up with a final, desperate plan to salvage the bout. He told Freddie that his only chance was to throw one big punch with his right. McCarney figured that Keys, who hadn't seen Freddie throw a punch with his right hand for eleven rounds, wouldn't be expecting it and he told his man to "start it back as far as you can get it and let it go". The Welshman followed his trainer's instructions and floored Keys with a right hook to the jaw after which the Australian's corner threw in the sponge. "You can imagine how much nerve it took to hit with all his might with that broken hand. But he did it. Keys whirled around and dropped for the count. Welsh almost fainted from pain," recalled McCarney.

The local Dayton press described it as the fastest bout ever pulled off in the neighbourhood and Freddie rather grandly claimed to be the champion of Australia and England as a result. The hand injury kept him out of the ring for a few months, however, and if there were no fights, there was no money. It was to teach him a valuable lesson. Freddie had a knockout punch in those days, and kept possession of it for several years, as his early victories proved. After a while he realized that if he was going to make a career as a professional boxer he had to take care of his hands and that he could not risk breaking them on hard, bony substances. "A boxer's hands are his most valuable assets," Freddie wrote, "and they are frequently the things he loses first unless he realizes as I did early in my career, that they must only be risked on something soft. I realized that I would have to take care of my hands if I was going to stay in the game."

His first fight back from the hand injury was against Jimmy Dunn of Newcastle, Pennsylvania. The bout was staged at the scene of his first and only defeat against Jim Callahan, the National Club in

Philadelphia on August 31st 1906. It was another setback and Freddie admitted that he had become a "trifle swollen about the head". He had begun to believe he was invincible, but the time had come for someone to come along and prove otherwise. Callahan had done the trick once and Jimmy Dunn was due to be the next performer. Freddie under-rated Dunn and paid the penalty, though the decision against him was once more only a newspaper one. Still Freddie "quite failed to relish it any the more, and thirsted sorely for revenge". He approached the Dayton Club to stage a return match. They were only too pleased to agree, as was Jimmy Dunn. Freddie's performance in the return bout, especially his work at close quarters, was a revelation, and surprised Dunn as much as anybody. He clearly outclassed his opponent and the Welshman's whirlwind style of fighting had Dunn reeling on several occasions. Freddie and the press thought he won, but the referee, who was allowed to give a verdict in the state of Ohio, thought otherwise and scored the fight a draw. The decision set the crowd raging and Dunn's swollen nose and puffy lips were evidence of the injustice.

Freddie returned to Philadelphia for a fight with an aspiring young boxer, Willie Moody. It was another routine win for the Welshman, who then turned his attention to luring Jim Callahan into another match. It was the only unresolved issue on his record. He needed to wipe it off the slate and Freddie tried every way to get Callahan to come up to the scratch. The American finally agreed to meet Freddie, in private, on October 22nd 1906 at Cincinnati. Both men had been guaranteed a purse of $1,000 with the privilege of a percentage, but Callahan failed to put in an appearance and made no excuse for his absence. So Freddie gave up the chase for Callahan and started to think of home. He'd been away from Wales for over two years and felt he had 'made good' and wanted to go back. He also got word from Pontypridd that his mother was far from well and she wanted to see him. He booked passage on the *S.S. Etruria* that was due to sail on December 15th 1906. It gave him enough time to take one more lucrative fight to swell the coffers before the journey. Kid Gleason, who Freddie had beaten in May, had been telling the newspapers that he had been out of condition then and that he was confident he could win a return. The Wayne Club in Philadelphia arranged the bout and it was set for December 12th. Freddie duly gave the 'Kid' another beating and with Fanny still in New York he set sail for England.

He returned to Pontypridd wearing a large black hat, a long black coat and an American accent. He found his mother's health was

actually much better than he'd been led to expect but that the money
he took home didn't last that long so his intention of taking a long
holiday wasn't possible. Freddie was fortunate to meet a local sportsman and former champion amateur boxer, Harry Marks, and the two
formed a close business and personal relationship. "It was while he
was here in South Wales that he was brought to me as a promising
fighter by Tom Toby, a character well known in Cardiff years ago,"
Harry Marks recalled. "Welsh on our first introduction was a spectacle indeed. Attired in a large black sombrero hat, with a long, clerical
looking coat, he seemed a typical foreigner. I took him in hand,
however, and I soon found he was full of British grit."

From that moment on Harry looked after Freddie's interests
whenever he fought on British soil. Any mention of Freddie's name
in the sporting press, if it was in anyway negative, was replied to by
Marks in the next issue. Harry had won the Lightweight Amateur
Championship at St James's Hall, Piccadilly in 1896 and was well
connected with the boxing aristocracy in England. He contacted
Peggy Bettinson, one of the founders of the National Sporting Club,
to tell him of Freddie Welsh. The Club had transformed the sport
from bare fisted brawling into an integral part of British sporting life.
Before 1891 professional boxing was illegal and fighters were often
arrested and dealt with as any other pair of street brawlers. The
National Sporting Club changed all that. It established a base at 43
King Street, Covent Garden, in a house that was believed to have
been built in 1636. One of the former tenants had constructed a
theatre room for variety performances and concerts and this made
the building particularly suitable to the needs of the new club. In
addition to the room used for boxing there was a reading room, a
restaurant and a spacious grillroom. It rapidly became the only place
in London in the eighteen-nineties where it was possible to watch
boxing in comfort and, usually, decorum. The management encouraged formality at the N.S.C. and many members dressed for dinner
and to watch the subsequent bouts in the boxing theatre, though
quite a number still came directly from their offices in the City or
their West End shops. They could get a good dinner of chops or
steak, with chips and cheese and a pot of beer for one shilling and
fourpence and any number of good fights for their subscription.

So keen were the members to uphold the fine tradition of the
Club that only boxers deemed to have reached a certain standard
could fight there. Freddie was approached by a few members who
expressed their concern that he was overmatched and that the Club
should have picked an easier opponent. "I got him his first fight at

the National Sporting Club with Seaman Hayes, who in those days was considered to be one of the best light-weights in the country," Harry Marks recalled. "Welsh was then an unknown quantity, and I was scoffed at for arranging the fight." Some of the sportsmen who ran the Club arranged a few tryouts for Freddie at the Irish Guards' Gymnasium nearby and he managed to satisfy them that he was no novice and should be allowed to grace their ring. By this time Freddie was of the opinion that he was the best lightweight in the world. "In my vanity I had believed that even the London public must have been following my career in the States, but I was soon to be undeceived," wrote Freddie.

On the night of his fight with Hayes, Freddie was the underdog in the betting, so he made full use of his status as an unknown. Freddie took the large odds against him winning to earn "a nice little sum". He beat the Londoner with ease, and the referee declared him the winner after six rounds. So pleased were the habitués at headquarters that Freddie was given a fifteen-round contest the following month with Alf Reed. Freddie stayed on in London, at the Cranborne Hotel, Leicester Square, but Reed injured himself playing football and a fighter called Young Joseph stepped into the breach. Joseph was a tougher opponent and once again the patrons of the Club were concerned that the good name of the establishment might be tarnished by a mismatch. Freddie proceeded to win every round and knocked Joseph to the canvas in both the thirteenth and fourteenth rounds. "Joseph had an idea that close-range work would suit his book and banged away hard with both hands," Freddie wrote of the fight, "but he wasn't used to the Philadelphian pace and soon had to hang on and hold." Only six-round bouts were legal in Philadelphia and the boxing supporters in the city demanded non-stop action. The fighters were therefore much quicker and Freddie believed that a six-round bout in Philadelphia was much tougher than a twenty-round fight in England.

With the National Sporting Club suitably impressed, Freddie returned to Wales. He was approached by one of Pontypridd's sports-men and academics, Professor Joe Smith, with the suggestion that they should run a series of boxing tournaments together. Professor Smith would look after all the arrangements and Freddie was to be the star attraction, ready and willing to take on any challenger. They decided to make a start at the Park Gymnastic Club in Pontypridd but the biggest problem with the plan was that no one of anything like sufficient calibre to extend Freddie showed up, so he took on three opponents in succession. They were the best Freddie could find, and they all had good local reputations, but they were all stopped inside six rounds. First up was Evan Evans who went out in about half a round; Charlie Webber was next and failed to stay a couple and though Gomer Morgan went after Freddie for two rounds he was put to sleep during the third. This made Freddie a "bit of a name" and Johnny Owens, the lightweight champion of Wales, promptly challenged him to a match for £25 a side and the title. The fight was staged on May 20th 1907 before a packed Victoria Hall with Harry Wheeler from Cardiff as referee. In truth it wasn't really a contest and the only applause for Owens came when he helped Freddie to his feet after a slip in the third round. In the next, Freddie hit Owens flush on the forehead and from that point on the champion kept dropping to the canvas without being hit. He was falling from exhaustion and Freddie appealed to the referee on more than one occasion to stop the fight. Wheeler, seeing that Owens was helplessly beaten, awarded the verdict to Freddie without the need to box the last two rounds. Freddie was the lightweight champion of Wales.

His next challenger was Sid Russell of Cheltenham, the ten-stone champion of the West of England. Freddie had to give a great deal of weight away because he still couldn't find anyone of his own division to fight him. The bout was staged at Taylor's Pavillion in Merthyr for a purse of £30. Russell never had a chance, but he fought gamely for seven rounds before his seconds threw up the sponge. Freddie returned to the Victoria Hall, Pontypridd, for his next fight and a £50 match against Young Lilley, the holder of the All-England championship belt of 1906 and winner of over fifty contests. Lilley gave up in the eleventh round having been battered for the previous ten. Freddie had found the Londoner was vulnerable to body shots and he pounded away at his mid section and so weakened him that he was forced to retire. It was after this fight that Freddie first crossed paths with the man who was the hero of Wales and who, for a short time, would become his great friend. Jim Driscoll and Freddie Welsh met at the St Mary Hill Fair in Bridgend. They treated the crowd to a six-round exhibition and Jim helped Freddie prepare for his next fight against Dick Lee of London. The bout was staged at the Merthyr National Athletic Club, but it was a disappointing affair with Freddie winning every round against Lee, a former amateur featherweight champion and the winner of over two hundred professional contests. Since his arrival on British soil Freddie had issued a challenge to fight any man in the Kingdom at 9st 7lbs but failed to get a match. What he really wanted was a match against the three men regarded as the leading lightweights in Britain: Jack Goldswain, Jabez White and

Johnny Summers. He entered into negotiations with all three men and posted money to cover the challenges, but for various reasons all the proposed fights fell through. Meanwhile Seaman Hayes, Freddie's first opponent on British soil, had expressed himself as having been very dissatisfied with the verdict of the first contest at the National Sporting Club and so he challenged Freddie to go fifteen rounds for £50 a side. The bout was sealed when the Victoria Hall in Pontypridd offered a purse of £100 to stage the fight there.

Hayes came at Freddie in his customary dogged fashion, but despite his well-deserved reputation for toughness and a gift for taking punishment, Freddie put him down twice in the fourth round and out for good in the fifth. It was the first time Hayes had been knocked out in a long career. Freddie was attracting ever larger crowds every time he stepped into the ring, yet he wasn't very well liked, especially in his hometown. Maybe it was his attitude, clothes or accent, but Freddie was very aware that there was no affection for him, and it hurt.

He'd been back in the country for only five months but Freddie had deeply upset the sportsmen of South Wales. He was considered too brash and his cockiness offended the rather conservative sporting fraternity. Freddie also refused to partake in what he saw as the overtly macho customs of this world. "Just because a man is strong there is no reason why he has to slap other men on the back, or squeeze their knuckles together until they squirm," said Freddie. "I hate to see a man indulge in this social demonstration of his physical powers." He'd returned home only to find that it no longer felt like home. Freddie was already planning his return to the United States and there were others in Pontypridd who were anxious to hasten his departure. A small group of wealthy gentlemen put together a purse to lure the Canadian middleweight Joe White to Wales to give Freddie a good lacing. The fight was made at catch-weights – a match between two fighters of different weight divisions. White was about four inches taller and at least two stones heavier, well outside what would normally be acceptable for a catch-weight contest. On the night of September 16th, in a warehouse loft in Pontypridd, about thirty of the sporting gentry of South Wales gathered to watch Freddie Welsh box 'Gentleman' Joe White for a fighting stake of £100 a side and a purse donated by a private syndicate. Captain Arthur Seaton, the chairman of the Pontypridd Urban District Council, put the warehouse at the disposal of the promoter, and a select gathering huddled around the roped square to see Gentleman Joe "burst the bubble that was Freddie Welsh". The match was staged in private and the thirty or so local gentlemen present secured their seats by ballot. The rounds were cut down to two minutes at White's request; he was the older, heavier man and was more likely to run out of speed. It didn't work. White was battered in a succession of one-sided rounds until the sixteenth when Gentleman Joe delivered an ungentlemanly low blow. Before the referee could interfere, Freddie jumped in, and taking no notice of the foul, asked his opponent to come on and fight. From here to the end of what was the last round, White was "receiver-in-chief", and soon after he had taken his seat his second, George Harry, gave in for him. In one contest Freddie became a local hero.

Word of his exploits against White led to a great demand for Freddie to ply his trade in public once more. A fortnight later, at the Mill Field ground, Pontypridd, Freddie undertook to stop two good men in ten rounds each. Arthur Ellis claimed to be the 9st 6lbs champion of England and Gunner Hart was the welterweight champion of the Navy. Freddie agreed to forfeit a side stake of £50 if he failed to accomplish the task of stopping both men in the limited period. Gunner Hart was first into the ring and for the opening two rounds neither boxer appeared to have the upper hand. But it was soon evident that Freddie had been measuring up his opponent and in the next round he clattered a flurry of unanswered punches into Hart's face that forced him to the ground. In the fifth Freddie dropped his opponent to the canvas once more and Hart remained down for eight seconds. He got up and Freddie rained in a series of body blows before the referee stepped in amidst the loud plaudits of the audience. Freddie sat in his corner and waited for Arthur Ellis to step through the ropes. Ellis at first looked to be very clever with his footwork, and appeared to be giving Freddie some trouble. But the Welshman was employing the same tactics as in the first encounter, devoting the first two rounds to measuring his man, and it was not until the third round that he brought to bear upon his opponent a sequence of painful short jabs. The referee threatened to disqualify Ellis for a foul blow after Freddie delivered a punch on the left jaw of the English champion. Ellis was badly beaten about the head in the fourth and he bled freely. In the next round Freddie floored his opponent three times in quick succession, Ellis once remaining down for nine seconds. The Englishman still evinced a desire to continue, but he was hopelessly beaten and the referee came between the contestants and declared Freddie the winner. At the end of the second bout, Mr Lewis Lewis of Treorchy, stepped into the ring and made an offer to match Freddie for a side-stake of £500 to £1,000 against any man of similar weight in Great Britain.

Right through the summer of 1907 Freddie had been trying hard to get a match with Johnny Summers, the man who was considered to be the British lightweight champion. But Summers could not be tempted into the ring and he set off for a tour of America. Freddie decided to follow him. The night before his departure Freddie was the dinner guest of Edgar Powell, the treasurer of Pontypridd Football Club, at the White Hart Hotel, who had agreed to accompany the boxer on his return to the United States. Powell decided to go on a four-month tour for health reasons – he had recently suffered from a 'throat attack'. They were travelling in the company of Wyndham Lewis, a well-known local footballer, and the famous singer Madame Polly Rowlands-Davies. Arthur Seaton presided over the banquet and in his introduction he stressed that the pugilist was by no means a common bruiser – a term which was often associated with the exponents of the noble art of self-defence at the time. In conduct and character Freddie served as a good model to all young men, claimed Seaton, who added that the boxer led an exemplary life and was a total abstainer and even a non-smoker. This wasn't actually true. Many years later Freddie admitted to being an "inveterate cigarette smoker in Pontypridd and in Montreal" and that he had developed a real craving for the use of tobacco. But at the time Freddie was anxious to cultivate an image of a young man leading a strenuous, clean life and that it would be difficult to find anyone whose morals and rectitude could stand greater scrutiny. Freddie received a large portrait of himself and was treated to an evening of song to wish him well on his journey. The following day he was given another send-off at the railway station. As his train pulled out the large crowd that had assembled burst into a rendition of 'Farewell My Own True Love'. Freddie left for America with an ambitious programme in front of him. He'd been a professional fighter for less than two years but Freddie Welsh had decided that he wanted 'the title'. When he started boxing, Freddie strove to equip himself to become a champion: because the champion made dollars while the boxer not a champion made cents. "Already I had started to dream that I should be lightweight champion of the world before I retired," Freddie later recalled, "but I was far from realizing how long and how weary the chase was going to prove."

Five

Victims and Dollars

As the bell sounded for the beginning of the forty-second round Battling Nelson was bleeding from his ears, mouth, nose and the mishmash of cuts that flapped open across his face. It was Labor Day, September 3rd 1906, in Goldfield, Nevada. Nelson and Joe Gans had slugged it out for over two hours and fifty minutes under a blistering sun in the longest gloved championship match recorded under Marquis of Queensbury rules. The brutality finally ended when Nelson could take no more and deliberately fouled Gans and was disqualified. Gans against Nelson was black against white, boxer against fighter for the lightweight championship of the world. If there had been any doubt before as to the rightful holder of the title, it was dispelled in the Nevada desert. Joe Gans held the lightweight crown, Battling Nelson had all but died in its pursuit and now Freddie Welsh was embarking on his long, painful quest to be champion. "In those days Joe Gans was at the height of his career, and he was my ideal of a boxer," Freddie later recalled. "I often thought if ever I became champion I'd try to be the kind of fighter that Gans was. But I was only a preliminary boy and whenever I mentioned any ambition to be champion I was laughed at."

The chase began in style however. Freddie, along with Edgar Powell from Pontypridd, sailed from Liverpool to New York on board the *Lusitania* on her first crossing after regaining the Blue Riband of the Atlantic for Great Britain. His days of sailing in steerage were over. Freddie spent the voyage relaxing in the lavish, gold-leaf covered, Louis XVI inspired lounges and dining halls of the Cunard liner. On arriving in the United States Freddie met Fanny in New York and the pair left for Philadelphia. He knew the city's boxing impresarios well and they managed to arrange three fights for him within a month of his return. The City of Brotherly Love was one of America's great fighting cities with a reputation for producing brave, all action boxers. A scribe once wrote that in Philadelphia even "in the subway, when you see two homeless guys fighting, they are throwing combinations".

Freddie's first opponent back in an American ring was 'Cyclone' Johnny Thompson who was regarded as one of the most serious challengers to Joe Gans. Freddie took Thompson's place in the pecking order with an easy six-round win. 'Spider' or 'Boxer' Kelly, otherwise known as the 'Graysferry slugger' was up next. That he was much bigger and heavier than the Welshman counted for little and Freddie used his opponent's head as a punch ball for most of the bout. Freddie spent Christmas 1907 picking up dollars and victims all along the Eastern Seaboard. In quick succession he beat Willie Fitzgerald, the 'Fighting Harp' of Philadelphia, Dave Deshler, Eddie Carter and Kid Locke – each one a respectable opponent, but the big name lightweights were out of town and it was time to move on. He and Fanny headed west and the first stop on the journey was Milwaukee, Wisconsin. A group of local sportsmen had challenged Freddie to fight Maurice 'Kid' Sayers, an old hand who had "put paid to the bill of some of the best of the boys". Good as Freddie was admitted to be, the men of Milwaukee thought the local man was sure to outpoint him. Freddie demonstrated his complete repertoire of punches to his new audience. According to newspapermen at ringside, he was particularly effective at shooting out left jabs deliberately wide of Sayers' face but in pulling back from the same lead he would land with the back of the glove. In one fight Freddie had won over another fighting city and Milwaukee's athletic clubs were lining up to offer the Welshman more bouts. He and Fanny moved into a lodging house in the city where Freddie soon incurred the wrath of his elderly landlady. It was a bitterly cold winter but Freddie, as was his custom, insisted on keeping his windows open throughout the night. It became a duel, with Freddie opening the windows and the landlady closing them as soon as she could. The issue was resolved one afternoon when Freddie returned from a walk to find a carpenter putting the last nail in the last window and the landlady declaring that she could not have her tenants frozen out by "fresh air fiends". They left for another boarding house that night and stayed on in Milwaukee for a match with Charlie Neary. It was to be a ten-round affair at the end of which the referee would decide the winner. Wisconsin was one of the few states where a referee's verdict was permitted. Because of widespread corruption in boxing at the time, most states insisted on 'no decision' fights and Freddie was soon to find out why this legislation had been put in place. He gave his opponent a terrible beating and after the first three rounds Neary's friends gave up all hope. When Charlie's nose stopped a few lefts some of the spectators groaned, though they soon got used to it. They watched their idol take an awful lacing; saw him miss continuously; saw him unsuccessfully try to out-fight his clever opponent; and saw him fall short with the majority of his left leads. But when the fight was over the referee raised the hands of both men to signify a draw. The crowd and the sportswriters knew that this fight was "one of those things". "And Al Bright called it a draw! Oh! Al Bright!!" wrote one local hack.

Bad as the decision in this fight was, Freddie's next experience in Milwaukee was far worse. In the 'grand old mob days' boxers and referees were a gambling asset in big matches where betting made the cost of 'fixing' a boxer a reasonable overhead. Even the world champion had been tainted by the whiff of boxing corruption. Before winning the title Joe Gans had fought well over a hundred contests and lost only five; twice when he was young and inexperienced and three times in obedience to the bidding of the moneymen and his manager. Fight fixing was so widespread that most of the States in the union banned referees from giving decisions at the end of a bout; paying off the referee was the safest way of ensuring the desired result. This was especially true in fights between two young, ambitious fighters who'd escaped the clutches of the mob thus far. So when the Badger Club in Milwaukee secured the contest between Freddie and Packey McFarland the only way to guarantee the correct result was to get at the third man in the ring. After the fight one leading boxing publication wrote:

> Whispers and rumours from time to time roll round the boxing world of there being places where men win or lose whether they like it or not, as many suit the betting-books of the proprietary, creating in the minds of all decent men a hearty desire to kick all such proprietors; but for real low down trickery the following takes the whole baking.
> A Chicago fighter was given the decision. A Chicago referee officiated.
> Chicago people offered bets of 3 to 1 on their man.
> These are three incidents in connection with the boxing contest on Friday night at the Hippodrome between Packey McFarland of Chicago, and Freddie Welsh, of Pontypridd, England.

McFarland grew up at the back of the stock yards in a tough section of Chicago. He learned to use his fists in fights on the street and in the handball courts and by the time he was fifteen he was professional. Packey and Freddie fought ten fast and furious rounds in Milwaukee at the end of which the Chicago man was given the decision. Suspicion that something was wrong with this fight started as early as the fourth round. A clear low blow from McFarland put Freddie on the canvas. It should have been a straightforward disqualification but the referee, Malachy Hogan, waved the fighters on. A doctor later told reporters that he examined Freddie after the fight and that he had been struck in the "groin area". A swelling formed where the blow landed. Referee Hogan said it might have been sustained in Freddie's previous fight a week earlier, but the doctor denied it and said the injury was definitely caused that night. Freddie recovered well from the low blow and by the eighth round he looked the stronger man. Packey's left eye was cut open and for the remainder of the fight Freddie kept working on the sore spot and had McFarland bleeding badly. But when the final bell sounded the referee raised the right hand of the blood-soaked McFarland. "Hisses and jeers followed his verdict, and there are few who believe the stockyards champion deserved the verdict," wrote one of the journalists at ringside, while another asserted, "the worst that was coming to Welsh was a draw". Cries of "rotten" came from the crowd as the referee made an undignified exit. But Malachy Hogan was used to unseemly endings to fights in which he'd officiated. In May 1900, Hogan took charge of a contest between Kid McCoy and Tommy Ryan. At the end of six rounds Hogan awarded the bout to a well-beaten McCoy. Ryan proceeded to summarily punch Hogan on the jaw and a near riot ensued. After the McFarland-Welsh fight, the Badger Club never employed Malachy Hogan again, even though he had been their regular official. Hogan had been a good referee, one of the most capable in America, but he found trouble when he was called upon to officiate in battles where Chicago fighters were involved. According to the *Milwaukee Free Press* the reason for this was evident. Hogan was in business in Chicago and he depended almost exclusively on the patronage of the element that patronized boxing shows. "Capable referees are few, and if Hogan is barred entirely it may be a difficult matter sometimes to find a man equal to the job," the newspaper commented. "When Hogan works in contests where his personal feeling is not an influence he generally gives satisfaction." By now Hogan's health was beginning to fail and there was a public outcry for his banishment from boxing. Within eighteen months of awarding McFarland the decision over Freddie, Hogan's friends were holding a benefit to raise money for the down and out old referee. He died on September 3rd 1911. The old adage that once the mob gets a fighter, they don't let go until he's washed up, blind, or dead also applied to referees.

Malachy Hogan was the only real loser in the whole McFarland-Welsh affair. Despite suffering the first reverse of his career Freddie received considerable compensation for his efforts. He got $900 for the bout, the first real money he'd ever made in the ring and he profited further from the publicity it generated. By virtue of a disputed defeat at the hands of a wonderful boxer like McFarland,

Freddie's name appeared in every major newspaper in the United States and he reaped thousands of dollars' worth of publicity out of the affair. Freddie immediately offered to meet Packey again for $1,000 a side on a 'winner-takes everything' basis, but the Chicago fighter had already moved out to the Pacific Coast in search of big money fights. In fact, in the spring of 1908, every leading lightweight in the world was heading for California and Freddie decided to join them. At the beginning of the twentieth century, the Sunshine State was staging some of the biggest fights in boxing, largely the work of the first real 'big time' promoter, Jimmy Coffroth of San Francisco. 'Sunshine' Jim had been fascinated from boyhood by the bare-knuckle matches held in clandestine spots around his home city. He was also the first boxing impresario to really understand the value of publicity. Coffroth used the press to build up the gate and he was able to lure champions to put their titles on the line with offers of cash guarantees that were far in excess of anyone else.

In the summer of 1908, one lightweight who desperately needed a cash guarantee was the champion Joe Gans. His manager, Al Herford, was crooked and had urged Gans to throw fights prior to his winning the championship. When Gans knocked out top contender Mike Sullivan, Herford vanished with the purse. To compound his financial difficulties Gans' body was wracked with tuberculosis and he was starving himself to make 133lbs. But he needed the money so the aging champion agreed to Coffroth's proposal of a return match with Battling Nelson. It was an easy fight for Sunshine Jim to sell after the claret drenched violence of their fight in Goldfield, Nevada two years previously. Gans had beaten Nelson then and despite his problems, was expected to do so again. In anticipation of the champion keeping his title Coffroth looked for other credible lightweight contenders to challenge Gans. One of the fighters on his list was Freddie Welsh. Coffroth offered Freddie a series of fights against some local favourites to work him up to a match with the champion. But at the time Fanny was sick in a Milwaukee hospital and the medical bills had taken most of the purse from the McFarland fight. Freddie was down to his last $100 so he stayed on in the city and planned to take a few more fights while he waited for his wife to recover. But more ill fortune struck the Welshman as an infected cut on his right hand forced him to withdraw from all scheduled bouts. Freddie and Fanny were virtually broke so they spent what they had left on train tickets to California and headed west. They knew they were in for a long stay. Practically all the other prominent lightweights were out there and had fixed up contracts with the leading promoters, and Freddie feared that he would have to wait around for engagements until Britt, McFarland, Nelson, Gans, and the rest had settled their differences. But fortunately for the Welshman it was at this time that the great Jim Jeffries was aiming to become the King of the Coast Promoters.

Jeffries never quite achieved his ambition, but he certainly travelled some distance towards it. Jim Jeffries was the former heavyweight champion of the world and one of America's true sporting heroes. He erected a gigantic arena in the town of Vernon, a fifteen-minute ride from the centre of Los Angeles and beyond the jurisdiction of the city officials. Inside the city boundaries only no decision bouts of ten rounds were allowed, while in Jeffries' arena he was able to stage contests of twenty-five rounds and to render a decision himself. Freddie was offered a match with Phil Brock on the first bill to be staged there and the arena wasn't finished until a few days before the contest. Freddie and Fanny stayed at Jack Doyle's place, within a short walk of the Jeffries' Arena in Vernon. Doyle was a local man who'd given up his job with the Southern Pacific Railroad to open a training camp for the big name fighters who were flocking to Los Angeles. Fanny took over the preparation of meals as Freddie found it increasingly difficult to find someone to prepare vegetarian food for him. He believed that discarding meat and substituting it with nuts, fruits and vegetables was better for building up solid flesh and bone. Freddie occasionally enjoyed a cup of milk and soft-boiled or poached eggs. "I'm not a sentimental vegetarian," Freddie wrote. "Some folks are vegetarians because they don't like to see animals killed. That's not my reason. It's because the diet makes me speedier and gives me more stamina." Fanny was also a vegetarian but she took an ethical standpoint and believed that "killing lambs and things to eat was most unkind".

The American press didn't find out that Fanny was Freddie's wife for many years and she was generally introduced as the training camp's chef. The deception was all part of an elaborate scheme to create the character of Freddie Welsh. The commonly held conception of a prizefighter was the man described by Jack London as "the human brute with tiger eyes and a streak for a forehead" while Freddie Welsh was a clean-living, abstentious vegetarian, who was not only the perfect athlete but also a gentleman and an intellectual. "Welsh is perhaps the only fighter in the business who customarily lives the life that is inductive of perfect physical condition," commented one Los Angeles newspaper. "He has not even the semi-bad habit of smoking which almost all fighters indulge in between battles. Aside from ale and weak wines which he uses periodically in moderation, Freddie's lips have never known the taste of intoxicants and the little Englishman has made it a life-long rule to get at least eight hours of sleep each night." F. Scott Fitzgerald created a character called Dexter Green, an embryonic Gatsby, who assembled himself as he assembled his wardrobe, with care. Green "recognized the value to him of such a mannerism and he adopted it". Freddie did exactly the same and was expert at publicizing his creation. The boxing writer Trevor C. Wignall wrote that Freddie was "the inventor of the kind of interview that is read by women as well as by men, but he was always careful to avoid overtaxing credibility". Freddie never made that blunder of speaking about subjects that he wasn't expert on. He dressed immaculately and spoke of the importance of healthy living, cleanliness and reading. This was the summer that Frederick Hall Thomas really became Freddie Welsh.

Jim Jeffries' press officers found it an easy matter to exploit the life of Freddie Welsh for the benefit of reporters. All Freddie's eccentricities, real and made up, were readily written about in the Californian newspapers. He was described as a "chronic vegetarian" and a "cold water faddist" and the people of southern California were fascinated by this fabulous foreign fighter. Freddie opened up his training camp to the public. Every afternoon between the hours of one and two o'clock the trams heading down Pacific Boulevard were packed with people going to the free show at Jack Doyle's South Side Athletic Club at the corner of Santa Fe Avenue and 38th Street. "Every east-bound car that crossed Main Street was crowded in such a way as to cause the regular patrons of the line to look askance at each other," wrote one reporter. Ever since he arrived in Los Angeles, Freddie had been regarded as a mild curiosity and was playing to large daily crowds. His training ring was placed under a large tent and every day more and more seating was rigged up. One very unusual feature of Freddie's audiences was the number of women, leading the boxing writer of the *Los Angeles Examiner* to conclude that the "fair ones like the boxing game as well as the sterner sex".

The glamour of the training camp was further enhanced by the arrival in California of Freddie's younger sister Kate. The Americans dubbed her "the daughter of the first regiment" and she was written of as a lady of distinction and good breeding. "Her contact with the glove men had no effect on her bearing," wrote one relieved journalist. "Miss Welsh, unlike the American girl, uses no slang; her English is perfect, and she reflects a cultured, refined training." Kate was on

Publicity photo for a fight on the 'wild' West Coast

a holiday of several months in the United States and travelled all over
the country with Freddie and Fanny. The two women imitated the
characters of Genevieve and Lottie, the sweetheart and sister respectively of the boxer Joe Fleming in Jack London's *The Game*. Freddie
was an avid reader of London's work, especially his stories about
boxing such as *The Abysmal Brute* and *A Piece Of Steak*. London
wrote *The Game* in 1905 and a few years later he and Freddie became
friends. Women were not allowed into the bear-pit atmosphere of
boxing clubs at the time so Fanny and Kate, just like the fictional
Genevieve, would bundle themselves up in a long coat and turn up
the collar to meet the cap that hid their hair. Freddie told the doormen
who they were and to let them in. The lights over the ring left the
remainder of the arena dark and very few spectators knew there was
a woman in their midst. "Whenever Fred fights I always let him know
where I am going to sit," said Kate, "and often when he is clinching
with his opponent he will look up at me and smile." Freddie described

Kate as his mascot and said that he couldn't lose when she was at his training camp. Throughout their summer in California Freddie, Kate and Fanny took frequent shopping trips into Los Angeles while evenings were spent boating in the lagoon at Venice Beach and nights at the theatre. During the build-up to the Brock fight Kate was of great interest to boxing writers who'd never had to type out a woman's name before. "Flourishing in coarse, uncongenial soil, I found a Welsh wild rose yesterday," wrote one reporter. "Slim, pretty and sunshiny, aged 18 years, with the delicate charm that belongs to the women of fierce little Wales, she thinks she is in her element in the garden cottage out on Santa Fe Avenue, where she can overlook the movements of her hero brother." One journalist asked her if her mother worried about her being in the United States in the middle of the fight game. "No, she doesn't worry," replied Kate. "She knows we all love one another very, very dearly, and my two brothers and I are not like most brothers and sisters, we are very close together, and she knows that Fred will take care of me, and it's not so far."

On the Sunday before the fight, Freddie staged a twenty-round exhibition in his training tent. Over 1,500 spectators filled the benches around the ring. Despite arrangements to accommodate as many guests as possible, many hundreds were turned away for lack of space. Freddie knew this stunt would cause the camp to be overrun with visitors and that it would give the Brock fight some judicious advertising and he was, after all, on a percentage of the gate. But this wasn't the only reason for the twenty-round affair. He'd taken very few long distance fights under any conditions and Freddie

Piloting the entourage at the lagoon in Venice, California.

The revolutionary headguard.

wanted to test himself in such a bout in the heat of a California spring afternoon. During the commotion of trying to fit everybody in, Freddie was enjoying his daily 'sun bath', lying on the ground at the rear of his cottage and baking his skin to a deep tan. Then at two o'clock Freddie was introduced to the crowd as "the lightweight and welterweight champion of all England". Freddie stepped into the ring; put on his homemade headgear (a customized American football helmet to avoid what Arthur Conan Doyle called "the slightly thickened ears of the fighting man") and the show began. He started by going ten rounds with Peter Sullivan, and with only the regulation thirty seconds between rounds, proceeded to fight for a further five rounds with a different sparring partner, Kid Carsey. The last five rounds were due to be fought with Charley Boesen, but Boesen was whipped in three having been "covered aplenty with the red fluid" and begged to be excused from finishing the bout. Sullivan ended the ten rounds bleeding from the right eye and right ear and Carsey was given a bloody mouth. After the exhibition and a brief conference with his sister at ringside, Freddie shadow boxed for another quarter of an hour to entertain the crowd.

On the eve of the fight, Baron Long, the "elephantine match-maker" of the Jeffries Athletic Club, made known his plans to stage a tournament in California to establish the true world lightweight champion. He wired an offer to Packey McFarland to meet the winner of the contest between Freddie and Phil Brock. Long's marketing strategy was in keeping with the deeply racist nature of American boxing crowds at the time. Joe Gans was due to fight Battling Nelson in San Francisco on July 4th and the black skinned world champion was expected to beat his challenger. In such an event Long intended to proclaim the man who prevailed between Freddie, Brock and McFarland as the "legitimate white world light-weight champion" and then fix up a battle of the races with Gans. Long told the *Los Angeles Herald* that in the event of Nelson "wrest-ing the title from Gans a fight between the durable Dane and the winner of the Vernon Fourth of July battle would decide who really is the best of the lightweights". Long's strategy confirmed that Freddie's quest for the title was gathering momentum. The Welshman had been back in America for just over six months and was within one victory of being installed as one of the four boxers contending the world championship.

Freddie trained faithfully for the fight with Phil Brock and left nothing lacking in his condition. He was thoroughly acclimatized and he finished his preparations in the belief that the battle was already as good as won. He went to a local barbershop to get his curly hair "clipped down to fighting style" and he told the assembled reporters that he had never been more confident of a victory in his life and that "contrary to the general idea of the meat eaters" he would show that he had more strength and stamina than Brock. But the carnivorous sportsmen of Los Angeles remained unconvinced and Freddie was the underdog in the betting. Very few people in California had seen Freddie box while his opponent was well-known and well-respected. The day before the fight, Brock's manager 'Cap' Tom McRae was offering anybody $150 against $100 that his man would win by knockout inside of fifteen rounds. Freddie and his friends were believed to have taken up the offer post haste.

The fight was held at three o'clock in the afternoon on May 30th 1908. Jeffries arranged for cars to ferry people from the centre of the city to his arena or, in other words, from where the authorities controlled boxing to where he controlled it. Another Jeffries innova-tion was the presence of a number of women spectators. This was the first time that women had been allowed into a fight in Los Angeles provided, of course, they were accompanied by male escorts. The club informed the public that "Manager Long will make every effort to provide for the comfort of his feminine guests. Many women have hesitated about going for fear of meeting with something in the nature of rowdyism at the pavillion but they are assured that nothing of the kind will take place." About 5,000 people made their way to the arena. The day being a holiday, Decoration Day, it drew a good crowd. The dollar seats were filled soon after the doors opened and the higher priced chairs were all taken by the time the main fight began. It was a fine day, although the air was chilly as the sun hid behind fleeting clouds for most of the afternoon. Freddie won the toss for the corner and took the southwest position that put his back to the sun. Brock had the American flag tied onto the post in his corner; Freddie had the Union flag fastened onto his. From the moment they stepped through the ropes there was a marked difference in the demeanor of the two combatants. Phil Brock seemed nervous and ill at ease as he sat on his stool. Freddie sat in the opposite corner, smiling as he looked over his shoulder to talk to Kate who sat a few rows behind him. Brock was right to be apprehensive and by the time he clambered out of the ring an hour and a half later he barely recognized himself in the mirror. His right eye was black and blue, and practically closed; his left eye was half shut; both cheekbones were red and swollen; his lips were bleeding and puffed to almost twice their natural size; and his back, arms, and body were a flaming scarlet. Brock bled copiously in every round, and in the clinches his face rubbed on his opponent and left Freddie covered in blood and gore. One ringside scribe commented that the Cleveland youth's countenance resembled a "piece of raw beefsteak more than it did a human face after he had covered the twenty-five-round route and taken the many dozen blows that Welsh showered in upon his features from every angle of the fight compass". Freddie smiled throughout the fight and left the ring unmarked. Many of the local sports took as much of a drubbing as Brock, losing good money betting on the American. He was outclassed in every way from start to finish and never had a chance to win. After the fight Freddie walked back from the arena to his cottage with a mob of men and boys in tow. He later enjoyed an evening strolling around the streets of downtown Los Angeles. "The city has another fistic idol and needless to say it is Freddie Welsh," enthused one paper. "With ordinary luck, the little Welshman will face Gans in a championship bout, and it would not be too much to say that if one of the present crop of lightweights is to defeat the dusky champion Welsh is the man."

But the full story of the fight didn't emerge until the morning after. One of the prominent sportsmen at the Jeffries' Club who often took a flier on the outcome of a ring battle was telling a journalist how he regretted not putting money on Freddie to win. The frustrated punter told how he spoke to Freddie a short time before the battle and asked him how to bet. Freddie replied that he had intended betting $250 on himself, but that he had hurt his foot while on the road and he was now a little afraid of blood poisoning. It emerged that Freddie had damaged his foot on a road run a few days previously and the bruise had festered. A surgeon cut a slice from Freddie's foot on the morning of the fight and he had kept it in an iced bandage right up to the start of the bout. He was lifted out of bed into a motorcar, driven to the arena and virtually lifted through the ropes. For the first six rounds he planted himself in the middle of the ring with his body weight on one foot and worked within a radius of just three feet. Then, just before the bell for the seventh round, "something seemed to burst through my whole system," Freddie explained, "a perspiration broke out all over me, and I felt the greatest relief. My foot became dead to all pain."

The morning after the fight, Freddie received a telegram from an old mentor to congratulate him on his great victory on behalf of vegetarians everywhere:

Battle Creek, Mich, June 2.
Mr. Welsh – Dear Sir: Hope you will go through the whole bunch of meat eaters.
BERNARR M'FADDEN

There was also a telegram from Packey McFarland agreeing to the terms offered by Baron Long for the Independence Day bout. But Freddie wasn't in a hurry to sign up to anything. Under the terms of the existing deal, he was to receive substantially less than McFarland and after the fight with Phil Brock Freddie wasn't about to play the supporting role any longer. Freddie knew he was as much of a card in Los Angeles as McFarland and demanded no worse than an even break on the money. They squabbled over the terms for a week before signing the articles. Initially Packey wanted a $5,000 guarantee but finally settled for $4,000. The fighters were to split 50 per cent of the gross receipts on a basis of 65 per cent to the winner, 35 per cent to the loser. Should Freddie win though, Packey still got his $4,000 guarantee. After an agreement had been reached Freddie and Packey sat a few seats away from each other at a fight in Los Angeles. Packey was heard to ask Freddie: "Where did you get that onion ear?" To which the Welshman replied, "Never mind you'll have one the same kind about this time on the Fourth of July."

Between the two fights Freddie took Fanny and Kate on a short trip to Mexico, then to San Diego before returning to Los Angeles to prepare for the contest. McFarland had arranged to train at Doyle's so Freddie moved his camp to the outlying neighbourhood of Venice. They checked into the Hotel De Novo but during the entire build-up to the fight Freddie slept outdoors. An old bathing pavillion near the beach was fitted up with his training equipment and a ring was set up by the banks of the Venice lagoon with enough seating for 2,000 people to watch specially arranged sparring contests. For the fortnight leading up to the event, Freddie donned his usual gymnasium suit of purple tights and dark blue shirt and put on the best show seen at Venice for many a year. Every afternoon he took on all comers at his open-air ring and over a thousand people routinely showed up to watch him perform. The Welshman became the crowd favourite because he allowed people to watch him train for free whereas McFarland charged his supporters for the privilege. Freddie continued with the same routine until two days before the fight. Running exactly the same distance over the hard-packed sand before returning to the same table exercises and rope-skipping stunts. This was followed by a long swim in the ocean before an afternoon of sparring and shadow boxing. According to one writer Freddie was "tanned as dark as a deep brown mulatto and is as hard as nails". These sessions were so frenetic and demanding that many old-time boxers were telling the papers that the Welshman was training too hard for the contest and that he would be stale by the time of the fight. "I've always worked this way even when I was fighting for a handful of change and training on egg sandwiches," Freddie explained. "I love to work and the more of it I do the better it agrees with me." He did suffer one major setback in his build-up to the fight when he cut the bridge of his nose on the bottom of a concrete pool after diving in. Every afternoon the cut bled profusely as each sparring session opened up the wound. Freddie refused to put a plaster over the gash so the public would understand that when the fight began McFarland didn't cause it.

Freddie's general politeness and the welcome that guests received at his camp won over even the most 'proper' people at Venice. "Gentlemanly is not superfluous when used in reference to Welsh," wrote one local reporter. "He is far and away ahead of the average American man of his profession and there is nothing of the 'put on' about him at that." He'd also impressed the boxing enthusiasts of

Venice with his skills and a syndicate was formed with $1,000 for the purpose of backing Freddie against McFarland. But despite this neighbourhood support and his showing against Brock Freddie was once again the underdog with the bookmakers and as the fight neared the money was going heavily on McFarland. By July 4th the cigar store booths of Spring Street were quoting the price on a victory for the Chicago fighter of 2 to 1 on. Such short odds were bad news for the legion of 'sportsmen' from McFarland's hometown. In the week before the fight there was a story circulating that Packey had damaged one his hands after being hit by a horseshoe during a game of quoits. The sports of Los Angeles didn't believe a word of it and the opinion was freely voiced that this was merely a clever ruse on the part of McFarland's manager Harry Gilmore Jr to influence the betting. The McFarland camp had a history of such stunts. The previous April they pretended to send Packey "through a severe siege of the Turkish baths" to give the impression that he was having difficulty making weight. This latest story of a quoits incident was enough to send Jim Jeffries, accompanied by the local newspaper contingent, out to McFarland's camp to discover that he had barely a scratch from the 'accident'. The night before the fight Freddie placed a bet of $1,000 on himself at odds of 10 to 6 and he placed another $1,000 at the same odds the following day.

The Joe Gans – Battling Nelson fight was to be staged at the same time at Jim Coffroth's Colma Arena in San Francisco. Even though this contest was for the title, most of the press attention was on the Welsh – McFarland bout because nobody believed that Nelson had a chance against the great Joe Gans. Then the news broke that Jim Jeffries had offered a $20,000 purse for Gans to fight the winner at his club on the third week of August. Suddenly Freddie was potentially just six weeks away from his shot at the title. Jim Jeffries wrote a letter to the *Western Mail* in Wales from Los Angeles on June 12th to inform Freddie's countrymen of his progress in America:

I am writing to you in regard to one of your townsmen – Freddie Welsh – who boxes before my athletic club on July 4. The Cardiff boy has made a decided impression on the lovers of the ring game in this section of the country, and I feel that his old-time associates should know of it. Welsh will box Packey McFarland, champion white lightweight of the United States, and from all advanced predictions a royal battle should ensue. It is looked on as the best card before the sporting public today, and we are expecting a crowded house when the clever lads finally enter the ring. As you may be able to use photos of the contestants, I am sending you some, together with the latest picture of myself. I will referee the bout,

and as no one ever knew me to do anything unsportsmanlike, all lovers
of clean boxing can expect an impartial judgment for one man or the
other, whether Welsh or McFarland proves the master.

By 1.45 pm, Independence Day 1908, the general admission tiers
of the Jeffries Arena were full. It was a hot, dry California afternoon
and the sun beat down on the red canvas ring. The reserve section
filled up rapidly and the betting at ringside was lively. McFarland was
still odds on to win but a lot of money was now going on the short
ender. Freddie was first into the ring wearing a long gray bathrobe
over his green shorts, followed by a goat, which he had painted in red,
white and blue stripes. Packey stepped through the ropes stripped
down to his boxing togs of short green trunks with an Irish American
flag on his belt and not to be outdone he was also followed into the
ring by a goat, which he'd painted green. Freddie won the toss and
elected to sit in the corner with his back to the sun. Howard Baker
and 'Young' Astle joined Freddie's chief second Eddie Robinson in
the corner. His trainer Pat Kinnealy, Harry Gilmore and Red Weimer,
surrounded McFarland. Two pairs of red gloves with blue laces were
tossed into the ring to a huge cheer from the sweltering crowd.

But there was a delay. Harry Gilmore objected to a big wad of tape
around Freddie's hands but after much discussion Jeffries decided
that the strapping was within the rules. Meanwhile, 'Megaphone
Cook' introduced a boxer by the name of Young Otto to challenge the
winner of the forthcoming bout. At 3.17 pm Jim Jeffries cleared the
ring. As he waited for the preliminaries to end Freddie sat under a
canvas canopy to protect him from the sun, while Packey sat under
an umbrella held by one of his seconds. Jeffries called the two men
together and they listened to his orders. Packey turned back to his
corner to wait for the bell. Freddie stayed in the middle of the ring.

From the opening exchanges the crowd rooted for the underdog
and they cheered every blow Freddie landed. And for round after
round they did a lot of cheering. Freddie's plan was to throw
constant left hand jabs to McFarland's face followed by a clinch to
protect himself and then a succession of sickening right hand blows
into Packey's kidneys on the break. It worked well in the opening
rounds and Freddie built up a big lead. At the beginning of every
round McFarland would come out of his corner with an expression
on his face as if to say: "Well, this is surely the round I'll get you." But
at the finish Freddie went back to his corner and smiled. Packey
managed to open the 'swimming pool' cut over Freddie's nose in the
third round and to cut him again in the tenth with a slashing blow

over the right eye. Freddie drew his first sight of blood in the fourteenth after slamming yet another straight left into Packey's nose. By the end of the fifteenth ringside opinion was that Packey would have to score a knockout to win. At this juncture there was an announcement that Battling Nelson had defeated Joe Gans and there was a new lightweight champion of the world. There was a great ovation from the crowd. "It's a great day for short enders, come on and win Welsh," shouted a ringside supporter. But this was very bad news for Freddie. He had a big lead in his fight but Joe Gans had lost the title and new champions tended to savour their new-found status as long as possible. After the announcement the direction of the fight changed. McFarland finished much the stronger of the two and during the last eight rounds he was chasing Freddie around the ring trying to land a decisive punch. For the most part Freddie made him miss with dozens of punches until, that is the final two rounds, during which the Welshman took a beating. Freddie blamed his cornermen for his poor showing in the final rounds. They soused him in water from the top of his head down and his shoes were soaked, slippery and heavy. "I could hardly keep my feet," claimed Freddie. "Then, right on top of that, they gave me a pint of champagne in the twenty-third round that did me no good." This was a favoured technique for reviving boxers at the time.

Just after they shook hands at the beginning of the final round, Packey caught Freddie with a hard right hook flush on the side of the jaw that sent the Welshman to the canvas. Freddie got up immediately without taking a count and raised his hand to his friends at ringside to indicate that he wasn't seriously hurt. He denied being knocked down and insisted that he slipped because of the water in his boots. There was no doubt that McFarland had won the twenty-fourth and twenty-fifth rounds quite clearly and by the finish he was clearly expecting to get the decision. When the final bell rang Packey turned towards Jeffries and half offered his glove, but then he saw that the referee was also going to take Freddie's hand to indicate he was calling the fight a draw. As soon as Packey realized what Jeffries had decided he turned his back and walked to the far corner where "he all but cried". Jeffries and Freddie were left in the middle of the ring with the Welshman's arm held up in the air. Many in the crowd thought the decision had gone Freddie's way until the official announcement was made confirming the draw. McFarland was furious and launched a vicious tirade of abuse at Jeffries. Odds of 10 to 7 on were freely offered on McFarland before the fight, and the Chicago contingent took the decision with very bad grace.

The referee justified the verdict to the journalists who fully concurred with his judgment. "I gave the decision as I saw the fight," Jeffries claimed. "In my opinion Welsh had a lead for nearly twenty rounds, and had not Packey made such a strong finish Welsh would have been declared the winner, but I do not believe McFarland finished good enough entirely to overcome the lead taken by Welsh in the first eighteen or twenty rounds." McFarland's manager Harry Gilmore claimed his man had been robbed of a deserved victory more by incompetence than corruption. According to Gilmore, Jeffries was either not capable of judging a winner or he lacked the courage of his own convictions. "Thousands of dollars had been placed on the little Englishman at odds of 1 to 2," said Gilmore, "and an even break to save this coin was clamoured for by the Welsh betters. It is our belief that Jeffries was puzzled and influenced accordingly by the shouts of the crowd." In the days after the fight most of the newspapers supported Jeffries. It was generally agreed that Freddie had won the vast majority of the first nineteen rounds and that it was only Packey's performance in the last few rounds that saved him from defeat. Gilmore's claims concerning the thousands of dollars wagered on Freddie were also dismissed. One newspaper claimed, "it would have taken a sledge hammer and a crow-bar to have loosened up a thousand dollars in Welsh money." Freddie had plenty of friends in the arena but few if any were willing to bet on him. Jim Jeffries certainly had no financial incentive to award the draw. The fighters' share of the gate receipts amounted to $7,500 to be shared 65 per cent to the winner, 35 per cent to the loser. McFarland had been guaranteed $4,000, which a winner's share would have adequately covered. By awarding a draw, McFarland's half of the fighters' money amounted to about $3,750 and Jeffries had to make up the remaining $250. Packey's "vigorous language" in denouncing the decision prompted Jim Jeffries to quit refereeing. "You can say for me," said Jeffries, "that McFarland is a dirty little rat. They couldn't get me in the ring to referee for him if they handed out $10,000. I am through with this referee business. It don't make you any friends and is a thankless job. I gave the only decision I saw and would repeat it 40 times if I had to do it over again." Freddie said very little after the fight. He sent a cablegram home stating: "Decision draw – Welsh won nineteen rounds easy, appreciate home sentiments."

Freddie and Packey were both dissatisfied with the verdict, and both professed straight away their eagerness for another meeting. But the real drama of the day was that Battling Nelson had knocked out the great Joe Gans and was the new champion. To cash in on his new title the 'Battler' had secured some vaudeville engagements and had also promised to give Gans a return fight. For Freddie and Packey the championship was out of reach in the short term so they went looking for other matches. McFarland had upset the boxing powers in Los Angeles so he headed north to San Francisco while Freddie took up Jim Jeffries' offer of another match in Vernon. His opponent was Johnny Murphy, described as being a strong, slugging fighter, greedy for punishment, and with a "punch that would upset brickwork".

Following the McFarland fight, the American press questioned Freddie's credentials as a top class fighter for the first time, highlighting what they saw as a lack of punching power. So Freddie changed his way of fighting completely for the Murphy fight. For the most part he just stood toe-to-toe with the 'slugger' and "flayed away like a wild man who had no knowledge of the finer points of the game". The contest went the full twenty-five round distance and the referee Eddie Graney had no hesitation in giving Freddie the verdict. Murphy managed to stay on his feet until the final bell though he was scarcely able to stand or see. Freddie was unmarked. Victor and vanquished spent the night of the fight staying in the same hotel. Murphy retired early to his room to recover from the terrible beating he'd received, while Freddie stayed up most of the night. He sent a cablegram to his mother to report another victory and he sent another to the National Sporting Club in London to accept challenges issued to him by three leading British fighters; Johnny Summers, Jack Goldswain and Jimmy Britt. They hadn't wanted to box Freddie when he was in Britain, but now he was a big draw and would attract a large purse. Freddie also informed the Club that it would have to wait a little while for his return because he still had unfinished business in California – the lightweight championship of the world. He had already signed articles with the promoter 'Uncle' Tom McCarey to fight Frank Carsey in Los Angeles on September 15th 1908. Freddie was collecting victims and dollars again. But there was much more at stake than a purse at the Pacific Athletic Club that night. The champion, Battling Nelson, had promised Freddie a shot at the title if he could knock out Frank Carsey before the ten rounds were up. Freddie duly delivered. A right-hand punch to Carsey's jaw in the fourth round rendered him unconscious before he hit the canvas. Carsey remained in that state for five minutes. After he came round Carsey sat in his corner for several minutes with his "head wobbling around like a cat with her face in the pitcher" and when he finally got up to walk to the dressing room he staggered across the ring and fell through the ropes.

Freddie's next opponent fared little better. Just a few weeks later McCarey matched Freddie with Harry Trendall of St Louis over ten rounds, again in Los Angeles. The Welshman turned up late for the fight because his car had broken down on the way to the arena, but he soon appeased an irate crowd with "as clean and pretty a knock-out as ever was pulled off anywhere". The end came in the sixth as Freddie drove his left glove into Trendall's solar plexus and hooked a right to his victim's jaw. Trendall was stretched out flat upon his back until Referee Eyton counted him out. When it was apparent that Trendall couldn't get up his seconds jumped into the ring and carried him to his corner. "When my fist landed on Trendall's basket, I could feel his backbone," Freddie said, "and I knew I had him in a position that I just couldn't help slipping over the sleeping powders." Freddie had been hurt by the remarks that he was a 'snowflake puncher' and he used the Carsey and Trendall fights to make a state-ment. It was also a sound business decision. American fight fans appreciated good boxers but they paid to see the big punchers. "I have to thank the Los Angeles sporting writers for my knockout punch," Freddie said after the Trendall bout. "They panned me so much for my lack of a wallop that I decided to bring it out of retire-ment and put it on exhibition again."

His style of fighting was very carefully thought out for any given contest. Freddie believed that cleverness was 'Class A' stuff while slugging came in the 'Class B' category. He always wanted the sure victory and so developed these two styles of fighting. If he considered a man dangerous Freddie made sure that his backers "cashed their tickets" by boxing cleverly and piling up enough points to clinch the win. If he figured that he had nothing to fear from an opponent Freddie would stand up and slug with him. He'd knocked out not just Frank Carsey but also Harry Trendall in a total of just ten rounds and had kept his part of the bargain with Battling Nelson. The champion also had a good September. Nelson had agreed to give the former champion Joe Gans a return match. Gans' health had deteriorated even further and despite a heroic effort he failed to last beyond the twenty-first round. After this victory Battling Nelson didn't need the likes of Freddie Welsh or Packey McFarland to make money anymore. He held one of the most prestigious titles in world sport and he intended to make the best and most lucrative use of it. So Nelson headed back for Chicago to write his memoirs. Freddie would just have to wait.

There was another leading fighter looking for a big fight in California at this time however. Abe Attell was the featherweight champion of the world, a title he'd earned by beating Jimmy Walsh back in 1906. He went on to make a record number of defences, fighting all the best featherweights of his generation. By the winter of 1908 there wasn't really a credible fighter left in the 126-pound division in America to challenge Attell and the public had lost interest. The only other featherweight Americans really wanted to see Attell fight was Jim Driscoll and there was much talk of the champion of the world fighting the champion of Great Britain for the undisputed title. But Peerless Jim wasn't due in America until the following year, so the San Franciscan decided to challenge bigger men in order to attract the promoters and the public once more. Attell was so good that he more than held his own against leading lightweights and had already fought Battling Nelson to a draw. His opponents were half-a-stone heavier than Attell and the crowds delighted in seeing the more skillful, smaller man giving the 'big guy' a beating. On October 29th 1908, Attell arrived in Los Angeles and sparked a scramble for his services by the city's two biggest matchmakers, Tom McCarey and Baron Long. McCarey was trying to secure a fight between Attell and a lightweight from Milwaukee named Ad Wolgast while Long offered the featherweight champion a bout before the Jeffries Arena with Freddie Welsh. Attell met both promoters on the same day but it was clear from the start that he regarded Freddie as the bigger drawing card with Los Angeles boxing supporters. Wolgast had 'flunked out' of two recent fights and wasn't well liked while Freddie was the most popular fighter of the year with the local customers.

Negotiations for the fight lasted several days. Attell, the smaller man, wanted the fight over ten rounds while Freddie held out for the twenty-five round journey. Baron Long suggested the compromise of a fifteen-round bout to which Freddie agreed immediately. A meeting with the fighters, their representatives and the matchmaker resolved all the other details regarding weight and money. The fight was to be held at the Jeffries Athletic Club on Thanksgiving Eve, November 25th 1908. Freddie had to make 130lbs by two o'clock on the day of the fight. Attell got $3,000 win, lose or draw and Freddie was to receive 30 per cent of the gate receipts whatever the result. Freddie and the fight promoters also got the motion picture rights. Attell waived these privileges in return for the guarantee. Just a matter of days after articles for the fight were signed confirming that Freddie was to be paid according to a percentage of the gate receipts, he made a startling announcement in the newspapers. Two great racing balloons were to be released the following week from Chutes

Park in Los Angeles as part of a transatlantic race. Freddie, in conjunction with race organizer Dick Ferris, made it known that he was going to fly in one of the balloons. "Sure, I'm going to take a chance at balloon racing," Freddie told reporters. "I used to watch the same kind of races start in England when I was a kid and I have always wanted to be lifted off my feet anyhow, I never found a boxer yet who could do it, so I guess the only way is to go up in a balloon. The only thing that would keep me from it is my contract with Attell, but I guess that if I get dumped in the middle of some ocean he will be satisfied that I haven't quit on him, and if the flight is successful I will be back here in plenty of time to give him all the attention he wants." The fight was one of the biggest to be staged in America during 1908 and it was well publicized in all the leading newspapers. But this stunt ensured that the build-up to the Thanksgiving Eve bout kept the press busy for weeks. Cartoons of Freddie in his ballooning outfit appeared in all the newspapers and it wasn't apparent if the journalists or Attell knew whether Freddie was serious or not. The day after the announcement, Abe felt compelled to issue the following statement:

> This is certainly a novel way of running out of a match. Ever since Welsh has signed with me he has been trying to find an excuse to sidetrack me; I guess he has found it in this. There is not one chance in a hundred that he will ever get back alive, so I guess I can't kick, although I would have liked to have the easy money a match with him would mean. If he does alight inside of civilization, the first thing I expect to get from Freddie is a telegram saying he will be unable to get back to California in time to train. I am going to get in good condition to meet Welsh, however, and when he definitely quits me I will be ready for somebody else just as easy.

Baron Long was certainly 'in' on the ruse. He let it be known to a *Los Angeles News* scribe that "the little English boxer decided to check his aeronautic ambitions for a time". This change of heart allegedly happened following a heated conference with Baron Long in which it was threatened that Freddie's forfeit money of $500, which was posted to insure his appearance in the ring against Attell, was going to be confiscated if he took to flight. "It was not without a stiff argument, however, that Freddie was persuaded to stay in the realm of ordinary individuals," reported the *Los Angeles News*. "Welsh had his heart set on the transcontinental aerial trip and in his stubborn English way threatened several times to let Baron Long, his forfeit money, Abe Attell and everything else connected with earthly affairs

go for the balloon route. Long had to talk to the lightweight like a
Dutch uncle before Freddie was turned from his resolution."
Questioned on his change of heart by the unwitting *Los Angeles News*
reporter, the Welshman predicted that Attell would soon wish that he
had sailed away in something less safe than a balloon when he was
done with him. It was only the "salmon livers" that were afraid to
take a chance, claimed Freddie but if it was going to cost him $500
and cause such an awful fuss he would stick around until after the
fight with Attell and then if there are any balloon races going on he'd
"make the ascension then".

With the contest nicely publicized, Freddie returned to his old
training camp in Venice to prepare. Even though he was under
pressure to get down to 130lbs on the afternoon of the fight, he kept
himself heavy for most of the build up, preferring to take off the last
two pounds right at the end. He kept up the same training routine
that had served him so well since arriving in Los Angeles. Running
in the morning, resting at midday, with gymnasium work and
sparring before an audience each afternoon. One day Freddie got a
visit from a promising fourteen-year-old boxer from a small town
called Sawtelle who went by the name of 'Young' Freddie Welsh.
Freddie senior allowed the boy to spar with him for three rounds that
afternoon. It was a happy training camp but Freddie knew that only
he could really lose on Thanksgiving Eve. For Attell the fight was just
a way of making money until better featherweight challenges could
be arranged. A defeat for Freddie by a smaller man could signal the
end of his chance of getting a championship fight. His training was
carried out at the usual frenetic pace. When he finished his day's work
his body was covered with beads of sweat – "labour's diamonds" he
called them. Referee Charley Eyton visited both boxers in their
respective camps a few days before the fight. Attell appealed to the
official not to allow Freddie to lay on him in the clinches. As the
smaller man he couldn't afford to have his bigger opponent hanging
on. Freddie meanwhile appeared untroubled. He was still enjoying
the late autumn California sunshine and was tanned to a dark brown
from exposure to the ocean breezes and the sun's rays.

The issue of the featherweight fighting the lightweight dominated
the debate and the betting in the week leading up to the fight. Neither
bookmaker nor scribe could call the contest. Attell was the
longstanding world champion at 126lbs; Freddie was half-a-stone
heavier but still a relative novice. Freddie also continued to tease
reporters about his diet. "A beefsteak stands out like a flag of danger
to me," Freddie told one writer. "I know myself just as an engineer

knows his machinery, and it is this food that gives me strength and stamina." Whatever he was eating, it seemed to be working. On the day prior to the fight Freddie had got within a pound and a half of his mark and by the time of the weigh-in the Welshman had decided to prove a point. He wasn't even going to give Attell the safety net of the weight issue as an excuse for losing the fight. The weigh-in took place as agreed at two o'clock at Jim Jeffries' Spring Street resort. "You won't object to me being a few ounces overweight, will you Abie?" Freddie joked. He then stripped to the skin and came in at 128lbs, two pounds under the required weight. Attell then stepped on the scales in his clothes and also weighed 128lbs.

The doors of the arena opened at 7.30 pm and the preliminary fights began half an hour later. But the crowd grew only slowly and there were storm clouds gathering. The paucity of spectators certainly wasn't due to a lack of effort in advertising on the part of the two leading protagonists. They had worked up more interest in a boxing contest than had been seen in Los Angeles in years. The fault lay with the promoters who decided to charge higher admission prices than usual and there was rain in the air. Just before Freddie and Attell stepped into the ring there was a downpour. Baron Long had prepared for the eventuality and had placed $5,000 worth of insurance against rain on the night of the fight. He'd also built a new roof over the ring to protect the fighters but the water was seeping through the crevices. The audience was hastily donning overcoats as Attell entered first, dressed in a heavy corduroy coat, sweater and cap. His hands were already bandaged. Surrounded by his seconds, the featherweight took a seat in the northeast corner. Freddie entered a minute later and got a much bigger cheer from the crowd. He was dressed in his old grey dressing gown. The ring was packed with photographers and attendants brushing away the rainwater.

Soon after the first bell sounded it was obvious who would win. Throughout the fight Freddie hammered straight left jabs into Attell's face and jaw that constantly shot his opponent's head back with a snap. His nose and lips were streaming blood from the middle rounds to the end. Seasoned followers of the boxing game saw something that they never expected to see – Abe Attell being out-boxed. One newspaper wrote that while Attell still held his world featherweight title, he did "lose the title that he has held for years, that of being the cleverest man in the game". The referee explained that he had no trouble in reaching a decision in Freddie's favour and that the Welshman won almost every round. When the fight was over Attell walked over to Freddie to shake hands and then turned to the newspapermen and asked "What did you think of it?" He didn't wait for an answer; he just shook his head and walked from the ring. The gross receipts for the fight were $8,447. Attell was guaranteed $3,000 and Freddie 30 per cent of the gross; $2,534. Only a few months prior to this fight Attell fought a draw with Battling Nelson. Such was the ease of Freddie's victory that the press was now clamouring for him to be given a shot at the title. Freddie was the biggest draw outside the heavyweights in American boxing and his celebrity produced offers from vaudeville, which he turned down, preferring instead to keep fighting in Los Angeles.

The Jeffries Athletic Club was trying to make a match for him with the old champion Joe Gans. A return with Packey McFarland was another lucrative option and Attell also saw the financial benefits of a rematch. He told the press the day after his defeat that he was going to stay in Los Angeles until Freddie agreed to go back in the ring with him. But the chase for the dollar wasn't Freddie's primary concern any more. He wanted the title, and as world champion the dollars would simply flow in. Battling Nelson was staying in Chicago at the time so Freddie wired the *Chicago Evening American* to challenge the champion to a forty-five round contest whenever he was ready, the weight and other terms to be to the champion's liking. Freddie informed the newspaper that he was also prepared to put up a $5,000 side bet. At the end of his letter he wrote: "Beat Attell as no other lightweight was able to do and trained for the fight on fruit and nuts." Nelson's reply was to publicly promise to fight Freddie the following January, but he made the terms so difficult that it was impossible to make a match. The *Los Angeles News* of November 29th, 1908 commented:

> Fighters of every weight, colour and description would raise themselves several notches in public estimation and assist materially in the promotion of their own game if they would follow the example of Freddie Welsh. The game little English fighter takes them all on, regardless of past reputation, and his only demand is they make his legitimate weight. Without an exception, boxers in the lightweight and all other divisions are wasting time and money in haggling over technicalities from the size of the purse to the colour of their opponent's hair. Among these Battling Nelson is first to blame, but even the Dane has his little forty-five-round hobby. Nelson refuses to go into the ring unless his adversary is willing to travel over a course that not over one fighter in a thousand can stand.

The other leading lightweight contender was Packey McFarland but he was having trouble making the standard 133-pound limit. He was demanding a weight of 135lbs at six o'clock or earlier in the afternoon to fight Freddie again. It essentially meant that he would be fighting as a welterweight. As for Attell, he knew that the leading lightweights were now out of his reach. He eventually fought Jim Driscoll when the Welshman came over to the United States in 1910. It was a ten-round no decision fight and although Driscoll failed to knock out the champion, the Welshman completely dominated the fight. Attell left the ring with one eye closed and a badly swollen nose while Driscoll was unmarked. 'Peerless' Jim claimed that he and Attell had agreed that the title would change hands based on the newspaper decision, but the champion refused to acknowledge that such an agreement had been made. But his title had been tainted, Driscoll was unofficially recognized as world featherweight champion and Attell eventually lost his claim to the title when he was defeated by Johnny Kilbane two years later. Throughout his career Attell regularly bet on himself during fights, a common practice of that time, but gambling would eventually tarnish his ring accomplishments forever. He was implicated in fixing the 1919 World Series between the Chicago White Sox and the Cincinnati Reds and was indicted after several White Sox players testified before an Illinois grand jury. Attell maintained his innocence and the charges against him were dropped when the prosecution could not produce enough evidence.

Kate had returned to Pontypridd after Freddie's fight with Trendall, after being in America for nearly twelve months. When news of her brother's victory over Attell reached Wales, she spoke to a reporter from the *Evening Express* and explained that there was nothing in the contests she saw in America to offend women. "I wouldn't like to see my brother hurt in a bout, but up to date he has escaped being seriously marked," said Kate. "As for the men he knocked out, of course, I feel sorry for them, but I know they are not injured. They sleep a few seconds and then arise and are as well as ever".

Freddie's decision to move to Los Angeles had completely changed his fortunes. California now offered the best chance for a young fighter to move through the ranks and in the winter of 1908 it looked like Freddie's sojourn on the West Coast would take him all the way to the world title. But he had to keep the pressure on Nelson while the champion tended to writing his memoirs and appearing in vaudeville, so Freddie looked for another big fight. There was no shortage of offers and he was kept busy using his paper cutter on telegraph envelopes. The one that really caught his eye arrived a week before Christmas 1908 and it came from his hometown:

Welsh, Los Angeles – Your countrymen crazy to see you. Cable if you will agree to meet the winner of the Britt-Summers battle. Welsh syndicate being formed to handle during March. Will give purse thousand pounds.

TED LEWIS, 3, Penuel Road, Pontypridd

A millionaire syndicate represented by Arthur Seaton, Harry Marks and Gerald Bruce, all of Pontypridd, had raised the money. Freddie also heard reports that Lord Lonsdale planned to present a gold championship belt to the holder of the British title in each weight division. His best chance of forcing Nelson into the ring was to be in a position to challenge him as the official champion of England and it would be prejudicial to his claim to allow anyone else to annex the trophy. He'd also been away from Wales for over a year and was feeling homesick. It was time to go back. On news of the offer, the *Los Angeles Examiner* editorial read:

> A mild-mannered, unassuming little gentleman of the prize ring, he came from the quiet hamlet of Ponty Pridd to play in Uncle Sam's big back yard.
>
> He won our friendship by his gentleness, and won as readily the laurels from the brows of our young champions from the Atlantic to the Pacific. He has left the name of Ponty Pridd indelibly stamped on our landscape. We have pitted our best against him and he has left them stripped of their titles. Then we awoke to find him an invader worthy of our steel and we stand ready to hand him all the credit that is coming to him for it.
>
> But Britannia calls him home. He has played long enough she thinks. "Freddie" she calls, "Freddie Welsh, won't you ple-e-ease come 'ome?"

Six

An Epidemic of Disgrace

Freddie wanted to go home as the world lightweight champion but the incumbent was celebrating Christmas 1908 back with his family in Chicago. Battling Nelson had won the title after a desperately brutal career and now he wanted to be paid in full for every fist that had smashed into his face and body over the past twelve years. He was a throwback to the early days of prizefighting; a man who stood there giving and receiving punishment without much thought for self-preservation. Nelson won his fights by being the last man standing in a brawl and one famous boxing scribe described him as having "the disposition of a junkyard dog". He had once engaged in a headbutting fight in his adopted town of Hegewich, Illinois, in which he and his opponent, hands tied behind their backs, lunged at each other cranium to cranium. After several shattering collisions, his rival was left with a gaping wound across his forehead while the 'victor' remained unmarked. After one medical examination a doctor told Nelson "he was of subnormal nervous organism", meaning his nerves were "less sensitive than those of the ordinary man, and did not carry shock to the brain in the normal way". So that winter Freddie spent every waking hour chasing a fight-to-the-finish with a man who could feel no pain. He was certainly the leading contender for a shot at Nelson's title but the champion was in no hurry to box anybody let alone the most dangerous young lightweight available. Nelson could recall the many years of self-denying labour, the many months of ridicule and the thousands of hard knocks it took to gain the title. When the possibility of losing it arose it was understandable that Nelson wanted everything his way.

Most boxing writers in America believed Nelson had retired. Just prior to his rematch with Gans, he told reporters that if he beat the former champion for a second time he would leave the ring for good to look after his business interests. Nelson duly beat Gans and declined all offers of another fight. The consensus in boxing circles was that Nelson would cling on to his title for as long as possible until public sentiment forced him into actual retirement. The title of retired champion was more lucrative than former champion. The theory was given greater credence when Nelson devised an elimination scheme whereby six of the best lightweights fought it out for the honour of a match with the champion. Such a series of fights would take at least a year to realize and in the meantime Nelson could gather all the profits associated with the world title. But Freddie wasn't prepared to wait that long. He issued a challenge to Nelson to talk business on or before February 18th 1909 or Freddie would claim the lightweight crown by default. "A champion can't be a champion when he refuses to defend his crown," Freddie wrote in his challenge. "So sincere am I in my desire to meet the Dane that I will allow him to dictate any kind of terms just so I get him in the ring with me. Nelson can't go on winning forever and I figure that I am the boy who can scale in at 133 pounds ringside and whip Nelson."

Public challenges of this kind were the staple of the sports columns and Freddie knew that the only way to win the title was in the ring. His intention was to consolidate his position as the 'next-in-line' and to raise public appetite for the fight. The greater the interest the higher the purse, and the champion played along. Before embarking on a ten-week theatrical tour of the southern states Nelson rebuffed talk of retirement. He told Freddie not to wait thirty days but that he could claim the title that day. The 'Battler' knew the public cared little for such claims and because of Nelson's fearsome reputation there was no way Freddie could force boxing fans to believe the champion feared him. "I fought tougher men than he ever will be and without a moment's hesitation," said Nelson. "Why should I fear a lad without a punch? Battling Nelson is on top now and they all use him for the purpose of getting some advertising. Go ahead, Mr Welsh, I'll get you soon enough."

With the champion treading the boards Freddie kept himself busy in Los Angeles. He bought a small orange grove on the outskirts of the city and he was also working with promoters to bring the Welsh middleweight Tom Thomas of Carncelyn over to the United States for a series of fights. He staged a three-round exhibition at the LA Athletic Club for the benefit of James J. Corbett, the former heavyweight champion of the world, who'd expressed a great interest in seeing him fight. But what he really wanted was another big professional contest and the most lucrative on offer was a third bout with Packey McFarland. Jim Coffroth cabled Freddie a proposal to stage the match on New Year's Day 1909. In the time since their second meeting Freddie and Packey's careers had gone in opposite directions. The public did not take kindly to the Chicago fighter's reaction to the result and Freddie's performances since that fight, especially his win over Attell showed he was still an improving young fighter. Packey's recent matches had been disappointing and he was having real trouble in making weight. Within just a few months the balance of power had shifted and now it was Freddie dictating terms. He wanted a guarantee of $4,000, the sum McFarland got for their previous fight in Los Angeles, and demanded that his opponent make 133lbs at ringside. McFarland's manager, 'Shylock' Gilmore as the press dubbed him, was insisting the match be made at 133lbs at three o'clock. This gave his fighter several hours to regain the four or five pounds he needed to be back to his comfortable weight that was now well over the lightweight limit. Freddie had "no possible use" for the extra two pounds he could gain in the same period. The senior boxing writers, who were in essence the unofficial governing body of the sport during this time, backed Freddie's stand. Even the great John L. Sullivan got involved in the debate and supported the principle of a ringside weigh-in.

The weight issue could not be resolved but Packey and Freddie's fortunes were entwined during the winter. Having failed to get a match with the Welshman, Packey took a fight against Jimmy Burns, or George Memsic as he was also known. Burns had once fought Joe Gans for the world title but a lack of care for his health and general physical condition sent Burns "down the toboggan at a fearful rate", but he rallied and was now considered to be a contender once more. McFarland's weight problems surfaced once again however and the Chicago fighter would not agree to a late weigh-in, so promoter Tom McCarey needed a replacement. He called Freddie and they arranged to meet. On the scheduled afternoon Freddie had gone to the races and "lost sufficient coin to make him realize that he was a real sport". Shortly before Freddie arrived at McCarey's office Jimmy Burns had called by and told the promoter to try and get the weigh-in at 133lbs at 3 o'clock. A few minutes after Burns left, Freddie arrived.

"Jimmy would like to make it 133 at 3 o'clock, Freddie," said McCarey.

"Can't do that, Tom. It'll have to be 6 o'clock," responded Freddie.

McCarey got Burns on the phone and gave him Freddie's ultimatum.

"All right," said Burns, and the match was on.

"Say, Tom, I want Burns to put up a forfeit for that weight, because I'm not going to go on with a welterweight, and they say he takes it on fast."

"Well, Jimmy usually puts up his diamond ring, and that's worth quite a lot," said Tom.

"Tell him to put up everything he has," said Freddie, "trunks and all. If he hasn't a pair of shoes to put up I'll lend him a couple."

So with Burns putting all his worldly possessions on making the correct weight the match was made. Freddie returned to his familiar routine at Venice. But during an afternoon sparring session he injured the forefinger on his right hand by mistiming a punch to the head of his partner Dick Winters. His finger was so badly bruised and he was in so much pain that he couldn't sleep that night. The doctor was called the following day and he lanced the bruise but this did not stop the swelling from spreading across his hand and wrist. One report suggested the injury was so serious that they were considering amputating his forefinger. Freddie was more concerned about the damage to his wallet. "Just to think, I was to get $1,000 for meeting Burns. It was just like picking up that much money," Freddie said. "Not only would I be able to grab off this $1,000 New Year's present, but I was hoping to whip Burns in such a decisive fashion as to show up Packey McFarland."

When Jimmy Burns mentioned that he had used up all his spare cash on training expenses for the bout, Freddie gave him $100 to cover the costs. Postponing the fight had already cost Freddie his $1,000 guarantee along with his own training expenses and doctor's bills. If that wasn't bad enough he was involved in an embarrassing scuffle with Billy Rose, a well-known hanger-on at the training camp who proceeded to tell journalists how he gave the champion boxer a "lovely thrashing". Freddie was furious and on the evening of January 12th 1909 he drove around the newspaper offices of Los Angeles "all aflame" after reading the story of his 'defeat' at the hands of Billy Rose in Venice. He took witnesses to the affair with him who swore that Rose went to Freddie's home and made accusations of a "dishonourable character" before getting the beating of his life. It transpired that Freddie made his traducer beg before he let him up off the floor. He publicly challenged Rose, who was a light-heavyweight, to a fist fight for a stake of $100 that Freddie intended to donate to a relief fund after he won. The challenge was never accepted.

The Jimmy Burns fight was to have been his farewell to Los Angeles and during the build-up Freddie was making plans for his return to Wales. He'd accepted the offer of a purse of £1,000 to fight Johnny Summers and he planned to fight his way across the United States before sailing for England. The West End Athletic Club of New Orleans invited him to fight Young Corbett there on a guarantee of $1,200 and 30 per cent of the gross receipts. Freddie held out for $1,400 and his rail ticket before accepting. From there he planned to carry on to Philadelphia and New York and take on any lightweight he could find. Freddie's injured hand was healing well enough for him to take the 'easy money' fight with Young Corbett and the New Orleans promoters wired Freddie to post a forfeit of $250 and they would send his transportation at once. But the railway ticket did not arrive and he was told that the club could not honour the $1,400 guarantee and that the fight was off. So Freddie stayed in Los Angeles and prepared for the rescheduled fight with Jimmy Burns. Burns was to get 20 per cent of the receipts for the bout but more importantly if he managed to win or draw, he was promised a fight with Packey McFarland within the next fortnight. At the beginning of 1908 Burns was considered to be a contender for the lightweight crown but he had had a poor twelve months with several disappointing fights and the likes of Freddie and Packey McFarland were now ahead of him in the rankings. This fight was a great opportunity and a victory would take him from near retirement to serious contention. This was a man who didn't even have the money for the forfeit and had to put his prized diamond ring up as a guarantee. A few old hacks saw this as a dangerous fight for Freddie. "Burns belongs to that class of fighters most dreaded by champions and aspiring candidates," wrote one, "he is an ambitious second-rater with the knockout punch." There were reports from Freddie's training camp at Horgan's Hall in Venice that he wasn't taking this fight as seriously as usual. Twice in the week leading up to the contest he broke camp curfew and went to the theatre. One afternoon, Freddie invited over his friends from the Burbank and Belasco theatres and put on an extended sparring exhibition for his thespian audience. On another occasion the famous comedian Nat Goodwin was Freddie's guest of honour. It all made for a good story and great photographs for the newspapers and Jimmy Burns was the bit-part player. "You would think that my fight with Welsh was already over and that Welsh had whipped me to a standstill," said Burns. "These boys seemed to have salted me away in advance without taking the pains to tell me anything about it." Freddie further fuelled speculation about his condition when he arrived for the weigh-in at the Hammam Baths in Los Angeles at six o'clock on the night of the fight. Burns was considered to be the one battling the scales but on the night it was Freddie who showed up three or four ounces overweight. He spent five minutes in the steam room and he scaled 133lbs exactly but it did initiate further speculation over his preparation for the fight. The truth was that Freddie had trained very well for the fight and his problem at the scales was caused by making the weight too easily. He was two pounds underweight that morning but as he drove in from Venice he was 'pinched' just outside the city limits for fast driving. While things were being squared with the constable

Freddie slipped into a nearby drugstore and drank a full quart of grape juice together with a raw egg.

Freddie had left nothing to chance. He wanted to say farewell to Los Angeles in style and he won the fight with ease. At the end of each round Burns trudged back to his corner with a dejected look on his face. He regrouped in the thirty seconds, came back out with renewed determination but slowly gave up hope as each round went on. Freddie fought most of the bout using just his left hand, protecting his injured finger until the end of the seventh round. With his first right hand punch he inscribed a large gash into his opponent's cheek just below his left eye. One writer commented that Freddie outpointed his man "outrageously". After the final bell Freddie turned to friends at ringside and proclaimed it the easiest fight of his life. A few days after beating Burns Freddie, accompanied by Fanny, started out on the long journey home. He told reporters at the railway station that when he returned to the United States he would make Los Angeles his home and he intended to persuade his mother to come with him. Freddie steamed out of the city on the 'Sunset Route', crossing through southern California, Arizona, New Mexico, Texas, Louisiana and into the Mississippi basin. At 6.45pm on February 9th 1909 Freddie and Fanny were met at the railway station in New Orleans by a small army of fans and a deputation from the Westside Athletic Club. It was carnival time and they were wined and dined at the city's Tulane Club where Freddie regaled a new audience with his heroic ring exploits. The following day he set up a training camp at the Young Men's Gymnastic Club and was given quarters near the City Park racetrack. Gene Lutz, a former boxer who'd become one of the city's leading racehorse owners, had arranged Freddie's visit to New Orleans. The two met up at the racetrack on Freddie's first morning to look over Lutz's horses, which were being exercised by a stable hand. Freddie decided he wanted to ride and chose a three-year-old mare by the name of Moscow Belle. The horse was bridled and saddled despite Lutz's protests. Freddie told everybody that he could handle "any bangtail breathing" and when he was told by the owner to do no more than walk around he just laughed. He tipped his hat to the friends who'd accompanied him to the track and gave the bridle a quick jerk to signal a gallop. According to Lutz, "the mare quivered from head to foot as Welsh jerked the bridle, then sprang away like a bullet, as though the barrier had been sprung and she was in a race". When the dust cleared, Freddie was seen struggling to his feet. "I went down from the opening rush, and just escaped a knockout," said Freddie. "I remember throwing my head as far back as possible as I struck the ground, and seeing that animal's ungloved hind foot shoot by my bean."

Freddie was left with his pride hurt and his left arm badly sprained. His first fight in New Orleans was only a week away but sparring was out of the question. His attentions were now elsewhere anyway. On February 12th 1909, over five months since he last fought, Battling Nelson finally made his intentions known. The world champion was on his way to San Francisco and wanted the promoter Jim Coffroth to fix up a fight with Freddie or Packey McFarland as soon as possible. This was six days before Freddie's deadline of February 18th when he intended to claim the champion's title by default. "Any news from Nelson is good news" was Freddie's reaction. He sent a wire from the Tulane Club in New Orleans to Coffroth accepting the challenge and offering side bets of $5,000 for a twenty-five-round fight or $2,000 for a forty-five round contest. Freddie was even prepared to waive his share of the purse just to get a shot at the world championship. All that was standing between the Welshman and his shot at the title was for Coffroth to agree a purse with Nelson. In the meantime there was the small matter of Freddie's New Orleans debut against Young Erne. Freddie had already beaten him as a novice back in Philadelphia and after twenty rounds at the Westside Club, Erne's face "was chopped raw, one eye was nearly closed, and a big lump was over his kidneys". Freddie had yet another victim, another purse and more bad news from Nelson. A few days after his fight against Young Erne word of the champion's financial demands arrived from San Francisco. The 'Battler' wanted $15,000 win, lose or draw to meet Freddie. This proposition was open to the promoters of the country until the next Fourth of July. If it wasn't met by that time Nelson would increase his demand to $20,000. This sum was then to be the only figure that would induce the champion to fight again. The promoters had until September 9th to do business on this basis. It was Nelson's 'anniversary day', exactly a year since his last fight, and unless he was signed up by this time he would announce his retirement. The two Los Angeles promoters, Tom McCarey and Baron Long, refused the demand immediately and there was a silence from other parts of the country. Nelson had succeeded in stalling Freddie's threatened 'jumping' of the light-weight championship and he'd managed to generate publicity for his music hall tour. The boxing writers denounced the offer as a stunt. "The American public hates a four-flusher," wrote the sports editor of the *Los Angeles Examiner*. "One has to deliver the goods to stay in the good graces of the people. Nelson has had a long enough rest. If he wants to retain his rank as champion he will have to come out of his hiding place and show some disposition to fight."

By the following week Nelson had devised an even more outrageous plan. There were five leading British fighters in the United States at that time: Freddie, Jim Driscoll, Owen Moran, Jabez White and Johnny Summers. Nelson made a proposition to Jim Coffroth that on July 4th he would allow the promoter to chose any two of these boxers and he would fight them both for $25,000, or any three for $30,000, four for $35,000 and any additional number for an extra $2,500 apiece. There was to be a fifteen-minute intermission between each bout but "maybe I won't need that much in some cases" he claimed.

While Nelson toyed with the newspapers and earned a good living by just *being* champion Freddie needed to keep on fighting. The Westside Club in New Orleans arranged another bout for him a few weeks later against Ray Bronson of Indianapolis, the self-proclaimed champion of the Mid West who had his championship credentials embossed on his luggage. Bronson arrived in New Orleans a week before the fight and declared that he had worked out how to beat Freddie Welsh. He refused to let scribes watch his sparring sessions for fear of letting the secret out. "I don't want these fellows down here to get next to my style of fighting. If they do they will run and tell Welsh. Pugs are like women in that respect," said Bronson. With about a minute of the thirteenth round remaining Freddie smashed Bronson to the canvas for the fourth time and his corner threw in the towel to avoid permanent damage.

The long-expected news that Battling Nelson had no intention of giving Freddie a chance at the title arrived soon after the Bronson fight. His latest plan was to defend the championship three times and then retire. Two of the opponents had already been chosen; Cyclone Johnny Thompson, who Freddie had already beaten and Dick Hyland. The identity of the third challenger had yet to be revealed but it soon became known that Nelson's management was talking to Packey McFarland. There was no mention of Freddie, who just carried on fighting. His third and final contest in New Orleans, one last payday before heading east, was against Young Donahue. It was an acrimonious affair even before they even stepped into the ring. From the time of the finish of the last preliminary bout to the main fight there was a delay of an hour and forty minutes. The crowd shouted for the fighters to come out, threatened to leave and at one point started to sing 'Home, Sweet Home'. The delay was due to Freddie's refusal to have a man named Dave Barry referee the bout, and the fight only went ahead after a Dr Wallace Wood was offered sufficient inducement and consented to officiate. Freddie also insisted that the management, in accordance with the articles he signed, pay him before he went into the ring. A compromise was reached whereby Freddie was paid in part beforehand. Despite being nearly a stone lighter than his opponent Freddie won virtually all ten rounds. But because of the controversy over the referee an agreement had been made that unless there was a marked advantage in favour of one or the other the bout was to be declared a draw. To set the record straight Freddie sent a telegram to H.M. Walker, Sporting Editor of the *Los Angeles Examiner*:

> Robbed of decision. I won in every round: inexperienced and over excited referee declared bout a draw. It was easier for me, and more one-sided than the Johnny Murphy fight in Vernon. New Orleans papers claim the unfair decision will be death knell to boxing here.
>
> FRED WELSH

Freddie and Fanny headed east the following morning. On their way to New York they stopped off at Baltimore and met up with the old champion Joe Gans. His tuberculosis worsening, he'd just boxed his last fight, a ten-round no decision contest against the former British champion Jabez White. Nat Fleischer wrote of the fight, "even though his body was full of death germs, Gans still displayed some of his famous punching power". The following year Joe died in his mother's arms. He weighed 84 pounds.

The couple travelled on to New York to meet up with an old friend, Jim Jeffries, the former heavyweight champion who had staged many of Freddie's biggest fights out in California. Since he retired as the undefeated heavyweight champion in 1905 Jim had spent his time farming and promoting other fighters in Vernon. But ageing and overweight, Jeffries had been pressed into a comeback to regain the championship for the white race. Jack Johnson held the most prized title in sport and there was a public clamour for a white hope to take the championship back. Jack London demanded that Jim Jeffries take up the white man's burden and relieve Johnson of his title and he penned an infamous commentary for the the *New York Herald*: "Jeffries must emerge from his alfalfa farm and remove the golden smile from Jack Johnson's face. Jeff, it's up to you!" London was a socialist who championed individualism; he espoused a spirit of brotherhood but wrote of the inferiority of the "coloured people". He was a friend of Freddie's whose own stance on the race issue was also full of contradictions. Freddie was a great admirer of Joe Gans, yet the Welshman also wrote of a gang of strikebreakers as being "as near savages as you would be likely to meet out of Central Africa". Freddie even contributed to the 'great white hope' debate by suggesting that a dragnet be taken through the Rhondda and Rhymney valleys to find the brand of Welshman that would "sooner fight than eat". He found the current 'hope', Jim Jeffries sweating off the pounds in a New York gymnasium. "Jeffries can whip any heavyweight in his present condition," Freddie told reporters. "I said he could get into condition but he has surprised me by his weight reduction and I think he can enter the ring in three months as good as he ever was in his life." When Jeffries eventually met Johnson in Reno, Nevada on July 4th the following year, he was hopelessly beaten in fifteen rounds.

Freddie and Fanny moved into apartments at the St Paul Hotel in New York. He signed for a fight against Dave Deshler at the Armory Athletic Club in Boston on the agreement that both fighters should weigh 133lbs at three o'clock. However, two days before the fight, Deshler's management informed Freddie's manager and the Armory Club that he wouldn't be able to make the weight. Dave Deshler was actually a rather heavy welterweight who would have entered the ring well over a stone heavier than Freddie who now had the money to turn down such propositions. Freddie arrived at the weigh-in to find that Deshler 'pulled down the beam' at 142lbs at three o'clock in the afternoon. By the time the fight started at ten o'clock that evening Deshler would have weighed a 147lbs or more. Despite the best efforts of the management to get Freddie to fight he promptly packed up and returned to New York on the 5pm train.

Freddie had been fighting professionally for over three years but had yet to box in New York. He finally made his debut in a match with Johnny Frayne at the Fairmount Athletic Club on May 7th 1909. Freddie won easily, but he didn't impress the locals. He certainly didn't make the same impact that Jim Driscoll had made in the months prior to Freddie's arrival in the city. The following day's edition of the *New York American* was typical of the press reaction to Freddie's Big Apple debut:

> The ringsters were somewhat disappointed in the showing of the Englishman, who was touted a wonder of the Jem Driscoll calibre. If Welsh is as clever as Jem, he didn't show it last night, especially from the standpoint of hitting. Welsh does not hit cleanly.

Freddie didn't want to go back to Wales without having impressed in New York and certainly not while being unfavourably compared to his countryman. He was stale from six weeks' hard work and the postponement of the fight up in Boston had upset his training programme. Freddie wanted to show New Yorkers he was a lot better than he had appeared against Frayne, so he challenged the city's lightweights to a match before setting sail for home. The first fighter in the queue was Jack Goodman from Greenwich Village. Jack was a great favourite with the customers and this was his first match with a boxer of international repute. Goodman had been in the crowd for the Frayne bout and told his manager to fix up the fight. Once again Freddie won easily enough but once again he was unfavourably compared with Peerless Jim. "While Welsh did not prove himself a second Jim Driscoll, he was fast and clever enough to stamp him as one of the best men of his weight in the world," was the typical sentiment of ringside reporters. Freddie returned to the Armory Athletic Club in Boston at the end of May. There was no controversy this time as Freddie put on a dazzling display against Phil Brock, his first opponent on reaching Los Angeles the previous summer.

He'd travelled from the East Coast to the West Coast and back again and now it was time to set sail for England to win the gold and diamond studded trophy that Lord Lonsdale was putting up for the championship of Britain and the Empire. If he could return to America with that belt around his waist no claimant to the world title could deny him. It was only fitting that when he and Fanny stepped on board the *Lusitania* there was one more Battling Nelson story to occupy Freddie's mind. Word reached New York that the champion had finally agreed to fight again. George W. Hancock of the Pacific Athletic Club in San Francisco had succeeded in getting Nelson to sign a set of articles to meet Ad Wolgast in San Francisco during Elks' Week in July. At the meeting Nelson had told Hancock he intended to retire in September and that he wanted him to arrange that his final fight would be against Freddie Welsh. A week later Freddie and Fanny landed in Liverpool. Freddie's sister Kate met them and they travelled by boat train to London. Among those to meet the party at Euston station were Harry Marks and Arthur Seaton of the Pontypridd and Cardiff syndicate. They all stayed at the Tavistock Hotel in London and the following day Freddie held court with the city's leading sportswriters. During their time in London Freddie, Kate and Harry Marks found time for a day at the Ascot races and also for a meeting with Johnny Summers at the National Sporting Club. Summers was the strongest claimant to the title of British lightweight champion and the Club's manager Peggy Bettinson confirmed to the two fighters that Lord Lonsdale had

promised a gold and silver belt to the winner of a match for the
British title. The basic agreement for the championship contest was
all but completed and now it really was time to go home.

Freddie was due back in Wales on the four-thirty London express
on Saturday June 19th 1909. Throughout the train journey he had
been wrapped in George Bernard Shaw's *Man and Superman* having
just finished *The Meditations of Marcus Aurelius*. An enormous crowd
turned out at Cardiff's Great Western Railway station. The platform
was crammed full and after the station doors had to be closed an
even larger gathering waited out in the concourse. The train eventually arrived at five minutes after five. As it steamed up to the station
Freddie's head protruded out of one of the windows. He stepped
from the carriage in a navy blue suit, straw hat and a leek as a button-
hole. He wore a scarf in which sparkled a diamond pin given to him
by Jim Jeffries. On his finger he sported a diamond ring "with a stone
as big as a green pea". Dangling from his waistcoat pocket was a
gold-mounted fob, to which was attached a gold medallion presented
to him by an old friend and pupil from a physical culture school in
Philadelphia. When he smiled he revealed an array of gold teeth. He
was besieged by the crowd and had to "undergo the ordeal of violent
handshaking". One of the first to greet him was Jim Driscoll. When
the crowd recognized Peerless Jim another loud cheer went up and
as Freddie finally got to his car he shouted at Driscoll to join him.
The vehicle made it's way through Penarth Road to St Mary's Street
where it was mobbed by so many people that it had to stop. It eventually made its way to the home of Harry Marks in Coldstream
Terrace. Newspaper reporters were waiting for Freddie there and he
spoke of his pride in "making good" and bringing back $30,000 to
Wales. One journalist wrote that he was "imbued with the spirit of
America – push, courage, enterprise, and a keen sense of the business
value of advertisement". The news of Nelson's offer to fight in
September had arrived before him and he informed the press that
he'd be very glad to return to America in August if this was authen-
tic and Nelson did not back out of it. When one reporter asked him
whether he would "marry a Welsh lassie and be happy ever after?"
Freddie just said, "they're all right; the Welsh girls. Wales can beat
anything America has got to show in the beauty line; but I want to
make a bit more before I settle down to the happy ever after life."
Meanwhile Fanny, officially the chef, said nothing. Only Freddie's
immediate family knew that he was married and Fanny spent most
of her time during this British tour working on the health farm that
Bernarr Macfadden had established in Chesham, Buckinghamshire.

'See, The Conquering Hero Comes': Pontypridd, 19 June 1909.

After a short rest at Harry Marks' home the party set off in various cars to Pontypridd. On the way from Cardiff the convoy was joined by hundreds of cyclists who followed its path up the valley. Surging crowds lined the road for several miles on the approach to Freddie's hometown. Along the way he recognized Jack 'Brandy' Davies, a former boxer and an old friend, who was persuaded to join the party. The crowds were singing, 'See, The Conquering Hero Comes'. When Freddie's car reached Pontypridd it took its place in a procession headed by four brass bands. Decorations were hung from every house and the town was ablaze with bunting. The population of Pontypridd at the time was 32,000 yet it was estimated that 80,000 turned up to see Freddie's homecoming. The car then headed for Merthyr and the house his mother had moved to since selling the Bridge House Hotel. As the car arrived in the town another procession was formed, this time headed by the band of the Merthyr Volunteer Battallion. The crowds had gathered outside his mother's house and because of the constant shouting for Freddie's appearance, Harry Marks advised them all to travel back to Cardiff with him. During the time he had been away Freddie had bought a number of houses in and around Merthyr in his mother's name. She collected the rents and lived on the income. After he started making money in the ring he also sent her £3 a week. Such was the reaction to Freddie's return to Wales that a few of the ministers in Merthyr spoke out against him. They detected in the welcome "a sign of moral degeneracy and encouragement of blackguardism".

The syndicate that lured Freddie back home put up a purse of £550 for his first fight against Young Joseph, the 'Pride of the Ghetto'. It was four times more than any previous offer for a bout in Wales. An enormous crowd was needed to cover such an investment and a venue had to be found to accommodate it. The Eisteddfod pavillion in the valleys' town of Mountain Ash was chosen and one of the syndicate members, Arthur Seaton, took charge of transforming the hall into a 10,000-seat stadium. Meanwhile Freddie took charge of filling it. Newspaper editors did not regard pugilists too favourably in Great Britain at the time. The important contests were reported, but there were very few articles dealing with a boxer's training, his likes and dislikes, or his views on general matters. Freddie changed this. Fred Dartnell, one of the leading boxing writers of the era, recalled how the Welshman was one of the first fighters in Britain to supply newspapers with material worth printing. "He needed publicity that was out of the ordinary, and he was sensible enough to realize that he could only obtain it by suggesting stories that had a wide appeal," wrote Dartnell. "He knew that a paragraph that was only suitable for the sports pages would not get him anywhere. It would be read by the few and skipped by the majority". So Freddie interested Fleet Street by discussing art and literature and espousing the view that meat eating was harmful, and explaining how he trained for all his contests on a diet of nuts and vegetables. He was featured in columns and half-columns that were usually given to crime, politics and fashionable divorces.

Freddie began his training in the seaside town of Porthcawl before moving to the Premier Baths in Cathedral Road, Cardiff, for a better choice of sparring partner. After one sparring session a scribe saw Freddie reading Epictetus' *Discourses* while his trainer was rubbing him down. When he was asked why he was reading the works of the great philosopher Freddie replied that training was such monotonous work that he'd go crazy if he didn't have something to think about. "Somebody ought to write a book on *Boxing as a Means to Grace*," Freddie told the reporter.

Young Joseph arrived in Cardiff two days before the fight and such was the interest in the contest that over a thousand people turned up at the railway station to welcome him to Wales. In addition to a side wager of £100 Joseph and Freddie entered into another novel bet. Joseph was soon to be married and on the result of the contest depended whether he would have to buy a drawing room suite or whether Freddie paid the bill. "If I win," said Freddie, "I don't know what I shall do with my suite. I shall have to store it somewhere, because I hope to make a lot more money in the States yet before I settle down."

The syndicate's gamble in offering such a large purse paid off handsomely. The gate receipts were over £4,000 and extra trains were organized to shuttle a crowd of over ten thousand to Mountain Ash. The men of South Wales had read about the exploits of Freddie Welsh and were now going to see "the cleverest boxer in the world" in action. The ring had been built in a cavernous pavillion with tiers of seats rising to all four corners. It was a hot, humid evening and there was barely a pause in the singing. The American journalist John R. Coyrell, who accompanied Freddie on his British tour, was at ringside. Boxing in Coyrell's hometown of New York had been confined to small arenas for many years and the State Governor was actively trying to ban the sport. After the fight he wrote home to say, "I remembered our own Governor Hughes was of Welsh extraction, and I sighed, wondering how he could have degenerated from his sport-loving ancestors."

For his part, Freddie treated the crowd to a display of boxing, the likes of which very few people in Britain had ever seen. He certainly wasn't the classic 'straight left' boxer like Wales' other hero Jim Driscoll. Freddie was blindingly fast and he threw punches from every conceivable angle. An American boxing journalist wrote of seeing Freddie fight:

> You may know when it is coming. The hazel eyes, at all times lustrous, sparkle with a dazzling light. It is as though an electric jet were suddenly turned up; a white fire seems to emanate from him, and he is inspired by a passionate energy that, like a seething mountain torrent of his own country that long pent up has broken bounds, carries all irresistibly before it – and in spirit you go with it. At such time Fred moves with incredible swiftness – far faster than the eye can follow, and his blows are as flying hail; anywhere, everywhere, from every possible and seemingly impossible quarter they come with the snap and precision of a flexible steel thong, and scourge unerringly again and again on the same weakened spot. Faster and faster goes the pace till the adversary, bewildered and weakened, can strive no more.

Joseph was forced to play the role of "receiver general" as battered fighters were dubbed by the American writers. Freddie began the fight with a demonstration of his favourite blow, the kidney punch. Many boxing historians actually credited Freddie for having introduced the kidney punch to the sport. Others vested the 'honour' on Ben Jordan, a former featherweight champion. Whether he was its originator or not, Freddie was certainly one of its leading exponents.

After just a few rounds a red patch the size of a man's hand became visible on Joseph's back. It was just above his belt and about two inches to the left of the spinal column. This red patch grew redder and larger in each round and in the fifth a lump as big as a goose egg made its appearance. Freddie smashed away at this lump whenever he had an opportunity. In the sixth round a sickening jab into Joseph's mouth opened up a wound that bled profusely for the rest of the fight. By the eleventh it was all that Joseph could do to cling to Freddie to be spared further beating. A right hook to the jaw sent the Englishman to the canvas and as he got up Joseph threw a low blow for which he was cautioned. A matter of seconds later Joseph did it again. The referee promptly disqualified him and "a scene of considerable excitement followed". Joseph seemed unable to understand that he had been disqualified, and shaped up to continue. The referee ordered him to his seat. Freddie, who appeared to be in pain, was also anxious to continue and it was not until referee Dunning had repeated his decision and one of his seconds took him by the shoulder that the winner retired to his corner. Meanwhile the ring was invaded by a large number of people and it was only by the exertions of the police that trouble was avoided. "If anything could get a boxing man into his 'hwyl' it is to have the chance of returning thanks to his countrymen for the demonstrative welcome they gave me when I returned to my home the other day," Freddie told reporters after the contest. "I am giving away weight – a big lump – a bigger lump than most people think, but there is nothing like taking a liberty about that or thinking too much of one's self in that. It's not my fault that no one at my weight will take me."

After the Young Joseph fight Freddie and Fanny took a vacation. They crossed the channel to Rotterdam and travelled on through Amsterdam, The Hague, Scheveningen, the Zuyder Zee, Antwerp and Brussels. From there they moved on to Paris. There was not time to see much but Freddie did contrive to see what Holland and Belgium had in the way of treasures by Rubens, Rembrandt and Van Dyck. While Freddie was appreciating the riches of the continent's art galleries one William Ecclestone or 'Jolly Jumbo' as he was known, walked "with the agility of a lightweight" into the offices of the *Sportsman* in London with a one hundred pound note and a challenge to the Welshman. Ecclestone was a well-known London sportsman who'd just returned from Paris where he'd discovered a new lightweight prospect, Henri Piet. Any French boxer was treated with a fair degree of cynicism by the sporting press in England at this time. On reporting the proposed match the *Sporting Chronicle* wrote "the French boxing man has been looked upon as a sort of person who would express profound regret to his opponent if the latter should receive anything in the nature of a severe blow". Freddie accepted Ecclestone's challenge and the South Wales syndicate agreed to put up the purse and stage the contest in Mountain Ash once more. Such was Freddie's popularity during the summer of 1909 that the syndicate's money would have been safe on any contest in which Freddie fought. But the newspapers were not impressed with the choice of opponent. Before the fight Jim Driscoll went so far as to say that it would "hurt the boxing game to have soft matches like this pulled off". Piet's perceived shortcomings did nothing to dim the enthusiasm for the fight throughout the valleys. As one newspaper reported, "boxing is at the boom stage in Wales, it is clear that her collier sons like nothing more than to see a struggle of fistic skill". All the popular price seats had been occupied for more than an hour before the preliminaries started. The pavillion was virtually full by the time Freddie reached Mountain Ash. He'd travelled up from Cardiff by car that evening and the crowds had gathered to cheer on the hero of the hour all along the route. Freddie stopped in Pontypridd en route just in time to see R.R. Day and F.C. Davies race the half-mile for the 'world's championship' on the town's athletic ground. By the time Freddie reached the hall it was packed to suffocation on a hot, late August evening. When the anthems were over, the crowd just kept on singing. Even Piet seemed to be impressed with a particularly vociferous rendition of 'Men of Harlech'. One of the Americans at ringside commented that the "thousands in the hall caught up the Welsh national anthem and sang it with an ardour and vim and correctness that set the blood leaping in one's veins. It is a trick these Welsh people have."

The fight was much better than anyone had dared hope. Despite the well-publicized concerns, Piet was an excellent fighter and for a few rounds at least he gave Freddie a good argument. The Frenchman's resistance finally ended in the eleventh round when Freddie hit him with five unanswered blows. The first was a right hook to the jaw followed by three consecutive blows under the ribcage. As he fell forward trying to suck in air after the impact of these body shots, Freddie threw a straight left between Piet's eyes that sent a spray of claret from a gaping cut on his nose. Blinded by sweat and blood and unable to breathe, Piet jumped back and with a sudden gasp clasped his hand to his knee. Freddie chased him and started to hit out at a terrific pace with both fists. Piet reached for the ropes and threw both arms in the air in a despairing gesture and offered his right hand to his opponent. Freddie shook it and the Frenchman limped to his corner. Unusually for a boxing crowd Piet's decision to quit was cheered sympathetically and he'd earned his share of the purse. Once the entire hall realized that the fight was over strains of 'See The Conquering Hero', first quietly but then quickly gaining in volume, filled the pavillion.

There was, however, an equally large and vociferous section of the public in South Wales that regarded Freddie as anything but a conquering hero. Following his defeat of Piet, one local newspaper reported a meeting held at a chapel in the village of Penrhiwceiber during which one of the deacons, a Mr David Jones, disparaged the young men of the congregation who'd been "drawn to the event". According to the *Aberdare Leader* Mr Jones, "speaking quite heatedly, said that the exhibition was entirely wrong and would be detrimental to the young generation". Another local minister thought it a shame that such eagerness should be displayed by thousands to witness "those brutal contests". He believed that prizefights encouraged gambling and betting and were the cause of "damnation of people". One letter to the same newspaper described the Mountain Ash fights as "an epidemic of disgrace". It was an epidemic that was out of control in South Wales in the summer of 1909. There was an insatiable demand to see Freddie fight and a third match was made at the Mountain Ash pavillion. Freddie was the only lightweight boxer in Britain capable of attracting large purses and offers for fights started to flood in. There was a rumour that Freddie would soon return to the United States to fight Battling Nelson for the world title so all the leading lightweights were trying to secure a large pay day before he left. After some wrangling over dates, weight and side stakes a bout was arranged with Joe Fletcher from Camberwell on September 6th 1909. The fight was for £100 a side and a purse of £500 of which the winner got sixty five per cent and the loser got the rest. The same syndicate that backed Freddie's two previous fights put up the money.

Freddie moved his training camp from Cardiff to Merthyr for this fight to be closer to his mother and sister. He couldn't find anywhere in the town to train to begin with but the local sportsmen organized the Tiger Hotel to be put at his disposal and the clubroom was transformed into a gymnasium for the duration of Freddie's stay. He damaged his right hand in one of the final training sessions but nobody was told and he went into the ring with as much bandaging as was allowed and a plan to use his right as sparingly as possible. It was one of the most one-sided contests ever seen between two men with any claims to being a top class fighter. From the fifth round onwards a cut along the line of Fletcher's left eye wept blood. By the seventh round the damage was so severe that he saw no more through the eye until the following day. Fletcher was hit to the canvas twice in the tenth round and one reporter commented that it would have been an act of mercy on Freddie's part to deliver the final blow. It eventually came in the twelfth. The sound of the bell ringing to start the round was still reverberating around the hall when Freddie chopped a right onto Fletcher's kidney and he fell forwards to the canvas. The Englishman got up at the count of three but one more vicious swing to the kidneys and another to the back of the neck finished it. Fletcher lay on the canvas for the count of ten and remained in the same position for a long while afterwards. Freddie raced from his corner to help his stricken opponent back to his chair. After the fight, Fletcher, barely able to prize his swollen lips apart, said that it was a mistake to think Freddie can't hit. One American boxing writer suggested that Freddie should join the "Lemon Pickers' Union" for lifting off "dead Queensbury fruit".

Whether Fletcher deserved such a disparaging report is arguable, but the difference in the abilities of the two men in the ring did serve to highlight the rut into which British boxing had got into at this time. Fletcher was considered to be a good opponent and one of the more credible claimants to the championship of England at a time when several men proclaimed themselves the legitimate titleholder. In an attempt to pull the sport out of the "dear old bad days", Hugh Cecil Lowther, 5th Earl of Lonsdale, an English nobleman, *bon vivant* and 'England's greatest sporting gentleman' intervened. He donated a championship belt for competition at fixed weights: heavy, middle, welter, light, feather, bantam and fly. Any fighter winning four contests at which the belt was at stake was allowed to keep it. A permanent holder was entitled, when reaching the age of fifty, to a pension of £1 a week for the rest of his days. Lonsdale believed the championship system would capture the public's imagination and enhance the importance and prestige of the National Sporting Club. He also hoped that the market value of a Lonsdale Belt holder would increase immeasurably and the champion would enjoy a status he could not have hoped for otherwise. He was right. The introduction of Lonsdale belts revolutionized boxing in Britain and did more to popularize the sport than anything else during the early decades of the twentieth century. Freddie desperately wanted to be the first man to wear one.

The only man left to dispute the lightweight title with Freddie was Johnny Summers, a Yorkshireman who boxed out of Canning Town.

The fight, with a purse of £2,200 and the Lonsdale Belt at stake, was fixed for October 18th 1909. After three fights in six weeks over the summer, Freddie decided to rest until the Summers bout. He did consider a challenge from a syndicate in Llanelli that was prepared to find an opponent but the deal fell through, so Freddie set off for Bernarr Macfadden's health farm in Chesham to be reunited with Fanny. Since they first met she trained right along with Freddie, she practiced and dieted and sometimes even sprinted and boxed with her husband. Both got into 'condition' at the same time. In America she stayed with Freddie until the master of ceremonies called him into the ring. She helped to keep him calm. But Fanny never liked to watch her husband fight because it made her nervous. During his fights in California the previous summer, Fanny used to go to a 'phonograph parlour' and listen to "all the crashy music they had". It relieved the strain for her and as soon as she knew the fight was over Fanny hurried back for the result. But the two were still anxious to keep their marriage a secret and so she stayed in England while Freddie returned to Pontypridd to prepare for the fight with Johnny Summers. Charles Trenchard, the proprietor of the town's Clarence Theatre put the establishment at Freddie's disposal. In the morning he would run from Pontypridd to Church Village and back – some seven miles. Freddie used the theatre stage for shadow boxing and sparring and welcomed the townspeople of Pontypridd to watch the sessions free of charge. Such was the demand that tickets had to be issued to control the numbers. Ladies were especially welcome and were excused the need for a ticket. Before Freddie's return from the United States the way boxers prepared for battle was shrouded in mystery. Stories would occasionally emerge from closed training camps of mysterious methods and secrets. Freddie changed that. He introduced the open training session and a hustling manner of advertising fights. *The Sportsman* commented on his ability to "quite fill the public eye in the matter of popularity almost entirely to the exclusion of any other man in the game".

But with less than a fortnight to go before one of the biggest fights to be staged on British soil to that date, Johnny Summers sent a telegram to the National Sporting Club asking for a postponement. He wanted the fight to be put back because of theatrical engagements in which he took on all-comers from the audience. His contract with the music-hall company extended a fortnight longer than he thought which left him insufficient time to train properly. Freddie was particularly annoyed because he'd turned down a £120 a week for a similar engagement and to make matters worse, he had been spending £80 a week training for a fight that would now be postponed. Freddie reluctantly accepted the delay but then there was another hitch. It transpired that Summers had already agreed to sail for Australia on the 12th of November and he'd have to forfeit hundreds of pounds to get out of this contract. It was reported that Summers was not in the best of health because of the worry and anxiety surrounding these contractual matters but that he felt a postponement would put him right. Freddie, Johnny Summers and their respective backers were called to the National Sporting Club to resolve the issue. A compromise date of November 8th 1909 was reached. The postponement cost Summers a forfeit of £50.

During the build up to the fight Freddie took on several charitable engagements, mainly to raise funds for disabled colliers. Just three days before the Summers fight he agreed to act as timekeeper for some exhibition bouts in Merthyr to "benefit a fellow sport" who was not enjoying the best of luck. His regular chauffeur was not available to take him so his old friend Councillor Arthur Seaton offered

Freddie and his brother Stanley.

to drive. Also in the car that afternoon was Freddie's brother Stanley who'd sailed in from the Black Sea to see the contest. Stanley was a seafarer and was trying for his officer's ticket. As they approached the village of Tonypandy Mr Seaton attempted to "show how the car should be controlled", but the greasy condition of a hill upset his calculations and the car skidded and made straight for a hedge. Arthur and Stanley braced themselves for the impact but Freddie decided to jump. The *Welsh Press Agency* reported that Freddie, "sensing the danger jumped out, landing heavily on one leg". He landed on his big toe and the impetus of his spring sent him forward onto his knee which was cut on the hard surface of the road. Arthur Seaton and Stanley were unharmed. "In one way the greasy condition of the road was fortunate," Freddie recalled, "as my knee on striking the ground slid somewhat forward, and so lessened the impact." Harry Marks drove up from Cardiff and took Freddie back to his house to avoid any further mishaps. The injured knee was massaged but the following morning it had stiffened up.

On the morning of the fight another huge crowd had gathered at the station in Cardiff. Freddie arrived five minutes before his train was due to leave and people were standing on the luggage trucks and at every possible vantage point just to see him. As the train pulled out, he came to the window and shouted goodbye to the crowd. A few hours later he was met by another packed platform in London's Paddington station. When Freddie left his carriage, accompanied by his mother and sister and the rest of his entourage, he was walking with a pronounced limp. From the station the party was driven across the city to the National Sporting Club for the weigh-in. Extra police were placed outside the building to keep back the crowds endeavouring to catch a glimpse of the two fighters as they arrived. Freddie was still limping as he took to the scales at two o'clock.

Long before the hour of the fight the Club was full to capacity; mainly populated by lords, baronets, knights and other "distinguished patrons of the noble art". Only two women were present, one of whom was Freddie's sister Kate. The Welshman entered first, his left knee painted with iodine and wearing trunks that he'd designed especially for the fight. The Union Jack, the Welsh Dragon and a leek had been embroidered along the silk belt. His seconds Jack Brandy Davies, Boyo Driscoll and Ernest Williams all wore shirts emblazoned with the Welsh dragon. The applause for the fighters only subsided with the cries for bets, and "much wagering seemed to be going on". This was also the moment when Freddie first showed his willingness to challenge the Establishment. It was a custom of the National

Sporting Club to ask the gentlemen in the audience to stop smoking prior to the main event and put out all lighted cigars. Lord Rothschild who was sitting just a yard or so behind Freddie's corner refused and carried on smoking a "big black cigar". Freddie instructed one of the ushers to kindly ask the lord to refrain from smoking because he found the smell sickening. Once again Rothschild refused, so Freddie sent Lord Lonsdale across the aisle who shouted at his fellow peer to put out the cigar or leave the building. Rothschild obeyed Lonsdale's orders as Freddie smiled in his corner.

When both fighters had reached the ring it became apparent that Freddie's hands were more heavily bandaged than Summers' and they were covered by a small glove with the fingers cut off. As soon as Summers' corner saw the arrangement they objected to the referee Tom Scott. Scott called Peggy Bettinson, Colonel Fox, the Chief of Army Gymnasia and Sir Claud de Crespigny to consult on the issue. They decided that Freddie had to remove the covering. So he left the ring and returned to the dressing room. The Lonsdale belt was exhibited to stop the crowd getting restless while the bandages were changed. It was taken to Johnny Summers' corner where the Londoner looked at it in wonderment. It was as close as Summers ever got to the belt. Freddie took the lead in the first round and continued to add to it in every subsequent one. One writer calculated that Freddie landed at least two hundred clean blows on his opponent's head during the contest. He drew first blood as early as the third round with a series of cutting blows to Summers' face. It was a rugged fight and Freddie was warned for butting in the fifth round having previously been warned for leaning on his opponent. Before the contest was half over odds of fifty-to-one on were being offered on the Welshman. As the fight drew to a close Freddie's hair and left shoulder were covered in the blood streaming from Summers' nose. Despite his overwhelming superiority over a badly beaten opponent a large faction of the National Sporting Club membership jeered Freddie because they considered some of his tactics, especially the kidney punching, as not sporting. "Ye gods! Some of the gentry who roar shouts of disapproval would give a bronze statue the headache," wrote one ringside reporter. "To hear their inane remarks, and to listen to the manner in which they develop their particular idea, is enough to make a person wish he were stone deaf for the period of the all too long contest with such undesirable company. I suppose it is not always the man who wears the cap and bells who is the greatest fool, and bitter experience teaches one to be very suspicious of the legions of obscure critics who made the night hideous with their cries."

It was a very different story back in Wales. A great crowd had gathered outside the offices of the *South Wales Daily News* in Pontypridd. This was the only place where the progress of the fight, round by round, could be followed. A huge cheer went up about midnight when news came through that Freddie had won. After the fight Freddie sent a telegram to the *Western Mail*:

> Delighted to bring championship to Wales. Summers hard puncher, gentlemanly boxer. I have been offered £250 weekly working halls. Home first though. Cymru am Byth.
>
> FRED WELSH
> (Lightweight Champion of England)

When the belt was awarded to Freddie shouts of "Clywch, clywch" (Hear, hear) were heard above the noise of the club. But his victory was not altogether a popular one. There were many at the National Sporting Club who disliked Freddie, as a man and a fighter. He was regarded as "irritatingly cold; cruel in his intensity of purpose, supremely confident, outrageously unconventional in his ideas as to what makes for physical fitness and outwardly a cynic". For the gentlemen of the Club these were appaling traits and now he was taking the Belt, their Belt, back to Wales. What Freddie did was to seize every advantage that the rules allowed; he stretched the law to its utmost extent. To his supporters it denoted a cool and experienced master of ringcraft. To his critics it wasn't sportsmanlike. The reaction in America was very different; it was as if one of its own had taken the first Lonsdale Belt from the mother country:

> They talk of the beauty of open boxing and straight from the shoulder punches; as if the last word on boxing had been said in the prehistoric days of the sport, and that it was something like blasphemy or lese-majeste or treason or anything else very awful to think of improving on the art of good old Tom Sayers – not to go even further back into the legendary days.
> When padded gloves were first put on boxing was born – boxing in the modern sense, anyhow, and all the old limitations that had hedged the sport about fell away. A new fistic science began to develop, and it has gone on developing. Moreover, it will go on developing. And if British boxers insist on keeping their eyes worshipfully fixed on the dead past they will continue to see themselves worsted in the game by those who look ahead, and who refuse to bow down to their fetishes.

Seven

I Don't Fight to Look Pretty

Freddie enjoyed being champion. He squandered a small fortune while travelling at a fast pace with his speedy companions in England, usually with the Lonsdale Belt in tow. The closest he got to a boxing ring for several months was to perform in a Drury Lane drama called *A 33-1 Chance* in which he sparred with Ben Jordan, Britain's first world champion of the gloved era. Freddie accepted a string of theatrical engagements in the music halls of London. It was lucrative work but it took its toll. He was keeping very late hours and was constantly catching colds dashing from steam-heated dressing rooms into waiting cars to be whirled to the next theatre. He felt slow, tired and stale and his thoughts turned back to boxing. Freddie was sure that now he was the holder of the British title Battling Nelson would be forced to fight him and the world championship would also be his. Life was good for Freddie Welsh in the winter of 1909. But a chance meeting on a wintry morning in London soon put an end to Freddie's contentment. He was walking along the Strand when he saw Packey McFarland walking on the other side of the road. "McFarland and I are not any too good friends although there is nothing between us, but instead of passing with a curt nod, as usual, McFarland stopped and waved to me," Freddie recalled. He walked across the street met Packey half way. The American had just found out that Battling Nelson had lost against Adolph 'Ad' Wolgast in San Francisco and there was a new lightweight champion. Packey and Freddie knew that for the last year or so Nelson had been "an easy picking for some young fellow" but they were both astonished that the previously unheralded Wolgast had triumphed. The two men who expected to do 'the picking' were chatting in the Strand and had been beaten to the prize by the 'Michigan Wildcat', a younger man who used to fight preliminary bouts on bills headlined by Packey and Freddie. The order of things had changed.

Battling Nelson had boxed a ten-round no decision contest with Ad Wolgast the previous summer. Because the referee wasn't allowed to give a verdict the only way the champion could lose his title was by knockout and Nelson regarded the fight as little more than an exhibition to cash in on his celebrity status. The contest descended into a demonstration of boxing's dark arts. Wolgast was seemingly as resistant to punishment as Nelson and had an equally large repertoire of dirty tricks. It was a blood-soaked brawl and the newspapers adjudged the underdog Wolgast the winner. It immediately propelled the Michigan based fighter to the head of the queue for a title challenge and it established a mutual hatred between the two men that lasted many years. The inevitable rematch was staged on February 22nd 1910. Wolgast was so confident of victory that he offered to let Nelson put a horseshoe in each of his gloves and bet him $2,500 that he couldn't be knocked out. It's often written of as the dirtiest fight ever held for a world championship under Queensbury Rules. In fact, for this fight the Queensbury Rules did not apply. One writer called it an "obscene orgy of eye-gouging, rabbit-punching, elbow-thwacking, and ball-busting". It went forty rounds during which Nelson and Wolgast punched, fouled and even bit each other. The referee finally stopped the carnage to save Nelson after he "received a beating such as old-time ring followers maintain was never before seen in the ring". By the time the fight was stopped Nelson couldn't see from either eye and as he protested to the official blood was pouring out of his mouth and onto the canvas. For years afterwards Nelson continued to insist that he was the lightweight champion because the referee hadn't counted him out. Nobody took him seriously and all Freddie's efforts to force a fight with Battling Nelson had been in vain. There was a new champion and the hunt for the title would have to start anew.

Freddie needed another big bout to reaffirm his status as a leading contender. One option was standing right in front of him in the middle of the Strand. Packey McFarland had sailed for England the previous month to look for a big fight of his own and he knew that a third contest with Freddie would fetch the best purse in town. He also knew that he was in a better position to dictate terms in England than in America. The championship regulations in the United States stipulated that a lightweight had to make 133lbs at ringside. McFarland was too weak at this weight but the National Sporting Club had set its lightweight limit a crucial two pounds higher and Packey could still just about make this. McFarland's arrival in England had aroused great interest among the nation's boxing aficionados. He was acknowledged as one of America's finest so there was a curiosity to see just how good he was. The large contingent within the National Sporting Club that disliked Freddie believed that McFarland was the very man to beat him. Freddie's attitude towards the conventions and traditions of the Club was not dissimilar to his reaction as a boy to the conventions and traditions of public school in Long Ashton. To the patrons of the Club boxing was the 'noble art' but to Freddie it was a 'noble business'. "I can't say that I ever worried much about what people thought or said of me," Freddie wrote. "I like to be liked, and have often wished that I could be as much loved as Jim Driscoll, say, but I have never been able to bow down to rules and regulations."

Peerless Jim had been one of the few men in boxing circles to take a genuine liking to Freddie but even that relationship became strained after initial, futile attempts to set up a contest between the countrymen. Driscoll was a great favourite at the National Sporting Club. He was the best living exponent of the classical English style of boxing and he was also considered to be a great sportsman and gentleman. Freddie of course had been tainted by the American brawling style and attitude that winning was certainly more important than taking part. The proposed match between the Welshmen floundered after a bad tempered meeting at the offices of the *Evening Express* in Cardiff. Freddie asked Albert Shirley, Driscoll's manager, under what conditions his man wanted to fight.

"To box under Queensbury rules," was the reply.

"How do you interpret the Queensbury rules?" asked Freddie.

"We want clean breaks," said Shirley.

The insistence on clean breaks was a reaction to Freddie's much criticised 'American' style of fighting. In English rings when the referee called 'break' the clinching fighters were expected to retreat without throwing any further punches. On the other side of the Atlantic the boxers parted in a flurry of blows and this just wasn't sporting according to the sensibilities of the National Sporting Club. After the meeting in Cardiff Freddie told the newspapers that Driscoll insisted on special stipulations such as the banning of 'infighting' before he agreed to the fight. Driscoll countered by promising to fight under any conditions and claimed Freddie only agreed to talk to him about a possible fight as a way to side-step Packey McFarland. The British press took Driscoll's side of the argument and then took McFarland's side in the long and often fierce newspaper battle that broke out between the American and Freddie in trying to make a match. No sooner was there an agreement as to weight than there was an argument over the venue. Freddie wanted to box in Wales; McFarland in London. When this was settled in Packey's favour the most serious row of all broke out about the referee. Freddie had accused McFarland of fouling in a previous fight so it was a matter of honour that the referee for the return match should have a reputation for 'squareness'. The man McFarland and his manager wanted was Eugene Corri whereas the Welsh party wanted four names to be put into a hat and a draw to made by Peggy Bettinson. It took several weeks and a transatlantic

newspaper war in which the British press generally supported
McFarland and the American press largely backed Freddie before,
finally, an agreement was reached. The contest was to take place at
the National Sporting Club on the Monday of Derby week, May
30th 1910. The weight issue was resolved at 9st 7lbs at two o'clock
in the afternoon. The purse was £1,500, winner take all.

Neither man had fought a single contest for several months so
both decided to take a warm up bout as part of the build up.
Rumours circulated that Freddie had not kept himself in as good a
condition as was his usual custom during his long winter break, so
there was great interest in his fight against Jack Daniels of Kentish
Town at the King's Hall in London on April 25th. It was his first
appearance in a ring since he won the Lonsdale Belt the previous
November. The fight was for a £100 stake and the purse. Daniels
managed to provide some resistance for six rounds but then in the
seventh Freddie hit him flush on the nose with a right hand and the
fight was over. He then travelled to Manchester for an exhibition at
the Central Academy where he sparred four rounds with Billy
Marchant of Salford before returning to Wales to prepare for Packey
McFarland. On his journey home word came from Detroit that Ad
Wolgast had turned down an offer of $20,000 from the promoter
James Coffroth to fight Freddie in a forty-five round contest during
the week of the Jim Jeffries – Jack Johnson bout scheduled for Reno,
Nevada later that summer. The champion wanted more money but
Coffroth refused to allow Wolgast to dictate the terms. Wolgast
wanted such consideration that former champions such as Joe Gans
and Battling Nelson had enjoyed when they held the title. The world
championship was out of reach once more so Freddie carried on his
preparations for McFarland. He staged boxing exhibitions in
Swansea, Bridgend and Tredegar before making his permanent training camp at the seaside town of Porthcawl. Freddie and his entourage
moved into a pair of cottages on a headland facing the Bristol
Channel. His morning runs were taken over the sand dunes to the
nearby village of Nottage and back and the weather was so good in
May 1910 that Freddie did all his boxing in a nearby field looking
over the ocean. On many an afternoon over two thousand people
flocked to the cliff sides to watch Freddie at work. Many of them
were Territorials from the Glamorgan Yeomanry who were in camp
in the next field and their ranks supplied Freddie with an abundance
of sparring partners. The windows in Freddie's cottage were never
closed for the duration of his stay. He slept eight hours every night,
and as soon as he awoke he'd take a sour lemonade to cleanse and

refresh the stomach. Half an hour's exercise on the pulley-weights and dumb-bells was followed by floor work for the back and neck muscles and ball punching, in which Freddie practiced all the blows he used in a fight. He then donned his road clothes and took a seven mile run along the beach and inland to get the benefit of both sea and country air. On his arrival back at the bungalow he jumped into a hot bath and then a cold one. After the bathing he'd go through an hour of massage by his trainer Jack Brandy Davies. Freddie taught his old friend the Swedish and German techniques he'd learned at Macfadden's in New York. He described it as "concussion treatment by the vibratory system". Another aspect of Freddie's training that confused boxing writers at the time was the copious drinking of water. Most boxers believed that water had a fattening effect on the lungs and stomach but Freddie told journalists that he believed that the insides were as much entitled to a wash as the outside. It used to be common around training quarters to see boxers break out with fever sores from the lack of water.

On his last night in Porthcawl Freddie put on an exhibition at the town's pavillion to thank the locals for their hospitality. His Lonsdale Belt was paraded and the audience sang 'Hen Wlad Fy'n Nhadau' before being treated to several rounds of sparring. His popularity in Wales was undiminished. Freddie left Porthcawl on the 7.50pm train to Cardiff on the eve of the fight and then took the 10am train to London the following morning. Nearly five hundred Welshmen made the journey to London. This is probably what accounted for Freddie being the 6-4 favourite though very little money was actually risked on any outcome.

The old theatre in Covent Garden was overflowing for the big fight. Two American sportsmen sent a desperate request for tickets by wireless from on board a liner due to dock in Southampton that morning. They were disappointed. No fight had attracted this many people to the National Sporting Club and it easily beat the attendance record. There had been considerable bitterness over the match, and the two men had devoted much time to personal attacks upon each other. It certainly helped to sell tickets. The National Sporting Club billed the fight as being for the "Light-weight Championship of the World," but the two fighters knew exactly who held the real title – Ad Wolgast. The extravagant billing was part of the squabble over the difference in weight limits on either side of the Atlantic. Just how much the American benefited from the British interpretation of a lightweight was clear to see at the weigh-in that afternoon. Packey stripped off, stepped on the scales first and just made the specified weight of 9st and 7lbs. "Is that good enough?" Packey asked, "I'm not a middleweight yet?" A few seconds later Freddie stepped up in his old dressing gown. He threw off the gown and took to the scales still wearing a shirt. Packey demanded that Freddie should remove it, and on doing so a 2lb weight fell to the floor. He was a few pounds under the limit after discarding all his excess baggage. By the time the two men entered into the ring nearly seven hours later they were in different weight divisions. When the fight started they also looked to be a class apart. During the opening rounds McFarland was so good that there could not have been a single supporter who did not think that Freddie would be beaten. Weighing in so early had allowed McFarland to enter the ring considerably heavier than his opponent and against a man obviously more muscular and harder hitting than himself Freddie decided to pay more attention to defence than attack in the early stages.

Packey concentrated his efforts on uppercuts into Freddie's ribs and right hooks onto his 'onion ear'. McFarland also used the bottom of his glove to mark up Freddie's face. This was the pattern of the first eight rounds. All were won by McFarland but by a generally decreasing margin as Freddie gradually worked out a way of taking all the punches thrown at him on the gloves or the elbows. By the halfway point the odds had changed to 2-1 on in McFarland's favour. But then in the ninth round the fight changed. Freddie had got McFarland "down to reasonable strength" and then he started to throw punches back. One newspaper gave Freddie every subsequent round from the ninth onwards but the general consensus was that Freddie had failed to claw back his early deficit. The master of ceremonies Peggy Bettinson leaned over to the referee's chair to catch the decision, and his face gave way to an expression of surprise as he caught the words, "a draw", and the official had to repeat them before the MC was certain that that was the decision, final and irrevocable.

At the end of the twentieth round, before the decision was given, McFarland sank down in his corner and said, "Welsh, you are the toughest man in the world". Initially at least, Packey seemed to be pleased with the draw. "After the decision was given he jumped up like a little baby with a new toy, and came across the ring and shook hands with me," Freddie recalled. "To use an Americanism, he was tickled to death. It was not until he got back to his dressing room and was told that the papers were going to criticize the verdict that he knew anything about it." After the fight McFarland told one reporter that he thought he had done enough to win "but the referee thought otherwise, and I can say right here that I have the same opinion of

Mr Scott [the referee] today that I had before the contest. I am
making no complaint. No doubt Freddie and I will meet again, and
if we do, why, we are sure to have another good go. Welsh is a great
fighter. There is not a man his own weight in the States today, or
perhaps in the world, that can hold him." A few senior American
writers, especially those on the West Coast, considered the fight to be
a moral victory for the Welshman. H.M. Walker of the *Los Angeles
Examiner* wrote:

> The recent drawn engagement between Freddie Welsh and Packey
> McFarland can in reality be looked upon as a victory for the game little
> English champion, not withstanding the prejudice-laden Press reports
> sent across the waters by British boxing critics who have been contin-
> ually knocking the Pontypridd boy ever since the match was made. All
> the flowery stories sent out by McFarland's friends combined cannot
> alter the one important fact that Freddie Welsh fought a welterweight.
> He was literally forced into a match with an opponent who out-
> weighed him by 6lb or 7lb, perhaps more. Every pound of weight
> advantage enjoyed by McFarland represented so much his inferiority
> to the English champion.

But the British newspapers were steadfast in the belief that
McFarland had been robbed of a legitimate victory. Even Lord
Lonsdale's approval of Tom Scott's decision did little to quell the
anger felt by Club members. It was the first time the gentlemen of the
National Sporting Club had ever shouted threats at the referee.
According to rumour, Scott had been 'bought' by a bookmaker who'd
taken a large bet on McFarland to win. Indeed Tom Scott was the
only loser that evening. A few years later Peggy Bettinson attributed
Scott's verdict as the action of a man who was on the verge of insan-
ity. "Poor Tom Scott should not have been allowed to handle the
contest," wrote Bettinson. "We did not know what we knew very soon
afterwards, that his mentality had begun to fail. He was a sick man,
else Packey McFarland would have been given the victory which he
undeniably won". Tom Scott had been a good amateur boxer and had
been involved in the sport throughout his adult life. He only refereed
one more contest, a novice competition a few weeks later, and was
shortly afterwards committed to a mental institution where he died.
"We are sure that poor Tom Scott to his dying day deeply grieved
that he was ever asked to fill the position. Indeed, he never looked up
afterwards; it was all very, very sad," wrote Bettinson.

No one present that night, including Freddie, thought the
Welshman had won the fight. But when the furore died down and the

moving pictures of the fight were studied there was a realization the referee may have called it right after all. It was sadly too late for "poor Tom Scott", whose reputation had been permanently tarnished. Photographs taken of the boxers after the fight told part of the story. Both of Packey's eyes had been damaged, his nose and mouth were bleeding, and his kidneys were swollen. Freddie wore barely a semblance of a mark on his face or body. The Welshman compared the contest to a bullfight with himself as the matador and McFarland as a rushing bull. The spectators had been impressed with the rushing but they failed to see that McFarland was charging into punishment. Privately though, Freddie acknowledged that his performance in this fight had been poor. Winning the Lonsdale Belt had satiated some of the hunger that drove him on through fight after fight in pursuit of whoever held the world title. But despite some adverse publicity he had emerged from the contest with his reputation just about intact. "All that the newspaper critics have said will be forgotten in a few weeks and the fight will go down in history as a draw," said Freddie. "When Greek meets Greek there is no discredit attached to the loser, and if I fight him again at some time in the future it will be no discredit or dishonour whichever anyone of us lose."

Freddie met up with Fanny in Chesham and sailed to France for a vacation just a few days after the fight. They intended to return to America in time to watch his friend Jim Jeffries' attempt to win the world heavyweight championship back from Jack Johnson. But they'd barely crossed the Channel before the offers of a huge purse for yet another fight with McFarland reached him. George Thomas, secretary of the Cardiff Skating Rink Company Ltd informed the newspapers that a syndicate of 'Docksmen' whom he represented would offer a sum of £1,750 to stage the fight at the American Roller Rink in Westgate Street, Cardiff. Within a few days the bidding reached £2,500 with offers from Dublin and an improved proposition from Cardiff and there was every probability that an offer of over £3,000 could be found. It would have been one of the biggest purses, if not the biggest, for a fight staged outside America to that point. But the choice of referee became a point of argument once more. This time the two boxers came up with a solution. Both men wrote to Lord Lonsdale to ask him to nominate the referee, a request to which his Lordship agreed. Everything had been settled, but with no remaining obstacles in the way of a fourth contest McFarland returned to the United States. He'd been promised a fight against the world champion Ad Wolgast and Freddie would have to wait. The contest wasn't even for the championship, McFarland was too heavy, and it was to be a ten-round exhibition bout. On his departure he thanked the many friends he made during his brief stay and for the "square deal" he was given. Suddenly it was Packey walking out on a fight and the British boxing writers were back with Freddie again. "Surely it is not true?" asked one of the London newspapers. "Has McFarland forgotten his request to Lord Lonsdale to appoint a referee? Has he forgotten that he wrote that request to his Lordship before Welsh wrote his? Has he forgotten that Lord Lonsdale has written to him – McFarland – telling the American that he has already fixed up the question of the official?"

The real reason for Packey's return may have had more to do with weight than the prospect of an exhibition fight with the world champion. Getting down to 9st 7lbs several hours before the fight had drained McFarland before the last contest and he struggled in the last eight or nine rounds. Boiling himself down again would be too difficult. Just how difficult was shown after his return to the United States when he had to forfeit the fight to Wolgast for failing to make weight. "I have been on the road for three weeks, and the very best I can do today is 148lbs," said McFarland. "I am not going to kill myself for a few dollars; in fact, I expect to quit the ring now for good."

So in the summer of 1910 Freddie found himself unable to get a fight of any note. Wolgast had priced himself out of a match, McFarland couldn't make weight and the National Sporting Club was unable to find a credible contender to challenge Freddie for the Lonsdale Belt. Attempts to lure the world featherweight champion, Abe Attell, over to England also floundered. But there was another fighter in Britain that summer in almost the same predicament. Jim Driscoll had won the Lonsdale belt for the featherweight championship and had run out of realistic challengers. He'd also been frustrated in a quest for a world title fight. Previous attempts to match the Welshmen had failed over seemingly insurmountable differences. But now they needed each other. They met when Freddie had just returned from the United States for the first time and was a virtual unknown in Wales while Driscoll was the star of British boxing. They became good friends and Freddie helped Jim prepare for a fight with Joe Bowker in June 1907. They remained on good terms until the value of a fight between them became too great to resist. "Before we were matched Jim and I were good friends," said Freddie, "but the minute the two sides met our friendship went to smithereens." According to reports in the newspapers in the summer of 1910, the relationship ended following an incident at Frank Guess' booth at St Mary's fair in Bridgend back in August 1907. In the tradition of the boxing booths, Freddie took up the barker's offer of £1 if he could stay six rounds with Peerless Jim. Not only did Freddie make it through the allotted period he turned the exhibition into a bit of a brawl with some hard infighting and hurtful kidney punching. Since that time the two had traded public declarations of mutual respect for each other's ability laced with the occasional caustic remark. It all made for the biggest fight staged in Britain to that point and it remains one of the biggest sporting events ever staged in Wales.

Even though there was a mutual need for the contest it took many months to reach an agreement. Freddie tried to keep himself busy picking up whatever work he could get. He took a fight at the Liverpool Arena in July against the best man the promoters could find, Joe Heathcote from Wigan. Heathcote was a middleweight and nearly two stones heavier than Freddie but after six of the scheduled twenty rounds the Englishman told the referee he'd had enough. And still the negotiations for the Driscoll fight rumbled on. Weight was the biggest issue. Freddie was the 9st 9lbs champion of Britain, Jim the 9st champion. Driscoll wanted a compromise of 9st 4lbs. Freddie said that a Welsh winter was too cold for him to work his way down to that weight. So Freddie took yet another warm up fight, against Dick Bailey of Bethnall Green, London at the Drill Hall in Burslem. Bailey was a lot heavier than Freddie but he was no more than a useful fighter. In the ninth round the Welshman floored Bailey twice and the referee stopped the fight. It allowed Freddie even more time to argue with Driscoll. By now they'd agreed a compromise of 9st 6lbs on the weight but then came a dispute over gloves. Jim was the lighter man so he wanted bigger, more padded gloves to cushion the heavier blows so he held out for 6oz mitts; while Freddie wanted 4oz. So they compromised on 5oz. The usual arguments about rules and referees kept the matchmakers busy throughout the autumn; but then suddenly it was all arranged. A meeting between the two men and their backers in Cardiff on December 1st 1910 resolved each and every point of contention and they signed the articles the following day at the offices of the *Western Mail*. The catalyst for the deal was a record purse of £2,500 put up by the Welsh Sports Club. Driscoll was to get £1,500 win, lose or draw; Freddie the remaining £1,000. The fight was to be staged at the Westgate Street American Roller Rink adjoining Cardiff Arms football ground. When the news was announced the *Sporting Chronicle* mused:

> Boxers are curious folk. Like racehorses and women, they are consistent only in their inconsistencies. Here we have Driscoll and Welsh

squabbling for the best part of a year about weight, hitting in holds, and all the rest of it, and then, when we have given the whole matter up as a bad job, they come together practically without flourish of trumpets or beat of drum, and arrange to meet in less than three weeks' time from the completion of the signing ceremony for the greatest purse ever given in this country.

The fight developed into much more than a contest between two men and it was described as "a boxing Test match". This was a contest to finally decide which was the superior style of boxing; the American or the British. Now the two greatest exponents of each method could settle the argument in the ring. The consensus of opinion in Britain was that whatever advantage in weight Freddie held over Jim it would be negated by Driscoll's classic English technique. All the old boxers, learned in the wiles of the game, rhapsodised over the 'straight left' and how many a great fighter had fallen after running up against a fist applied as 'old Jem Mace' taught subsequent generations to use. To these men the new-fangled methods of getting close in, the American way, was inherently inferior. The American newspapers had long since identified Freddie's problems in Britain with his lack of respect for the old traditions and techniques. The *Los Angeles Examiner* claimed that "it is, in fact, the Americanisms which he has picked up here that detract from his popularity with the sporting world of London". When one of his London critics kindly called his attention to this lapse of propriety on his part Freddie replied that he didn't fight to look pretty; he fought to win. Freddie believed the Americans in their six and ten-round bouts had developed a style that was better than either the slugger's or the boxer's, for it combined the two. "I have not changed my ideas as to the benefits of boxing as taught in my own country, but when in Rome it is advisable to do as the Romans do," Freddie wrote. "I have learned to blend the English or orthodox style and the unorthodox style of the American ring, and as a consequence I'm quite at home with almost any kind of boxer I may be sent against." But there was still a significant sector of Welsh society which didn't view the contest as a match between two great boxers or two styles of fighting. For these dissenting voices it was a matter of right against wrong or even good against evil. The churches and chapels of Wales had picketed Freddie's previous fights in the Principality and the Evangelical Free Churches Council for Cardiff and District wrote an announcement in the *Western Mail*:

It is our duty to express the strong views we hold on such matters, and to call upon all Christian ministers to use their influence by protesting against such occurrences, and to urge all teachers of day and Sunday schools to do all they can with their young people to create disgust for such degrading exhibitions. The moral well-being of the community is so seriously threatened that this must be our excuse for writing.

The community's well-being was facing another, more immediate threat in the winter of 1910. This was a time of great concentration of ownership in the South Wales coal industry, the most notorious example being the expansion of the Cambrian Combine. The company absorbed several collieries until it employed a total workforce of 12,000 men in the mid-Rhondda alone and it became the focus of a bitter dispute, centred on the coal seams where working conditions made it impossible for a collier on a piece-rate to earn a living wage. In an attempt to drive down costs the Cambrian Combine cut back on the customary allowances made to these workers. When a new seam subject to these abnormal conditions was opened at one of the Cambrian pits, the miners demanded a suffi-cient rate to guarantee them an income they could live on; the company responded by locking them out. The dispute escalated as the whole of the Cambrian Combine struck in support. Further action was called in other parts of the coalfield and by November 1910 some 30,000 miners were on strike in South Wales. It soon turned violent as striking miners tried to stop others from going to work. There were riots in the town of Tonypandy with open fighting between colliers and the police. Winston Churchill, the Liberal home secretary of the day, sent massive detachments of police and troops and the Rhondda became an 'occupied territory'. The workers stayed on strike for almost a year until they were forced to return on the owners' terms and conditions. It was to this bitter and divisive atmos-phere that Freddie Welsh and Jim Driscoll returned to their hometowns to prepare for a contest that served to cause further bitterness and division. Freddie went back to the Clarence Theatre that was converted into a gymnasium tailored for his needs. The auditorium was packed for every session and he decided to charge a small fee for admission and donate the entire proceeds to the Pontypridd Cottage Hospital. It was a particularly tough period of preparation for Freddie. He had developed a system of controlling weight that was different to other boxers. The usual method was to work gradually down to a fighting weight but Freddie's theory of conditioning was to go under the required limit first then gradually build back up. But he had to get down to a lower weight than usual for this fight and Pontypridd in December was not the ideal environment. He did all his work under several large woollen sweaters after the cold, damp weather made it difficult for him to take the pounds off. Driscoll was also having problems at his camp in Cardiff. Some of Jim's friends were privately concerned for his health because he'd contracted malaria during his recent trip to the United States. Several scribes asked him about his illness but Driscoll dismissed the stories. The fighter insisted his only problem was a "slight festering" on the left ear that had stopped him sparring on the Friday before the contest.

The promoters were also having a difficult time. It cost £1,000 for the necessary alterations to convert the skating rink into a boxing arena to seat 8,000 spectators. This was in addition to the £2,500 purse and the venture was becoming a serious risk for the backers, especially as the coal strike was still biting hard and was likely to deny thousands of potential spectators the means to attend. Originally the lowest fare for admission was to be one guinea, but in response to a general appeal the promoters allowed 2,500 tickets to be sold for ten shillings each. They had no difficulties in selling the expensive seats for the contest however. Lord Lonsdale alone booked thirty seats in the bandstand at the price of two hundred guineas.

The weighing ceremony was held, in accordance with the articles, at the skating rink at two o'clock on the afternoon of the contest. The scales were fixed at 9st 6lbs and Freddie was the first to step on. The balance didn't move. He'd made the weight. Jim followed dressed in a sweater, trousers and boots. Again the scales didn't move. Some people at the weigh-in noticed that Driscoll had a small plaster on the left side of his head between the temple and ear to cover the remnant of the festering. Driscoll wasn't a fighter who looked naturally fit and the difference in physique between the two men was quite striking. By the time the gates opened Freddie was favourite in the betting, mainly because of his weight advantage, and was generally quoted as 2 to 1 on to win. But this was a highly partisan market. Both boxers had a large band of admirers and the audience was sharply divided into two distinct camps over the question of who was the better man. It all made for an acrimonious night.

The mood of the crowd was not helped by events leading up to the main fight. Two ten-round bouts and one six-round contest had been scheduled as preliminaries to the main event. There was some entertaining and lively boxing in the first two fights but unfortunately the third bout ended prematurely in favour of a Corporal Darley on a foul by his opponent in the first round. This meant the audience had to endure a wearisome wait of three-quarters of an hour until, just

before nine o'clock the men in charge of the cinematographic apparatus went to work. Suddenly the arc lights over the ring were turned
on and the brass band started playing. But then nothing. Freddie was
late and the crowd became even more irritated. It was just after nine
thirty when the man from Pontypridd eventually entered the ring
followed by his array of attendants and seconds. Driscoll then stepped
through the ropes and got a much louder cheer. Several people
remembered seeing the plaster over Jim's left ear that according to
one scribe "looked rather bad". With both fighters in the ring,
Driscoll's seconds objected to the bandages on Freddie's hands; then
Freddie objected to the bandages on Jim's hands. After a long consul-
tation, Peggy Bettinson in 'Solomon-like' judgement, decreed that
both men should remove their bandages and substitute them with
fresh ones of lighter material. It was a further twenty minutes before
bandages and gloves were readied for the fight. By now proceedings
were running nearly an hour behind schedule.

When the opening bell finally rang the noise from the arena
boomed across Westgate Street. Two of the world's great boxers, two
Welshmen, were finally in the ring with each other. The fight was too
close to call according to the morning's newspapers but they all
agreed that it was sure to be an extraordinary exhibition of the noble
art. But there was nothing noble about this fight. One American
newspaper described the contest as a "bunch of abattoir athletics".

Jim Driscoll, the consummate exponent of the purely English
style of boxing, standing upright with straight rapid blows was
surprised to find that Freddie intended to fight that way too. He
genuinely believed he was better than Driscoll at all aspects of the
game and so the first scoring punch was an immaculate straight left
from Freddie. At the end of the fight Freddie told the press that he'd
decided to fight that way because he wanted to show the public that
he could out-box the Peerless boxer. It didn't work in the opening
round and despite taking the first blow most of the newspapermen at
ringside scored it to Driscoll. Freddie responded by winning rounds
two, three and four quite decisively. The betting in the arena changed
from 2 to 1 on to 5 to 1 on in Freddie's favour. Up to this juncture it
was a good sporting contest and at one point when Driscoll slipped,
his smiling opponent helped him to his feet. But then the whole tone
of the fight changed suddenly. Freddie had managed to strike his first
serious blows on Jim's left ear and they were to be the first of many.
By the end of the fourth round the plaster on Driscoll's head was
crimson red. It became apparent that Freddie was ruthlessly target-
ing the festered area above Jim's ear. Driscoll's kidneys were the

Freddie helps Jim to his feet after a slip.

second most popular port of call for Freddie's gloves. Freddie had
the peculiar faculty of protecting himself with one hand and inflicting body punishment with the other and at the same time to keep
smiling through it all. To a British audience kidney punches were
considered to be an 'Americanism' and if they just about fell within
the letter of the law they certainly were not within the spirit of the
game. With each assault on Driscoll's kidneys the jeering got louder
and Peerless Jim's back got redder. The booing increased in the fifth
and sixth rounds as Freddie realized that these blows were having the
desired effect of weakening his opponent.

As the bell sounded for the beginning of the seventh, Freddie
stepped within range and planted a vicious hook to the red target on
Driscoll's back. The fighters clinched and Freddie continued to drive

The 'head butt' cartoon from *Boxing*, 31 December 1910

his gloves into Jim's kidneys. The Cardiff man had his head tight resting on Freddie's chest and as the blows reigned in on his back he snapped his head upwards into Freddie's chin. Driscoll was cautioned and from this point the contest degenerated into a brawl. The referee, Peggy Bettinson, was one of the most influential figures in the history of boxing in England, and had his own ideas on everything. If there was one thing he did not like it was having the referee in the ring. He officiated from his ringside seat and as a result he missed almost everything that went on in the clinches from both men. Protests from Driscoll to Bettinson that he was being fouled came to nothing so Jim decided to take his own disciplinary action. For the remainder of the fight the pair elbowed, gouged, mauled, and butted each other. An astonished crowd looked on as the gentleman of the British ring became incandescent with rage. Freddie just smiled at him and the angrier Driscoll became the more Freddie smiled.

In the ninth round Driscoll looked as if he could stage a recovery and he forced Freddie around the ring. Jim seemed stronger and by some force of will and magnificent boxing skill he was back in the fight. But not for long. At the beginning of the tenth round the two men clinched and Freddie continued his assault on Jim's kidneys. Driscoll had the top of his head under Freddie's chin and he rushed his opponent back to the ropes with a series of at least half-a-dozen head butts. Bettinson jumped into the ring at once and ordered Driscoll to his corner and pointing to Freddie declared him the winner. Peerless Jim burst into tears and made a desperate appeal to the referee to let him fight on. Freddie walked over to shake his opponent's hand but Jim refused and motioned to his opponent that the fight should continue. By this time the rival seconds were in the ring and a fight ensued between Boyo Driscoll and Badger O'Brian that recommenced the next day in the street outside Cardiff railway station. The scuffle between the seconds prompted a general invasion into the ring and the police had to intervene. Driscoll was still in tears as his gloves were taken off and he was escorted to his dressing room by a group of sympathisers. Freddie sat downcast in his corner throughout the melée. Boxing writer Fred Dartnell ('Long Melford') described the scene:

> Immediately the decision was given, the hall where the fight took place was in an uproar. The inflammable Celtic temperament easily takes fire. Before you could say knife, as it were, there were scores of fights going on in various parts. To crown the tempestuous proceedings, the chief seconds of the two rival boxers had a fierce set to with the knuckles in the ring itself. As I had to telephone through to London, for the purpose of giving some impressions of the evening, I was glad to get as quickly as I could out of the pandemonium. It was, however, no easy matter to steer clear of the chairs and forms that were upset all over the place, and the heated partisans who were supporting their arguments with deeds in the most disagreeable fashion.

Another ringside reporter, Trevor C. Wignall, was hit to the floor by a uniformed policeman. "He was anxious to get at another constable – with whom he afterwards fought – and I happened to be in his way," wrote Wignall. "But the punch was fortunate in one respect; it sent me to my knees, where I remained until the chairs and bottles and other missiles ceased flying." By the time the police had parted the warring sides, the riot had added very considerably to boxing's bad name in Wales. One London publication blamed "the inflammable Celtic temperament" adding as a rule "your Welsh spectator is not a bad fellow [but] he has a natural bent to partisanship". Soon after the fight, four petitions, one of which bore as its first signature that of the Bishop of Llandaff, were presented to the Lord Mayor protesting against the staging of any further prizefights in the city.

The enduring image of Driscoll is of a fighter standing by the ropes, badly cut with tears streaming down his face. The day after the fight Jim told reporters that his actions had all been in retaliation for the fouls Freddie committed. "He was butting me all the time. Look at the blow on my eye! Is that a punch with a glove? Am I not entitled to do it if he is?" Driscoll asked. "I asked the referee to stop him a dozen times, and my seconds were appealing to him all the time. The referee allowed Freddie to butt me till I couldn't stand it any longer. I thought I'd let him see that I was a better goat than he was. But I got disqualified. I certainly did butt him." The referee, Peggy Bettinson, was not without sympathy. "Welsh, I admit, is a most exasperating man to fight, and I can fully sympathise with Driscoll in losing his head," he said. In England the sportsmen professed to believe that fouling, particularly butting – was peculiarly American. Yet there was unflinching sympathy for Peerless Jim. The *Sporting Chronicle*'s editorial expressed the opinion that there were few men more capable of annoying an opponent than Freddie. "He would smile as he went up to the serious-faced Driscoll, smile as he landed a blow that was good either because of the force of the hit or because he had got one in when it was obvious that Driscoll never thought he was in danger of being hit, smile when Driscoll punched and missed; and Welsh's smile was always one of those face contortions that are meant to express something like – 'Well, you are a duffer!' "

It had been a contest and an event in which nearly everyone involved lost. Driscoll lost the fight. The promoters of the fight lost money with the outlay eventually exceeding the receipts by several hundred pounds. Freddie, the winner of the fight, had also lost in several key respects. His reputation as a cynical, unsportsmanlike fighter had been further enhanced. He'd beaten the most popular boxer in Britain by corrupting a man of previously impeccable behaviour and dragging him into an unseemly brawl. He knew that such an outcome would be damaging. "I didn't want to win like that. It is the most disgusting thing in the world to win a fight like that. I believe he was beaten, and he got wild." But the record books now showed that Freddie Welsh had beaten Peerless Jim Driscoll, a man considered by experts on both sides of the Atlantic as one of the world's greatest boxers. Freddie had beaten everybody of note in Britain and he could return to America and force Ad Wolgast to fight him for the world title. In December 1910 Freddie genuinely believed that there was nobody at or near his weight who could beat him. It was a dangerous mindset:

> It was at this stage of my career that I am afraid I suffered most from a swollen head. I was going downhill and didn't know it. The contest ought to have warned me. Jim boxed very badly indeed, for him, and I forgot or overlooked the handicaps under which he was labouring. I forgot that he had been suffering from an abscess in the ear, and that he had consequently been unable to sleep. All that I knew or thought about was that I could boast of having beaten the great, the peerless Jim Driscoll. But an awakening was at hand.

Eight

I'm a Boxer, not an Undertaker

Freddie had been in possession of the Lonsdale Belt for fifteen months but owing to the lack of competition and the absence of a challenger of sufficient class to please the members of the National Sporting Club he had still to defend the title. The Club committee had tried to find a man that could scale 9st 9lbs and was prepared to risk a stake of a couple of hundred pounds, but failed. The British champion was on the verge of packing the belt in his trunk ready for his return to America when the challenge of Matt Wells and his backers became known. Wells was an ex-amateur champion who hadn't long entered the ranks of the professionals. He'd made a name for himself on a tour to the United States but nobody really gave him much of a chance against Freddie. When the match was announced one London newspaper claimed, "Master Matt's courage was more commendable than his prudence". But Wells' money was down as an earnest of his own and his backer's confidence and the National Sporting Club was only too happy to accommodate the challenge. The match was made for February 27th 1911.

Wells trained for the fight at the Black Bull in Whetstone. But in truth Wells had been preparing for his night in the ring with Freddie Welsh for many years and there had been very few better-planned schemes to capture a prize than that orchestrated by him. When he turned professional he travelled from London to Mountain Ash to watch Freddie make Young Joseph's kidneys sore. He was challenged from the ring "for any part of £50" by Harry Marks on behalf of a local fighter, Fred Dyer, but remained silent. At all Freddie's proceeding fights Wells was there – watching, studying. Sitting next to him during his eighteen month vigil was a trainer from Swansea, Dai Dollings who devised a fight plan to beat Freddie Welsh. Dollings had noticed that Freddie began his fights by sizing up his man so the attack was prepared accordingly. Dollings told Wells to "get at him" in the first half of the fight and then "keep away from him" until the final bell. Not a single leading boxing writer thought he could do it.

After the Driscoll fight Freddie travelled to London for a short rest before taking on music hall engagements where he'd box exhibition bouts against sparring partners and all comers from the crowd. It was good money, but it was exhausting. "I did not hit the primrose trail, as many thought," Freddie later wrote, "but was up against a hard theatrical game which sapped my strength and speed more than any training campaign I ever went through." He decided to take a holiday on England's south coast around the cities of Portsmouth and Southsea. He was soon back at work and the sailors stationed at the Naval bases in the area provided a generous supply of fresh sparring partners. When the match with Matt Wells had been signed Freddie returned to the Clarence Theatre in Pontypridd to prepare for his title defence. Once again he opened the doors every afternoon so that the public could watch him train. He gave charge of the box office to the St Michael's Boys Home committee with the proceeds going to the orphans in their care. At the end of his training stint in Pontypridd Freddie gave money to all sixty boys at the home.

After the publicity generated by his fight with Jim Driscoll the build-up to the Wells bout was low key. Very little money had been placed on the outcome because Freddie was such a short-priced favourite. At the weigh-in Freddie stepped up dressed in a vest, shirt and collar and did not pull down the beam. Wells was stripped naked and was still half a pound over the 9st 9lbs limit. Freddie didn't think his challenger was in the same class as him so he did not object to Wells' extra weight and the fight was on. Wells stepped into the ring first and was given a thunderous cheer. In marked contrast when Freddie stepped through the ropes he received an "Arctic reception" with not a single hand or a solitary voice to cheer him. The sympathies of the house were clearly with the underdog. Every successful punch that Wells landed was "cheered to the echo" and whenever the challenger successfully dodged any of Freddie's returns many in the audience laughed. One journalist at ringside wrote, "Freddie might have been rapidly excused had he displayed signs of temper at this obvious partisanship". But Freddie displayed no real emotion at all, and just as Dai Dollings had predicted the champion started the contest very cautiously and was content to stay out of danger. Wells, as instructed, chased Freddie around the ring. The challenger built up a big lead after the opening rounds and by the time the champion realised the danger he was in it was too late. Freddie won every round from the eleventh to the eighteenth but the last two rounds were too close to call and Wells was given the decision. The verdict was greeted by a wild outburst of cheering throughout the house. It was a very popular result. The *London Morning Post* commented that Wells' victory "should do the sport a lot of good". Freddie accepted his defeat with good grace. He congratulated his opponent and politely told the referee that he was disappointed not to get the decision.

The following day Freddie was in a spirit of subdued reflection at

Haxell's Hotel in London. "I believe Mr Douglas [the referee] thought it was an absolutely fair and just decision," he told one reporter. Freddie also bemoaned no moving pictures were taken of the fight to show how he chased Wells all round the ring that in the latter part of the fight. In the absence of film, Matt Wells' face provided sufficient evidence of Freddie's ultimately futile assault. After the contest the new champion was pouring blood from several cuts all over his face. To reach his dressing room Wells had to go through the kitchen, where the cook threw her apron over her face because she couldn't bear to look at his injuries. "If that's the winner what must the loser look like," she asked. Freddie was unmarked. But his treasured Lonsdale Belt had gone. Its new owner wasn't obliged to make a defence immediately and Matt Wells intended to reap the rewards from his champion status for a while. A rematch could wait. Fortunately for Freddie the American newspapers were generally prepared to accept the fight as an aberration and the promoters were not unduly worried by his defeat. Tom O'Rourke, on behalf of the National Sporting Club of New York, offered the former champion a series of five fights. So Freddie and Fanny set sail for America on board the *Lusitania* on March 11th 1911. On his departure Freddie sent a telegram to the *New York Journal*:

> There is a new lightweight champion of England. Of course you know that already. What is much worse is that I know it.
>
> I'd like to say for Matt Wells that he is a very strong, rugged fighter and much cleverer than he has been supposed to be. I didn't box my best, but that was my lookout. He kept flicking me with some very pretty double-barrelled straight lefts, till he finally waked me up.
>
> I don't mind telling you that when the final gong sounded I turned toward the referee with a cheerful smile on my face, fully expecting to hear him say those delightful words, "Welsh wins". I have heard them so often. Out of seventy-three battles I have fought this is the second time I have heard my opponent pronounced the winner.

They arrived in New York on St Patrick's Day, March 17th 1911. Freddie, in particular, made quite an entrance stepping off the ship dressed in a long coat with a fur collar and silk lining. From his necktie gleamed a large diamond to complement the three stones laid in the ring on his right hand. He and Fanny moved back into apartments in St Paul's Hotel on 60th Street and Columbus Avenue, near to Central Park. Freddie had a fortnight to prepare for his first fight against Pal Moore from Philadelphia. Moore was the ideal opponent; he was still a teenager and many of the leading boxing writers were sure that they were watching a future world champion. He had defeated an ailing Jim Driscoll the previous summer and Freddie was anxious to avoid any more unfavourable comparisons with Peerless Jim in the American press. Every morning he went for a six-mile run through the pathways of Central Park before heading downtown to train at Jack Lee's gymnasium on Bleecker Street. Freddie did all his training under electric lights to accustom himself to the shadows in the New York boxing halls. But his preparations hit a snag one afternoon when he strained a tendon in his left shoulder during a sparring session. It stopped him working for a few weeks and the fight was delayed. While he was recovering from the injury he received a visit from the Mountain Ash Welsh Choir whose presence at the gym Freddie described as being "as inspiring as a breeze from my Welsh mountains".

His recovery from the shoulder injury coincided with a terrible tragedy that unfolded just yards away from his training camp. Late on Saturday afternoon, March 25th 1911, a fire broke out in the Triangle Waist Company, a clothes factory occupying the top three floors of a ten-story building on Washington Place in Greenwich Village. It was only a few blocks away from Jack Lee's place and Freddie walked past the building every day. He never spoke or wrote about the events of that Saturday afternoon but other witnesses told of desperate young women jumping to their deaths from windows eight or nine floors up. By the time the fire was under control 146 of the 500 employees had been killed. Most of the factory workers were recent Italian or European Jewish immigrants: women and girls as young as 15 years old. The *New York Times* on March 28th 1911 published a list of those who'd sent money for the victims' families to the mayor's office. One of the biggest donations listed was for $100 from Fred Welsh.

Freddie's fight against 'Philadelphia' Pal Moore eventually took place on April 12th. Packey McFarland sat at ringside to watch Freddie win nine of the ten rounds against an opponent many scribes thought would be too good for the Welshman. The *New York Herald* reported that "when Pal went to his corner he looked a wee bit like a hamburger steak without the trimmings, which he sadly needed – onions are good for discoloured eyes I believe". The contest transformed Freddie's prospects. Before the fight there was considerable talk about him having "gone back" but now all the leading promoters were sending the Welshman telegrams once more. The one that interested him most was from Milton T. Clark in San Francisco. The city was the only place in the United States that could compete with New

York for the biggest bouts and the fattest purses. Freddie and Fanny prepared for another journey to the Pacific Coast. Freddie met a Welsh baggage handler on the train and between them they turned one end of the baggage car into a temporary training quarters. Freddie worked the pulleys, lifted dumbbells, shadow boxed and did his floor exercises. They were due to arrive in San Francisco on June 7th and Clark and a deputation of newspaper reporters set off to the ferry depot to meet him as scheduled but there was no sign of Freddie. He and Fanny had stopped off in Chicago to visit Bernarr Macfadden and stayed the night there. They arrived on the Santa Fe overland the following day.

When they reached San Francisco the couple spent some time sightseeing with Freddie's friend, the promoter Baron Long. The American press was still unaware that Fanny and Freddie were man and wife and so Mrs Welsh was introduced as Mrs McFadden, allegedly Freddie's married sister. Long had travelled up from Los Angeles to look after Freddie while he was on the West Coast. They took a bay trip to Sausalito to look over Long's new yacht *Sweetheart* that had just arrived in the harbour after a stormy passage from San Pedro. Baron Long was known as a man "who deals big cards" and as someone who never hesitated in the matter of money when he wanted something. He had been the sporting editor of the *Fort Wayne Gazette* but quit journalism to seek his fortune in California. His first foray into boxing cost him $15,000 through paying fighters too much money at failed promotions in Los Angeles and with only $3.50 in his pocket he moved to San Francisco and started an agency selling Chinese medicines. The venture made him a rich man and he returned to Los Angeles to prove that he could make it in the boxing game. He established the Vernon Country Club under the protection of local ordinances that permitted him to stay open all night as opposed to the bars in Los Angeles that had to close by 1am. He made $100,000 out of this endeavour in the first year and he opened a second bar out in Santa Monica. Long built a reputation for being a "thoroughbred sportsman" and Freddie considered him to be his best friend and backer in all of America.

Freddie's opponent for his San Francisco debut was Matty Baldwin of Boston who'd recently held his own in a twelve round contest with world champion Ad Wolgast. Freddie's real incentive for travelling to the Pacific Coast was to force the winner of the forthcoming Independence Day bout between Wolgast and the Englishman Owen Moran to fight him. San Francisco was an important boxing town and he needed the patrons in the city on his side to

get a championship fight. Boxing there a week or so before Wolgast
was scheduled to fight increased the pressure on the champion. But
Wolgast and his manager Tom Jones were not about to let Freddie
dictate the terms for any future challenge. Jones told the newspapers
that he thought a fight between Wolgast and Freddie was unlikely
because the Welshman didn't have the money to put up a stake for
the contest. According to Jones, Freddie had lived a pretty decadent
lifestyle when he was in England and as a result he'd lost his prowess
in the ring, as witnessed by his defeat to Matt Wells, and he'd also lost
his money. Jones claimed Freddie was broke and was obliged to box
anywhere and everybody in order to "accumulate a bankroll to
replenish his depleted exchequer". Wolgast's manager said Freddie
had spent his money lavishly while cutting quite a dash in England
the previous summer and now he was fighting "pork-and-beaners" to
make both ends meet".

When Freddie read the story he "went up in the air" and started
to look for bankbooks to show newspaper reporters at his training
camp that he wasn't broke. "It will take more than a typewriter to
send me into bankruptcy," Freddie shouted. "I'll admit that I spent a
lot of money, but I saved more coin than I let go of." Freddie claimed
to have earned $70,000 during the previous eighteen months. Of this
amount he admitted to tossing away $30,000 in having "what I
thought of as a good time". He told the scribes that if it came to a
showdown he could cash in $100,000 right then and not feel the
strain because he'd been saving and investing his money from his
first important fight on. The insinuation that he was financially
embarrassed had struck a very raw nerve and Freddie kept up the
rant at his accuser for much of the afternoon. "This fellow Jones
didn't know what he was talking about when he made that statement," said Freddie. "If he is a good sportsman I will convince him
that I have some money. I am willing to make a match tomorrow with
his fighter for the lightweight championship and bet him $10,000 on
the result. I would bet every cent that I possess that I can beat
Wolgast and will bet it at evens. Why Jones should ever make a statement like that I don't know. I have made plenty of money boxing and
saved most of it." At this juncture Freddie spied his 'sister' in the
gymnasium and he instructed Fanny to go and fetch his account
books to show the gentleman present that he was financially sound.
She made for the stairs but the reporters assured her that Freddie's
word was sufficient.

Having succeeded in getting the desired reaction Tom Jones drove
to San Francisco. He made directly for a bank and armed with a

certified cheque for $10,000 set off for Freddie's training camp to accept the Welshman's bet to fight Wolgast over twenty rounds. An agreement was put in place within days. All that was needed was for the two men to win their respective bouts that July and Freddie would finally get his title shot out on the West Coast before the year was out. It was big news. One journalist wrote the affair had "created more talk than anything that has happened since the matching of Jim Jeffries and Jack Johnson". Meanwhile Moran and Baldwin, the two forgotten opponents, did not take the news with any degree of enthusiasm. Both boxers felt their opponents were being a trifle discourteous in discussing terms and posting guarantees before the outcome of their fights was known.

It was the first time Freddie had fought in San Francisco and the publicity surrounding his championship challenge ensured there was great interest in him and his activities. Every day packs of reporters turned up at the training camp in Colma, just outside the city. Freddie kept them entertained with boxing exhibitions, lectures on the benefits of vegetarianism and even the occasional history lesson. After one strenuous session in the gymnasium Freddie sat at the end of his massage table to educate the gathering about how the original settlers of old England were driven to the mountainous regions of Wales, where they maintained a sort of guerrilla warfare for many years and were finally taken into camp by a trick played by Edward I.

The fight itself was generally regarded as one of the best staged in San Francisco for many years. Every round was full of action and the big crowd was gripped. The first ten rounds were pretty even but from then on Freddie was far too good for Baldwin. By the end of the night Baldwin's face was badly cut up. Freddie started the 'crimson flow' in the opening round and Baldwin "never had a chance to sidestep the blood swallowing process".

Freddie had lost ground during his trip to Wales and England and the defeat to Matt Wells had harmed his credibility in America. The victories over Pal Moore on the Atlantic Coast and Matty Baldwin on the Pacific Coast had repaired the damage. Freddie convinced the American boxing press that he was worthy to fight Wolgast, who'd watched the Baldwin fight from ringside. The Welshman had kept his part of the bargain in the ring but there was one more issue to resolve before the championship fight could be made. When Freddie originally challenged Wolgast for a stake of $10,000 he said he could produce the bankbooks to prove he had the money. It was a bluff. He didn't have the $10,000 to match Jones' cheque and had to wire his backers in Wales:

Marks, Cardiff – Won easy twenty-round decision from Matty
Baldwin. May fight Wolgast September. Must find two thousand
pounds side stake. Back in form. Will bet thousand pounds own
money. Can you raise thousand pounds from Husks, Seaton, Bruce
and friends? Cable quickly.
FRED

The 'Bruce' referred to was Gerald Bruce, a millionaire resident of
Pontypridd and the nephew of Lord Aberdare.

On July 4th Ad Wolgast successfully defended his title against the
Englishman, Owen Moran. Wolgast made a punch bag of him as
Freddie watched from a seat just behind Moran's corner. The follow-
ing night the champion gave a banquet for friends and family at Tait's
in San Francisco. He invited Freddie and Baron Long to join the
party. The dinner was largely a celebration of Wolgast's victory over
Moran but a little business talk was injected into the proceedings.
The outline of the deal was agreed and the match was scheduled for
September. That night Jones and Wolgast took the train south to Los
Angeles. Freddie was nervous. He still didn't have the stake money
and there'd been no reply to his message from Wales. He sent Harry
Marks a second cable, "If two thousand pounds not posted immedi-
ately Wolgast will back out. Send draft care of *Examiner*".

The following day Freddie got the telegram he'd been waiting for.
Harry Marks wrote that he would back him "for the full £2,000
($10,000) against Wolgast". The telegram also allayed Freddie's
concerns that his backers had lost faith in him. "Before I lost the
decision to Matt Wells I could have got backing to the extent of
$50,000," he remarked, "and it is gratifying to know that my friends
in England still believe me capable of winning the world championship." Freddie immediately followed Wolgast to Los Angeles. He
and Baron Long travelled by steamer. The scribes reported it as a
chase to Los Angeles on the trail of Tom Jones and Ad Wolgast. In
fact it had all been arranged. The four men met on July 11th at two
o'clock at the offices of the promoter 'Uncle' Tom McCarey. Both
boxers were good friends of the promoter and McCarey had
brokered a deal. There had been so much publicity surrounding a
possible fight that it was inevitable that terms would be reached.
After a couple of hours' wrangling over money, the choice of referee
and motion picture rights the fight was on. The articles were signed
the following day. The contest was to be staged at the Vernon Arena
in Los Angeles on Thanksgiving Day, November 30th 1911. The
champion was to get $13,500 and 51 per cent of the motion picture
rights; Freddie was to get the remaining 49 per cent and $5,000. It

was good business for McCarey as the gate was expected to be in excess of $30,000. It also transpired that the whole saga surrounding Freddie's 'impoverishment', the $10,000 side bet, the transatlantic cables and money drafts were all in vain. There was no mention of any $10,000 wager in the articles. Against the wishes of the two principals, McCarey had insisted the bet be called off. The promoter informed them that the anti-gambling statute made it a felony to bet on the result of "any contest of endurance or speed between men or beasts", and that not only would all concerned be arrested and probably convicted, but the bout itself would be endangered. Freddie and Wolgast were fully aware of this of course, but the story made their fight into one of the best-publicized events of the year and they were now to contest a big money fight without either man having to risk a cent. It was also good news for Freddie's backers who could now put their money on Freddie at much better odds. Their man was certain to start as the underdog and they could expect a price of $20,000 for their $10,000 on the betting market.

Finally, after nearly six years as a professional boxer, Freddie was going to fight for the lightweight championship of the world. But with the articles already signed there was a problem. Despite his previous promise not to engage in any more bouts until his fight with Freddie in November, Wolgast announced on July 17th that he would probably take at least one ten-round contest in the meantime, although it would not be against any lightweight of the top rank. What made matters worse for Freddie was that Matt Wells who'd taken his English title back in February had arrived in America in the summer of 1911. Having taken Freddie's Lonsdale Belt, Wells now threatened to derail his world title aspirations. Wells' manager George McDonald announced that he'd signed an agreement with Tom O'Day of the Metropolitan Club of San Francisco for a fight between his charge and Wolgast on Labour Day, the first Monday in September. "I feel sure that Wolgast will not let this opportunity slip by," said McDonald. "Wells is champion of Great Britain and is here to meet champions. He is the holder of the Lonsdale Belt, having won it decisively from Freddie Welsh at the National Sporting Club in London, so that, in making a match with Welsh, Wolgast is agreeing to fight a man whom Wells has already beaten." But McDonald's problem was that his man wasn't capable of attracting the sort of purse in America that would make the fight worth the risk for Wolgast. The champion was promised $13,500 to fight Freddie and he abandoned any plans for an intervening contest.

Freddie headed straight back to his old haunt at Cottage 86, Tent

City, Venice to spend the summer and prepare for the fight. The first priority was to install the library that followed him around wherever he travelled. A typewriter was first placed on a table and then the books arranged in a specific fashion. Among the volumes of current reading were Robert Ingersoll's speeches, three books by George Bernard Shaw, a copy of Emma Goldman's *Anarchism* and a volume on Yogi philosophy. Freddie read for hours every evening. "It was a big match and I didn't want to worry about it," he told one friend. "When I'd finish my day's work I'd read. I used to forget I had a match on hand. Books helped me as much as my gymnastic stunts." Freddie's 'sister' was once again the focal point for the newspaper reporters. She informed the press that she'd left her duties as assistant manager of Bernarr Macfadden's health home at Chesham, Buckinghamshire and had married a Mr Horace G. Church. She wanted to be known as Katie Welsh Church.

During the summer Freddie was compelled to cross the continent once more. On his return to the United States in March he'd agreed to take on a series of bouts at the National Sporting Club in New York. The promoter Tom O'Rourke had arranged three fights at $4,000 each and another three fights for $2,000 each. He'd named all six opponents, one of whom was Ad Wolgast in the $4,000 category. Freddie fought Pal Moore in the first of the proposed contests before travelling to California to fight Matty Baldwin. O'Rourke then wrote to Freddie to return to New York where he'd provide him with the remainder of the promised contests. So Freddie packed his bags and, accompanied by Dan Sullivan, a well-known middleweight and athlete who was a member of the 1906 USA Olympic track team, Freddie took the train east. A match with Tommy Murphy was arranged but when the question of money was raised O'Rourke couldn't even give Freddie $2,000, the lowest price they'd previously agreed upon for any contest. Freddie refused the fight and O'Rourke filed a complaint against him with the boxing commission in New York. After explaining his case to the commission Freddie was exonerated but O'Rourke got even by influencing other promoters in the city to freeze out Freddie. O'Rourke knew that the sport was in difficulty in New York at the time and the other promoters were anxious to keep purses down as far as possible. Freddie failed to get a single contest so he made his way back to his training camp in Los Angeles.

He allowed himself several weeks more preparation time than usual for the fight with Wolgast. It was of course a world title fight but there was another reason for the prolonged training period. His performance against Jim Driscoll and then the defeat by Matt Wells had shaken Freddie's self-belief for the first time in his career. He started to believe that even at the age of twenty-five he was beyond his best already. Freddie realized in his fight with Driscoll that he'd lost speed. He didn't regard this as a sign that he was going backwards, but he figured it was time to start fighting along different lines and he planned to go in for more solid punches. "I also looked at the Driscoll experience as a hint that I must train hard and conscientiously for every important battle I engage in," he wrote. So it was back to the old routine – morning runs, exercises and afternoon sparring – only with added intensity.

Wolgast prepared for the fight at Jack Doyle's gymnasium in Vernon. It may have lacked the science of Freddie's training camp but it certainly didn't want for passion. Wolgast was one of the hard men of the ring, an old-time boxer who prepared for fights by fighting. One writer who moved between both camps compared it as a match between "the lightweight fighter who trains on vegetables, doesn't smoke, drink or chew and reads high-brow books" and "the champion, who lives mostly on beef, smokes black cigars by the dozen, and combines all this with the punching ability proportionate to Jack Johnson and the grit of Battling Nelson". Both camps attracted thousands of spectators daily just to watch the boxers train and there was plenty of drama to keep them entertained. On the Sunday before the main event a journeyman fighter by the name of Charlie Dalton was employed by the Wolgast camp as a sparring partner. He hadn't read the script properly, hammered Wolgast on the jaw and stunned the champion. Tom Jones rang the bell and stopped proceedings immediately. Word reached Freddie's camp so they also decided to employ Dalton's services as a sparring partner. Dalton boxed four rounds with Freddie at Venice in full view of the press. Freddie floored him three times before the session was stopped in front of the biggest audience ever to have attended a training camp in Los Angeles. Wolgast paid the challenger back for his audacity a few days later. Freddie was doing his morning roadwork when a cloud of dust got up and a car screamed past him and his 'pacer' on the bicycle. It came so close they had to jump into the side to avoid being hit. The car was carrying Tom Jones and Ad Wolgast. The champion recognized Freddie and stood up in his open topped car and shouted, "Keep it up, that's the way I got my start." Wolgast was on his way to Wheeler Springs in the Ventura Mountains. Every morning he'd scale the inclines and then rest in the afternoon by taking sulphur baths. Ad wanted to escape the "tobacco smoky air" of a city training camp.

The tickets for the fight went on sale at 10 am on November 22nd 1911. Such was the demand that special care was taken to ensure the scalpers were not able to buy up the seats and charge extortionate rates. Then with only a few days to go it looked likely the whole event would be called off. The man named in the articles to referee the fight, Eddie Smith, died. A replacement had to be found and Wolgast insisted on Jack Welch, who'd officiated in his last defence against Moran. Freddie opposed his selection because Welch was well-known for being slow to break clinches. Wolgast was renowned for being a rough fighter and Freddie knew that long clinches would allow Ad to use his repertoire of tricks. He also knew that Jack Welch and Tom 'Ten per cent' Jones were both San Francisco men and had known each other a long while. Freddie was unlikely to knock out a man like Wolgast so his best chance of winning the fight was to get the official's decision. The choice of referee was therefore critical and the row nearly ended in blows one morning. Tom Jones was furious after Freddie had issued a statement alleging the articles of the fight had been doctored after Eddie Smith's death to allow the champion's camp to choose a replacement referee. Jones met Freddie by chance as he was walking down Windward Avenue in Venice and when he saw the Welshman the "cloud lifted and he sailed in and called Freddie all the names on the list from A to Z". Freddie stood back and smiled, as Jones became increasingly angry.

"Say you, I have a good mind to knock your block off and save Wolgast the trouble," said Jones, "just you come around in the alley and I will show you that the manager of the champion is some scrapper himself."

"Jones, I would not run the risk of breaking or dirtying my hands on your face," replied Freddie laughing. "You can't get anything by this and it looks like kid work to me. I thought you were a grown up, man. I can make $5,000 and win the lightweight title by licking Wolgast, but if I knocked you down I'd only be arrested for hitting a fat man."

According to onlookers it was only Freddie's brisk pace of walking that prevented a riot as 'Ten Per cent' had "worked himself up into a state of excitement bordering upon explosion".

A few days later Jack Welch got involved in the argument by defending his interpretation of the law on holding. Eventually Freddie decided to bring the squabble over the referee to a head himself. He had no choice. Wolgast was the champion and he refused to fight unless Welch was the referee. There was to be no arbitration. Freddie told Wolgast that "rather than lose the chance to whip you for

the world's championship I will accept Welch". The confirmation that
Welch would referee moved the betting even further in Wolgast's
favour. In heated exchanges in the press the impression was created
that there was a lot of bad blood between the two men, though they
were very good friends. They started out at the same time and they
saw each other fight quite often. Freddie was the senior in the
relationship and at one time was a sort of fatherly adviser and instructor to Wolgast. Indeed Wolgast had often taken part in preliminary
fights on a card in which Freddie topped the bill and the man who
was now world champion used to write to Freddie out in Los Angeles
to recommend him to promoters for bouts. Freddie mentioned his
name to Baron Long who fixed up a few fights for Wolgast. He did
well in these fights and became a name. The last time Freddie was in
California the two had met by chance at Long's office. Wolgast asked
Freddie if he'd mind posing for a photograph to "have our mugs
taken together". Wolgast said he was going to send the pictures all
over the country and "they'll think that I must amount to something
or you wouldn't be in a picture with me, savvy?" Freddie posed for
the photograph and Ad proceeded to order several hundred copies
and he mailed them to every newspaper between Los Angeles and
New York. He gave Freddie fifty copies that the Welshman dumped
in the bottom of a trunk. While posing for the photographs they had
spoken of Battling Nelson and how the champion was there to be
beaten. Freddie told Wolgast that he didn't think Nelson would ever
agree to fight him and if Ad got the opportunity to "get him first and
down him I'll come back and lick you for the title".

After Wolgast became champion Freddie was approached by
members of the National Sporting Club in London who asked him
about the new champion. Freddie remembered the photographs and
in less than an hour all fifty had been handed out to curious boxing
supporters who were taking their first look at the new world title
holder. And Wolgast had been an impressive champion. His
manager, Tom Jones, claimed that during his time as champion
Wolgast had earned $240,000. Half the fortune was made from
fighting, the other half from theatrical engagements and investments.
And even though he hadn't given Freddie the first shot, he had at
least given him an opportunity to fight for the title. The scribes
thought the contest was one of the few great battles that would be
decided upon negatives. Freddie could not win unless the fight went
to the twenty round limit, in which event he would probably win by
out-pointing the champion. Wolgast could not win unless he ended
the fight by a knockout. Despite the champion being the odds on

favourite in the betting none of the journalists ventured to call a winner. "What will the loser, Wolgast or Welsh, do for an alibi?" asked one. "The alibi is the thing that the defeated boxer brings to the newspaper office the next day after the fight with his indigo eye and oyster-shell ear effect?" Freddie had no doubt that he was going to be champion at last. He closed up his training camp the night before the fight and told the reporters: "I'm so sure of winning that I have been wondering what the first thing for me to do will be after the referee has awarded me the decision. I guess I'll dive for Newspaper Row and shake hands with you fellows."

But on the eve of the fight Freddie got a message from the Clara Barton Hospital in Los Angeles. Wolgast had returned from his run that morning complaining of slight pains in his abdomen. The pain subsided and the champion finished his training, he ate a hearty supper and went to bed. Wolgast slept in one of three beds in a large room at the training camp; the other two were for his sparring partner, Hobo Dougherty and his manager Tom Jones. At four o'clock in the morning Wolgast, groaning in pain, woke up Dougherty.

"Hobo, I can't sleep comfortable on either side. What's wrong with me?" asked the champion.

Dougherty woke Jones. Wolgast was rushed to the hospital where physicians diagnosed an acute case of appendicitis and that he'd need an operation to save his life. When Ad was told he agreed but refused to have any of "that sleeping stuff". Wolgast told the doctors to take him into the operating room and strap his arms and legs down so that he couldn't fling them about and then to go ahead. "I can stand it all right but I don't like that sleeping stuff," he said.

By daybreak a notice was posted outside the Pacific Athletic Club on Broadway in Los Angeles that the fight was off. Several rumours abounded the following morning. One was that the champion was simply shamming illness having realized he was going to lose the fight. Another was that Wolgast had been drugged. And still another was that he was dead on the operating table. Anyone who'd bought a ticket was told to call and get their money back if they so wished. The advance sale of seats had reached $12,500 and with the reservations it was fully $35,000. Uncle Tom McCarey went straight back to his office at the club to try and rescue the bill. There was no shortage of offers for a replacement. The first to call in was a palooka lightweight by the name of Frankie Conley who assured Uncle Tom that Welsh could never stop him and that he'd be a good draw. McCarey put his arms around the fighter and thanked him for the offer but said it was impossible. The promoter had another plan. He'd been told that up in San Francisco a young local boxer called Willie Ritchie had been keeping Packey McFarland honest in several sparring matches during the previous fortnight. He was a little heavy for a lightweight but he was fit and in condition to give Freddie a decent workout. Ritchie travelled to Los Angeles on an over-night train to take the fight. He was certainly a good opponent but Ritchie weighed at least 140lbs so Freddie was fighting a welterweight. The Welshman didn't have to take the bout but in the end he consented. Little did he know then that this novice fighter would play such a central role in the rest of his career. "I don't know what to do or say," Freddie told reporters. "Tom Jones called me up this morning before daylight and I thought that I was still in bed having a bad dream. I'm very sorry for Wolgast. I'm sure this is as annoying to him as it is to me. I hope he comes through this operation all right. This has put a crimp on all my plans and I am up in the air."

In fact Freddie was devastated. He was renowned as one of the most restless men in the business, and before a fight he always prowled around until finally he was able to sleep. Then, after the battle was over, Freddie found it impossible to close his eyes, whether he had had an easy time of it in the ring or not. The night before the Ritchie fight Freddie didn't make it to bed at all and he spent the time pacing through the neighbourhood with a raging headache. He lost three and a half pounds that night through "the nervousness and sleeplessness". Freddie tipped the scale at only 128lbs but still the fight went ahead.

The newspaper reports were pretty consistent in scoring the fight fourteen rounds to Freddie, three to Ritchie with three even. The referee had no hesitation in awarding the contest to the Welshman. He'd won the fight but he was nowhere near his best. According to the *New York Times*, "Welsh got the decision, but Ritchie had him groggy on two or three occasions. After the mill the main topic of conversation among pugilistic followers centred on the question, 'How long would Welsh have lasted against Wolgast if the latter had been in the ring?'" The fight did nothing to dispel the suspicion that Freddie was past his peak. When he arrived back in the United States the influential sports writers had been prepared to forgive him his defeat to Matt Wells as a one-off. But even though Freddie had won all three fights on his return, against three leading contenders, he didn't look like the boxer who'd left America in the spring of 1909. He needed several good, hard fights to get back the prestige he lost that day. His performance against Ritchie damaged his ability to draw the big purses and reduced his chances of getting another shot at the title.

Freddie argued that he'd won all three contests clearly. "I'm a boxer, not an undertaker," he snapped after a question regarding his inability to knockout Willie Ritchie. But when he had time to recover and reflect on the whole affair Freddie was actually a relieved man. Had the original bout been staged a night earlier he would have been world champion but he may also have killed a man. "Believe me, it was a close call for Wolgast, and a closer one for me," said Freddie. "If I had hurt him I would have been haunted for the rest of my days."

On December 4th Tom Jones announced that the champion had passed the crisis of his illness. Wolgast spoke to reporters from his hospital bed just before his release. His immediate plan was to go to Venice, California, to recuperate for three or four months. After that he intended to go in to the Ventura Mountains for a week or two, and then make a trip to Savannah, Georgia, and then on to Philadelphia. After the trip he would come back to Los Angeles to begin preparing for a fight with Freddie Welsh on Independence Day 1912. It was a detailed schedule but most of the newspapers suggested Wolgast was finished as a fighter. Considerable time and column inches were devoted to the question of who actually was the world lightweight champion? Did a champion cease to be a champion the instant he was unable to defend his title? At this time a championship was not a tangible thing: it was based only on a man's ability to predominate. The moment you ceased to have that ability; you ceased to be champion. Billy Nolan, the manager of Battling Nelson, argued the title should now revert to the former champion. Nobody took this claim very seriously except for the Battler himself. Freddie had a bit more support for his claim. He challenged the champion for his title and through misfortune Wolgast was obliged to default. The title therefore naturally passed to Freddie just as it would in a tennis match. "Certainly a champion can't retire into a hole – from whatever cause – and drag the championship in after him," commented one newspaper. But public sympathy was with Wolgast and it was generally agreed the champion should have at least a year before any decision was made on the title. Journalists estimated the illness cost Wolgast $100,000. Freddie knew he would have to wait on Wolgast's progress before pressing his own claims any further. The elusive championship was as far away as ever. In fact *Boxing* believed that this was actually the end of Freddie's title aspirations:

> Freddie has had the cup dashed from his lips once more, and this time, seemingly, for good. For it certainly doesn't look as though the pride of Pontypridd is going to be afforded many more chances.

Nine

Goodbye to the Enemy

Al Levy's Café was the first major movie business hangout. It stood on Spring Street between 7th and 8th streets in downtown Los Angeles. In the dying moments of 1911 Freddie sat with the fashionable set in one of Levy's three lavish dining rooms listening to the house orchestra play in the New Year. As the twelve o'clock chimes sounded he pulled out his watch and stared at its face to confirm 1911 had passed. He told his friends: "Goodbye to the enemy". It had been a bad year. He lost his British championship to Matt Wells in London, squandered $30,000 playing the 'good fellow' game and lost the chance of a world title fight through no fault of his own. "In every one of the twelve months I felt the grip of the hoodoo," said Freddie. "Here's hoping that it doesn't follow me in 1912." It did.

After the disappointment of the fight that didn't happen with Ad Wolgast and the fight that did happen with Willie Ritchie, Freddie worked solidly for six weeks to try and get mind and body back into shape. After his last appearance in the ring Freddie compared himself to a piano player who does not play for several months at a time and then, after trying, finds his fingers stiff and his execution slow. He felt tired and lethargic. To get his speed back Freddie had helped out two young boxers, Joe Rivers and Frankie Conley, to train for their bout on New Year's Day. He went from camp to camp continually offering himself as a sparring partner to get as many workouts as possible. He sparred at the St Ignatius Club and at Doyle's against any boxer who was preparing for a fight and needed some help. When he felt good and ready Freddie set up his own training quarters at Venice, where Ad Wolgast visited him while recuperating from his operation. Two bouts against journeymen fighters were set up to ease Freddie back into competitive boxing. With his preparations for the first contest complete, Freddie decided to indulge in a 'light' wrestling match with trainer Dick Wheeler. Then he went riding on a motorcycle along the beach in Venice and up into the Santa Monica canyon. When he returned he complained of a 'poker neck'. A massage seemed to ease the discomfort but he was awoken the following morning by a terrific pain on the back of his head. A doctor was summoned from Los Angeles who diagnosed an acute attack of torticollis caused by luscated vertebrae. In simple terms he'd dislocated his neck. He couldn't lift his right arm or move his head forward at all. One of his sparring partners recalled how pitiful it was to hear Freddie plead with the doctor to try and rid him of the pain so that he could fight.

A surgeon at the hospital told a scribe that Freddie's injury was serious and that it would be many months before he'd fight again. But barely a week later he signed to fight Jack Britton in San Francisco as part of the celebrations for George Washington's birthday on February 22nd. Freddie and Fanny sailed on the *Harvard* from Los Angeles to San Francisco and the ship was several hours late due to stormy weather and high seas. The following day Freddie started training at Millett's gymnasium and within a few hours he broke down again. It was a recurrence of the injury that had stricken him in Los Angeles, only this time the attack was worse. Reporters found Freddie lying on a heap of pillows in his hotel room. "Every once in a while a groan would escape Welsh," one of them wrote, "not a loud groan but one of those low soft ones. You know the kind that almost tear a fellow's heart out." Freddie was certainly down on his luck, lying helpless while rumours started that he deliberately called off the match with Britton. This certainly wasn't true; promoter Coffroth had guaranteed him $1,500 and as Freddie admitted at the time he "needed money badly enough now". He was in poor shape: physically, mentally and financially. His right side was completely paralyzed and he was unable to get out of bed for five days. Freddie had cancelled three ring engagements inside as many months and now he was in trouble. One physician advised him to rest for at least a year to allow the displaced muscles to be restored and strengthened. Freddie knew that if he took this advice his career was just about finished. A year of idleness would mean he would be in the 'has-been' class and Freddie had no appetite to figure in that role. Old friends on the West Coast said the Welshman was so discouraged that he didn't care if he ever donned a glove again. He began to talk about retirement plans to bring out his mother to California and open a health farm. But more than anything else he wanted to go home to Wales for a while.

As soon as Freddie was physically able he and Fanny left San Francisco and headed north, stopping in Portland and Seattle before crossing into Canada. Even though he was still badly handicapped by the injury Freddie needed money so he looked for short exhibition bouts. He spent a few days with his old friend and sparring partner Eddie Carsey, who had given up fighting for good and was running a successful hardware and grocery business in Winnipeg. When the management of the Empress Theatre heard he was in town they arranged a four-round exhibition bout with Young O'Brien who claimed to be the champion of Manitoba. Freddie and Fanny then crossed back into the United States and met up with the sportswriter Tommy Andrews in Milwaukee. From there they moved east to Chicago to stay at Bernarr Macfadden's health farm for six weeks to try and find a permanent cure to the injury that threatened Freddie's career. More bad news arrived while he was in Chicago. Wolgast had recovered from his surgery but had decided that his first fight back was to be against Joe Rivers on Independence Day 1912. This was the young boxer Freddie had helped just to keep busy. Freddie and Rivers had been in the ring together while Wolgast was recuperating but these sessions were more akin to demonstrations than sparring. Now the pupil was getting his shot at the title while the master was forced to look on. To make matters worse Freddie had agreed with Wolgast and his manager Tom Jones not to take the $2,500 forfeit they had posted for the fight if they promised him the first shot at the champion after he'd recovered. Freddie didn't ask him to put anything on paper because "it wasn't a time when you asked someone to do anything of the kind".

"Jones agreed by all that was good and holy that Wolgast and myself would meet when Wolgast was himself again," Freddie explained. "With that understanding I didn't take Ad's money. But once they had their forfeit money in their pockets it was a different matter. He's agreed to fight Mexican Joe Rivers on July Fourth. That's the match I was promised. Would you believe that I am sick and tired of chasing after the lightweight championship?"

He and Fanny stayed in Chicago for over two months and by now they needed money very badly. Freddie planned to go to New York where he could get plenty of six-round club fights and also challenge the winner of the forthcoming fight there between McFarland and Wells. They were the only two men to have gained a verdict over him in the ring and a bout against either man would attract a good purse. On his way to New York Freddie stopped off in Buffalo where he'd been offered a fight against the local champion Jimmy Duffy. He was about half-a-stone overweight stepping into the ring with Duffy. It was certainly the heaviest Freddie had ever been for a fight and it slowed him down. Each of the ten rounds was very similar with Freddie allowing Duffy to lead with jabs that he comfortably blocked before punching his opponent in close. It was a routine ten-round win but at least he was back in the ring and making money again.

Freddie and Fanny stayed in Buffalo for a few days after the fight. They went to visit the Niagara Falls, the first time Freddie had been there since his hobo days, and stayed with another old friend, Elbert

Freddie with the 'Sage of East Aurora', Elbert Hubbard.

Hubbard. Hubbard was an author and publisher who'd been inspired by the English socialist William Morris to establish the Roycroft Printing Shop at his home in East Aurora. It was part factory, part social experiment. He employed the best bookbinders along with young people and 'fallen women' to produce the finest handmade books of the time, the best examples of which were purchased by Henry Ford, Theodore Roosevelt, Queen Victoria and Freddie Welsh. The Roycrofters prospered into a completely self-sufficient community, operating their own factory, blacksmith shop, farms, bank and an inn that still stands today. Hubbard was a believer in 'rugged individualism' and his writings held great appeal for Freddie. "He taught the philosophy of being yourself and not depending on others," claimed Freddie. From the time he started boxing professionally Freddie had relied less on managers, trainers and seconds than most other fighters. "No good fighter depends on his second – he doesn't need a second any more than a great baseball player needs a signal or a rule." Freddie and Elbert Hubbard became great friends and often discussed the possibility of jointly establishing a health farm in the vicinity of East Aurora. The day after he'd beaten Jimmy Duffy, Freddie took a picnic with the Roycrofters and under the spreading branches of a big chestnut tree he gave a lengthy lecture on physical education after which he put on a boxing exhibition. By the spring of 1912 Freddie had grown tired of the chase, the training, the travelling; tired of just taking the blows. But the time he spent with the Roycrofters changed everything. He'd been in constant training for eight years and now he decided to employ a different approach. Instead of the gymnastic work, he chopped wood. Instead of the roadwork, he went for long tramps in the forest with Elbert Hubbard – and the 'Sage of East Aurora' practiced on Freddie the lectures he was getting ready to deliver. "I was a pretty fair audience I think," Freddie recalled, "it got my mind out of a rut, and I came back." He left the Roycroft estate with a renewed determination to regain the British title and to renew the chase after Wolgast. Freddie was a contented man for the first time in a long time.

When he eventually reached New York Freddie discovered that it was far more difficult to get fights as a former champion than it had been as the possessor of the Lonsdale Belt. He'd been out of the ring for a while and there was a feeling among promoters and boxing writers in the city that Freddie was finished. He cut a sad and lonely figure. Freddie sent a letter to the *New York Evening Herald* challenging Packey McFarland to a fight and according to the newspaper it was written on "beautiful paper with deckled edges, headed in red ink: Fred Welsh, Pontypridd. Lightweight Champion of England." Freddie added on the bottom of his note:

> P.S. You will have to excuse my using this paper. I never expected to lose the English title, and laid on a large stock of paper. F.W.

McFarland meanwhile was more interested in the current world champion Ad Wolgast than a fighter who was no longer considered the best in his own country. Freddie had to get back on the road to find work so he travelled to Columbus, Ohio, to fight Grover Hayes. There was a long argument before Freddie stepped into the ring. The event was promoted by the Pastime Club but a lack of financial backing made the event a 'gambler's chance' and Freddie was booked in the hope his name would fill the venue. The Club had guaranteed Freddie $1,000 but took only $650 in receipts. Grover Hayes was promised 30 per cent of the gate. Freddie and Grover discussed the matter beforehand and agreed to take a "financial trimming" rather than kill the sport in Columbus for the other clubs. They fought ten two-minute rounds for which Hayes got $200 and Freddie $300. Many in an already empty house left before the main bout started. When it eventually began Freddie looked something like the fighter he'd been eighteen months previously. Hayes was a very good lightweight and the Welshman outclassed him.

Freddie moved on to Winnipeg, Manitoba, following an invitation from John McKee of the National Sporting Club to take a couple of bouts in the city. While he was in Winnipeg he stayed with Bob Lewis of Cardiff, who was now an official of the Canadian Pacific Railway, and Griff Davies of Aberdare who ran a motorcar dealership. The first of his two bouts there was against Grover Hayes again. He beat him very easily once more and just over a week later he was matched with Phil Knight from Kansas. Knight had boxed a draw with Packey McFarland and according to the press cuttings he carried with him, he hit so hard that "a whole hospital corps has been at its wit's end to revive a victim of its terrible consequences". Unfortunately for the man from Kansas he was in no condition to hit anything after the first six rounds but Freddie kept him on his feet to ensure the bout continued. This was probably Freddie's best performance for two years. Before the fight Knight told reporters that he'd be happy to take twelve punches from Freddie just to land one. He didn't even make one in twelve and in the last round gave out a shout to his opponent, "For heaven's sake stand still!"

A rejuvenated Freddie Welsh returned to New York to get back on the champion's trail. Wolgast was scheduled to defend his title against Packey McFarland at Madison Square Garden but the fight was beset by financial problems. Wolgast failed to sell his share of the motion picture rights so he demanded more than the $15,000 guarantee offered him and the Garden Athletic Club refused. The boxing press reported the incident as yet another attempt by the champion to avoid the best lightweights. There was certainly no prospect of Freddie being able to force a match with Wolgast but there was some good news to cheer him in New York. A cable arrived from Harry Marks informing Freddie that a rematch with Matt Wells for the Lonsdale Belt had been agreed in principle and that he should

come home. The fight was scheduled for the first week of October
1912 at the National Sporting Club in London. While he was waiting
for the first available berth on the *Mauritania* Freddie read newspaper reports regarding the demise of the Jeffries Athletic Club in
Los Angeles. The club had made several of Freddie's biggest matches
and he had several good friends there, the closest of which was Baron
Long the promoter. Before he set sail Freddie cabled Long to inform
him that he had $7,000 in cash, only part of which he would need for
the trip. He offered Long half to tide him over. The promoter wired
back his gratitude but that it really wasn't necessary. Still, Freddie
mailed a cheque for $3,500 just in case he needed it. He also found
time to interpret the history of prizefighting in England for the
benefit of an American journalist knowing that his words would
arrive at the National Sporting Club in Covent Garden before he did.

Now a fighter has every opportunity to become a scientist, an artist, a
psychologist, and a moralist. Formerly he was a slave, and had no
means of self-development. In England he was kept like a fighting dog
by some unscrupulous English gentleman, called a governor. If his
governor was crooked he would fake fights and cheat the public. He
had no self-respect, no ambition, and no morality.

I felt the cloud over the fighting profession when I began. But now
I see how conventional I was. I see it is only the holy pedants who don't
understand life who think that any strenuous occupation may not
develop the best there is in the mind, the heart, and the nervous
system. A fighter is a citizen of the world, and if he has any brains he
learns to see the humour of life.

The gentlemen of the National Sporting Club knew well enough
what the message was. Freddie was returning to Great Britain to fight
his way, on his terms and with the intention of tucking Lord
Lonsdale's belt into his trunk and returning to America. Here was a
boxer who'd studied the noble art of self-defence, the time-honoured
British game, the artistic and scientific system of fist play developed
and perfected by Broughton, Gentleman Jackson, Jem Mace and
goodness knows who besides, and had found it wanting. Freddie
believed that the "traditions of the British prize ring, which it was
thought would endure for all ages like the lion and the unicorn and
the other things which go to make up the British coat-of-arms, have
been swept aside". While he was sailing the Atlantic, *Boxing*
commented "you couldn't say that Fred is exactly a popular man
among his fellow professionals from either the three kingdoms or the
Principality. But that is because he has pointed out a road which
none of the others has had the wit to follow."

Freddie took a warm-up fight in Liverpool as part of his training for the contest with Matt Wells. He was matched with Jack Langdon, an Englishman who, like Freddie, had done most of his fighting in the United States. The contest generated great interest because it was the first opportunity for British sportsmen to decide whether reports of Freddie's declining powers were true. Nearly two thousand people had to be turned away from the stadium but those who managed to get in saw Freddie box to his very best form. He was back in peak condition and returned to Pontypridd to complete his preparations for the championship fight. He used much of the time to see old acquaintances and to rekindle a friendship that appeared to have died. Jim Driscoll and Freddie Welsh had been friends for many years before the two were lured into the same ring by a huge purse. When it became obvious that a second fight would benefit neither man they became friends once again. They spent the autumn of 1912 helping each other prepare for defining fights in their respective careers: Freddie's against Wells and Jim's against Owen Moran. It was at this time that Freddie also met the man who within just a few years would become the third member of a triumvirate of Welsh boxing heroes. On the Saturday before the contest with Wells, Freddie made his final public appearance at the Olympia Rink, Merthyr. He boxed a total of eleven rounds with four different sparring partners. As part of the show a young boxer from Tylorstown, Jimmy Wilde, battered an opponent in the second round.

At just after a quarter past ten on Monday December 16th 1912, Freddie now in the role of challenger, entered the ring of the National Sporting Club. He won the toss for choice of corners and duly sent Wells into the corner in which Freddie himself had sat when he lost the title in the same ring eighteen months previously. It was the only thing Freddie won for quite a while. He started the fight very slowly and lost the first four rounds. The turning point came in the sixth when a right hook to the jaw shook the champion and Freddie followed it up with a blow to the back of the neck and another sickening thump into Wells' ribs. From that point onwards the champion was perceptibly slower. Freddie had cancelled out his deficit by the tenth of the twenty rounds. Blood was now flowing freely from the champion's nose as his unmarked challenger landed blow after blow into his face. As the fight went on Freddie got faster and Wells got slower. Up in the gallery Jim Driscoll was telling the boxing fraternity that it was now 10 to 1 on his countryman. It had been just as brutal as their first encounter and the last few rounds descended into a desperate slugging match in which both men tried to knock each other out. By the final bell Freddie's right eye had been closed with swelling but he knew he'd won long before the announcement was made. He was carried triumphantly back to the corner. "The real Fred Welsh won back the title of lightweight champion of Great Britain at the National Sporting Club last night, scoring a very easy victory over Matt Wells," reported the *Daily Chronicle*. "Welsh's was a display of boxing that left one wondering how the art could be brought to such a high degree. Wells is a fine boxer, but in the contest he was hit so frequently that he might have been the veriest novice."

A huge crowd had gathered outside the offices of the *Western Mail* in Cardiff and for over two hours the newspaper staff were kept busy informing those assembled of Freddie's progress and answering telephone inquiries from all parts of Wales. Meanwhile outside the National Sporting Club several hundred London Welshmen lined the Covent Garden pavements and after several renditions of 'Sosban Fach' and 'Hen Wlad Fy'n Nhadau' they marched down the Strand, still singing, into the night.

Harry Marks was back at the National Sporting Club the following day for a meeting to discuss the possibility of a bout with Hughie Mehegan, the lightweight champion of Australia. Mehegan had beaten Matt Wells in the summer and had stayed on in England after being promised another fight at the Club by Peggy Bettinson. Had Wells kept his title this would have been an easy promise to keep but Freddie was the champion once more and he made it clear that any future matches would be made on his terms. He knew that Mehegan was a 'big' lightweight so he instructed Harry Marks to agree to the fight at 9st 7lbs, the American limit, and not 9st 9lbs, the British limit. Bettinson was enraged and said the committee at headquarters would not tolerate a fight according to American regulations. He pointed out to Harry Marks that Mehegan had stayed on in England just to make this match and now Freddie was trying to stop it. A few days later a second meeting was convened at Covent Garden and this time Freddie and Mehegan were present. It was late starting because the Welshman was delayed returning from an engagement in Liverpool but it soon became apparent what Freddie really wanted from this fight. After the two boxers were introduced to each other Bettinson turned to Freddie and told him that the committee had agreed to offer a purse of £1,000. "Mehegan accepts it, and it's up to you now Welsh. He wants to box in December for an international championship." Freddie asked Bettinson what championship it was for, to which Bettinson replied that it would be for the lightweight championship of the world.

"If we box for the lightweight championship title, will the Club put up a belt?" asked Freddie. Bettinson was not prepared to answer his question. "I am given certain latitude by my committee, and I cannot go any further," was his reply.

"Well, I have been made a bigger offer by an opposition, and promised an empire belt, but I would much sooner box at the Club for less money than anywhere else," said Freddie.

Realizing that the negotiations would go nowhere unless a belt was put up, Bettinson agreed. At this point in the proceedings the argument between Freddie and Bettinson became very heated and the Press was instructed not to report it. Freddie had already extracted a promise from Bettinson beyond his remit, but he wasn't finished quite yet.

"I suggest that a belt be put up for this particular contest, and it to become the winner's own property," suggested Freddie.

Ignoring the long-term future of the belt, Bettinson moved on to the issue of stake money. "If this match is made, what side stake do you require?" he asked, adding, "Mehegan has got £1,000 lying at the *Sporting Life*. And all he wants is a square deal, so that if he returns home defeated he will have no excuses to make. We look upon you, as our champion, to defend the old country."

"I would not care to box for a big stake outside the club, but at the same time I should like to do something definite about the belt. I had been offered a £2,000 purse outside the club, and furthermore a belt. I will be willing to sign articles if you give a belt. I don't mean one that will cost £1,000 or £500."

"If the Club gives a belt, it will be a good one," snapped Bettinson. "I will put it before my committee, and I don't think you need worry very much."

The discussion moved on to the motion picture rights and weight. It looked as if everything had been settled and Bettinson tried to get everybody to sign the articles. But Freddie was still concerned about the belt. "Well, we don't want to sign and be put into a false position," said Freddie. An exasperated Peggy Bettinson had to go back and get his committee's approval for the belt, insert the clause into the articles and finally a few days later Freddie signed the document. The stake money of £1,000 a side was the largest that had been put up for a fight in Britain. A rich Australian backer put up Mehegan's money, while Freddie put up a large part of his stake personally. The story that kept the newspapers busy however was the Club's announcement that the fight would be for the championship of the world. The decision to bill the fight as being for the lightweight

title was part of the National Sporting Club's efforts to establish their
rules and weight divisions as the globally recognized standards. Even
the British newspapers questioned the wisdom of such a strategy
now that Ad Wolgast was fighting again and was the undisputed
lightweight champion. But one low blow in an American ring
changed everything.

On Thanksgiving Day, November 25th 1912, exactly twelve
months to the day after his fight with Freddie had been cancelled, Ad
Wolgast was making a title defence. His opponent was Willie Ritchie,
the relative novice Freddie beat as a substitute on the day that Wolgast
was struck down. The champion was a 10 to 6 favourite in the betting
and for most of the contest he was easily the better man. But this was
another night in the ring when time as well as the opponent would
catch up with and eventually beat an ageing champion. Ritchie was
younger, fitter and stronger and he floored Wolgast twice before the
desperate champion threw two low blows and was disqualified.
According to one reporter at ringside, "at the finish, just as he fouled,
Wolgast's eyes were glazed, his legs shook, and he tottered around the
ring". The news that the Americans were now hailing Willie Ritchie
as champion strengthened Freddie's case considerably. The old
champion had refused to fight him and he'd already beaten the new
one; but before any claim to a world championship could be made
Freddie first had to beat Mehegan. He had returned to Pontypridd to
train but his preparations were badly disrupted by a sparring
accident. Freddie and his partner Dai Roberts ducked at the same
time and clashed heads. He was cut along his left eyebrow and was
unable to do any hard boxing in the week leading up to the fight. By
the night of the contest the wound had healed to the point where it
was barely noticeable but Freddie was still concerned that it would be
a serious handicap. "While the outside cuticle of such a cut would
indicate that it is a strong adhesion, the inner flesh is still tender and
susceptible," Freddie explained. "I knew Mehegan would read of the
affair, and I also gave him the credit for the brains to take advantage
of his knowledge. I would do it; so would any boxer who uses his
mental powers. If he landed a good blow on that damaged eyebrow it
would be sure to reopen, and the blood from it might temporarily
blind me." The accident had been reported in the newspapers but no
mention had been made of which eye had been damaged. So Freddie
got Harry Marks to pencil in a "clever imitation" of a wound over his
right eye just before the weigh-in. He partially covered the artwork
with a plaster that was kept on for the fight.

It was by all accounts one of the best fights ever staged at the

National Sporting Club. Freddie boxed brilliantly and several of the
London papers wrote that he had never boxed better in his life.
"Round and round the ring the men fought, swapping blows as
fiercely as the greatest pugilistic glutton could desire," wrote one
ringside reporter, "Mehegan was a Samson in a net, and Welsh was
the net." In the course of the fight Freddie took several sickening
blows from Mehegan and he took longer to recover from the effects
of this bout than after any previous contest. For three or four nights
he found it difficult to sleep because of the pain. Freddie told
Mehegan, "Hughie I can't put the point of a needle anywhere on my
body, from my ankles upwards, where I am not feeling sore. It isn't
only where you punched me; it's where I had to brace myself up as
well." Many years later Freddie spoke of how he very nearly lost the
contest. At the end of the eighteenth round he was cut on his lip, so
his seconds used collodion mixed with ether to stop the bleeding.
The fumes were so strong that he almost went out on his feet. He
fought the last two rounds in a haze and collapsed when he returned
to his dressing room.

With great commercial savvy Freddie announced that his win was
due in part to Stren-tho, Macfadden's new cereal preparation that
had helped him gain even more strength. The gold belt that he had
pressed for in the negotiations was presented to Freddie on
Christmas Eve. It was made by Messers Mappin & Webb. The quality
of the fight, the sublime performance of the winner and the tenuous
nature of Willie Ritchie's claim on the title left the British press in no
doubt that Freddie Welsh was, finally, the lightweight champion of
the world a title second only to the heavyweight crown in terms of
prestige. The following Sunday the *News of the World* reported the
lightweight championship of the world had returned to Britain for
the first time since Dick Burge lost the title to Kid Lavigne in 17
rounds at the National Sporting Club on 'Derby Night' 1896.

America can shout, but the fact remains that we have the lightweight
champion of the world in our man. Packey McFarland would not meet
him and Wolgast has been beaten by a man Welsh made rings round.
How does that strike you? It strikes me in a manner that will not admit
any discussion.

Publicly Freddie was prepared to play the role of champion. He
told the *News of the World* that it had been a long road, a winding,
halting, and oft-times rough road that he had travelled, and it had
taken him five years to pass over it; but he had reached his goal at
last. Freddie proclaimed that now he was content, and when he

looked back over all that he'd endured, the weariness, the disappointments, and the only too frequent discouraging set-backs he wouldn't
have one step of it altered. "The prize I have won is all the more
precious to me for the troubles and obstacles I have encountered in
the winning of it," said Freddie. But privately he knew he hadn't won
it. So did the American boxing scribes. One writer claimed that he
had no protest as long as Freddie stuck to the title of champion of
England, or Canada, or New Zealand, "but once one speaks of the
world – well there is America! And America is the only breeding
place of champions." The dispute over the rightful holder of the
championship was rooted in the cancellation of the Wolgast fight the
previous year. Freddie's victory over Mehegan and Wolgast's defeat
to Ritchie highlighted the injustice. English publications such as
Boxing argued that a default was equivalent to defeat: "It is clear as
the sun at noon-day that Wolgast forfeited his title when he defaulted
to Welsh after having weakened its value quite as much as Nelson did
by picking and choosing opponents." Another English boxing scribe
argued, "the first principle of the boxing game has always been 'Play
or pay' from time immemorial, so where does Ritchie come in?
Especially as Welsh clearly and decisively defeated Ritchie on the
very day when Wolgast first defaulted him."

While the battle for the world championship was being fought in
the press Freddie and Fanny moved into 12 Pitman Street, Cardiff.
He intended it to be a short-term stay before heading straight back to
America with his Lonsdale and 'world' championship belts in his
trunk. "I haven't enjoyed too much luck chasing American champions
and as things are now I can't help thinking that it is Ritchie's turn to
come chasing me," claimed Freddie. But during the Christmas of
1912 his priorities changed. His mother became very sick and within
a few weeks she died. Every night following her death Freddie placed
her photograph inscribed with the words, "to my darling boy, Fred,
from Mamma" over his bed. Any plans to chase Willie Ritchie would
have to wait. Following his mother's death Freddie felt a need to stay
close to home. Yet he was also restless, and he decided to take a tour
around Wales. He'd crossed the United States and Canada several
times yet his experience of his homeland was largely confined to the
industrial valleys of the south. For the next four weeks, Freddie and
his sparring partners, Young Joey Smith and Munroe Grainger drove
around the country putting on exhibitions in over fifty towns and
villages throughout west and north Wales. Instead of sparring for
three short rounds as was usually done in exhibition bouts, Freddie
boxed ten three-minute rounds with his sparring partners and any

New York World, 7 January 1913.

The Chapel response to boxing.

local boxers that could be engaged. When he played in more than one house on the same night he fought twelve and occasionally eighteen rounds in an evening. He did disrupt the tour to take on a few professional bouts. The first was against the French fighter Paul Brevieres at the Aberdare Market Hall. The bout lasted a total of eight and a half minutes after which Brevieres threw down his hands and cried "enough". The crowd was furious at the submission but Brevieres had broken his thumb and was in great pain. The best contest of the evening was between the local Free Church Council and the promoters. 'Chapel pickets' were stationed in various locations in Aberdare to try to induce members of their Churches away from the Market Hall. They lost and over two thousand men turned up to watch the fight. Freddie's ability to attract enormous crowds had been a concern for the religious authorities in South Wales since the summer of 1909 and the three epic events staged at the Mountain Ash pavillion. Pamphlets were printed proclaiming that "neither Freddie Welsh nor any other man can save you from the boxing God will give you if you die out of Christ." Freddie was still a very young man when he first became the focal point of the anti-boxing protests and it troubled him. But in the intervening years he'd spent a great deal of time with Elbert Hubbard whose publication, *Philistine*, once asked:

> If our Christian friends are right, Heaven if full of murderers, rapists, burglars, and handmade liars who repented at the last minute and so slipped one over on Saint Peter and passed into Paradise. Where will you spend eternity? Not with such a bunch, I hope.

A few days after the Brevieres fight Freddie met up with Jim Driscoll at the annual assault-at-arms in Pontypridd in aid of St Michael's Orphan Home. The event was the public introduction of Fanny Weston as Freddie's 'good lady'. From there the entourage moved on to Aberystwyth on the west coast where Freddie put on an exhibition at the town's Colliseum Theatre. They moved north to Llandudno, Caernarfon and Rhyl before taking a short holiday in the mountains of North Wales. On the way back to Cardiff Freddie boxed in Brecon, Pembroke Dock and Ammanford. The exhibitions made good money and kept him sharp. With plenty of running through the mountains of north and mid-Wales Freddie was in good condition for an upcoming fight with Young Nipper at the Canterbury Music Hall in London. This was the first time Freddie had boxed in London outside of the National Sporting Club for three years and he was anxious to put on a show for people who did not generally get the opportunity of witnessing contests at what he called "the prim little club at Covent Garden". He did not disappoint. The following morning *The Times* reported "as an exhibition of the Champion's wonderful artistry it was well worth seeing". He moved on to Sheffield for a match against the French champion Raymond Vittet. Freddie knocked him to the canvas three times in the tenth round of the scheduled twenty and the referee had seen enough. "The referee's heart was touched by the hopelessness of the situation," wrote one reporter. Four nights later Freddie was fighting in Liverpool against Eddie Beattie. It was his last contest in Britain before sailing to America and it was a night when Freddie came very close to seeing all his hard work come to nothing. Beattie was one of the best welterweights in Britain and a much bigger man. For the first nine rounds this advantage counted for little, then he threw a punch which very nearly ended the Welshman's world title aspirations.

Without looking to be in any danger Freddie was hit with a vicious blow to the body that sent him reeling to the canvas. It looked to be a low blow and the referee J.H. Douglas, undecided about the legality of the punch, delayed the start of the count. The few seconds of reprieve gave Freddie time to recover and he made it to his feet on a count of nine. He went on to win the fight comfortably. With that victory his latest British campaign was over and it had been a great success. This time he was sailing back to the United States with the Lonsdale Belt in his possession and his reputation restored. As he prepared to leave Wales once more Freddie genuinely believed that this time the undisputed world championship was within his reach.

He was given a farewell party by his aunt Mrs Parry-Thomas at Pontypridd's Bunch of Grapes Hotel. Freddie travelled by car from Cardiff in the company of 'Miss' Fanny Weston, who was now introduced as his fiancée. On his arrival the crowds that lined the streets sang 'Auld Lang Syne' and 'Hen Wlad Fy'n Nhadau'. Councillor Arthur Seaton took charge of proceedings and made a speech in which he told Freddie with a "good deal of his ready wit" that the eyes of the world were upon him. Freddie spoke mainly of his defeat to Matt Wells on his previous visit and how the reverse had been beneficial as it "kept a man on the ground and prevented swelled head". Fanny then gave a speech in which she thanked her Welsh friends. "I love the Welsh people, and I love sport," said Fanny. "I think sport is the play-spirit of grown-up people, and it is a good thing to keep up. People admire a champion because he is the ideal of what they would like to be. But to be a champion needs concentration. You have to make up your mind for one goal, and make for it. I am very pleased to be associated with Mr Welsh, and if I have helped him to success I am very happy."

Freddie and Fanny boarded the *Mauritania* in Liverpool on the morning of March 22nd 1913. On the morning of his arrival a week later the *New York Journal* wrote:

> When you hear the big guns at the various ports in the bay booming and the sirens of the steamboats sirening and the little whistles of the dainty tugs whistling to-day, put a little bet down hurriedly that Freddie Welsh is right on our front doorstep.
>
> The last time he arrived here sans title; the brass bands that met him were notable by their absence.

Ten

Industry Without Art is Brutality

The boxing men said it couldn't be done. Once a man was beaten for his title he lived for the remainder of his life in fear of his conqueror. The only successful comeback in boxing before 1911 had been Stanley Ketchel's victory to reclaim his middleweight title from Billy Papke. Freddie was only the second fighter to contradict the old maxim that "they never come back". Even American sportswriters were impressed by his recent achievements. There had also been a significant revision of Freddie's fight against Willie Ritchie. Just over a year previously it was an unimpressive performance over a novice; now it was a twenty-round whipping of the current world champion. Freddie's popularity was further enhanced when Ritchie announced that he wanted a guarantee of $15,000 to fight the Welshman. One leading boxing scribe wrote that Ritchie had "already impaired his reputation with the followers of the roped arena by hugging to his bosom the title, which many think he secured by a fluke, and refusing to defend that title in the prompt and business-like manner that characterized all his worthy predecessors". Three of the four big boxing countries – England, France and Australia – acknowledged Freddie as champion of the world. The United States, the most important one, did not. Freddie knew that he'd never win the debate in the newspapers and annex the title by consensus. He had to beat Ritchie and the American had shown no enthusiasm for such a contest. So Freddie employed the services of Harry Pollok, the man described by the *New York Evening Sun* as the "only man in the world who can be wrong and get away with it". Pollok was one of New York's most flamboyant sports impresarios. He staged cycle races, managed champion boxers and wrestlers and was one of the best publicity men in the business. Pollok was one of the breed of prize-fight manager "who would never admit to waiting for a telephone call that costs less than a dollar".

Freddie, Fanny, their prize-winning bulldog 'Welsh' and the two championship belts arrived in New York on March 29th 1913. The first thing Freddie asked his reception committee as he got off the boat was "where's Willie Ritchie?" There was no sign of the champion but Harry Pollok was at dockside, "in a wreath of 25 cent cigar smoke and a hair-cut", orchestrating the reporters and photographers. Getting a match with Ritchie, even with Pollok's help, would be very difficult. The Frawley Law that allowed boxing 'exhibitions'

Freddie and 'Pontypridd'.

in specially licensed clubs had caused a dramatic increase in the number of venues staging fights in New York. For a world champion this was a lucrative and sensible way of using the title: a champion's purse was always high and because the contests were of the no decision variety his title could only be lost by knockout. The only 'decision' contests were staged out on the Pacific Coast so Willie Ritchie and his manager Billy Nolan stayed in the east picking up fights in New York and Philadelphia. As soon as Freddie arrived back in America Billy Nolan announced that the champion would not fight anybody for four months because of a European trip to fulfil theatrical commitments. While the champion trod the boards Freddie embarked on a tour of the United States and Canada, fighting as often as he could. He needed the fights to be in condition to take on Ritchie at any time and they also helped reinforce the impression that while the champion had abdicated the heir apparent was prepared to take on all-comers.

Freddie's first public appearance on his return to the United States was an exhibition contest as part of a benefit night to raise money for the flood ravaged Ohio Valley. Old-time boxers joined

Freddie, Boyo Driscoll and the prize-winning
bulldogs.

current day champions at the 22nd Regiment Armoury in New York
and Freddie sparred with Jack McAuliffe who became the first ever
world's lightweight champion back in 1887. Such was Freddie's
stature in the sport that he became the inadvertent champion of the
campaign to legalize boxing across the United States. Elbert
Hubbard had written an article about Freddie in the *Philistine* that
was read by an "un-named but prominent" senator. The senator
shared Freddie's passion for the writings of John Ruskin and when
the politician learned that Freddie boxed according to Ruskin's
belief that "industry without art is brutality", he wrote to the
Welshman to ask him to front his proposed Bill on the legalization of
boxing. Meanwhile Freddie's first contest in the ring was at the
Union Boat Club in Bridgeport, Connecticut, against local fighter Al
Ketchel. The venue was packed and many hundreds climbed onto
the roof to get a view of the British champion. Freddie displayed his
two championship belts to the crowd before giving his opponent a
terrible beating. "Welsh closed Ketchel's eye in the fifth round,"
wrote the *Journal Courier*, "and used the latter's face for a punchbag
thereafter."

After the Ketchel fight Freddie travelled to Canada for a series of bouts starting in Winnipeg, where he had a good following. His first opponent was Jack Redmond, a veteran fighter who'd punched it out with most of the leading lightweights except Freddie. Redmond took an awful amount of punishment and was forced to hold on in the last round to escape a knockout. From Winnipeg, Freddie and Harry Pollok travelled on the Canadian Pacific Railway to Edmonton, Alberta. On the afternoon of their arrival, fighter and manager were invited to meet with Bob MacDonald, the president of the Edmonton Athletic Association. MacDonald told the two men that he had $25,000 to stage a bout between Freddie and Willie Ritchie in Edmonton on Dominion Day, June 1st 1913. It was the first offer likely to satisfy the champion's financial demands and it provided Pollok with further ammunition in the newspaper war. Freddie's main reason for going to Edmonton was to box a local fighter called Louis 'Kid' Scaler who was reported to have a "bacon bringer" in either hand. The fight was staged at the Thistle Rink and the young men of the town were invited to bring their lady friends to the contest. The management assured the very best of order would be preserved and insisted that spectators refrain from any unseemly remarks. Despite the great interest in the fight it was a subdued evening, in part due to a very large police presence instructed to eject anybody who misbehaved. The fight was also overshadowed by news from Calgary that a boxer by the name of Luther McCarthy had died in the ring with suspected heart failure. Because of the tragedy it was agreed that Freddie and Scaler should fight a no decision contest. Freddie won the fight by common consensus and according to the newspapers he barely took a single blow through the entire fifteen rounds.

The Canadian tour moved on to Moose Jaw in Saskatchewan. Freddie was pitched against the best local fighter the promoters could find, Billy Farrell. It was staged at the town's curling rink and Freddie dispatched Farrell in quick time. A right to the jaw and two lefts into the stomach left the local man fighting for breath and his seconds threw in the towel in the fifth round. Freddie and Harry picked up the purse and headed off that night by train to Vancouver where a group of about fifty Welsh ex-pats staged a banquet in his honour at the city's Elysium Hotel. According to one Canadian reporter the greater part of the evening was spent in the "rendition of stirring Welsh songs in solo and then by the entire company". After hearty renditions of 'Sosban Fach' and 'Comrades In Arms' the 'foreigners' present were amazed and delighted at the volume of harmony that came in with the soup and continued to the coffee. By now Freddie was introducing Fanny as his wife. Also present were his uncle and aunt – Mr and Mrs Hall from Cardiff – Freddie's mother's brother and his wife. In submitting a toast to the King, Dr J. Ellis Griffith said that there were no more loyal subjects than the natives of "gallant little Wales". The national anthem was lustily rendered followed by 'God Bless the Prince of Wales'. To round off the evening Freddie's aunt gave a speech and told how as a child he was always full of mischief but that he was always good to his mother and sister.

The first of his two fights in Vancouver was against Ray Campbell of San Francisco. Freddie was late because the car in which he was travelling to the arena broke down. It was a wild stormy night but that didn't stop a large crowd turning up and they forgave Freddie after being treated to fifteen amazing rounds of boxing in which Campbell was given "an artistic lacing" in almost every round.

Freddie and Harry broke off their Canadian tour in early July 1913 to go to San Francisco to watch Willie Ritchie's return to the ring. The champion had completed an extended run in vaudeville and declared himself through with theatrical arrangements and that from then on his business was fighting. His opponent was 'Mexican' Joe Rivers, a novice who wasn't expected to give Ritchie any difficulty. But against all expectations Rivers outfought the champion for much of the bout until Ritchie salvaged the fight with a knockout blow in the eleventh round. This was all good news for Freddie. The champion wasn't impressive and would come under even more pressure by the newspapers to fight him. To ensure he kept his name firmly in the frame Freddie decided to reveal one of his great secrets. In an interview with the *Evening Express* he admitted that he and Brahna 'Fanny' Weston, a young lady of Jewish parentage, were married. The ceremony had taken place in New York City in 1905 when Freddie was just a novice boxer on the East Coast six-round circuit. "We decided that it would be better for his professional prospects not to make our marriage public," Fanny told the reporter, "although all of our relatives knew of the ceremony. Keeping our marriage a secret grew to be a habit with us and we have had many a laugh at the 'soubrettes' who set their caps for Freddie." They also had many a laugh at the scribes who'd dedicated all those column inches to Freddie's 'sister', the Welsh rose who'd prepared all his special meals before the fights.

It was as Mr and Mrs Welsh that Freddie and Fanny returned to Vancouver that summer. In his second engagement in the city Freddie fought Young Jack O'Brien, the most formidable opponent he'd been matched with since returning to the American continent.

O'Brien had beaten the former champion Ad Wolgast and Willie
Ritchie thought him enough of a threat to issue a statement that he
would box the winner of the Welsh – O'Brien contest for the highest
bid offered. O'Brien had impressed the locals with his training
displays and as the day of the fight approached the odds on him
beating Freddie got shorter almost by the hour. The fight justified its
billing. It was a fast and furious fifteen-round affair and Freddie got
the referee's decision. The general reaction was that O'Brien gave
Freddie "a worthy argument" but the consensus on the scoring was
that O'Brien only had one round to his credit, the tenth, when he
rallied and carried the fight to Freddie; ten rounds belonged to the
British titleholder, while the other four were called even.

With an important victory in his ledger Freddie's tour through
Canada continued on to the town of Fernie, British Columbia. He
picked up a $1,000 for battering Martin Murphy of Seattle for seven
rounds before knocking him out in the eighth. Freddie returned to
Vancouver once more where Harry Pollok was finally beginning to
make some progress in securing a fight for the championship. Harry
Foley, who looked after Ritchie's interests, sent a letter to the newspapers stating that the champion was prepared to take on any fighter
with any promoter for the biggest offer available. Ritchie knew that it
was only a match with the Welshman that could generate the purse
of $15,000 that he was looking for. The first two promoters to
indicate that they were interested in staging the fight were James
Coffroth in San Francisco and Chester McIntyre in Vancouver.
Coffroth declined to go anywhere near the figure that Ritchie wanted
but McIntyre agreed to meet the demand of $15,000 for a
September 1st date, Labor Day, at the Brighthouse Arena in
Vancouver. While the negotiations proceeded Freddie got involved in
a stunt to break the Canadian land speed record over one mile. That
summer he became friendly with 'Speed King' Bob Burman. Freddie
sat in with Burman as he broke the record by travelling the mile in
50.8 seconds in his Blitzen Benz. "It was like a runaway train coming
down Pike's Peak," Freddie recalled. "That big machine didn't look
safe, didn't smell safe, and didn't act safe. When we were going pretty
fast, at the rate of sixty miles per hour, I remarked to Burman that
'we are going pretty fast'. He intimated that he thought I wasn't satisfied with the speed, and let out another notch." Freddie now had the
distinction of having ridden faster in a car than any other boxer.

While Freddie was breaking speed records and the promoters were
bidding for the fight, Willie Ritchie set off for a ten-day hunting trip
to shoot deer. The world champion was informed that the Canadians

15. Speed King Bob Burman and the world's fastest moving prizefighter.

had agreed to meet his financial demands at his mountain retreat near
Salinas. On the night of August 5th 1913 Chester McIntyre received
a cable from Ritchie: "Bout is on. Send complete articles at once.
Letter following. Rush articles." Ritchie was to get $15,000 win, lose
or draw. If the bout drew a gate in excess of $30,000; he would also
get 5 per cent of the extra income. The promoters immediately sent
three return trip tickets for the journey from San Francisco to
Vancouver to Ritchie's manager, Harry Foley. As the fight was being
made many of the leading San Francisco sportswriters claimed that
Freddie had outgrown the lightweight division and would have trouble
making the limit. To dispel any doubt Harry Pollok staged a public
weigh-in at the beginning of Freddie's training in which the Welshman
weighed only 130lbs – three pounds below the limit before he had
even started to work. Pollok also managed to secure the services of the
former world middle and heavyweight champion 'Philadelphia' Jack
O'Brien to help Freddie prepare for the fight. Jack was the brother of
'Young' Jack O'Brien who Freddie had fought that summer. McIntyre
meanwhile was negotiating with the Canadian Pacific Railway and the
Great Northern Railroad for the provision of special trains at lower
rates to bring the crowds to Vancouver. He also arranged for extra
boats to be laid on from Seattle, Tacoma and Victoria.

Freddie set up his training quarters in Vancouver. He took an
apartment out at English Bay and was given the use of the Imperial
dancing pavillion every afternoon for sparring and gymnastic work.
He did his roadwork through Stanley Park nearby. But suddenly

Reaction from the *Evening World*, 19 August 1913.

Freddie's plans received another blow, this time self-inflicted. He'd turned on his ankle in training but believed that it would heal with a little rest. When he started to train in earnestness he was rounding a corner on a run around the park and his ankle gave way again. Freddie was taken back to his quarters by ambulance. This happened on the day before Ritchie was due to arrive in Vancouver. Freddie could barely walk for a week and he spent his time composing a 35-page letter, neatly typed and dispatched to the offices of *Boxing* magazine in London. The letter is dated August 25th, 1913. The first section was addressed to his brother Stanley:

> If you were here right now I would grubstake you to the Shushanna Gold Rush up in Alaska, which seems to be opening up with another Klondike. I have been seriously thinking of going up into the goldfields

and staking a claim, and would certainly do if it were Spring now instead of Autumn.

I have been feeling so sick of this fighting game with its disappointments that lately I have felt that even the search after pure gold nuggets, with its hardships, privations, and elusiveness, cannot be more disheartening than this 'will-o'-the-wisp' title that I have been chasing these last seven years.

Freddie rambled on in a stream of consciousness about his future plans, which included various fruit growing and town planning schemes in California – all with an eye on the opening of the Panama Canal. He also dreamt up wheat-growing schemes along the Mackenzie River which he prophesied would be one of the richest farming areas in the world within a few years. The letter made it clear that Freddie seemed resigned to defeat against Ritchie because of the choice of referee. This issue had yet to be resolved but Freddie knew Ritchie would insist on Jim Griffin, an old friend of the champion who'd worked in his corner. Freddie wrote that he was so sick of the whole business that he left the matter entirely in the hands of Harry Pollok who would probably accept Griffin as referee. Ritchie did insist on Griffin and Pollok did agree and it was obvious from the tone of the letter that Freddie was tiring of the chase.

Well, whatever happens, I shall be out of the game inside the next two years. I have made up my mind on that point. I am as tired of it as I can well be. It wasn't so bad before, but ever since I set out to chase the title, ever since I got busy after Nelson, Wolgast, and Ritchie, it has been nothing but wranglings, delays, disappointments, and uncharitableness – and I am heartily sick of it all.

Still, I suppose it is up to me to pick up all I can while I am still in the business, so once I am through with Ritchie I guess I will have to be getting around as quickly as I can.

By the way, I would like to hear from a few friends at home. So you can tell them all that Sylvia Apartments, English Bay, Vancouver, B.C. will always find me.

The training accident had given Ritchie a grand opportunity to shake down the promoters for a little more small change. He demanded and was given $1,000 for his inconvenience. After Freddie's ankle injury Ritchie called him a "broken down old man". The initial prognosis was that Freddie's injury would keep him out of the ring for six weeks and an editorial in *Boxing* asked if Freddie was haunted. This theory was given further credence during the Welshman's convalescence. While he was in Vancouver that summer

Freddie became very friendly with Jim B. Reid, the proprietor of the
English Bay Tea Rooms near his training quarters. Reid was an
Englishman who helped Freddie for several weeks but who wouldn't
take any kind of payment for his services. Freddie suggested that as
Reid kept an eating-house, it might be a bit of an advertisement if he
lent him the two championship belts to display in the window of the
restaurant. Reid was delighted and offered Freddie a guaranteed
cheque of $10,000 as security for the trophies. "Of course I wouldn't
take that," explained Freddie, "but I had to accept his undertaking to
make good if either or both of the belts got lost." Freddie didn't think
the belts were worth stealing. Their actual value was about $200 each,
which is what he'd insured them for, but they couldn't be sold intact
because it would be obvious that they'd been stolen. Melted down
they'd be worth even less.

The belts had been displayed in the window of the diner on the
corner of Davie and Denman Streets for a week when a gang of five
or six men entered the restaurant and started to order several items
from the menu. This had the desired effect of sending three of the
four girls who waited there into the kitchen. The last girl was asked
for cigarettes, which had to be fetched from a back room. The
moment the restaurant was cleared of its employees one of the men
raised the back panel of the window display and grabbed the nearest
belt – he didn't have time to take both – and made off with the
National Sporting Club trophy without being noticed. A few days
later a man claiming to be a lawyer approached Freddie and
suggested that he could arrange the belt's return but that it would cost
"quite a few dollars". Freddie had expected something of the kind,
and he refused to have any dealings with a "sneak thief" who would
run the risk of being sent up for five or six years for such a paltry
prize as a belt that could not be worth more than £10 or £20 melted
down. Freddie told the lawyer to tell the thief that he could keep what
he'd got. That was all he heard of the matter for ten days when he was
notified that the belt had been found in Seattle. It was in the possession of an Australian named Henry Beckett, a former jockey who was
on the boat from Vancouver to Seattle. He was wearing the belt under
his coat but as he went into a lavatory on board ship his coat got
slightly caught on a door handle and a steward caught a glimpse of
the gold. The steward, believing the man to be a smuggler, reported
the incident to the purser who in turn informed the customs officials.
Beckett was seized on arrival in Seattle and asked if he had anything
to declare and when he said he hadn't he was searched. Beckett made
a run for it but succeeded only in running up a blind alley and was

trapped. He told the customs officials the belt was his and he was in fact, Freddie Welsh. One of the customs officials who had seen Freddie fight told the thief that while the Welshman was now a veteran for a fighter he certainly wasn't as old as his captive looked. Beckett was 45 years old. The thief and the belt were now in the safekeeping of the American Customs officials but there was still no guarantee that the trophy would be returned to its rightful owner. American Customs insisted that Freddie prosecute Beckett and get him sent back to Vancouver; otherwise they would confiscate the belt as smuggled goods. The newspapers had reported the belt was worth $5,000 and this meant grand larceny and six years in the pen for Beckett. The thief and the belt were returned to Canada where Beckett sent for Freddie and pitched him a hard-luck story. Freddie obviously believed him and set off to see the judge to explain the belt didn't "amount to a row of beans" and that its worth had been greatly exaggerated, apart from its sentimental value. Freddie recalled his days as a hobo and his real horror of the 'pen' and didn't want to see anyone he knew of sent up. The judge took a lot of convincing, but Freddie pointed out that Beckett was nearly fifty, that he had a wife and children dependent on him, and that he wouldn't amount to much when he came out. "There was more human nature about that judge than there is about most," Freddie recalled, "and after a while he listened to my tale and agreed to make the charge petty larceny, and so Mr Beckett got off with six or nine months, I forget which."

As the summer of 1913 turned into autumn it appeared that Freddie's fortunes were finally improving. His belt had been returned, the injured ankle had healed and articles were signed for the contest with Ritchie. Both men had posted forfeits of $2,500 and training resumed. The Vancouver press was impressed by the number of women who attended Freddie's sparring sessions. Before each bout Freddie made a speech to the men present asking them not to smoke as a personal favour to him on account of the ladies present. "Welsh is an old fox," wrote one of the reporters. "I noticed the smoke was bothering him, and you have to hand it to him for putting it up to the ladies." Freddie and Ritchie were holding public training sessions every afternoon and there was great interest in the fight. The huge gamble by the promoters to offer the champion such a large guarantee seemed to have paid off until early on the afternoon of Tuesday, September 9th, when a rumour circulated that Willie Ritchie and his entourage were leaving town. In the absence of any definite word from the champion the promoters and journalists started to look for him. The first sign that the story was true came from the Ebrune Hotel where Ritchie's room had been cleaned out. He had gone to a friend's home and issued a strict instruction that any enquiries as to his whereabouts should be met with the answer that he was "not there". Ritchie remained in seclusion all afternoon. The hunt for the champion eventually ended at the dockside in Vancouver where his trunk had been taken on board the *Princess Victoria* at 10.30pm. A few minutes later the gangplank was raised and on board ship was Willie Ritchie, Harry Foley, Jim Stack and Ray Campbell, one of the sparring partners. "Certainly I'm going," Ritchie told one reporter. "I am tired of being made an office boy of by these people here, and I'm not going to stand it any longer." One of the reporters present wrote that Ritchie was "plainly nervous, and throughout his conversation exhibited a spirit of childish pique little becoming the champion in the popular class of pugilism".

The reason Ritchie later gave for his displeasure was a disagreement over advertising rights in connection with the motion pictures. This was the revenue from the big signs on the arena walls that consequently appeared prominently in the films of the fight. Ritchie also wanted a concession on the refreshments and programme sales written into the contract. It was a strange request because there was no liquor sold at the Brighthouse Arena so this clause would bring no more than 'pin money'. The promoter Chester McIntyre had agreed to Ritchie's demands and the clause was inserted into the. typed articles. A few days later Ritchie met up with Hugh Springer, who had put up the money for the fight. Springer told the champion that he was unaware of any problem with the advertising rights but he was surprised that Chester McIntyre had rather exceeded his duty in inserting the clause. Springer also told Ritchie that it was "a small thing to have trouble about" and that he would leave it until the original telegrams could be found to ascertain exactly what had been agreed about these rights. Springer claimed to have left Ritchie on good terms and heard nothing else until receiving the news that the champion had left town. "They simply got Ritchie's goat," claimed one of the champion's friends. "He did not sleep a wink last night. Willie felt that if they would repudiate one section of the agreement by saying that McIntyre had no authority to sign they might repudiate it all." On reaching Seattle, Ritchie told reporters "If they want me they can follow me over to Seattle where I will dictate terms. But I expect to be in San Francisco by Saturday or Sunday."

"Who ever heard of a champion running away before for such a tiny amount of money with so much ready assured him?" replied Harry Pollok. Freddie's manager later revealed that Harry Foley had approached him to turn the contest into a no decision bout and when Freddie refused Ritchie ran off. Pollok had the letters to confirm his story; Ritchie had written to ask if the bout could be a fifteen-round no decision affair. Freddie had replied: "Nothing doing – championship or nothing!" Further evidence emerged that Ritchie did not just suddenly decide to leave town. Two days before he set sail for Seattle the champion had gone to the promoters to demand that he got the $1,000 for the delay due to Freddie's ankle injury. He got his money but on the same day he wired his bank in San Francisco to stop certification for the $2,500 cheque he had posted as a forfeit for weight and appearance. The official stakeholder for the match was Al Hagar, the manager of the New England Fish Company. Hagar sent both Ritchie's and Freddie's forfeit cheques away to be certified but the American had stopped his before it reached the bank. Consequently Freddie and the promoters had no chance of recovering Ritchie's forfeit for non-appearance. Hugh Springer issued a statement that included a list of facts on the affair. He offered $5,000 for every fact that Ritchie could disprove. Springer claimed that Ritchie had wired a friend in California to tell him the fight was off. He also claimed the champion had asked advice on stopping a certified cheque by wire and then subsequently proceeded to stop his forfeit cheque in this manner. Springer offered to lodge the money with James Woods, Police Commissioner of San Francisco, together with evidence that it was not the advertising concessions that caused Ritchie to cancel the fight. Springer asked Ritchie to deposit his $5,000 and his evidence with Woods and both men would have to abide by the Commissioner's decision. His challenge was declined.

The newspapers were split as to what really happened. Many writers branded Ritchie a coward. The *Philadelphia Ledger* alleged, "For the first time in the history of the ring in this country the champion of the lightweight class is being labelled a 'quitter'." The Pacific Coast writers were more charitable to the San Francisco fighter especially as they had been sceptical as to how the Vancouver promoters could guarantee Ritchie so much more money than promoters in the United States. The consensus was that the champion was suffering from the lack of an experienced manager to look after him. The man who guided him to the title, Billy Nolan, was an experienced boxing impresario but he'd been sacked after a disagreement and Ritchie's trainer, Harry Foley had taken over since when the champion had been the victim of too much bad advice. According to one scribe, Ritchie's unfortunate predicament showed "that a champion pugilist cannot look after both ends of the game without suffering a severe reverse at one end or the other, and it will take a lot of good management and a lot of sympathetic sporting editors to again set him on the pedestal from which he has fallen by the force of his own foolishness."The manner in which Ritchie had left Vancouver – under cover of darkness without explaining his actions – was very damaging. On arriving in San Francisco Ritchie claimed the real reason he fled was that he felt "out-generalled" by Harry Pollok who'd purposely annoyed him in the making of the match and had thereby upset his training. Freddie and Harry decided to keep the pressure on. They told the press they would track Ritchie all the way to his home if necessary and demand a match. Freddie announced that he intended to turn up to the venue as planned on the Saturday afternoon to shadow box for a few rounds. Having beaten his imaginary opponent he would claim the world championship, demand Ritchie's forfeit and set in train the legal machinery to obtain damages from the American for the several matches he had lost waiting for the champion to fight him. He even prepared a detailed timetable for Saturday's events:

> Weigh in at 12.15pm at 135 lbs; hop through the ropes an hour later; shadow fight an imaginary Ritchie; land an imaginary knockout; declare himself world's champion; visit his lawyers, and make a claim for the $2,500 forfeit money.

But Ritchie had already stopped the forfeit cheque and Freddie wasn't even reimbursed for his training expenses. He was left in Vancouver and the champion and the championship had eluded him once more. So Freddie and Harry set off in pursuit. They moved on to Seattle on their way across the continent to New York and the plan was for Freddie to fight several times on the journey. The first port of call was Butte, Montana, for a bout with 'Fighting' Dick Hyland. The boxers had to share a gymnasium to train for the fight. Hyland did his work first, from 3 pm until 4.30 pm when Freddie took his turn. The British champion, despite all the disappointment of the Ritchie affair and the fact that he hadn't boxed for over three months, fought brilliantly. He won every round against Hyland and the contest was so palpably one-sided that the audience lost interest after it had gone a few periods. Five nights later it was the same story against Leo Kossick in Billings, Montana. Freddie and Harry crossed back into Canada once more, to Winnipeg for a match with Milburn 'Young' Saylor. It was a tough, dirty fight and Saylor was warned a number of times by the referee to raise his punches. In the ninth round he drove a right-hand punch into Freddie's groin that dropped him to the floor, writhing in agony. With Freddie on the canvas there was a commotion in the arena. Ray Bronson, Saylor's manager, and his seconds claimed a victory for the Indianapolis boxer and hugged and kissed him in the middle of the ring. When the decision was given to Freddie on a foul Bronson threatened the announcer and accused Freddie of having a "yellow streak" and cheating Saylor out of the fight. The referee was supported by Dr William Black who examined Freddie after the fight and said "a livid blotch showed where Saylor's glove had landed". A victory, or at least a moral victory, against Freddie Welsh would have ensured Saylor better fights for bigger purses. Even though the referee 'Bun' Foley avowed that the punch was a foul, he was later 'persuaded' to give Saylor a signed statement that he had won by a knockout. Foley claimed to have done it to "help the lad along". Unfortunately the controversy served only to lead the authorities to suspend boxing in the town, a course of action that had been threatened since the death of Luther McCarthy in the ring with Arthur Pelky. A few weeks later, the Winnipeg promoter issued a statement concerning the fight:

> I intended to say nothing either way, but now that Saylor is sending records to Australia with 'The man who knocked out Freddie Welsh' in big type I feel as if I ought to speak. The blow that ended the fight was a rank foul, as plain a foul as ever was struck, and no doubt about it.

After Freddie had recovered from the Saylor fight, he and Harry continued to chase Ritchie. They arrived in New York in time for the champion's next defence against the 'Fighting Dentist', Leach Cross, at Madison Square Garden. The fight was a big success for Ritchie as he comfortably outpointed the local man and his performance was so good that it completely repaired the damage to his reputation. By now Ritchie was enjoying life as world champion. Before leaving New York for his San Francisco home he was given a box party at the Winter Garden as a farewell tribute, hosted by two of the stars of *The Pleasure Seeker*, William Montgomery and Florence Moore. The previous night Ritchie had been the guest of honour at a dinner hosted by the promoter Billy Gibson at the Bronx Theatre restaurant at 149th street and Third Avenue. Over fifty of the most prominent businessmen, boxing devotees and newspapermen of the Bronx attended. During the many speeches Ritchie was lauded for his performances in and out of the ring. The *New York Times* reported that "as a talker Ritchie proved as much of a surprise as he did in the ring Monday night". Back in England *Boxing* wrote that there was "something of a conspiracy among the New York papers" which had

supported Ritchie's version of events in Vancouver, and agreed that
Freddie was a spent force.

Freddie boxed in New York for the first time in nearly three years
against Phil Bloom at the Atlantic Garden Athletic Club on
November 25th 1913. He told boxing writers that he took the fight
to show New Yorkers that he deserved a match with Ritchie. Bloom
had recently cut a swathe through the East Coast lightweights and
this was a very important bout for Freddie. He had never boxed at
his best in New York and he'd generally been considered in the city
to be an inferior version of Peerless Jim Driscoll. He took the fight
seriously and went to train at Dal Hawkins' roadhouse. Hawkins was
an 'old-time' fighter who once boxed Freddy Bogan for the
American featherweight title. They had fought for seventy-five
rounds until the fight was stopped at five o'clock in the morning.
They resumed the next day and the fight eventually ended in the
ninetieth round.

Freddie built a good lead in the early rounds against Phil Bloom
but seemed to tire and had a very uncomfortable final period. The
city's sportswriters wrote of a fighter who had "begun to feel the
touch of Time's inexorable fingers". The boxing scribes didn't think
that Freddie could hit hard enough to be considered a credible
contender for the world title. "As a scientist Welsh ranks high,"
proclaimed one reporter. "He is a wonder at blocking, a good fighter,
has speedy footwork and superb ring generalship, but with it all he
gets nowhere. With one short arm jolt Ritchie can do more damage
than Welsh can accomplish in ten rounds of the most frantic
exertion."

Ten days later Freddie was back in a Canadian ring. His opponent
was the New Yorker Arthur Ellis and the fight was staged in
Montreal. After toying with his opponent for four rounds, Freddie
smashed a right to his jaw in the fifth and Ellis had to take a count.
He made it to his feet only to be hit again with the same punch and
this time he did not get up. After the fight Freddie pushed the cheque
for $500 into his pocket and told reporters that he got $35.71 per
minute for his work that evening. This was the city in which he used
to earn $1 per day working for the Canadian Pacific Railway.

Freddie travelled south to New Orleans for Christmas. He was
frequently seen in the city's restaurants, often dancing the night
away. "When Freddy has the floor, the majority of the other dancers
stop and watch him," one local newspaper reported. "His good looks,
good tangoing, cheerful disposition and intelligent conversation have
led him into the highest society that frequents the café after the

theatre." His main reason for visiting the city was a bout with Johnny Dundee on New Year's Day and Freddie kept the New Orleans press entertained throughout the build-up. He spoke to a female reporter of his support for the suffragette movement though he stressed that he didn't "believe in throwing bricks into a fellow's window". He also took time to defend George Bernard Shaw against a reporter who questioned the writer's sincerity. "When I first read his *Quintessence of Ibsenism*, I was amazed that any human being could have such thoughts and be brave enough to put them on paper," said Freddie. "Since then I have just concluded that Mr Shaw just thinks ahead of the rest of us. I believe the world will come around in the next couple of hundred years to adopt a lot of his most apparently scandalous ideas." He'd charmed New Orleans and one writer commenting on his pursuit of the title described Freddie as the "best little gloom-chaser" he knew of, adding that if the Welshman had lived in Job's day he could have given that "old scout some pointers on patience".

Mrs Welsh meanwhile was on a world tour with her sister and spent Christmas in Australia. On his arrival in New Orleans Freddie received a cable from his wife that had been sent on from the St Paul Hotel in New York:

Awfully lonesome. Arrive France end January. Can you join me? Answer. Steamer Macedonia. Adelaide. Love. FANNY

To which Freddie replied:

Care of S.S. Macedonia. Cannot go France. Welcome you New York. Come quickly. Love. FRED

In the midst of all the merriment Freddie seemed to ignore the fact that he'd travelled to the city for a match with Johnny Dundee, a fighter that was being touted by the American press as a contender for Ritchie's title. Freddie confessed to having "loafed around" for quite some time before the fight and he was carrying more weight than ever before. He worked hard to shed it but by the night of the contest he was still a few pounds overweight and as the opening bell sounded it looked as if Freddie would pay dearly for his Christmas in New Orleans. Dundee drew first blood in the opening round with a short left hook that split the Welshman's lips. Freddie lost that round and then the second. But that was the last round he lost. A vicious hook in the sixth round flattened Dundee's nose and the blood flowed for the rest of the fight. Freddie went back to his corner at the end of the sixth and smiled. He made sure of the win by battering his tiring opponent in the tenth round. Freddie won a unanimous newspaper decision and it was generally agreed to have been the best bout staged in New Orleans. After the fight, Dundee's manager Scotty Monteith said his man had won the fight but had lost the "wire game". The accusation was that Harry Pollok had wired all the important New York newspapers with reports of a victory for Freddie before the 'true' accounts of the fight could be dispatched. So Pollok "sent out for a bottle of vitriol, dipped his pen into it" and sent a letter to all the leading sports editors to clear up any confusion. "Scotty Monteith must be full of Dundee jam. He is making a yell that could be heard in the Fiji Islands that he was the victim of the wire game," wrote Pollok. "Monteith is very self-sacrificing in trying to lift the load of defeat from Dundee's shoulders by acknowledging that he is a bush league manager, but he is practically accusing each and every one of the New Orleans sporting editors of being unfair and biased."

The row was, of course, good for both men and the New York papers had devoted much more space to the fight than they would have otherwise. Freddie's victory over a good opponent increased the pressure on Ritchie. Dundee, as the younger fighter, had emerged with a great deal of credit from a fight in which he gave away weight to his more experienced opponent. Freddie kept the copy rolling. On the eve of the fight he'd stayed at the Grunewald Hotel in New Orleans. He told reporters that he'd been awoken by loud banging noises and that Scotty Monteith had arranged somebody to make the racket outside his window. He managed to fall back asleep but was awoken again by banging noises an hour later. He got up to read and turned on the light but then snapped it off again when he realized that it would encourage the tormentors to know they had disturbed him. He went back to sleep only to be awoken a third time. Then Freddie remembered that it was New Year's Eve and that it was the firecrackers that had disturbed his sleep. But Freddie decided to accuse Scotty Monteith anyhow. When a reporter put the allegations to him Monteith replied: "Do you mean to say that they let off at 4.30 o'clock? Why, I paid the bloomin' chaps to keep it up until 7, and they double-crossed me. Curses on 'em."

Straight after the fight Freddie went back to his room in the Grunewald, donned his heaviest clothes and ran in circles around the room for twenty minutes. He shadow boxed four rounds and sparred three light rounds with one of his trainers. He was still carrying surplus weight and needed to take it off quickly. The plan for the month of January was to take a fight a week, in a different city, and by meeting the local favourite he could get an average guarantee of $1,000 per fight. From New Orleans Freddie and Harry moved on

Boyo Driscoll and Freddie in 'mental' training.

to Atlanta, Georgia. Only five days after beating Johnny Dundee he was back in the ring to box the 'Fighting Carpenter' Frank Whitney of Cedar Rapids, Iowa. Count Lou Castro – ball player, comedian, prizefight promoter and prince of good fellows, was promoting the fight. Freddie gave several interviews to the Atlanta press and told them about his love of the philosophy of Maeterlinck; of the gloomy and at times baleful influence of Ibsen; of the brilliant satire of Shaw; of the wonderful human understanding of Count Tolstoy. Freddie had spent much of the journey around Canada and the United States during the winter of 1913 reading Russian literature. He liked the way they "went down into the bones of things". "When a man takes to Tolstoy," said Freddie, "well, he doesn't leave off until he's read all the Tolstoy there is. After him, Maxim Gorky comes naturally, don't you think so?"

During the few days he spent in Atlanta, Freddie boxed for nearly 200 newsboys at the Sunday American and Georgian Newsboys' Club. After the sparring was over he gave a speech to the boys: "Don't ever get into a fight unless you have to. Fighting is a bad business. But learn to be able to protect yourself in case you are forced into a fight." Freddie was carried out of the clubhouse on the shoulders of the boys. He had been booked to give another exhibition at the Atlanta Athletic Club a few days before the bout with Whitney but that had to be cancelled due to yet another automobile accident. Freddie and several friends were taking a spin along country roads when the machine "threw a front wheel". None of the party was hurt but they got back too late for the exhibition.

The most noteworthy feature of the Whitney fight was Freddie's weight. He was still having difficulty in shifting the extra pounds, especially around his waist. He weighed 144lbs – more than a stone heavier than when he beat Willie Ritchie a few years previously. But it didn't stop him putting on a dazzling performance. "I did not know a fighter had so many hands," wrote one journalist, who added that Freddie "had it over his opponent like sunshine over a hayfield".

Freddie and Harry continued eastwards to Philadelphia for a match with Sam Robideau. It was Freddie's third fight in three different cities in ten days. It was also his third win, a third superb performance and at last his weight was coming down. Straight after the fight they took the train west to Kansas City. Offers for fights were pouring in. Pollok never asked for an opponent's name when approached by a promoter and each offer was replied to in the same way: "Name your guarantee, date and weight and we will be on hand if terms are satisfactory". The fight in Kansas was against the promising young Mickey Sheridan, an Irish American from Chicago. It was staged at the Academy of Music and Sheridan underwent "thirty minutes of torture and considerable humiliation". Freddie sent Sheridan to the canvas several times but refused to knock him out even for the benefit of the majority of those in the hall that favoured the rough and ready stuff. Freddie didn't come in for much applause at the end. "Those who went to see gore and fancied the surroundings of slaughterhouse decorations were disappointed," wrote one ringside scribe. The following day there was enough time for a round of golf with friends at Swope Park in Kansas City before boarding the train for Cincinnati to take on local boy Earl Fisher. The bout attracted the largest fight audience seen in the city. The pair fought for ten rounds and Freddie was barely touched by his opponent, while Fisher fell through the ropes three times after swinging and missing. During his stay in Cincinnati, Evan Lloyd a boyhood friend of Freddie's, put on a banquet in his honour attended largely by the city's Welsh ex-pats. Straight after Freddie jumped on the train to St Louis where he beat Leo Kelly "without as much as getting his hair ruffled".

After six fights in a month Freddie returned to the St Paul Hotel in New York to rest. The old 'victims and dollars' routine had the desired effect of swelling his bank balance and reducing his midriff. It was a year since his mother had died, his wife was still away on her round the world trip, the leading American sportswriters were still calling him a 'has-been' and he was no closer to Ritchie. Freddie and Harry implemented a new strategy; to travel to the West Coast and fight as many of the championship contenders as possible with the expressed aim of eliminating several of Ritchie's potential challengers as credible opponents. On their journey west they stopped off at St Louis to take an eight-round contest with a young fighter called Jimmy Duffy. Freddie's spirits had been raised by the arrival in St Louis of his brother Stanley, but physically he was still recovering from the relentless schedule he'd undertaken. The countless punches he'd landed on various heads and bodies in recent weeks had taken their toll on his hands, especially his injury prone right. By the time Freddie stepped into the ring against Duffy, Harry Pollok had arranged several important fights in California and he needed his charge to be in the best condition. Throughout the bout with Duffy, Freddie was content to stay out of harm's way and just use his left hand with Pollok shouting at him not to use the right. It was a no decision contest but many of the newspapers gave the verdict to Duffy and Freddie was stung by the criticism. Before setting off to Los Angeles he wrote a letter to the city's sports editors:

I see where you criticise me for boxing second raters in "tank" towns. What am I to do? Ritchie is deathly afraid of me since I whaled him so unmercifully in your city. Wolgast passes me up like a bad check. I have started the year of 1914 by winning six battles in January, and am going better than ever in my life before. Do not put me before the public as a bragging boxer. I am merely writing facts to substantiate my claim for a match with Ritchie.

Freddie arrived in Los Angeles on March 3rd, accompanied by the newly returned Fanny, his trainer, his brother (introduced to the local press as Sir Stanley Cornwallis-Thomas), eight trunks, a slender cane and a bulldog. He decided to train at Jack Doyle's instead of his usual haunt at Venice but the change in location disorientated the Welshman. One morning he took a wrong turn on his morning run and ambled all over the southwest end of the city for several hours until a friendly motorist finally recognized him. Freddie's displeasure at his new environment deepened when his routine of never going to bed before midnight and never getting up before 10 am was disrupted. A gang of boilermakers were working near to his hotel and they began early every morning. Freddie couldn't sleep and promptly moved hotels. One journalist commented that Freddie looked a "little haggard and with overwrought nerves". Indeed most of the writers agreed that Freddie didn't look good enough to beat his next opponent, Joe Rivers. Despite being six years younger than Freddie, Rivers had already had two opportunities to be champion. His first had come against Ad Wolgast on July 4th 1912. It produced one of the most bizarre endings to a world title fight in boxing history. In the thirteenth round both fighters landed with instantaneous punches. Both hit the canvas. The referee Jack Welch, who'd been selected for the bout by Wolgast, raised the champion off the canvas and supported him under one arm while counting Rivers out with the other. On Independence Day twelve months later Rivers got another chance against the new champion Willie Ritchie. Rivers had a good start but was knocked out late in the fight. When the match was made the younger man was the favourite in the betting but by the fight it was even money. The newspapers found it impossible to pick a winner but they were all agreed that the bout was a "last stand for both men". Rivers had already lost twice in title challenges and was unlikely to get another chance if he was defeated again. Freddie had just celebrated his twenty-eighth birthday and no lightweight had ever won the title at such an 'advanced' age. Many of the American writers already regarded him as a 'has been' and to lose to a fighter many years his junior would confirm this view.

The summer of 1914 arrived early in California. By St Patrick's Day, March 17th, there was a withering sun that promised an afternoon of agony for the boxers who toiled under its burning rays, as well as for the spectators who sat in a shirtsleeved mass around the ring. Freddie won the toss for the corner and duly sent his opponent to sit in the glare. From the beginning of the first round until the shadows of the arena covered the ring, Freddie kept the sun directly in Joe's eyes. Rivers tried every way to change positions but only succeeded once when Freddie allowed him to take the much-coveted advantage, and as soon as he got it, the Welshman slammed several lefts to Joe's sore nose. "Joe Rivers' efforts to outbox Freddie Welsh reminded one of a child trying to open a Yale lock with a soup ladle," wrote one of the ringside reporters. Nearly every round was a repetition of the one preceding it; Freddie pecking away at Joe's nose with his left hand and hammering the right into his kidneys. When Referee Eyton stepped forward at the final bell Rivers turned his back, voluntarily acknowledging his defeat. After the fight Freddie had enough energy to run back along the dusty quarter of a mile track from the arena to Doyle's training quarters still dressed in his boxing trunks and bathrobe. He had forgotten to bring his street clothes and declined the offer of one of his trainers to go back for them. Meanwhile one of the world's leading lightweights sat in his dressing room nursing a badly swollen and cut nose, weeping cuts over both eyes and split lips. The following day one local sports editor who'd tipped the Mexican to beat Freddie wrote: "Rivers saw more boxing gloves in one afternoon than ever before in his career and the smell of leather should sicken him during the remainder of his life."

After enjoying a celebratory dinner Freddie explained that he'd long since worked out a way to beat Joe Rivers and that his victory had been one of the mind as much as the body. "I knew, as every scientist knows that the shortest distance between two points is a straight line. Rivers did not," said Freddie. "I hit only in a straight line and after a time those short, hard punches told even more than Rivers knew they did. They drove his good intentions out of his head and fogged his brain even more than they hurt his body. You see I figured out Rivers' mind. I knew what he would do. That is science." He was in a particularly exuberant mood after this fight. One of his friends showed him a week-old copy of an English newspaper that carried a report regarding King George V's enthusiasm for boxing and that he'd put the royal seal of approval on the sport. So Freddie decided to send the King a cable. He took out his pen and wrote His Majesty a 'heartfelt' word of thanks for his support:

> After defeating Joe Rivers, the Mexican and Southern Californian light-weight champion on St. Patrick's Day, the sons of St George, St David, Hibernians and sport-loving Britishers here have conferred the honour on me to represent them in expressing their delight at the encouragement you have graciously given them to the sport of self-defence in the old country, and in assuring you of their loyal appreciation of your British sportsmanship. A reply would gladden the hearts of thousands of patriotic Britishers.

Freddie got a royal reply the following day:

> London, March 18. Freddie Welsh, Los Angeles. I am commanded by the King to thank you and those who associated themselves with you for the loyal message contained in your telegram.

Nearly every major newspaper in the United States and the United Kingdom printed the correspondence in full. H.M. Walker, of the *Los*

A heartfelt note of gratitude to the King.

Angeles Examiner, described Freddie as the cleverest press agent in America. The cable probably cost the King a couple of pounds but it was worth a thousand or so to Freddie in the matter of grabbing column space. When the Welshman was questioned about the sincerity of his patriotic gesture he replied: "I'm not going back anyhow, and I knew he'd never have the chance to run me off the dock. And, my word, what does the old boy go and do but slip me an answer. Pipe."

After the Rivers fight Freddie and his entourage set off on a yachting tour of the Santa Barbara Islands on Baron Long's boat, the *Sweetheart*. But even while he was adrift on the Pacific Ocean Freddie was determined to keep his name on the sports pages. Buoyed by the successful cable to King George V, a telegram was sent to all the major newspapers informing them that the Constitutionalists had captured Freddie Welsh:

San Diego, March 29
I Mexican revolutionist just escaped from San Quentin, Mexico. Next cell mine was Freddie Welsh, who the Constitutionalists imprisoned for sailing boat Mexican waters. They say he was bringing powder shot for revolutionists, which is lie, although he like see us win.

   Freddie say he cruise Mexican waters just snapshot pictures and hook fish. He good boy let me out prison so I get through lines and tell

you see British Consul save him, wife, brother and ship. United States consul must save two citizens, captain and cook. Freddie he no care, but worry about sailing boat, which Mexicans say they burn up pretty soon. Freddie say act quick.
JOSE MIGUELO

Rumours of a kidnapping helped draw attention to the fact that before Freddie had set sail for the Santa Barbara Islands, he agreed terms with Tom McCarey to box the 'Fighting Dentist', Leach Cross in Los Angeles on April 28th. The match was very much of Freddie's own making. He was keen to advance the idea that Cross was one of the toughest lightweights in America and that in defeating him he was ticking off yet another contender. Cross didn't really have any pretensions to be world champion. He was reputedly the wealthiest lightweight in America and worked for dollars not titles but had the reputation in his hometown New York of never training properly for a contest. After working in the gym Leach was too concerned with rushing back to his dental practice. But out in California he had a month to train without worrying about teeth and his friends thought he'd beat Freddie Welsh.

Freddie enjoyed his yachting tour and came back from the trip "as fat as a Japanese wrestler". This may have been some exaggeration but he was having difficulty making weight even in the California sunshine. Even though he continued the pretence of being a vegetarian fighter throughout his career all his friends knew otherwise. Freddie regularly slipped quietly away to some secluded roadhouse where he was known to indulge in his favourite dish of Chicken Maryland. But he'd certainly lost the appetite for training by this stage in his career and he found it easier to stay fit by boxing regularly rather than through his old, punishing gymnasium and running routines. "It doesn't take a game man to fight, but it takes a game one to train," Freddie explained. "Each year it is harder to hit the training stride, and it surely becomes a monotonous affair." To relieve the boredom Freddie spent several afternoons at the circus and he became a friend of a performer called Death Valley Scott. During the lead up to his fight with Leach Cross, Freddie took his entourage to the Buffalo Bill circus at Sells-Floto. Before the show they walked around taking photographs and Freddie entertained the party with great tales of his horse riding exploits back in Wales. One rather sceptical sparring partner dared Freddie to ride the black steed that Daredevil Indian Chief Carlos rode. The Welshman was straight up on the animal's back and away it went, rearing and plunging, while Freddie held on for dear life. A Native American named

Cabash made a wild plunge at the horse's head and managed to bring the animal under control.

Freddie had also taken time away from his training to watch Willie Ritchie fight in San Francisco. It was all part of the chase; wherever the champion boxed Freddie and Harry could usually be seen at ringside. Their idea was to box better opponents than the champion and beat them more convincingly. After seeing Willie Ritchie struggle against 'Harlem' Tommy Murphy, Freddie returned to Los Angeles and beat Leach Cross with consummate ease. The critics rhapsodized over his performance, but the contest was so one-sided that by the end of the eighteenth round hundreds got up to leave and filled the exits. Hundreds more booed and hissed. Freddie was too

20. Freddie astride one of Buffalo Bill's broncos.

21. Freddie and another friend from the circus.

clever, and the fight had been too free from heavy punching, too
devoid of blood. "As an exhibition of boxing the bout was sensa-
tional," commented the *Los Angeles Tribune*, "but as a fight it was a
failure". Leach Cross tried furiously to land one single 'sleep-
producing punch' but he got nowhere near. It didn't improve the
crowd's humour that Freddie appeared to take the whole thing as a
joke; even Cross had to smile at his useless attempts to hit the
Welshman. This wasn't what the public had paid to see and even
when Freddie scored a knockdown in the thirteenth round the
jeering continued. The following day one sporting editor
commented: "They say that the sporting public loves a winner, but if
Freddie Welsh was to win a few more fights he'd be so popular he'd
have to ask the police for protection." Freddie and Harry Pollok
continued their relentless pursuit of Willie Ritchie. They told
reporters that they would stay on the champion's trail "until both of
them are sent to the home for the aged and infirmed".

Eleven

"Cymru am Byth!"

Freddie and Harry Pollok had been trying to sign Ritchie for a championship bout for over three years. Pollok made the champion's life miserable, sending him telegrams and letters almost daily. Ritchie simply ignored them and by spring 1914 the Welshman and his manager had become a little discouraged. Finally the boxer told his manager that if "he would keep off the game for a few days" Freddie would see if he could get Ritchie interested. Harry agreed and Freddie sent Ritchie a telegram that read:

> Please let me know in confidence if you will consent to a championship bout to be decided in England, providing you get a satisfactory guarantee. Answer yes or no at once, as I have several matches pending, and I want to find out where I stand with you. The answer will be treated in strict confidence.

Freddie held Ritchie in high regard as a person and he was sure he'd get a reply. The following day came word that he would agree to the fight for the right money. Freddie and Harry were aware that Bob Vernon, a famous English-born sportsman based in New York, had been charged with luring Ritchie to London to defend his title. He was representing the promoter Charles B. Cochran who was prepared to offer the champion a purse of $25,000. Cochran was a well-known London-based impresario who had lost big on two or three occasions during his career but had always been able to coax money back again. When Cochran first approached Freddie about the match he asked the Welshman what sort of guarantee he was looking for. "I'll share with you," said Freddie, and up to the moment the articles were signed not a scrap of paper passed between the two men. Each depended on the other's word. "It isn't worth $15,000 or $25,000 to the world to see Willie Ritchie fight, of course, any more than it is worth as large a sum to hear Caruso sing," said Cochran. "But these things are all determined by market values. If the world will pay these sums to hear a very excellent Italian gentleman put on pink tights and sing or to watch Willie Ritchie smack a respectable young man in the face with his left hand – well, the wilful world must have its way. That's all there is to it."

Ritchie had boxed only three times since winning the title and by the spring of 1914 the American boxing writers were beginning to succumb to Harry Pollok's constant claim that the champion was 'side stepping' Freddie Welsh. Pollok had convinced the newspapers that the champion was damaging the honour of American boxing. The *New York Evening Sun*, one of the newspapers that had derided Freddie's world title claim after beating Mehegan reported:

> Ritchie must accept a bout with Welsh or stand discredited in the estimation of the American sporting public.
> The fact than an English champion is permitted to ridicule a world's title holder without fear of retaliation is not relished by followers of the ring in this country. Ritchie must fight Welsh!

Freddie was so confident the match could be made he told Vernon to cable the Olympia Theatre in London to ask for its use as the venue and to book the newspaper advertising space. This was a big gamble. When a bout was arranged in the United States the promoters had to make arrangements with the press for publicity. But in England the boxers had to guarantee to spend a certain amount on advertising to get a certain amount of reading matter. Once an advertising contract was signed the papers protected the promoters by taking no other fight advertising for an agreed number of weeks before the contest. In anticipation of Ritchie's signature, Freddie had his newspaper space secured. His next move was to find out exactly how much money Ritchie wanted. The sum of $25,000 had been mentioned in the press and this had been enough to frighten off the Californian promoters. Freddie was convinced this would be the maximum Ritchie would ask for. Freddie and Harry had lambasted Ritchie unmercifully since he won the championship so the American figured out the probable size of the gate and insisted upon such a big slice of it that there would be nothing of consequence left for the Welshman and the promoter to split up. Ritchie didn't want Freddie and Harry to make anything off him. When the champion's answer came, Freddie said it "would have made a horse laugh".

> Will accept for all interests and services in match with Freddie Welsh to take place June 30, for my end fifty thousand dollars and round-trip tickets for three. These are my best terms. WILLIE RITCHIE

Freddie was committed to a few thousand dollars of preliminary expenses and had advertising contracts on his head that would set him back more money than he cared to think about and now Ritchie was asking an impossible sum. When the news of the champion's demands for $50,000 win, lose or draw were made public, the *New*

York Evening Mail commented: "All along Broadway – aye, even down into the side streets – 'de gall o' dis guy Ritchie' has chucked a bombshell into the camp of the fight followers and then touched it off." Ritchie knew $50,000 was out of the question but he did think there was probably just a "little more money" waiting for this match. London sportsmen had gone without a world's boxing champion for a long while and were willing to pay a stiff price for the opportunity of bringing a championship 'back home'. He was right. Pollok got in touch with Cochran whoand he agreed to put $40,000 in the hands of a New York banker to ensure the fight went ahead. Under the agreement Ritchie received $10,000 for advertising rights, a $15,000 guarantee, $10,000 for the moving picture rights and 50 per cent of the various privileges that he could expect to bring in at least another $5,000. The promoter also stipulated that Ritchie could not take any more fights in the meantime. In other words, Ritchie had to refuse all other fight offers for about six weeks for $40,000.

"A sane man would have thought that Ritchie would have jumped at the offer," said Freddie. But Ritchie had different ideas of his own worth and after a series of cables he wired his acceptance of the $40,000, but that he would not think of "tying himself up" for that sum and had to be allowed to fight as many times as he pleased in the interim. He had already signed for a ten-round no decision fight with Charley White in Milwaukee. The London syndicate relented but stipulated that Ritchie had to defeat White or the fight with Freddie would be off. In the meantime Freddie was committed to take a bout on his journey back from California to New York. He enjoyed going to New Orleans and he had agreed to a ten-round contest there against Joe Mandot on May 26th 1914. On previous visits to New Orleans Freddie became a fixture on the city's social scene. He would go to restaurants and clubs in the company of businessmen, sportsmen and politicians. This time his brother Stanley, who was celebrating passing master mariner's examinations, accompanied him. They spent much of the time going to baseball matches in the afternoon and heading for the tango restaurants in the evenings. "Welsh is a great dancer," wrote the *New Orleans Star*, "and sometimes keeps late hours because of his enthusiasm for the tango, but he never dissipates in any other way. He is not on speaking terms with the stuff that sparkles." Freddie managed to retain enough energy to win a unanimous newspaper decision against Joe Mandot, although most of the writers agreed that there was only one round to choose between the two. Not only did he win but he impressed the American press by hitting Mandot hard. Freddie knocked his opponent to the canvas and had him tottering around the ring a few times. Mandot ended the fight with two heavily swollen eyes and a gash on his cheek while Freddie emerged unscathed. All attention now switched to the Willie Ritchie – Charley White fight in Milwaukee the following night.

The first punch, or practically the first, which Charley White got home very nearly decided the issue. It staggered Ritchie and laid him open to a battering from which he was never able to recover. Both his eyes were nearly closed shut by the final bell but somehow he managed to stay on his feet until the end of the fight. "White made Ritchie look like San Francisco after the fire," commented one ringside sport. After his lacing in Milwaukee Ritchie had been backed into a corner and it forced the champion to realise his position. It was White or Welsh, if he wanted to retain the respect of the sportswriters. He had to defend his title and he had to do it against one of these two men. As soon as Harry Pollok heard how White had given Ritchie a beating, he approached Freddie and asked:

"I know you are a good sport, Freddie, but are you a good gambler?"

Freddie replied that he thought he was and asked what was on his manager's mind.

"Are you willing to waste all your years of hard work for a good big chunk of money?" Pollok asked.

"Sure," replied Freddie, "if the chunk is big enough."

Pollok then showed Freddie a telegram he wanted to send to Ritchie. It read: "Promoters have called off match with you. Want us to meet White."

"Send it along," said Freddie, "I don't think he will call the bluff."

Freddie had spent several thousand dollars of his own money on the advertising, he had a chance at the title he had chased for years, now he was prepared to risk it all to try and cut down Ritchie's guarantee. But he knew his man. The next morning saw a telegram from the champion. "Call off nothing until I see you," was the message. The following day Ritchie accepted a $25,000 guarantee and $1,500 expense money. "That fight with White saved us almost $15,000," Freddie recalled, "quite some sum when one considers the game we were playing."

Just three days later Freddie was scheduled to appear in New York to fight another leading lightweight, Johnny Dundee. Freddie had narrowly beaten Dundee on New Year's Day 1914, but this time the local press expected the Welshman to lose. "From the general opinion gleaned from sporting circles, the Briton will run second,"

wrote the *New York Times*, "close followers of the game figuring that
Dundee has improved enough over his last fight with Welsh, when he
lost the shade decision, to take the British title-holder into camp."
The fight was to be the main event in a night of boxing to open the
Twyford Athletic Club at Ulmer Park, Brooklyn. But as the night
progressed it became obvious that the public wasn't that interested
and at 10.45 pm the management, after counting up the receipts,
found that the total taken was only $1,300. Freddie and Dundee had
been guaranteed $2,000 and $1,000 respectively and they insisted
upon receiving the full sum promised before entering the ring. Many
New York clubs were struggling to pay the attendants let alone the
fighters and the manager, Jimmy Twyford, was unwilling to incur the
loss by honouring the contract so he offered to give the two boxers
the total receipts to share between them. Both men refused and
Twyford was forced to call off the bout and offer a refund to the
patrons. An immediate rush to the box office followed and long
queues formed. It was well after midnight before the disgruntled
spectators got their money back by which time Freddie and Johnny
had long since left the building. In the aftermath, Billy Gibson,
manager of the Stadium Athletic Club, offered to stage the fight the
following week. Gibson told their respective managers that as the two
men had trained for the fight and were in good shape it was a great
opportunity for them to settle their differences in the ring. But once
again the price demanded by the boxers was too high. With no other
fights scheduled for either Freddie or Willie Ritchie, all that was left
to do was to sign up for the match and for the two men to book
passage across the Atlantic.

The provisional articles were finally signed in New York on June
9th 1914. Freddie wasn't at the ceremony so Pollok signed for him.
Ritchie set sail for England the following day on board the *Aquitania*
and landed in Fishguard on June 16th. It was his first visit to Europe
and the world champion was accompanied on the voyage by his
manager Emil Thiery and his brother Henry Steffens. "I am certainly
glad that the match did not fall through," Ritchie told reporters at the
dockside. "I was determined not to sail until every detail had been
arranged. Now I know just what to expect and have nothing to worry
about." Harry Pollok sailed for London on the same crossing.
Freddie cabled Fanny, who was pregnant and had stayed behind in
California, to follow him to England and he and Stanley set sail on
the Hamburg-American liner, *Imperator*. Freddie left in such a hurry
that as soon as he was on board he found that he'd stowed all his
boots in a big trunk in the hold. For the duration of the crossing and

Signing the articles. Standing: Harry Steffans (Ritchie's brother), Colin Bell, Bob Vernon. Seated: Freddie, C.B. Cochran, Willie Ritchie.

the landing in England he wore 'dancing pumps'. To while away the days on board Freddie tried his hand at writing poetry. But when he was asked a question about the correctness of his metre, he confessed that a friend implored him not to read his poems a second time. His verses were destroyed but some of his writing from this voyage survived, including a letter to the *Mirror of Life* and *Boxing*:

> At most times I am a vegetarian, and nature made me an optimist; this happy combination helps to make a sound body and a cheerful mind, but my seemingly fruitless pursuit of Trans-Atlantic title-holders had almost converted me into a pessimist. Hopes sprung up at different times that I would be given my wish of a contest with the champion, only to be badly crushed.
>
> I am now entering the final lap of a six years' race, and though the prize is always worth winning, it will be all the more welcome in my case, considering the many obstacles that have had to be surmounted in this most stubborn chase.

Freddie stepped from a first class compartment at Waterloo station shortly after eight o'clock on the night of June 12th 1914, having travelled by train from the docks in Southampton. He told reporters at the station that it had been a most agreeable passage and that news had reached him on board the *Imperator* that he had become a father for the first time. His wife had given birth to a baby girl, Elizabeth, "weight ten pounds at cribside". As soon as both were fit to travel they would follow Freddie across the Atlantic. That night the Welshman and his entourage stayed at the Waldorf Hotel in

23. Fanny, Freddie and baby Elizabeth.

London and took the 1.10 pm train the following day to Cardiff. Since leaving Wales on March 28th 1913 he had travelled over 50,000 miles and engaged in 22 contests and won them all.

The following week Welsh and Ritchie met at the Piccadilly Hotel in London to draw up final articles for the contest. Ritchie had been expected to argue about the referee and it was feared the champion would demand an American official, but he surprised all present and asked for Eugene Corri, the most popular referee in England. Corri was officiating at contests throughout London on a nightly basis in the summer of 1914 and whenever he stepped in the ring the spectators gave out a yell to which the referee responded by waving his hat "like a popular politician at convention time". The champion also agreed to weigh in according to the British regulations. For most of the meeting Freddie sat in almost disbelief at the straightforward nature of the negotiations. "I was going to kick because it never does any harm to object to the other fellow's terms," said Freddie afterwards, "and then Ritchie took my breath out by granting me the English lightweight limit of 9 stone 9lbs, weigh-in at 2 o'clock. That suits me – except that I didn't have a chance to enter a protest!" The

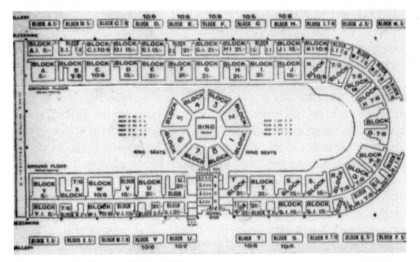

The floor plan for the Olympia Theatre.

only slight sticking point was the exact date of the contest. The provisional articles called for the fight to take place between July 4th and 11th. Freddie wanted the contest on a Saturday to enable the Welsh colliers to be present and C.B. Cochran asked for a few days to fix the date with the venue. The initial idea was to meet again the following day but Ritchie had accepted an invitation to go to Ascot for the horseracing and they eventually reconvened two days later to sign the contract. The fight was signed and sealed for July 7th at the Olympia Theatre, London.

Freddie returned to Cardiff for a few days before starting his training in earnest. He stayed with his uncle, Tom Williams, a retired Board of Trade inspector. Such was the interest in the fight back in Wales that it wasn't possible for Freddie to stay in the capital for long. He hoped for a quiet night at the Cardiff Empire theatre and he booked a lower box on the left-hand side of the stage for an evening performance. But as soon as he took his seat Freddie was spotted and there was a loud cheer from the crowd. A stream of limelight was turned on him and the orchestra played 'For He's A Jolly Good Fellow'. Freddie bowed in acknowledgement but there were loud calls for a speech and he had to respond: "My dear friends, it makes me very proud to have such an enthusiastic welcome home to Wales. I am not much good at speechmaking, but I hope you will receive me with as much enthusiasm after the 7th of July as you have tonight."

Later he was guest of honour for a special matinee performance at the Cardiff Cinema in aid of the Queen Alexandra Fund. Freddie used the event to talk about the prejudice, especially in Wales, against boxing. He attributed this sentiment to the traditional antipathy aroused by the brutality which, in the past, was not only associated with boxing but with other kinds of sport. He explained that just as fencing was now practised with protected foils, the boxer's weapons, his hands, were thickly padded, and those who took part had to lead an "abstentious and pure life". Freddie claimed the brutalities of boxing had been eliminated by the introduction of the Queensbury Rules to the point where even ladies were interested in the game.

With just a fortnight to go to the fight Freddie set up his training quarters in Porthcawl. He moved into a small villa named Canford on Victoria Road, just yards from the seashore. His sister Kate was in charge of the catering and his brother Stanley was the chauffeur, driving around in a new Buick that Freddie had bought as soon as he arrived in London. Freddie said it had been especially built for hill climbing and he would be touring the Welsh mountains after the Ritchie fight. He attached a brass plate to the car with the words "Freddie Welsh, Lightweight Champion" engraved on it. But on his first day of training, after the afternoon's gymnasium work was done, Stanley failed to show. Fearing a cold, Freddie swathed in towels, a rug and a dressing gown, made a rapid run through crowded streets with his entourage in tow. In his anxiety to "efface himself" Freddie made for a doorway but it was the wrong one. "A mother fainted,

Freddie and Stanley in the Buick, with Harry Marks' daughter in the back.

children screamed, while a father rushed upstairs for an old rifle, apparently fearing a foreign invasion," he recalled. Boyo Driscoll, his training partner, stammered out an explanation to the effect that they were in the wrong house in the nick of time.

The weather was so good during his fortnight at Porthcawl that Freddie had no trouble in making weight. Temperatures approaching ninety were recorded most days and he slept in the open air every night. Freddie covered eight miles on his morning runs but he was in such good condition that occasionally he would break this routine. One morning when he was out on the road, fully attired in training sweaters, he suddenly made a wild dash over the rocks and took a headlong plunge into the sea. Boyo Driscoll rushed in after him to persuade Freddie to come ashore. While being rubbed down on the beach, Freddie explained that he felt further sweating to be unnecessary and he had come to the conclusion that this was a far more pleasant termination to the run. His afternoons were spent sparring before the public at the Coliseum in Porthcawl and every afternoon queues stretching for several blocks formed outside the theatre. A story from Freddie's training camp claimed the sparring partners had gone on strike to demand that Freddie wear bigger gloves so that they wouldn't get hit so hard. To add to his general feeling of contentedness came the news that Fanny was on her way from America with his new baby daughter. The baby was born scarcely more than a fortnight prior to the contest, yet Fanny ventured to cross the water after a week's illness:

Much happier with baby. Getting stronger. Baby prettier daily – dark hair and dark eyes. Have written. Will start for England about end of June. Address letters Brooklyn. Love – FANNY

Freddie's final public appearance was staged on the Sunday before the contest with the proceeds going to the Porthcawl Rest. His most trusted sparring partner, Boyo Driscoll, had to sit out the exhibition after an accident at the beach that morning. Freddie and Boyo had been standing on the rocks looking out to sea when they were hit by a far bigger wave than they expected that cut off the two men from the land for a moment. Freddie escaped with nothing worse than a good shower, but Boyo was knocked over and was badly cut on the forearm. A suitable replacement was found to spar with the challenger and after twenty minutes of shadow boxing Freddie treated the crowd to a dozen rounds with Arthur Greenstock, Joe Beckett, Joey Smith and Arthur Evans. When the session was over he thanked the people of Porthcawl for the welcome they'd given him and he left them with a pre-fight message of guarded optimism: "I am as fit as the proverbial fiddle, and I hope to take to the ring at my very best. This is the contest I have had before my mind for the last nine years. Ever since I began to box professionally it has been with the aim of qualifying for the highest honours at my weight. All those who follow boxing will know how, time after time, I have been baulked in my desire. I have, therefore, left nothing undone now that my chance has come to gain my desire."

The following day journalists were allowed into Freddie's temporary home in Victoria Avenue, Porthcawl, but were respectfully told by his sister not to bother him too much. The visiting reporters arrived to see the boxer stretched out on a table he had especially made for his daily massages. Freddie was draped in towels while his sister doused his head with a sponge soaked in local seawater breaking occasionally to place small pieces of ice into her brother's mouth. Freddie was relaxed and talkative and it was certainly a happier camp than the champion's.

Ritchie trained for the fight in Brighton. American writers who visited him feared that Ritchie was carrying the telltale flush of a tuberculosis victim. The British boxing scribes didn't entertain the remotest possibility of the champion retaining his crown. *The Times* commented that Willie Ritchie justified George Bernard Shaw's description of the modern boxer as "by no means a knight errant of these latter days", and that he was in the main a painstaking and perplexed man of business who was anxious to make as much money as possible before he lost the power of drawing a crowd. Ritchie was so badly beaten in his last fight against Charley White the American boxing writers demanded he prove himself a bona fide champion by fighting a leading contender. The only two credible candidates were Charley White and Freddie Welsh and Ritchie chose the man who could offer him the most money.

The closer to the big fight, the more partisan the coverage became. It reached a crescendo on Independence Day. De Witt Van Court wrote in the *Los Angeles Times*:

> The Fourth of July is our greatest American holiday, the anniversary of when we broke loose form Johnny Bull, and from that time since, he has won little or nothing in the athletic line except rowing.
>
> English boxers have never won any kind of a world's title in the boxing game, but we have to hand it to them for trying and admire their gameness for developing fighters who are willing to try and take a chance.

It was certainly true that since the sport of boxing crossed the Atlantic in the nineteenth century the Americans had dominated the prizering. While men like Jim Driscoll and Joe Bowker had staked a claim to a title no Briton had been truly recognized as a world's boxing champion in the first decade and a half of the twentieth century. The last undisputed British world champion was Dick Burge who'd lost his title to the American George 'Kid' Lavigne in London in 1896. Freddie and Willie Ritchie were fighting for one of the two great titles in boxing, and the fight had taken on an even greater significance for a large faction of the American sporting public that believed it had already lost one of the titles to the 'negro race'. Jack Johnson had battered all the 'great white hopes' of the heavyweight division for the past six years and now Freddie Welsh was intent on annexing the lightweight crown for Britain.

It was said at the time that no boxing bout in the history of the sport had been billed like this contest. The promoters used the entire sides of large buildings to publicize it. On arriving in London one American journalist wrote that "as one would ride on top of a bus on the Strand, around Trafalgar Square, or skirting Hyde Park, no matter in which direction the eye turned, immense letters, world's championship battle, painted by expert sign painters, met your gaze... England is mad about the gentlemen of the mitt."

A great crowd assembled at the Cardiff Great Western Railway Station to see Freddie depart for London. The Welshman looked well, though a trifle concerned, and there was a slight bruise on the bridge of his nose due to the close attention of a sparring partner. It was a very long train and it moved out before half the party had realized. Freddie was absolutely the last man to scramble on board. Each member of his entourage sported an Alexandra Day rose. Freddie spent much of the journey reading, contributing very little to the scant conversation that occasionally broke the silence in the carriage. The train arrived on time at one o'clock but the crowds that gathered to welcome the challenger couldn't find him until he was spotted exiting from the rearmost carriage. A mighty cheer went up, reverberating from end to end of the huge station. Freddie greeted his friends, shook many hands and made what was a triumphal procession from the train to the waiting Buick, sent up a few days previously. As the car was driven through London groups of men recognized Freddie and there was "much raising of hats and hearty greetings". Freddie headed for the Waldorf Hotel before the weigh-in at the Olympia Theatre. By the time Freddie's car reached the arena the officials were forced to shut the gates to limit the admission to the hall to those who had tickets for the weigh-in. Most of the contingent that had travelled up from Wales didn't have one but their wait was not in vain and when Freddie arrived he persuaded the men at the door to let them in. Such was the interest in the fight back in Wales that special trains had been organised to carry the supporters. Two packed trains arrived in Paddington from Cardiff soon after dawn and every London-bound locomotive from Wales that day was pulling nearly twice the usual number of carriages. "So notable an occasion was it that hundreds of Welsh toilers were prepared to forego the excursion trains and pay for the more comfortable experience of travelling by day at the full fare," wrote the *Western Mail*. Little could these men have imagined that the next time the vast majority of them would leave Wales it would be for the trenches of the Somme, Verdun and Ypres.

The weigh-in took place in the Purces Room, a commodious chamber within thirty yards of the ring. When the clock struck two Freddie had not yet arrived while the champion was stripped to his underclothes and socks ready for the scales. Ritchie suggested they wait but there were cries of "time's up", and the champion mounted the scales. "He's just underweight," declared Arthur Wormald and immediately a cheer went up and Ritchie dressed. A mild protest was audible from the crowd that nobody representing Freddie was there to check the champion made the weight. "Well, it is his own fault," replied one of the champion's supporters and Ritchie did not weigh again. Two minutes later Freddie walked in. He shook hands with his opponent, and, stripped naked, took the scales and the verdict was announced that he was just a quarter of an ounce under the required weight. Another loud cheer went up and Freddie got dressed. The Welshman was an acknowledged expert on judging his weight. George Considine, the American sportsman who routinely accompanied Freddie to many of his fights was with him at the weigh-in. They walked into the Olympia together and Freddie handed Considine his big diamond ring just before stepping on the scales. Had Freddie kept the ring on he would have been overweight. It was a matter of comment that very few were prepared to bet on the contest. Boyo Driscoll offered to put 50 to 40 on Freddie to win on behalf of his man, but nobody present was prepared to take it up. After the ceremony Freddie went back to the Waldorf Hotel with his friends to relax before the fight. His wife and baby had landed in Fishguard on board the *Lusitania* at five o'clock that morning along with Bertha Weinstein, Fanny's sister. They were met by Stanley and so began the chase to get to London in time to watch Freddie fight for the title.

The Willie Ritchie – Freddie Welsh contest became *the* social event in London in the weeks leading up to the outbreak of war. The fight attracted a crowd in excess of 10,000 paying anything from 5s. to 10 guineas for a seat. The most novel aspect of the audience was the presence of a thousand ladies that according to one scribe "imparted the contest with the distinction never before known in the history of British boxing". For the most part they were ladies moving in high circles in London society. It was whispered that there were titled personages among them and that they were all attired à la mode, and lent to the great arena a grace and dignity more akin to a night at the opera. The *Western Mail* claimed "no contest which has ever taken place on English soil has brought together a larger aggregation of gentlemen in evening dress". It was, so far as the more expensive seats were concerned, a gathering of British aristocracy. Many of the peers of England who in a variety of ways had helped to foster and purify English sport were in the audience. Among those present were Lord Lonsdale of course, Lord Clonmell, Lord Tweedmouth, Lord Howard de Walden, the actress Ida Adams, known as the "million dollar show girl", the tenor John McCormack, and John Wanamaker Jr. The Welsh 'aristocracy' was also well represented. Lord Ninian Crichton-Stuart MP was a regular at Freddie's fights. He was joined by D.A. Thomas, one of Wales' richest and most powerful coal barons. The Welsh professional classes – doctors, barristers, solicitors and mining experts had turned up in their hundreds. A large American contingent had also made its way to the Olympia for the fight. One 'big American sportsman' was reported to have accepted £650 to £400 that Ritchie would win. American supporters included many theatrical people including William H. Crane, George Tyler, Charles Klein and Joseph Coyne. The Harvard and Union boat crews were in attendance and *The Sporting Life* commented that the connoisseur was much in evidence: "the men who reckon boxing as one of the great concerns of their lives were there in force". The fight was not scheduled to start until nine-thirty in the evening but the cheap seats were already filling up by five o'clock. Before the Welsh invasion Ritchie was the favourite in the betting, but such was the backing for Freddie from his supporters that by the time the fight started the odds had switched, with Freddie being the favourite at 7 to 4 on.

It was a quarter to ten when the master of ceremonies for the evening, Rev John Harvey Boudier, stepped into the ring in his clerical garb and got a good round of applause. Popularly known as Father Boudier, the burly clergyman was quite a character and was

well-known to many of the Welshmen in the crowd. He had been a
curate at St Mary's, Bute Street, Cardiff and also at St Anne's in the
Roath area of the city. During his time there Father Boudier established a temperance saloon in which he placed a large crucifix over
the bar. The venture was a big success. Father Boudier had a voice
that "would not disgrace a Thames pilot" and declined the use of the
megaphone. He announced in what the *New York Times* described as
"stentorian tones" the next fight on the card was the lightweight
championship of the world between the holder Willie Ritchie and his
challenger Freddie Welsh. He then introduced the promoter C.B.
Cochran to the crowd as the man who'd organized the contest. As the
impresario took his applause twenty great electric lamps blasted into
life for the benefit of the film cameras.

The fight had been scheduled to start on the stroke of nine-thirty
but Freddie wasn't even in the building by this time. A section of the
crowd got rather restive as five, ten and then twenty minutes went by.
Freddie apparently had a great deal of difficulty getting to the
Olympia Theatre because of the crowds. When he eventually arrived
at the hall he was already dressed for the fray and went straight from
his car into the arena and into the ring. By this time Willie Ritchie
had been sitting in his dressing room for nearly half an hour. It was
a little before ten o'clock when an enormous cheer greeted the
challenger as he made his way, draped in a rich silk gown and looking
rather grim-faced, into his corner. Then as the cheers died out a
strange hush descended on the arena. The silence was broken by a
quiet refrain of 'Hen Wlad Fy Nhadau' from a small section of the
crowd. The singing gradually grew louder as a "great volume of
trained voices sang" and Freddie stood up and turned to face the
crowd. Unplanned and unaccompanied a choir of several thousand
Welsh voices conjured a performance of "note perfect intensity".
Willie Ritchie sat in his dressing room throughout both verses and
choruses of the Welsh national anthem and a complete rendition of
'Sosban Fach'. Five minutes later the American ventured into the hall
and the preliminaries began. Both boxers were attended by a crowd
of seconds. Freddie's corner consisted of his brother Stanley, Boyo
Driscoll, Harry Marks, Arthur Evans, Victor Beckett and Billie
Baxter, while Ritchie also had a Welshman in his corner, Dai Roberts.
Ritchie wore a dark red and violet cloak and sported a plaster above
both eyes. His hands were heavily bandaged to protect his knuckles;
Freddie did not have nearly so much padding. Both men chose their
gloves and Ritchie's seconds smeared the lids of his eyes with red
ointment. Mrs Ritchie reached up and shook hands with her

husband; Mrs Welsh was yet to arrive. The referee tossed the coin for choice of corners. Freddie won, and kept the corner to which he'd originally entered.

The general opinion before the fight was that Freddie was the more skillful boxer whereas Ritchie had the harder punch and it took just thirty seconds of the opening round for Freddie to realize just how hard the champion could hit. Ritchie thudded his right hand onto a spot just over Freddie's heart, but the challenger simply smiled and then confounded the experts by opening up on the champion instead of settling in to his immaculate defensive style as predicted. As the bell sounded for the end of the first round Freddie walked to his corner sporting a broad grin. After three rounds of masterful boxing odds of 2 and even 3 to 1 on were being offered on the Welshman. By the end of the next round the odds had shortened even further. Freddie's boxing prompted huge cheers from the Welsh contingent in the crowd and he was given a standing ovation as the bell sounded for the end of the fourth. Freddie smiled back at them. "I think in that moment he could see the title almost within his grasp," wrote one ringside reporter. But Ritchie was a notoriously slow starter and his friends and supporters waited for the pattern of the fight to change. The champion seemed to pin all his hopes on landing the punch that made him famous and carried him to the title – an uppercut that had sent many an opponent to sleep. But every time he tried it Freddie had long since left the spot at which the punch was aimed. One writer compared the Welshman to the elusive Pimpernel of Baroness Orczy's novel. "Welsh was never there," he wrote, "and once or twice Ritchie nearly fell as the result of a mighty smite which found no greater resistance than the air it cut."

Ritchie did manage to get a hard right to Freddie's jaw in the sixth round and for the rest of that period the challenger was not so aggressive, and it was one of the very few rounds in the fight that was clearly the champion's. Other than the sixth and the thirteenth the rounds were very similar. Whenever Ritchie threw a lead he found the blows either blocked or avoided but when Freddie led his left hand almost always found its mark and as early as the third round the champion's lips were bleeding and he was cut under the right eye. As the contest wore on his face became more puffed. From the tenth round onwards, in spite of the protest of the officials, Ritchie's seconds were shouting words of encouragement to their man:

"He knows it's coming!"

"Fight him Willie."

"Push him off!"

The referee instructed them to be quiet to which Emil Thiery, Ritchie's manager, could only say: "Could anyone be quiet? Could you in my position?"

But still Ritchie was strong and Freddie could not afford to take chances. The champion's best round was the thirteenth during which he caught Freddie with three unanswered right hooks. Each shot caught the Welshman on the retreat however and the blows were largely robbed of their force. Later on in the fight Freddie became over-confident and fell into a right counter that shook him to his heels. He fell into a clinch to get some time to clear his head. It was a near thing and Freddie stayed away from Ritchie and kept the fight at long range until the bell sounded for the end of the round. After this scare the fight resumed its usual pattern. By the end of the sixteenth round everyone in the arena knew that only a stoppage would deprive Freddie of the championship. In the corner Emile Thiery was clearly heard telling his fighter this was his only hope of victory. In the seventeenth round one of Ritchie's wild swings not only missed the challenger but missed by such a distance that he got caught in the ropes trying to hit a target that had long since left. On another occasion a right hook failed to land on his opponent and hit referee Corri. In the last few rounds Freddie knew he had a big lead and was more cautious and watchful. All he had to do was stay on his

Another Ritchie right hook misses its intended target....

And Freddie ducks under another straight left.

feet for a few more minutes and he'd be champion of the world. There were a few uncomfortable periods for Freddie in the last three rounds but the man who even the American writers admitted to being the finest defensive boxer at any weight was not going to make any mistakes now. Freddie was heard to say to Ritchie: "You've lost the belt, old man, it's all over, the scrap is mine. Let's quit."

At the end of the seventeenth round a pair of empty seats at ringside were finally filled. Fanny and her sister had arrived at the Olympia as the fifth round began but didn't move to where Freddie could see them until near the end of the contest. They reached the front in time to see the best three minutes of the contest. From the opening of the twentieth until the closing bell the two fighters stood toe-to-toe and battled. At the end of the fight Freddie was cut above the left eye and had further cuts on his nose and lips. Ritchie's lips and eyes were also badly cut up at the final bell.

The cheer for Wales' first world boxing champion went up long before referee Corri announced the decision. The Welshmen in the crowd sang once more, and this time their rendition of 'Hen Wlad Fy'n Nhadau' was a victory song. Freddie described it as one of the three great moments in his life. The other two were listening to Ernestine Schumann Heink sing in an amphitheatre in the California hills and wiring his mother after winning the Lonsdale Belt. As soon as his gloved hand was raised Fanny was helped into the ring and husband and wife were reunited in a long embrace. Her first words to the new champion were: "Oh, Fred don't you want to see the baby?" She was followed into the ring by hundreds of other spectators as the referee, Ritchie and his seconds were all brushed aside by the crowds swarming around Freddie. Before he had the chance to take off his gloves the new world champion was lifted on the shoulders of the mob and carried through the auditorium to his dressing room. Freddie wasted no time in hurrying back to the Waldorf Hotel to see his daughter for the first time. From that day onwards Freddie always carried bundles of photographs of his baby in his pockets. "She is an eugenics baby," he would tell people, explaining that as both parents were athletes his baby girl was sure to grow up fit and strong.

After the fight the streets of Covent Garden were full of hymn-singing Welshmen celebrating a famous victory and a profitable evening. More than £500,000 is said to have changed hands in the betting after the fight. Sir John Courtis, Mr D.A. Thomas and other gentlemen in evening dress left the Olympia theatre to be jeered by throngs of Welsh supporters wrongly believing them to be Ritchie's backers. When one of the crowd shouted out: "What do you American millionaires think of it now?" The reply came, "Cymru am byth!" The *Western Mail* relayed the news to the people of Wales. It had a telephone at ringside from where round-by-round updates were dispatched. The newspaper made an announcement at Cardiff, Swansea, Newport, Merthyr, Pontypridd, Penygraig and various other towns across South Wales.

When the referee raised Freddie's hand at the end of the fight, Ritchie broke down in tears. One of the journalists who later saw Ritchie in his dressing room wrote the former champion had "his head dropped forward into his still gloved hands and he sobbed – sobbed the sobs of a still strong man who was as powerless to retrieve what had been lost as though he were shackled with the iron chains of materialism". Another wrote that Ritchie looked up at him with eyes that "looked just like some woman's with the agony of her own child's death in them". The American refused to talk to anyone until he'd left the arena and was back in his hotel room. When he'd composed himself Ritchie spoke to a journalist from the *New York Times* and appeared to have taken the verdict in good grace:

> I am defeated but not humbled. A good sportsman always wants the best man to win. Welsh earned the decision. I know I disappointed my friends, but I could not get going right. The strong arc light over the ring was too dazzling and I could not measure the distance. I never fought before under such a glare and it affected my judgement. My friends cannot feel the defeat more keenly than I do. I am sure I can beat Welsh. He did not hurt me with a single one of his blows. I can outpunch him, and the result will be different next time.

Eugene Corri later wrote in his autobiography *Gloves and the Man* that the fight was the greatest event in his career as referee. "I can see Ritchie now clenching his teeth as he strove to accomplish his object," wrote Corri. "When all was over the game young American accepted my decision without a murmur." The consensus of scoring around the ring gave Freddie ten rounds, Ritchie five with five even. The British writers gave Freddie an even bigger margin of victory, the Americans thought it closer. A special cable installation into the building allowed the American journalists present to wire updates directly back to their newspapers. The *Daily Telegraph*'s New York reporter wrote that every American ringside correspondent believed the Welshman had outclassed Ritchie.

Freddie spent the day after his victory in a suite at the Waldorf Hotel overlooking the Strand in London. The only sign betraying that he'd fought for the world championship the previous evening was a slight graze on the bridge of his nose. For most of the day telegrams and cables of congratulations arrived from around the world at a rate of over a hundred an hour. There were several offers to appear on the music hall stage and magazines and book publishers approached him to write about his exploits in the ring and his ideas on physical culture. There was an immediate call to present the champion with a belt or some other trophy which might be held by any British boxer who had accomplished some particularly notable feat, such as winning one of the world's championships. Lord Lonsdale was approached and expressed his cordial approval of the scheme and his willingness to assist. The *New York Evening Herald* remarked that

Daily Citizen, 9 July 1914

trying to calculate the amount of money Freddie would make through being champion, and the most popular champion England ever had, was enough to make one dizzy. But all this would have to wait a while because Freddie spent much of the following week getting drunk. Many years after his great victory Freddie told a boxing writer that after the fight he felt the need to relax. "The training and the scheming to get the champion in the ring against me had told on my nerves. Do you know what I did? I went out and kept 'lit up' for five days, and I felt better for it. I believe I added a number of fights to my career by doing it, and when I added fights I turned a good business deal. It was just like a good buyer getting more goods for his money."

Now suitably 'relaxed' Freddie decided that his first tour of duty as champion would be back in Wales. He told reporters that he won the title by being patient, silent and a stoic. "It's natural with us Welshmen to sit the thing out," Freddie remarked. "I'll never forget watching the men of my race squatting around, smoking their pipes. They're all miners. They're used to squatting down in the coalmines for hours at a time, with hardly room to move, picking away at the coal with short little backs. Then when they come up out of the mines after the day's work and want to rest they will sit quietly, each alone with his thoughts. I inherit that spirit and it was that alone that gave me the courage to wait patiently for my whirl as a world's champion."

During his tenure as champion Willie Ritchie had earned at least $100,000, mainly from the stage and the occasional no decision contest. This was the dilemma for any champion. The paying public would only tolerate a titleholder reaping the benefits of his status for a certain time before calls to take on credible challengers became impossible to resist. Ritchie had certainly reached this point by the time agreed to fight Freddie. What his friends and indeed the reporters who called on him to fight the Welshman couldn't understand was his decision to take the fight in England. It was seen as bad business. He'd been lured over the Atlantic by an enormous guarantee instead of staying in America to fight for less money but with a much better chance of retaining his title. One of the newspapers published in Ritchie's hometown, the *San Francisco Bulletin*, commented:

All we have to say is: "We told you so, Willie Ritchie." The champion made a bone-headed play, that's all. Had he remained in California and boxed Charley White, as so many of his friends wanted him to, he might have won. Then he could have gone over to England and handed over his belt to the marvellously fast but punchless Freddie Welsh.

The general result, of course, would have been no different. Freddie would have won the championship in the end.

When it came to settling the financial affairs a few days later it emerged that Freddie's gamble to reduce Ritchie's guarantee had been an unnecessary risk. The Welshman had agreed to take 50 per cent of whatever was left over after Ritchie had taken his guarantee of $25,000 and the expenses were deducted. It transpired that the gate didn't even cover these costs so Freddie was left with 50 per cent of nothing. He'd fought for no money at all for the first time in his career while Ritchie at least had the compensation of a small fortune to console him on his journey back across the Atlantic. The American cartoonist Rube Golberg wrote, "Ritchie was sorry to lose his title but there were a lot of lords present who would have changed their titles for Willie's share of the gate receipts." Freddie got his title; Ritchie got his money but the promoter C.B. Cochran ended up with nothing but a shortfall out of the whole venture. "I think that purses have gone as high as they can because I do not believe the public will pay more to see fights than they are paying now," said Cochran after the fight. "But understand me, this is all up to the public. If the men who want to see the fights are willing to pay guineas a seat to see a scrap instead of shillings I'll find them a pair of fighters who are as nearly worth guineas a seat as any two men can be."

He'd made very little money out of winning the fight, but Freddie knew how lucrative the title could be. While negotiating the contract for the Ritchie contest Freddie was already thinking well beyond the actual purse for his evening's endeavours. In 1914 the place that most people saw the big fights was on the cinema screen and the new champion made sure that he got a substantial percentage of every ticket sold. The day after the fight a sum of $13,000 was offered for the cinematograph rights in Australia, Canada and New Zealand alone. The first opportunity Wales had to see its new world champion fight was a showing of the film the following night at the Castle Cinema in Castle Street, Cardiff. Freddie decided to "till whatever ground" was presented to him. He determined to always be ready to fight in the belief that "every mickle makes a muckle".

One obvious way of making a lot of money very quickly was to give the former champion a rematch. The fight in London had generated huge interest in the United States especially as Ritchie and his manager were now claiming the American had been robbed of his title. Immediately after the fight Ritchie said Freddie had "earned the decision". The following day Ritchie claimed the worst he should have got was a draw. By the time he had arrived back on American soil the former champion was telling reporters he thought the referee had been swayed by the shouts of the crowd when the bout ended and he truly believed he won the fight. The hunted was now forced to use the language of the hunter. Freddie was the champion and he was the one who would dictate the terms for any possible rematch. Ritchie had made the Welshman chase him around America for nearly three years before agreeing to a contest and had unwittingly imposed the conditions upon which he could have a return match. Ritchie had forced Freddie to find him a $25,000 guarantee for the London fight. Now Freddie was going to ask the same of Ritchie. For this sum the new champion was prepared to fight the former champion in his home state of California, with a Californian referee, with the fight to take place six months after Ritchie had secured the finances.

On his return to America, Harry Pollok ensured the story of the fight remained in the news. He accused Ritchie of being able to "outshine Baron Munchausen" in his ability to tell exaggerated and fantastic tales. "Distance seems to have stretched Ritchie's imagination," said Pollok. "Immediately after the match he stated that 'the worst I should have had was a draw.' Now that he has planted his feet on American soil he says he 'won all the way'." Long before he won the title Freddie told friends he'd prefer to fight Ritchie in California than in London. He felt there wouldn't be a "holler about English prejudice" if he won the title in America. There had been an atmosphere of suspicion in American sporting circles since the match was announced. It was intimated that there was a "smart set of New Yorkers in London with plenty of money to invest if there was an 'ace in the hole'". The talk was that Ritchie's $25,000 was being guaranteed in whole or in part by Arnold Rothstein, who some years later became infamous as the man who fixed the World Series baseball final. In 1919 a group of players from the Chicago White Sox, the favourites to win the World Series that year, were paid by a group of professional gamblers to 'throw' the series to the Cincinnati Reds. The Chicago players performed so badly that after the second game Ring Lardner walked through their train compartment singing 'I'm Forever Throwing Ball Games'. The accepted wisdom is that Rothstein did not arrange the fix but knew about it and bet accordingly.

The full story of what happened before the Welsh – Ritchie fight only emerged a year after the event. In the summer of 1915 the sporting world was abuzz with rumours that the heavyweight championship fight between Jack Johnson and Jess Willard had been fixed. One afternoon, Freddie was part of a group discussing the many theories put forward as to why Johnson may have thrown the fight. Freddie listened to the conversation and then intervened: "Speaking of 'one of them things,' did you ever hear the true story of how I won the championship?"

A few days before the fight, Freddie's training schedule was disturbed by some extraordinary news from Harry Pollok. "So far everything had been running on the level," Freddie recalled. "I was

out to get the championship and all that we pulled was strictly legitimate. Pollok and I both looked at the matter in the same light." It was
to Freddie's great surprise therefore when Harry remarked that he
had turned down a fairly good proposition. Pollok never did any
business without consulting Freddie.

"Something of no importance?" Freddie enquired.

"I wouldn't say that," said Pollok, "in fact, it's the biggest thing
that ever came your way."

Pollok told of how a ring of London gamblers had offered him
£50,000, a quarter of a million American dollars, for Freddie to
throw the fight. The betting was 5 to 2 on Freddie at that point and
the gamblers could have cleared a fortune. "Fifty thousand pounds
is a mighty lot of money, but we neither could see it," said Freddie.
"My friends were tied up with me and I was after the championship.
We decided to go after the title and to this day I have never regretted
that the Welsh – Ritchie bout was not 'one of them things'."

After the contest the newspapers were satisfied "there was not an
atom of foundation for the rumours, for if ever two men tried to win
from each other Ritchie and Welsh are the two". But Willie Ritchie's
defeat to Freddie Welsh at the Olympia Theatre on July 7th 1914 did
leave a long term effect on boxing champions from the United States.
It would be another twelve years before an American defended a
world title on British soil. On January 12th 1926 the *New York Times*
reported that Mickey Walker, the then welterweight champion of the
world, was considering an approach to fight Tommy Milligan in
London that year. According to the newspaper the decision given to
Freddie over Ritchie was still disputed twelve years later. "Americans
who witnessed the match," the paper reported, "asserted Ritchie
clearly defeated Welsh on points." It became an accepted part of
American boxing folklore that Ritchie had been robbed of his title, yet
the day after the fight not a single newspaper questioned the verdict.

Freddie was scheduled to return to Cardiff on the 3.30 pm train
from Paddington on the Saturday after the fight. Tens of thousands
congregated around the railway station to welcome the champion
home, but Freddie very nearly missed his train, boarding the carriage
as it moved away from the platform. Freddie hadn't left the Waldorf
Hotel until 3.15 pm and arrived at the station with only two minutes
to spare. His family was safely installed in a carriage and Freddie
went to organize the luggage. The guard's whistle blew, and the train
began to move, but there was no sign of Freddie or the luggage. He
appeared at the end of the platform running alongside a porter and
a trolley of luggage. They reached the moving carriage door, threw

the cases on board and then Freddie took off after the train and managed to jump it. His experience as a hobo was still useful even now that he was world champion.

The train arrived in Cardiff at 6.36 pm and it was with great difficulty that Freddie's party reached their waiting cars. Someone from the crowd shouted, "Show us the baby, Fred," and Fanny raised Elizabeth, who was fast asleep, up for all to see. There was a "chorused approval" for the champion's daughter. They proceeded to Pontypridd and there were large crowds cheering him on in every village en route. Once the new world champion had reached the town of his birth he called on his aunt, Mrs Parry Thomas at the Bunch of Grapes Hotel. Freddie was then ushered over to the Clarence Theatre and introduced to the packed crowd. He also visited an old family friend, Mrs McKenzie of the Castle Hotel before making his way to Merthyr. The crowds increased in density as they drove up through the valley and as a result Freddie was very late for an exhibition he'd agreed to stage at the town's Drill Hall that evening. A huge concourse had blocked the traffic in Merthyr in anticipation of the world champion's arrival. When he eventually got to the hall wild cheers rang out and prior to boxing with Young Hatto, a local boy and former Welsh amateur champion, Freddie made a short speech. He spoke of his pride in bringing the title to Wales and of his plan to keep the championship for two years before retiring undefeated. When the exhibition was over Freddie took his friends to the Castle Hotel in Merthyr for a raucous celebration. A few days later, after he'd had time to reflect on the scale of his achievement, Freddie wrote, "I believe, or, rather, I hope in spite of all this, that I have learnt how to think a good deal less of myself than I did in those days, for I remember saying that after my long chase and the persistent side-stepping of Battling Nelson, I almost felt entitled to sign myself Fred Welsh, 'lightweight champion of the world'. You can understand, therefore, that I am glad to-day that I didn't, and that I am also glad that I have always refrained from doing so ever since, in spite of the fact that the first boxing club in the world, the National Sporting Club, of London, told me I was world champion two-years ago, when they presented me with a belt as evidence of their opinion."

But this was July 1914 and Europe was on the brink of an unprecedented catastrophe. Sam C. Austin, writing in New York's *National Police Gazette* speculated on what the future now held for the new champion:

Freddie Welsh will probably sidestep the glory of serving with the

British colours in the pending difficulty, and may soon be expected back in America, where the somewhat belated profits to be accrued from his championship victory over Willie Ritchie awaits him.

Freddie may be counted upon to tackle all the aspirants for the lightweight title if the money is in sight, but first he will put in a few weeks on the American stage. Then there will be three weeks or a month to get into shape after his easy life, so chances are it will be well along toward the spring before the new lightweight boss gets into action again.

In picking up the soft money before fighting again Freddie is only following precedent. Nelson, Wolgast, Jeffries, Corbett and a host of others grabbed off the footlight coin.

Twelve

From Roy Rogers to Gunboat Smith

It had taken nearly ten years of fighting and tens of thousands of miles of travelling and finally Freddie was back in Wales as champion of the world. But this was July 1914 and Europe was on an irreversible slide to a catastrophic conflict. Just twenty-five days after Freddie's victory, Germany declared war on Russia and the Great War began. The championship fight had been part of a great carnival of sport that Britain enjoyed in the summer of 1914 but the war ended the festivities. Eugene Corri later wrote that it was "as if the gods, feeling a little ashamed of what they had plotted, had decided to let their playthings have a half-holiday before the storm broke". The boxing boom, a major feature of this 'national playtime', was over. The young men who had flocked to see the big fights were now boxing themselves in training camps under the tuition of the professionals they'd paid to watch a few months earlier. Freddie's planned stage career, the traditional route for new champions to exploit their status, was curtailed. He appeared in Liverpool, Weston-Super-Mare, Aberdare, Ferndale and Tylorstown but when the war started he lost more than $50,000 in European music hall engagements alone. Freddie had planned to take a series of fights in Britain as the world champion but this was now out of the question. Within weeks of hostilities starting, his sister Kate went to war as a Red Cross nurse. Stanley was on one of the merchant ships sunk by the German cruiser *SMS Emden* and it was nearly a month before Freddie got word that his brother survived. Thanks to a manager on the White Star Line, Freddie, Fanny and Elizabeth obtained first class passage on board the *Olympic* at a time when dozens of millionaires were riding in steerage. The ship docked in New York on Friday August 28th and after a coat of naval grey paint, it made a high-speed run back to England. According to Bat Masterson, "the Champion was lucky to get back to this country before the English Government grabbed him and sent him to the front to aid in whipping the Germans. Welsh, if he could shoot with a rifle as he can with a boxing glove, would make a splendid soldier, and it is surprising that the English Government let him get away without giving him a chance to show what he could do with a gun."

Other leading American sportswriters went as far as to call Freddie a coward for returning to the United States after war had been declared. Freddie and Harry Pollok had had a public feud with Bob Edgren, the editor of 'The Best Sporting Page in New York' in

'What's the war in Europe when there's a fight like this coming?' – *Toledo Times*.

the *New York Evening World* since the night of Freddie's postponed
fight with Johnnie Dundee at Ulmer Park in May 1914. Edgren had
printed a story to the effect that the Welshman had tried to "stick the
club up", that he was afraid to fight Dundee and that he had not even
showed at the club. After the article appeared in the newspaper
several men came forward and said they'd seen Freddie in his dressing room stripped and ready to fight that night. When the error was
reported to Edgren he refused to publish a correction. Just a few days
later Freddie sailed to England for the Ritchie fight and the matter
was largely forgotten. However on Freddie's return Edgren not only
repeated the allegation of spinelessness on the night of the Dundee
fight but he also accused Freddie of cowardice in not enlisting in the
English army. After the article was published, Harry Pollok sent a
letter to several of the leading newspapers asking what Edgren was
doing when the Spanish-American war broke out. Pollok had found
that the war records failed to show Edgren's name among those
enlisted to serve their country.

Freddie was world lightweight champion at twenty-eight; an age at which champions in this weight division had come and gone, had their opportunities and made way. His first public performance on returning to the United States was at Hammerstein's Victoria Theatre in New York. He invited many of the city's leading sporting men to the opening performance. The new world champion gave a short talk on how he finally managed to corner the elusive Ritchie and then gave a demonstration of his training methods followed by a spotlight exhibition of shadow boxing. He wound up the evening with a wrestling challenge. Freddie was willing to wager anyone in the audience for any amount of money that he could keep them pinned to the ground for three seconds. Every night the biggest men in theatre would try and throw off the lightweight champion but to no avail. He performed at Hammerstein's for a week but Freddie had pledged not to become a "champion actor or an actor champion" and he was going to defend the title against all-comers. He had offers of fights from cities across the country. It seemed that nearly every lightweight in America, no matter what his reputation, issued a challenge to the new champion and the leading promoters got busy in an endeavour to secure his services. Jimmy Coffroth of San Francisco was the first to come forward with a substantial offer. As soon as Freddie's ship docked in New York, Coffroth sent a cable offering $50,000 for three fights. One of these contests was stipulated to be against Charley White, who had given Ritchie a beating before he'd lost to Freddie. White was considered by most American writers to be the boxer with the best chance of regaining the title for the United States. It was a particularly attractive offer because the money for the remaining two fights remained good even if Freddie lost his title in the first contest. But just as the war had closed down Europe as a venue for professional boxing, legislation was passed in California banning the sport in the state. On hearing the news Freddie commented that when they were handing out horseshoes somebody made a mistake and gave him the left hind shoe of a sick mule. "If it was raining rubies and diamonds I'd have cramps in both hands," he said.

When he started fighting the sport was in danger of being killed off by legislation in the United States. Boxing needed a period of rehabilitation and the boxers had to take the best they could – ten-round no decision contests – or have no boxing at all. These bouts had the effect of legalizing the game in several states where it had been an offence just a year or so previously. When Freddie became champion there were only two states in the union that allowed twenty-round bouts to a verdict, Colorado and Louisiana. The big fights held in these states were naturally held in Denver and New

Orleans respectively. Championship fights were also staged in war-ridden Mexico and Cuba. So when Freddie returned to the United States it didn't make business sense to risk his title unless there was a large guarantee available but no promoter in Denver, New Orleans, Juarez or Havana offered a purse that was worth risking the title for. Freddie held out for $25,000 because that was what the world champions before him had received for their services. Having waited so long for the opportunity he wasn't going to be pressurized into selling his crown cheaply. If he'd won the title in the days of the old Horton Law in New York which permitted twenty-round bouts instead of the days of the Frawley law then it would have been worth his while to take longer fights and a referee's decision. The city was big enough to support big events and ensure guarantees.

Freddie needed an alternative strategy for maximizing the financial benefits of being champion. With very few places able to hold championship fights his plan was to box every leading lightweight in the country in ten-round no decision contests, in which the referee was prohibited from giving a verdict. If Freddie was still on his feet at the end of ten rounds he would retain his title. These contests were not as lucrative as bona fide championship bouts over twenty rounds, but as the titleholder Freddie could pick up $5,000 on an almost weekly basis without being too concerned that anybody was capable of knocking him out. Only one championship had ever changed hands in such a bout: when Al McCoy knocked out George Chip in Brooklyn at middleweight. Freddie didn't mind too much if any boxer got a newspaper decision over him by this point; he'd fought for over eight years and won as many fights as he wanted and achieved his aim of winning the world title. Now it was about 'the coin'. On this basis Freddie named his price and let the promoters select an opponent. The only exception was Willie Ritchie. Freddie took what he admitted to be a "spiteful stand" against the former champion and to box him only on the condition that for doing so he would get what Ritchie demanded for the London fight.

Freddie knew that he wasn't destined to be a popular champion because light-hitting, clever fighters were not popular with American boxing fans. They much preferred their champions to be hard-punching brawlers like Battling Nelson and Ad Wolgast. These were fighters immensely proud of their physical dominance and were prepared to die in the ring rather than admit that another fighter could beat them. The American champions "strewed their paths with the prostrate carcasses" of the men they knocked out. It was a matter of pride to them that any man who would dare take their championship was carried out of the ring. Freddie was unconcerned about knocking anybody out and occasionally he deliberately avoided doing it. At this stage his aim was to make as much money as possible and he was largely indifferent as to what the customers thought of it. The contenders would continue challenging, Freddie would accommodate them all and the crowds always turned up in the hope that that the champion would be beaten. Freddie later wrote that the American audiences would sit up in the gallery and "yell for my downfall until they are blue in the face".

While Freddie was treading the boards Harry Pollok matched him with seven fighters in seven weeks. Before undertaking the campaign Freddie and his family travelled to East Aurora to visit his old friend Elbert Hubbard. When the time for resting was over Fanny and the baby stayed at the Roycroft estate while Freddie, accompanied by Pollok, travelled around the eastern seaboard to fight. "Show Welsh the kale and he'll box anybody from Roy Rogers to Gunboat Smith," commented one newspaper. While he was staying at East Aurora, Freddie repeated his intention to fight for a further two years before retiring as the undefeated champion. His plans to open a health farm on Hubbard's estate were well advanced but he needed to keep on fighting to raise the capital. He didn't demand a big guarantee for his appearance in the ring and took his chances on a percentage. Freddie knew he'd make more money in the long term because he'd get more bouts than if he waited around for big guarantees.

His first fight as champion was in Boston, Massachusetts, at the Atlas Athletic Club, on October 27th 1914, against Matty Baldwin. Freddie arrived in Boston on the day before the fight but there was no one to meet him and he got lost trying to find the hotel. His trunk had also been lost so he transformed his quarters at the Copley-Plaza Hotel into a gymnasium. Freddie moved all the furniture into the middle of the room and kept running round and round until he figured that he'd covered a distance of five miles. He wanted to set a precedent that he was not going to take "soft game", and Baldwin was a well-respected lightweight and the fight drew a good crowd. American boxing fans had read conflicting reports about his victory over Ritchie and a ban on the shipment of fight films had denied them the chance of making their own judgement on the contest. Freddie won ten of the twelve rounds against Baldwin and was given the decision. He impressed everyone in the hall and by the end of the night blood poured from four separate cuts on his opponent's face. Baldwin said he did not know of anyone in the country who stood much chance of wresting the belt away from Freddie. After the fight, the champion, accompanied by Harry Pollok and Bob Vernon, went straight to Boston's South Station and took the Owl Train bound for New York. He arrived unmarked after twelve rounds with Baldwin and was ready for a fight at Madison Square Garden with former champion Ad Wolgast in just one week's time. The promoter, Jimmy Johnson, claimed the war in Europe had now reached New York. Wolgast was born in Michigan of Dutch extraction and that was near enough to being German for the purposes of selling a fight. "Yes, it will come to pass that the war will be shifted to this scene of quietude and peacefulness," said Johnson. "T'will be some war, for Freddie is a bloomin' Englisher, while Adolph turns over to sleep softly murmuring 'Hoch the Kaiser'."

Ever since he lost the championship to Willie Ritchie on a foul in November 1912 Wolgast had claimed he was robbed of his title. When Freddie subsequently won the crown from Ritchie, Wolgast wrote of his pleasure in typically frank manner: "I don't care whether I ever fight any more or not, since the championship is back with the white race again. Ritchie is far from being a white man to do such dirty tricks as he has done...Welsh is a good fellow and a good fighter and I'm satisfied now to sit back and watch the other fellows fight him. I'll never demand a match with him, but would if the public wanted it." The public wanted it badly enough to ensure a near capacity crowd at the Garden. The prices ranged from $1 to $7 and nearly ten thousand New Yorkers paid up even though money was tight around the city. For Freddie the fight represented another opportunity to prove that he had been the best lightweight in the world for many years before finally becoming champion. He'd lost the opportunity to win the title when Wolgast was forced to pull out through illness three years previously and the man from Michigan had refused to give him another chance.

Altogether it was a typical night of boxing at Madison Square Garden. A canopy of cigar and cigarette smoke hung over the ring, there were women in men's clothes in the audience and a fistfight broke out in one of the ringside boxes. The women turned up in riding costumes over which they wore heavy automobile coats and they covered their heads with soft hats of the 'prevailing fashion'. They sat on the Fourth Avenue side of the Garden and the sharp eyes of the throng that packed the gallery detected their appearance in the arena at once. They were shown to their seats by a "rather shamefaced escort" to a chorus of catcalls and shouts. The crowd was with Wolgast and there was very little applause when, just after the first bell, Freddie threw four unanswered jabs onto his opponent's nose. It may have been a coincidence, but it was well publicized that after Wolgast lost the title to Ritchie, and in one of his phases of attempted retirement, the Michigan Wildcat tried cosmetic surgery. His flattened nose was reshaped by injecting it with paraffin. It was not a great success as one publication reported:

> The other day a pimple appeared on Ad's nose. It bothered him. He squeezed it. He kept on squeezing it. And when he finally finished, his nose sagged in the middle. All the paraffin had leaked out through that pimple.

Apart from the blows to Wolgast's deflated nose the first few rounds were fairly even and it looked on a few occasions that the old champion was hurting the new one with hard blows to the stomach. After the fight was over Freddie got a bit peeved when the press picked up on these punches. One writer suggested that it was Freddie's vegetarianism that was to blame and that "being grass fed, he was not in condition to stand the blows as well as if he had dallied with the festive roast a little". Freddie had always prided himself on being able to take harder blows to the stomach than any other boxer. After the opening exchanges Freddie was too fast and too strong for Wolgast. The definitive moment in the fight came towards the end of the fifth when Wolgast used his right arm to block an uppercut. The blow was enough to break his ulna three inches above the wrist. Wolgast fought on for a further three rounds in a futile attempt to hide the injury. He couldn't even close his right hand but he still occasionally threw it as part of the disguise. Each time Wolgast returned to his corner between rounds his seconds implored him to retire but he refused. As the eighth drew to a close Freddie smashed a right upper cut onto his opponent's jaw that sent the former champion into the ropes. With only one good hand to defend himself, Wolgast was battered with a flurry of blows and looked set to be knocked out just before the bell sounded. Wolgast finally realized the hopelessness of the situation. He turned to his corner and shook his head despondently. Wolgast slowly sat down and finally nodded consent to having the contest stopped. His cornermen cut the glove off his right hand and with tears streaming down his face the former champion protested that he would have knocked Freddie out. A big crowd rushed into the ring and surrounded Wolgast, while Freddie sat in his corner not realizing the fight was over.

Most of the reporters at ringside agreed that this was the best Freddie had ever fought in New York. Wolgast was one of the roughest, toughest and hardest hitting fighters in an American ring so

Freddie decided to beat him up. "He was Wolgast's master at all styles of fighting and boxing," wrote one ringside scribe. Freddie had become the first man to stop Wolgast but there were still plenty of column inches dedicated to Freddie's lack of a knockout punch. By this time he'd been fighting for nine years and there was a pronounced swelling above the knuckles on his right hand. It was an injury that followed him throughout his career and now that he was champion it could seriously damage his ability to cash in on his status. The wisdom of Freddie's more conservative approach to battering opponents was well illustrated by a cursory glance at the high points of Wolgast's medical resume: 1906 – left ear cauliflowered; 1907 – right ear cauliflowered; 1908 – bones in hands cracked; 1910 – broken arm and rib; 1911 – appendicitis; 1912 – bones in both hands broken; 1913 – ribs cracked; 1914 – two broken arms. If that was the price of popularity with the public Freddie wasn't prepared to pay.

He left New York the following day and travelled to Chicago to train for a fight with Charley White in Milwaukee. He worked at Harry Forbes' gymnasium for five days. Some of the fans that routinely turned up to watch him train were disappointed not to see the Welshman sparring because he was saving his right hand for the fight. All they got to see was Freddie shadow boxing, working the pulleys and performing his floor exercises. During the week Freddie and Fanny visited a loop café following a visit to the theatre. Freddie was seen to order grape juice highballs. When the waiter brought the drinks, Freddie, noticing all eyes on him, asked if it was pure Scotch. The waiter nodded yes and Fanny tested it to make sure it was not. The word was immediately passed around that Freddie was up until the wee small hours partying away drinking Scotch highballs, and every person in the café the following day reported that Freddie drank too much.

At the end of training in Chicago, Freddie's party moved on to Milwaukee for the fight. By this time the swelling in his hand had gone down and he was able to put on the gloves again for a few rounds of sparring. It was a return to the city where Freddie received his first significant purse for a fight. He graduated from the $50-a-night rank to the 'wind up' class when he fought Packey McFarland in Milwaukee in 1908. That fight was one of only two defeats on his record and it was widely predicted that Milwaukee would also be the scene of the third. The American boxing writers were convinced that Charley White would take the world championship title, and even gave White a great deal of credit for Freddie being champion. It was

White who gave Ritchie a beating over ten rounds in Milwaukee just weeks before Freddie fought him for the title. He was also the type of fighter Americans liked – a man with a 'jaw-breaking' punch and there was a real expectation that Charley White would be able to land one on Freddie. Such was the interest in the contest that Max Goldstein, a Milwaukee businessman, was prepared to lodge a $30,000 wager against the gate receipts. A leading real estate agent, Goldstein offered to give the promoter and the two boxers a certified cheque for this amount in return for the takings. Promoter Tom Andrews, Harry Pollok and Charley White's manager Nate Lewis met to discuss the offer and decided to turn it down.

When the boxers entered the arena Freddie got as warm a welcome as the local man. There was a thunderous clatter of flash-lights and then a panic. Two bags containing flash powder used for taking a picture of the crowd ignited and flamed up. A couple of Milwaukee's finest put out the flames and the fight was allowed to start. White soon regretted that the building hadn't been engulfed in fire. Freddie won the first eight rounds. His opponent was the leading challenger for his title but Freddie looked to be in a completely different class. White was totally baffled and his perform-ance was described as a "magnificent spectacle of wasted energy". The challenger didn't win a round until the ninth which he shaded on a few newspaper reports while others called it even. The tenth and final round was the best of the contest. Soon after the men left their corners there was a clash of heads that slashed a deep cut over Freddie's right eye. The champion stepped back and put a glove to his eye. When he brought it down it was stained deep crimson. The blood poured from the wound for the remainder of the round and all those sitting anywhere near the ring could see Freddie's flesh gaping out of the wound. The blood blinded the Welshman and he had to keep wiping away the fluid from his eye. White saw his opportunity. He tore at the champion, hooking and slashing away, but Freddie's defences were immaculate even with one eye. "Never before did Charley punch so many holes in space," wrote one ringside reporter. When the final bell sounded Freddie turned to his corner and smiled. White looked disconsolate as his second chance to become champion had slipped by.

Freddie had defeated the best American lightweight and barely lost a round. The champion, who was allegedly too old to be anywhere near his best according to the 'dope', was much fitter than his much younger challenger and he lasted the ten round pace much the better of the two. A few Chicago sportswriters, who for the previous week had been boosting the stock of their hometown fighter in the hope of influencing public opinion, maintained that White had held Freddie to a draw. All the other reporters at ringside dismissed these reports. By the time the fight started Freddie was the 2 to 1 on favourite so there was a great deal of money to be made if White was given the newspaper decision. The sports editor of the *Chicago Tribune* revealed that an attempt had been made by a bunch of 'sure thing' gamblers from the Windy City to bribe his writer to give White the decision. Many punters who had wagered on Freddie to win were robbed of their money through decisions given by certain sections of the Chicago press. Boxing was still illegal in Illinois at this time but there were moves afoot to have the ban lifted. "Far better that there be no boxing in that State if it is not to be more fairly conducted than the Chicago connection with the Milwaukee bout," wrote one commentator. One sports editor called it "the greatest scandal that has occurred in the boxing game in years", while a writer from New York concluded that "a lightweight who fights Charlie White, the Chicago boy, in Milwaukee has as much of a chance of securing the popular verdict over White as Kaiser Wilhelm has of being banqueted next Sunday by King George and Czar Nick". The only disappointment for Freddie was that the gate receipts amounted to $24,000 – they should have taken the businessman's wager.

After beating Charley White Freddie returned to Chicago for a three-night theatre engagement during which time his manager Harry Pollok was involved in a fight of his own. He was battling with the management of the Queensbury Athletic Club in Buffalo over terms for a match between Freddie and another leading lightweight, Jimmy Duffy. Duffy held a disputed newspaper decision over Freddie and there was an argument over whether the American fighter had knocked the Welshman to the canvas in that fight. Freddie maintained that it was a slip. In many ways Duffy's career mirrored that of Freddie's in always being a dangerous challenger that no champion wanted to risk his title against. Accordingly Freddie gave Duffy his first ever shot at being world champion. Harry Pollok said they'd take the fight on condition that the Buffalo club raise its normal admission prices to $2 for the cheap seats and $20 at ringside, with a sliding scale of prices between the best and worst tickets. These were the prices that the Milwaukee club raised for the White fight but the Buffalo matchmaker didn't think he could sell seats at these prices. Whereas the boxing starved populace of Chicago supported Milwaukee fights, Buffalo had no large city to call on for support. An easy compromise was found with seats being sold for $1.50 to $7 with Freddie getting a guarantee of $5,000 to sooth the deal.

Freddie trained at Elbert Hubbard's Roycroft estate in East Aurora and he travelled to Buffalo the day before the fight. Hubbard and around twenty of the Roycrofters turned up on the night to lend their support and Freddie continued his imperious form of late. Even in front of a partisan crowd that wildly cheered Duffy's every move Freddie was given the newspaper verdict by anything ranging from a round or two to a landslide. The world champion was completely unmarked at the end of the contest and even the cut that he sustained in the clash of heads with Charley White a week previously didn't bleed though it had yet to heal. Duffy was a mess at the end. His lips were split open and badly swollen. In the sixth round Freddie burst open one of Duffy's cauliflower ears and his nose bled for most of the fight. Freddie had fought four times in little more than three weeks and no world champion had ever been so busy. Even though they were sceptical about his status as champion and disliked his way of fighting the American boxing press was impressed at his business acumen. The influential *National Police Gazette* wrote:

> Judging from the busy little manner in which Freddie Welsh is meeting opponents, one is forced to accept the idea that opportunity has come his way and he's got brains enough to make it pay a premium. Instead of crawling into his shell and accepting only theatrical engagements, which, by-the-way, are never fraught with danger, he is throwing down the gauntlet to all aspiring contenders. Hand Welsh forty-five per cent of the gross receipts and he doesn't care a rap who his opponent is or who the promoter selects to pit against him. He asks no guarantees – unlike some of our modern champions – but is willing to gamble and take a chance. Thus far it has helped fill his coffers with gold.

The gamble was paying off. Over ten thousand people paid to see Freddie fight in Buffalo; before he won the title he wouldn't have attracted a tenth of them. It showed that the word 'champion' tacked to a boxer's name was a great financial asset. Freddie also used his title as a social asset. He and his family lived in glamorous apartments near Central Park and his friends now included the former American secretary of war, Senator Elihu Root, the playwright and theatrical producer David Belasco, founder of American Tobacco Company Thomas Fortune Ryan and Hudson Maxim, the inventor of the machine gun. This was not the company prizefighters usually kept and many of the sportswriters believed that Freddie was now harbouring ambitions way beyond his station as Donald O'Brien wrote in the *Los Angeles Times*:

Freddie Welsh is a young person who feels himself to be superior to his job. His manager is a somewhat older person who frankly and thoroughly despises boxing as a business. The result of which combination is that Mr Welsh is the worst failure of a lightweight champion who ever held the title.

Flattered by the society and companionship of these men, Freddie has but one idea, to be one of them. The world's championship means to him only the money and the increased glitter of fame that will make his position the surer among the men into whose circle of life he hopes to scramble.

In a few months, Freddie will make a face at the championship; poke his money in his pocket and the name of Fred Hall Thomas will go on the lists of some club and Freddie will begin the real fight of his life – to "break in".

Just five days after beating Jimmy Duffy in Buffalo, Freddie was in Boston putting his title on the line once again in a decision contest with local fighter Fred Yelle. He wasn't doing any real training by now and was staying fit by fighting. At the start of the ninth round, with both men in the centre of the ring, Freddie caught Yelle with a right hook to the jaw that laid the American flat on his back. Yelle got up after a count of eight but he was staggering. A few seconds later Freddie sent another right hook crushing onto the same spot. The American went straight down to the canvas and just about beat the count while Freddie was wincing in agony after feeling the bone in a knuckle crack. In his fifth fight in as many weeks Freddie's right hand finally failed. He fought the last three rounds with one hand and got the referee's decision. After the fight Freddie and Harry Pollok were keen to deny that there were any broken bones because Freddie had another two fights (and another $10,000) lined up within the next eight days. For the first of these he travelled to Syracuse for a ten-round bout with Young Brown of New York. Fighting with just his left hand, Freddie was far too good for his opponent and emerged with a victory, a few thousand dollars and no further damage to his injured right hand. Next it was back to New York to demonstrate once again his willingness to take on other boxers who, like himself, had been avoided by previous champions. It was also good business. Joe Shugrue of Jersey City was popular with New York fight crowds and the match guaranteed another healthy payday. An even bigger crowd turned up at Madison Square Garden for this title defence than had attended the Wolgast fight in November. But the fight was a disappointment.

The effects of his constant training and fighting told on the champion and he came very near to losing against Shugrue. He

New York Evening Globe, 27 November 1914.

entered the ring looking tired, pale and nervous, and still protecting the hand he'd broken in Boston. According to one ringside reporter, "Shugrue seemed to realize that the moment of his career had arrived". But the champion had designed a system of boxing that guaranteed him the maximum return for the title. He fought by throwing out lightening fast left hand jabs and then holding on to his opponent in a way that came in just within the limit of the rules. Without exactly holding on he kept his opponent's arms "spraddled out like the wings of a chicken on a very hot day". The referee couldn't disqualify Freddie for holding because he wasn't really holding his opponent even though the effect was the same. One writer commented that he kept his opponent's arms as "immobile as a trussed pig". For the entire ten rounds against a dangerous fighter like Joe Shugrue Freddie boxed largely with his left hand, using his right just for protection. Freddie's defences were impregnable and Shugrue failed to hurt the champion let alone deliver a knockout blow. The newspapers were split over the decision but most gave it to the Jersey City fighter. The general consensus was that it was a draw although a few writers awarded the fight to Freddie. What everybody agreed upon however was that Freddie needed a rest. He was due to box again in Grand Rapids, Michigan, later that week, but Freddie took his doctor's advice and rested. By the time he stowed away his share of the receipts for the bout with Young Shugrue it brought his earnings for five weeks to more than $50,000. Freddie fought more men in thirty-five days than the previous champion, Willie Ritchie, had boxed during his two and a half year tenure. No world champion in any division had ever fought that many men in the same period of time. "He will find himself supreme in his class," wrote one American journalist, "but with little honour." Freddie had devised a new and novel method to capitalize on his title. He gave every credible boxer in America a chance to fight him, at the right price, knowing all that was required to retain his crown was to be standing at the final bell. It was certainly a different approach from his predecessor: Willie Ritchie believed in fighting as few times as possible and getting as much as he could for each bout. Ritchie's idea was to make the appearance of the lightweight champion an important occasion and demanded at least two or three times more money per fight than Freddie was asking. The *National Police Gazette* thought Freddie's idea a masterstroke:

> As Welsh has started out to do a two-a-day act his profits in the long run are bound to exceed those of Ritchie by many thousands of dollars. There is not one chance in a thousand that Welsh will ever lose his title in a ten round bout in which the referee's decision is not given.

Ten-round bouts without a decision are meat for a boxer of the Welsh type. He is a splendid ring general, a wonderful defensive boxer, and entirely too wise to take any chances.

In taking on the very best challengers so regularly, many of them young fighters who'd had time to prepare for the fight, it was inevitable that Freddie would lose the popular decision in many fights. From the outset he was resigned to the challenger taking the newspaper honours: what the champion wanted was the 'coin'. Boxing for the glory of it ended for Freddie on the night he took the title from Ritchie. He won the championship at the worst possible time – the Great War was underway and times were hard. Anything he did had to be done quickly and as often as possible. He had to hustle. If he got stale doing it, that was just an occupational hazard. "I'm horribly sick and tired of fighting," wrote Freddie as 1914 came to an end, "you don't know how I loathe it all." He'd been obsessed with becoming world champion for nine years and after he'd achieved it boxing became just a business for him, and an unpleasant one at that. The art had gone and all he saw now was the brutality.

Thirteen

Kill that Englishman!

Freddie, Fanny and Elizabeth spent the festive season of 1914 in their New York apartments. Freddie was celebrating his first Christmas as a father and as the world lightweight champion. It was everything he'd always strived for, always fought for, but he felt tired and jaded. When he was a contender in the ranks he had a host of American 'friends' always boosting for him. They wanted to see him win. Once he won the title all Freddie heard from ringside were shouts of derision. He had started the year believing that if he became world champion it would lead to a life of untold riches and happiness. As 1914 drew to a close Freddie was left feeling disillusioned and contemplative. He spent much of his time reading Ibsen and Maeterlinck alone in his library and he wrote of his own belief that in the end "everything comes back to one".

Others may believe that man is a spirit with an immortal destiny, or may believe that he is a bacillus germinated in the cultures of decaying planets, or may believe that man is a speck of some cosmic consciousness, entangled for an instant in a grain of matter, like a portion of air enclosed in a film of water bubbles below a fall – or people may decline the question. No matter what they believe, at some period in their lives they will find it difficult to dissent from the conclusion that there is abound in the universe a power not ourselves which makes for righteousness.

When the holiday season ended Freddie returned to the business of being world champion. He attended the annual reception and ball of the Avonia Athletic Club at the Manhattan Casino. During the ball the stars of the prize ring were introduced to club members when, as promised by the billing, "for one night in the year at least, thoughts of ring contests are replaced by an evening of jollity, with dancing as a most important feature". Freddie socialized with many of the men who either had or would fight him for his title; Kid Williams, Joe Shugrue, Ad Wolgast, Johnny Dundee and Leach Cross.

Freddie planned to end his enforced absence from the ring with a ten-round fight against Charley White at Madison Square Garden on January 26th 1915. He was quartered at Jim Donovan's Park Hotel at Oceanport, New Jersey, to try to get back into shape following the lay-off. Donovan was an old-time boxer from Ireland who Freddie met when he first arrived as a teenager in the United States.

The Irishman had long retired from the ring and had settled on New Jersey's Atlantic coastline. Having the world lightweight champion visit was a big event in the town and nearly all of Oceanport was present when Freddie opened up his training camp. A constant stream of cars and tractors arrived at Donovan's and when Freddie and his sparring partners came into the gym on their first afternoon in Oceanport the crowd was lined up two deep against the walls. But just as the champion was about to start boxing the lights in the gymnasium failed. So Freddie, with his team and the entire crowd in tow, walked across the street and took over a bar room. All the tables and chairs were cleared to the side and Freddie boxed ten rounds against three different opponents, finishing off with 'One-Round' Hogan. One of the scribes invited to watch him train wrote of Freddie as "a very obliging chap and impresses one as being more of a scholar than a boxer," adding that he "would sooner answer a question than speak first".

The clean air of Oceanport was having the required effect and Freddie soon recovered from his staleness. The New Jersey seaport town provided the sort of environment he loved to train in. Most of his work was done outdoors and he banned anyone from smoking at his camp. He woke up at nine every morning and breakfasted on prunes and a glass of sugarless lemonade. The day's training began with an exercise routine on his unique system of pulleys and weights. This was followed by a series of floor movements intended to work every muscle. Next came twenty minutes of breathing exercises during which Freddie opened the door of the gymnasium to take in a deep breath of sea air. With arms folded behind him, he violently threw his upper body forward until his head nearly hit his knees. He maintained that the thrust forced oxygen into all parts of the lungs. He moved onto a twenty-minute shadow boxing session. He threw countless left jabs for five minutes followed by right uppercuts for the same duration. For the next ten minutes he threw all the different punches in his repertoire in a variety of combinations. His punching routine ended with several rounds of hitting the heavy bag, at which point the training partners were called together for a road run. They ran for fifty minutes, Freddie taking one deep breath every hundred yards and holding it for as long as possible before exhaling. On his return to camp Freddie was wrapped in blankets to continue sweating before taking a hot bath followed by a cold shower and a massage. He ate no lunch but rested for an hour or so, reading and writing letters. With the day's correspondence completed, Freddie strolled around the farm with his dog Nellie. Along the way the world

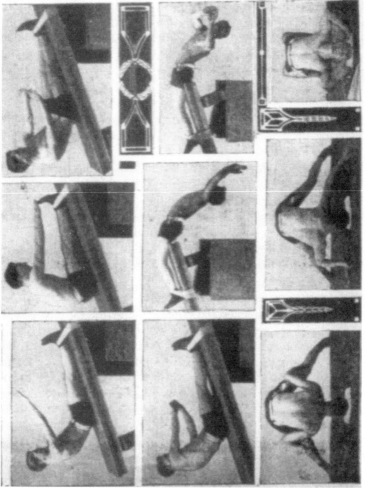

Freddie's 'patent' abdominal and neck-strengthening exercises.

champion helped out on a local farm, chopping and sawing wood, feeding the chickens, cows and horses, and carrying logs back to the farmhouse. At four o'clock sharp, every afternoon, Freddie was back in his boxing togs ready to take on all four of his sparring partners in succession. A final rubdown completed the day's work. Supper consisted of three eggs, a glass of tea and, if he was particularly hungry, a few oysters. One afternoon Freddie invited a few of his New York friends to join him on the farm and he drove to the railway station to collect them. With not enough room for everybody in the car he gave the vehicle to his friends while he ran the two miles back to camp. He beat the car by several minutes.

Freddie also found time to become a local hero in Oceanport, although in truth he nearly destroyed the entire town. He was dining in the hotel one evening when he heard the crackling of burning wood, preceded by the smell of smoke. Freddie ran upstairs to rescue Nellie and her six puppies. The smoke was pouring out of the upstairs room he'd been using for a gymnasium. Freddie opened the door to find that a bottle of inflammable rubdown fluid had been left too near a hot stove and had exploded, setting fire to the walls. He picked up a big rug and began to smother the flames. When he had them under control he dowsed them with a few buckets of water from the nearby showers. His host, Jim Donovan, was so thankful that he ordered a banquet in Freddie's honour. Donovan had just spent a small fortune renovating the hotel. At the dinner, Freddie was presented with a diamond horseshoe pin and was made an honourary member of the Oceanport fire department and was given a red shirt and helmet. According to one report "the lightweight champion extinguished a conflagration that threatened the whole town", adding that "after a strenuous half an hour's work Welsh and his assistants had the fire safely under control".

While Freddie was rejuvenated in Oceanport, all was not well at Charley White's New York camp. Two days before the fight rumours began to circulate that the Chicago boxer was sick in bed with a high fever. White's manager issued a statement that his fighter was in good health and had left his hotel room for a stroll. Yet less than two hours later, Jimmy Johnson, matchmaker of the Garden Athletic Club, announced the fight had been cancelled as White was suffering from a severe attack of the grip. Threatened with pneumonia and a number of other complications, White was confined to his bed with two doctors in constant attendance. Freddie wasn't told of the postponement by the promoters and was informed of his opponent's illness by a local newspaper reporter. It was a disaster for the Garden Athletic

Club with thousands of tickets for the show already sold. Jimmy
Johnston tried to get Johnny Dundee or Leach Cross to substitute for
White, but they declined to take on Freddie at such short notice. On
the morning of the event the club finally turned to one lightweight
who was always ready for a fight, Willie Beecher, the protégé of well-
known crime boss John 'the Barber' Reisler. Beecher was in good
shape because he was in training for another fight and relished the
chance to fight the world champion. He was regarded as a good, old-
fashioned, rib-tearing brawler, which made him very popular with
New York fight fans. It had been Beecher's long held ambition to fight
Freddie and now he was a knockout punch away from becoming
world champion, at least in theory. Beecher entered the ring with his
body smeared in olive oil, which dries into the skin at first but when
the perspiration begins to flow it makes the skin very greasy and
slipping in and out of clinches becomes much easier. Beecher
wrongly figured that Freddie would try and hold him and fight defen-
sively. But in a very bad-tempered fight Freddie decided to batter his
opponent without mercy. The American rushed out of his corner in
the first round and tried desperately to throw the one big punch that
could make him world champion. Freddie watched the wild swings go
by and then nailed Beecher on the jaw. It was the start of a terrible
beating for the substitute and confirmation that the rest had done
Freddie a great deal of good. For much of the second half of the fight
Beecher's blows were all below the belt and it looked to the crowd that
the American was trying to get disqualified. After the fight the referee
Billy Roche remarked that it had been a very impolite battle. "They
were calling each other a lot of pert names that wouldn't look good in
print," said Roche. "When Beecher, unintentionally or otherwise, hit
Welsh low a couple of times Welsh said, "Stop that you ___ ___, or
I'll knock your chin off." "Go ahead you English this and that, you
couldn't knock anybody's chin off," replied Beecher.

Buoyed by his return to full fitness Freddie instructed Harry
Pollok to line up another gruelling series of fights. The contenders
continued to challenge and Freddie continued to accommodate
them. Next came Johnny Griffiths in Akron, Ohio. The fight was
staged just five nights after his defeat of Willie Beecher and established the pattern for much of his term as champion. To ensure the
biggest possible gate Freddie travelled to the hometown of the
challenger. The fights were reported by local writers who'd always
give the decision to 'their' man. These stories were wired to newspaper desks across the country for boxing fans to read about the
champion's latest 'defeat'. In the dozens of fights that Freddie fought

as champion the headlines and introduction to a story would report that the Welshman had been beaten while the detailed description of the fight contradicted this impression. Freddie hardly took a blow in twelve rounds against Griffiths yet the local press gave the local boy the decision. But by this point in his career Freddie barely stayed in a town long enough to read the following day's press. "Griffiths was a youngster. He was fighting before his friends, and they were naturally carried away with his efforts," said Freddie after the fight; he was not without sympathy for his opponent. "I'd rather be the champion of the world being panned than an aspirant for the honours being boosted. I served my time in that boosters club, nine or ten years of it, and I know just how Griffiths felt about it."

Ring Lardner, one of the most famous writers in America at the time, often dropped Freddie's name into his work, both fiction and non-fiction. Lardner saw Freddie box many times and was present at several fights the champion was alleged to have lost. When reports of Freddie's 'defeats' began mounting up Lardner penned a satire of the champion's treatment by the press:

It's Getting To Be A Habit

HOME TOWN, Ohio. Feb 2
(Special). – Joe Smith of this city made a monkey of Freddie Welsh, lightweight champion, in a twenty round bout here tonight. The Home Town critics were unanimous in awarding the decision to Smith after one of the most one-sided fights ever seen here. The local miller had the better of the ninth, first, fourth, third, sixth, eleventh, twelfth, second, eighth, and fifth rounds. The seventh and tenth were even, and Welsh won the rest.

Smith came within an ace of de-throning the champ in the third with a clean knockout. He started a hard left swing for Freddie's jaw, but Welsh blocked it. If that blow had ever landed, etc.

So dazzling was Joe's display of boxing skill that Welsh never got started till the first round. Then he tried desperately to make a showing that would offset Smith's earlier advantage, but it was too late.

In the second Freddie was unable to do anything but beat a tattoo on Joe's kidneys. On the other hand, Smith paid no attention to Welsh's body and tried only for the face. It is estimated that he would have landed four blows to the champion's one but for the latter's ducking, which was evidence that Freddie did not care to take the chance of having his block knocked off. If Joe had been able to land even once in this session it would have been all over with Freddie.

The third was Smith's best round. Aside from just missing with a knockout punch he clearly outsprinted Freddie from gong to gong. The fourth was also Smith's best round. So was the sixth. The fifth was

32. *New York Evening Sun*, 19 November 1915.

even, with Smith having a slight shade.

Joe got really busy in the seventh and punished Welsh severely with a series of jabs on the ulna and radius bones. The eighth was even. Welsh closing both of Smith's eyes, and, in return, receiving three straight lefts that started a flow of crimson from his gloves. As the boys came together at the start of the ninth the crowd was yelling loudly for Joe to finish the Britisher, but Smith had forgotten to bring his shotgun.

The tenth was even. Welsh being outpointed by only the narrowest of margins. The eleventh and the twelfth were about even, as were the ten preceding rounds.

It must be admitted that Welsh did all the landing and most of the landing, but Smith's punches had more steam, and would have done twice as much damage if they hadn't missed. Smith would have won by a wider margin if he hadn't been tired from the first round on. The killing pace began to tell on him in Round One, and he wasn't as effective thereafter.

When the bout was over Smith showed no marks except that two of his eyes were discoloured and closed, one of his noses was broken, his left and right ears were puffed, and thirty-two of his teeth were missing. Welsh was unmarked, but probably was injured internally.

This is the champion's eleventh defeat in his last twelfth battles. The twelfth was a draw.

He is still the champion.

Freddie returned to New York from Akron in good condition for the following week's bout with Joe Shugrue at Madison Square Garden. In the build-up to the fight, Pete Fitzgerald, Shugrue's manager, challenged Freddie to a championship match wherever such a contest was legal. Fitzgerald said he would post a $5,000 forfeit as a guarantee to make any weight Freddie may name, and another $5,000 as a side bet. Shugrue had been trying to beat all the other claimants to a title fight just as Freddie had done. Fitzgerald and Shugrue were in exactly the same position as Freddie and Pollok had been for so many years and $5,000 was certainly not going to be enough to entice the Welshman to risk his title. So Shugrue had to settle for another ten-round contest and the chance of knocking out the champion to take the title. Their first fight just over a month earlier had certainly whetted the public's appetite for the return. Shugrue had won but it was obvious that Freddie fought with just one hand and still managed to hold off one of the leading contenders for his title. It ensured another big crowd at the Garden for the return and another big payday for the world champion. Interest in this fight received a further boost when the gangster John Reisler decided to sue the Athletic Association in the Supreme Court of New York City for barring him from the bout.

Jimmy Johnston, the matchmaker at the Garden Athletic Club, responded to Fitzgerald's criticism of Freddie's holding tactics in the first bout by announcing he would enforce an 'anti-clinching' rule. Referee Billy Roche was told not to tolerate any holding or rough work and to disqualify the first man to break the rules. A disqualification would cost Freddie his title. Before the fight the Welshman used his status as champion to impose a concession of his own. He persuaded Johnston to establish a new rule at the Garden banning spectators from smoking during the main bout. Freddie complained that during recent bouts there the smoke impaired his boxing. Some spectators had complained that the smoke was so dense it had become difficult to see the ring from the gallery and balcony.

The boxing press in New York expected nothing less than a repeat victory for Shugrue over a boxer well past his best. The *New York*

Times, however, sounded a warning for Shugrue. "Welsh never boxes a man twice in the same way, and the generalship which he may employ Tuesday night may be something that will cause bewilderment to the Jersey lightweight. Shugrue on the other hand, will be more of an open book to the Briton." The *New York Times* called the fight exactly right. It was another defensive masterclass from Freddie and even though the newspaper verdict went to Shugrue, the challenger rarely laid a glove on the champion and there was never any danger of the title changing hands. The American press was now openly hostile to Freddie and his determination to hold onto the title. "The ten-round game as played by Freddie is as safe as betting on the toss of a coin with two heads," commented one writer having seen another highly lauded aspirant for the title fail in his quest.

The following day Freddie, Fanny, Griff Davies and Harry Pollok left New York and headed west to Grand Rapids, Missouri, for a fight with local favourite Jimmy Anderson. After taking a total of two punches from his opponent and landing several hundred, the champion and his party took off for Chicago to prepare for another fight with Charley White. They were joined in the Windy City by former champion Willie Ritchie. Since losing his title Ritchie had developed a vaudeville act with his sister Josephine entitled 'From the Ballroom to the Gymnasium'. It was a hit and broke all records at the Empress Theatre in San Francisco. He had had offers to take the show to Chicago and New York but rejected both to win his title back from Freddie. Ritchie had failed to get a promoter to come up with a big enough offer to lure Freddie into a twenty-round championship fight so he agreed instead to fight the Welshman in a ten-round no decision contest at Madison Square Garden. Ritchie's plan was to give Freddie such a beating that the champion would be forced to take a lower offer to defend the title in a long contest. To promote the upcoming matches Freddie, Charley White and Willie Ritchie met up at the offices of the *Chicago Herald*. Freddie forgot about the meeting and had to be telephoned at the gymnasium to be reminded. He dropped his work, rushed through a bath and chartered a taxi. He arrived "dressed in the height of fashion", shook first White's hand and then Ritchie's and complimented both on their looks. The photographer prepared the poses while the world's three leading lightweights gossiped. Freddie was anxious to talk to Ritchie about dancing: "You know I'm interested in the fancy steps myself and I have been following your work. Your write-ups have been simply wonderful and before you leave town I want you to show me a few new steps I have not yet learned. What do you think of dancing as a conditioner?"

WILLIE RITCHIE   FREDDIE WELSH   CHARLIE WHITE

'The race for the title' – caption suggested by Freddie to the *Chicago Sunday Record*, 28 February 1915.

Ritchie spent some time explaining how much time it had taken him to master the new glides and how it was harder work than training for a boxing match. The former champion said he was preparing for a long theatrical career after he finished boxing and that he'd already become part owner of a hat-making factory in San Francisco. The conversation turned to Charley White's car and then Freddie's clothes. "You know I'm having a deuce of a time getting shirts from

Paris," Freddie moaned. "I have a friend over there who looks after my haberdashery and my last order has been delayed. I suppose the war had something to do with it. How do you like these Paris dress shirts?" he asked the other two.

Boxing was banned in Chicago at this time so Freddie, Charley White, their respective entourages and the crowds had to go to Milwaukee for the second contest between the champion and his most obvious challenger. This was a time when boxing really was a hard game. In Milwaukee, a policeman sat in every corner and if a second or a handler let out a peep he'd be marched out of the building. For Freddie it was the first in a series of fights that would see him box all the leading lightweights and make a lot of money in a very short space of time. It was the first time he'd agreed to make the lightweight limit since becoming champion. He was nearly thirty years old by now and the strain of making 133lbs was telling. But he'd made a special effort for this fight because of the publicity following his last encounter with White. This time he wanted to make sure the Chicago man didn't win a round. Once again the leading scribes were predicting the championship would change hands by knockout. Once again they were disappointed. Freddie was back to his best and far too good for the man considered to be America's leading lightweight. In the ten-round no decision contest, Freddie was adjudged the winner by the unanimous opinion of the ringside sportswriters. Even Chicago ringside reporters were forced to admit "that Welsh is far superior to White seems beyond argument now". Before the bout was half-over the crowd that had been hollering for White was cheering Freddie and laughing at the challenger's efforts to hit him. Freddie appeared to take the bout as a joke and he came back to his corner after each round with a smile on his face. In the fifth, when White actually managed to land a punch, Freddie looked over to Harry Pollok, smiled, and shook his head. He had humiliated the heir apparent to his title.

The bout with Willie Ritchie was set for Madison Square Garden a couple of weeks later so Freddie returned to the sea air of Oceanport on the New Jersey shore. He let it be known that he was in the best possible condition following a daily schedule of boxing, running and bag punching. But during this spell in Oceanport he spent more time preparing for retirement than for Ritchie. By now Freddie hated the grind of training and he and Fanny made several trips to Long Island to look at property that was on the market for around $75,000 and was suitable for conversion into a health farm. When boxing was legal in California they used to divide their time

Elizabeth and Freddie Jr.

between their cottage by the beach in Venice, Los Angeles and the apartments at the St Paul Hotel in New York. Since the Pacific Coast closed for business Freddie and Fanny were compelled to spend more time in Manhattan and they were tiring of city life. Mr and Mrs Welsh had met each other at Macfadden's Institute of Physical Culture and both remained staunch advocates of the doctrine taught there. Now they had baby Elizabeth to consider it was time to move to the country. "There is nothing finer for babies than a ride in a park, where they can enjoy the bracing air and the warmth of the sun's rays," declared Fanny. "It's not half as hard as some people imagine to bring up children healthy, respectful and ideal in every respect. I would advise mothers to do what I have already accomplished – healthy babies and holding aloof doctors, who prescribe foolish medicines and break you financially if you allow them to." Freddie felt that a change of environment would help him regain an appetite for boxing once more.

Before his title fight with Ritchie in London eight months earlier Freddie was trained to perfection. He was honed to his best fighting weight, his reactions were razor-sharp and his body was hardened to take any blow. Freddie was the hunter who'd stalked Willie Ritchie until he ripped away his title. This time he was the quarry. "A champion has a continual worry on his mind, something I am free from now," Ritchie told reporters. "I have forgotten all about my fight in London and am like a kid with a new toy, anxious to get the gloves on again." The contest between the world champion and the man whose title he took was a major event in New York. The management of Madison Square Garden spent an extra $1,000 to print counterfeit-proof tickets, such was the demand for seats. Boxing fans poured in from Philadelphia, Boston and other cities across the Eastern Seaboard. There was a general feeling that the Californian had a much better chance to win than he'd had in London. There Freddie had been familiar with the English rules and methods of conducting a bout, and had the home crowd. He had all to gain and nothing to lose; but now the positions were reversed.

The crowd at the Garden filled every seat and overflowed into the aisles and passages at either end of the building. Freddie had trained very badly for the fight and Ritchie tore at him from the sound of the first bell in a frenzied effort to get the all important knockout. But Freddie was too clever to be cornered, and was content to duck or sidestep out of harm's way. He'd decided to take no chances whatsoever against the man he considered to be his only real challenger. The American deliberately dropped his guard several times to try to coax Freddie into close quarters, but the champion didn't fall for it and instead flicked jabs into Ritchie's face from long range. By the seventh round the crowd began booing and the jeers reached a crescendo at the sounding of the final bell. "What do they want me to do, stick my jaw out and let him win back with one punch, that which took me eleven years to earn?" asked Freddie. "If it's a slaughter they want to see instead of good, clean boxing, why not go to the packing houses and watch them fell the beef with a hammer?" he added.

Every leading lightweight in America had attempted to take the title from Freddie in ten-round contests. Some had tried twice. Ritchie was seen as the last hope and when he came no closer than the others the boxing press descended into a state of collective depression tinged with anger. Frederick G. Bonfils, professional gambler and publisher of the *Denver Post*, wrote to Willie Ritchie with an instruction that Freddie be offered $15,000 for his end of a twenty-round fight to a decision to be held in Colorado on July 4th. Ritchie received the offer before the fight at the Garden but held it back until the following day. "I hoped to knock him out then, but there was too much deer in him," claimed Ritchie. When he finally put the proposition to Freddie, the champion wouldn't listen to a fight unless he got $25,000, the amount that was guaranteed to Ritchie in London. It looked like the end of the matter until Ritchie offered to add to Bonfils' guarantee of $15,000 by betting Freddie $10,000 on the side. "He ought to jump at this chance to gather in $25,000. I'm willing to gamble $10,000 on my chances though. I don't need the money – I've got plenty – but I want to whip this fellow to the satisfaction of every American in the land. I'll retire when I do," said Ritchie. When Harry Pollok read about Ritchie's offer he replied: "We will bet him dizzy if he will risk enough. Here is my proposition. If Ritchie will get us a $25,000 guarantee we will bet him the whole guarantee, at even money. If he is so sure he can win then he can give us the guarantee himself."

Ritchie was never able to raise the guarantee that Freddie wanted for a championship fight. He fought on for another twelve years but never regained the title. But at least he got out with his health intact and served as Chief Inspector on the California State Athletic Commission from 1937 to 1961. He died on March 24th 1975, in Burlingame, California.

Freddie was back in the ring just six days after his fight with Ritchie. Fanny and Pollok accompanied him on a 585-mile train journey to the Majestic Theatre in Fort Wayne, Indiana, to box local favourite Hal Stewart. It was hostile territory for the champion. During the first three rounds the home crowd jeered and hurled so much abuse at Freddie that the referee had to stop the fight to instruct the crowd to be quiet. "You are doing a world's champion a lot of injustice," announced referee Dickerson. "He is a grand boy, a wonderful fighter and is afraid of no one in the world. Kindly show him the consideration that a fellow of that sort is entitled to." For the rest of the fight Freddie stood toe-to-toe with his novice opponent and battered him into a state where even the local papers gave the Welshman the 'shade'. The party left Fort Wayne as soon as Freddie collected his dues. They headed north to Canada for an eight-round fight with journeyman fighter Patsy Drouillard in Windsor, Ontario. For the first five rounds it resembled an exhibition bout; Freddie hitting his opponent at will and not taking a blow in return. Then in the sixth a section of the audience objecting to the lack of blood dripping to the canvas started to chant "fight, fight". It seemed to anger Drouillard who threw out a right hand that caught Freddie on the tip of his nose. From that point onwards Freddie planted his feet in the centre of the ring and slugged it out with his opponent. "The crowd wants one man to put the other fellow out of business," said

Freddie after the fight. "They are eager for the spectacular, even if the blow is a foul." "Kill that Englishman!" was becoming a regular cry at many of Freddie's fights.

Freddie, Fanny and Harry left Windsor for a city in which the champion was always welcome, Montreal. They stayed at the Windsor Hotel and Freddie spent much of the week meeting up with old friends. A ten-round contest had been arranged with Johnny Lustig and Freddie carried his opponent through the majority of the ten rounds. After the fight Freddie announced that he'd be leaving for Havana in a few days for a forty-five-round fight with Battling Nelson. In the spring of 1915 a procession of the world's leading boxers made their way to Cuba in the wake of a world heavyweight championship fight to be staged on the island between the holder Jack Johnson and the latest 'great white hope' Jess Willard. Jack Johnson had been convicted of violating vice laws after several high-profile romances with white women. He fled the United States to escape a prison sentence but he was still in possession of the heavyweight title and white America wanted it back. Johnson's ascent to the championship triggered a crusade to avenge what was considered to be an historical inaccuracy that the so-called "inferior race was superior to the white man in this, the most supreme of all contests between two men". The promoter Jack Curley lured the heavyweight champion to Cuba to defend his title for $35,000 and an illusory promise about a pardon from the United States government. His challenger was Jess Willard, a six-foot-six-plus, 260-pound white heavyweight from Pottowatamie, Kansas. The mercury hit 103 as the first bell sounded and the searing heat appeared to take its toll on a wearied, overweight champion. The end came in the twenty-sixth round when Willard knocked out Johnson and for the racists the 'Dark Age' of boxing was over. Just how exactly it came to an end is still debated today. Within months of his defeat Jack Johnson issued a confession claiming that he'd agreed to let Willard win sometime between the tenth and twentieth round but because his opponent was so inadequate he had to wait until the twenty-sixth to make it remotely credible. Jack Curley, meanwhile, became known as the man who got the world heavyweight boxing title back to the white race.

Whether the fight was fixed or not the Cuban authorities were unimpressed by the boxing circus that had encamped on their island. On the day after the Johnson – Willard fight a bill prohibiting any kind of boxing in Cuba was put before the legislative bodies of the Republic. It was passed within a week only to be challenged and thrown out by the Supreme Court the following day. The court rendered its decision by dismissing a test complaint against Governor Bustillo of the Havana Province alleging that he was guilty of an infraction of the law by personally attending the heavyweight title fight. But in the confusion surrounding the legality of boxing in Cuba the proposed match between Freddie and Battling Nelson fell through. Freddie returned to the United States from Canada and arranged a series of alternative fights but for Battling Nelson the cancellation was a disaster. He'd followed Freddie around the United States for months for an opportunity to win back the title. Nelson went to Indianapolis for a meeting with Freddie and Harry Pollok only to find the two had already left town and were in Toronto. Nelson telegraphed and got a reply which read, "How do you do? How are you? Good luck and goodbye." Freddie decided to treat Nelson in the same way as the 'Battler' had treated him when the roles of champion and challenger were reversed. When the articles were finally signed for the fight in Cuba Nelson set sail for the island immediately. He cancelled over $8,000 worth of theatrical engagements, spent over $2,000 in cash, fought three fights and trained for three months for the contest.

With the trip to Cuba cancelled, Freddie and his party moved on to Toledo, Ohio, for a hastily arranged fight with a novice boxer called Billy Wagner. A slightly overweight champion gave the young fighter a lesson in the finer points of boxing but Wagner gave Freddie two painful lessons in the art of gamesmanship. Towards the end of the fight Freddie slipped and as he got up one of Wagner's seconds yelled to referee Matt Hinkel that the champion's glove was covered in resin. Freddie stepped back and dropped his hands to wipe the gloves only to receive a terrific hook to the jaw. He clinched and proceeded to make up for the punch with a volley of rights and lefts. Later on in the same round Freddie fell for another trick. Wagner told the champion that his bootlace was loose. Freddie dropped his eyes for a second and Wagner smashed another right hook onto his opponent's jaw. Freddie had to smile at the audacity of his young opponent.

Freddie completed his tour around the Great Lakes in Hudson, Wisconsin, with a ten-round match with 'Red' Watson. Freddie peppered Watson's face so often in the first four rounds that his opponent fought the last six with one eye open. But what nobody at ringside had realized was that for the majority of the fight it was a case of a one-eyed fighter against a one-armed boxer. Freddie's right shoulder left its socket early in the fight but he had to continue on or the title would have gone to Watson on a technical knockout. As soon as the contest was over Freddie was rushed to a doctor who put his dislocated shoulder back into place. He was told to rest it for a month and Harry Pollok immediately cancelled two bouts scheduled for the next few days with Johnny Harvey in Columbus, Ohio, and Gilbert Gallant in Boston. The injury also forced Freddie to withdraw from a much bigger contest. This particular fight was staged in a courtroom and is docketed in the records as the "United States vs. 3,542 feet of motion picture film representing a prizefight". The film in question was of Freddie's fight for the title against Willie Ritchie and the case would establish a critical precedent for the future of boxing in the United States.

Newsreels of the big fights were very popular in moving picture theatres throughout America in the early years of the twentieth century. But when Jack Johnson won the heavyweight championship in 1908 church groups and local governments became very concerned with how and where these films were shown. Johnson's initial victory over Tommy Burns was not as important as his retention of the championship title; one win was easily passed off as a fluke result against a poor champion, but successive defences of the title confronted white theatre goers with an "unprecedented image of black power". The audiences grew with each new film of a Johnson victory until the hysteria to reclaim the title for the white race reached its zenith in Reno, Nevada, on July 4th 1910. Johnson battered American hero Jim Jeffries, which resulted in an eruption of racial violence across the country. More than a dozen African-Americans were killed and over a hundred were injured. The authorities were concerned the situation would worsen if film of Johnson knocking Jeffries to the canvas was shown in the theatres, but they had little power to restrict screenings. By the time Johnson fought Jim Flynn on July 4th 1912 Bills were introduced in both the House and Senate as a pre-emptive measure to ban the distribution of the fight films. The successful measure, authored by Representative Thetus Sims of Tennessee, was designed to ban the importation of boxing films into the United States and any interstate commerce of moving pictures of prizefights. The stated aim of the legislation was to protect the public from the violence of two men punching each other but the image of a black man beating a white man was what really troubled men like Sims. They were especially concerned about the effect that films of Johnson smiling over his white victims had on black audiences. In order to suppress these films the movement of all prizefighting footage had to be banned to "prevent the display to morbid-minded adults and susceptible youth all over the country of representations of such disgusting exhibition". The Sims Act cost promoters and boxers hundreds of thousands of dollars and it was inevitable that someone would challenge the legislation in the courts. Any such action would need to show that modern prizefighting was not the "disgusting exhibition" of old but an athletic pursuit, and a noble art. If anyone personified this transformation it was Freddie Welsh, gentleman and lightweight champion of the world.

Freddie's friend, the New York promoter George Considine, had taken several reels of the world championship fight in London back to America as part of his personal baggage on board the *Aquitania*. Customs officials in New York, acting on instructions from Washington, seized the films at dockside. The United States government contended that the films were "subject to forfeiture". Considine lodged an objection on the basis that his films were of a pugilistic encounter not a prizefight and the Government moved for a trial by federal judge without a jury.

The case was heard on May 10th 1915, before Judge Hough in the Federal District Court in the Woolworth Building in Manhattan. The Assistant United States District Attorney submitted a brief in which he gave dictionary definitions to show that a prizefight and a pugilistic encounter were the same and that consequently the films should be barred. Freddie was to tell the court that he won the title from Ritchie in a scientific manner but he was a reluctant participant from the outset and the shoulder injury saved him from testifying. This was a great disappointment to the court, which had hoped for a firsthand account of how the world champion had won a famous contest. Considine's attorney, Frank S. O'Neill, who was also a State boxing commissioner, argued the film did not come within the meaning of the act and that modern boxing as practised by Freddie and Willie Ritchie was far removed from the immoral spectacle of the prizefight of old. Judge Hough was not without sympathy for O'Neill's argument but he ruled in favour of the Government. He referred to the contemporary *Murray's New English Dictionary* in which a 'prizefighter' was defined as "a professional pugilist or boxer, who fights publicly for a prize or stake". The judge contended that although the defence had argued the Welsh – Ritchie fight was a boxing match, it was impossible to hold that the use of another name had changed the substance of the fight. "Both Ritchie and Welsh were professionals," said the Judge. "If the modern dictionary definitions be accepted, it is impossible for me to say what they did was not a modern prize fight, even though it may be admitted that the wearing of gloves and the limiting of the number of rounds would have prevented its acceptance as a prizefight fifty years ago. It is, therefore, concluded that according to the modern acceptance of the phrase the Ritchie – Welsh affair was a prizefight, and it was beyond question an encounter of pugilists." As a result of the Judge's decision the film of Freddie's fight with Willie Ritchie in London was never shown publicly in the United States and Considine's copy was destroyed together with thousands of feet of motion picture film of contests in various countries around the world.

He may not have been fit enough for the legal fight but Freddie's dislocated shoulder kept him out of the ring for a mere thirty-five days. He returned to Montreal to box Frankie Fleming, the feather-weight champion of Canada. It was a bad-tempered fight and Freddie was visibly annoyed on two occasions during the bout. The first flashpoint came as a few spectators at ringside became sarcastic and started to belittle the champion. Freddie sailed into Fleming, backed him up against the ropes with his left hand and then hammered two stiff rights onto the same point on his jaw. Freddie was noticeably grinning at his tormentors while he was doing so. On the second occasion one of Fleming's seconds taunted Freddie and asked him to "land one for him". Freddie duly obliged and hit Fleming with six unanswered blows. His next match was scheduled to be with Milburn Saylor in Indianapolis on May 28th. It was a long-held tradition that the city held a boxing match the day before the famous 500-mile motor race at the speedway and this year Freddie was to be the star attraction. But Mayor Joseph E. Nell decided unexpectedly to ban boxing because he considered that the sport had degenerated into fake prizefights conducted solely for money. The cancellation cost Freddie a few thousand dollars but it did give him a break from the ring of over a month and the rest proved to be very beneficial.

To mark the first anniversary of becoming champion Freddie signed for two matches in New York in the space of a week. He had a longstanding arrangement with John Weismantle, manager of the Brooklyn Sporting Club, to fight Johnny Lustig on June 28th. Unbeknown to Freddie, Weismantle had also made an arrangement with Leach Cross and Johnny Dundee to fight on the same bill. Freddie wasn't happy with the idea that he'd be overlooked in the advertising for the show so he sent Harry Pollok into battle. Consequently Freddie was offered a large flat guarantee instead of a percentage of the gate receipts while the other three boxers had to accept a reduction in their share. Such were the privileges of being world champion.

New York Globe, 9 May 1916.

The Brooklyn show was staged in the open air on a hot, sultry night at Ebbets Field. It attracted a crowd of over 10,000 which the New York Times described as a "a cosmopolitan gathering where patrician rubbed elbows with plebeian". It was a lively evening and there was certainly no restraint on the part of the crowd in expressing its approval or disapproval of events in the ring. Most of the abuse was aimed at Freddie. He was lean, fit, fast and far too clever for Johnny Lustig and according to one reporter Freddie's "monotonous advantage over his inexperienced adversary, sent many of the spectators away before the tenth round came". Freddie was, by now, several years past his best as a boxer but none of the contenders with the youth and strength to beat him had been able to so much as jar the champion. Charley White was still considered the best of the American fighters and Freddie agreed to give him a third opportunity to win the title at the Brighton Beach race track in New York. Freddie trained hard for this fight and he moved from the bustle of New York to Rest Inn, Long Island. He breakfasted every morning among the cherry trees and dined by the seashore. He swam in the river, ran through the woods and performed his exercises in the hot sun of a chicken yard. Every night he slept out in the orchard. On the occasional day when it rained he worked in an old church nearby and showered under a garden hose with rose bushes providing the privacy of bathroom walls. He returned to New York in peak condition.

From the opening round Freddie carried the fight to White, and though he never tried for a knockout blow, the persistency of his left jabs had his opponent's nose bleeding early. After the fight was over Freddie sat in his dressing room and smiled. "Well, that's three tries that the world's hardest hitter has had to knock me out. I'll tell you now, as I've told you before. I've got that fellow's number. He can't land a knockout on me and he knows it. I've got him hypnotized, that's all." Freddie's first year as champion was over. He'd put his title on the line twenty-one times, against the best men the promoters could find, but nobody had come close to relieving him of the light-weight crown. Bob Edgren, Freddie's most vociferous critic was left to ponder whether Old Father Time was the only credible challenger in the field:

> Freddie Welsh's term of office in the lightweight division is on the wane. The world's lightweight title, which he has in his keeping at the present time, will not remain in his possession much longer. This prediction is warranted by his latest exhibition. Just which boxer will relieve him of his championship cannot be foretold, but it has become quite evident that the Briton is slipping, slowly, 'tis true, but none the less surely. His retrogression has been suspected for some time. He is the oldest lightweight to hold the title since Joe Gans, and nature alone is due to extract her toll of him.

Fourteen

Jack This and Tommy That and Benny Somebody Else

In his apartments at the St Paul Hotel in New York Freddie's library contained a large number of Elbert Hubbard's finest books. The centrepiece of the collection was a set of three large leather-bound scrapbooks given to Freddie by Hubbard to record his achievements in the ring. Stamped on the spine of each, in gold lettering, were the words "Welsh" and "Champion". Fanny gathered all the letters, newspaper articles and photographs for the volumes and Freddie dedicated the books to her. Another of the lightweight champion's prized possessions was a collection of Hubbard's works entitled *The Note Book of Elbert Hubbard*. One of the essays in the anthology was about the sinking of the *Titanic*. A number of Hubbard's close friends and acquaintances were on the ship and lost their lives. In the piece Hubbard reflected on the final moments of a couple that he knew:

> One thing is sure, there are just two respectable ways to die. One is of old age, and the other is by accident. All disease is indecent. Suicide is atrocious. But to pass out as did Mr and Mrs Isador Straus is glorious. Few have such a privilege. Happy lovers, both. In life they were never separated and in death they are not divided.

On May 7th 1915 Elbert Hubbard and his wife Alice were passengers on the *Lusitania* when it was torpedoed by the Germans off the coast of Ireland. Like the Strauses the Hubbards died together, along with 1196 others. Elbert and his wife were sailing to England to begin a lecture tour and while he was there Hubbard intended to write a story entitled, *A Little Journey to the Home of Freddie Welsh, Lightweight Champion*. Only the accident of a delayed telegram kept Freddie from sailing with the Hubbards. One of the last letters Elbert wrote to Freddie included the line, "Well, Freddie here's a hand grasp to you. May you be blessed and happy in this world and if there is no squared circle in the next one, you and I will arrange one." Hubbard had also given Freddie a ticket to the Roycroft Inn upon which he had written: "Expires never". When news of the *Lusitania*'s sinking reached the United States Freddie was asked to write a word or two about his friend for a memorial publication:

Dear Friends: It is easier to philosophize optimistically about death when one is not so close to the subject or not right up against it, as Elbert and Alice Hubbard were. However, it is but logical to suppose that both faced death as they had faced life – game and unafraid. Knowing Hubbard as I did, I picture him using the last moments in this world speaking words of love and encouragement to Alice, his mate, who was to take the final little journey with him on the ship that carried them to Valhalla.

Elbert Hubbard did not believe in sham, hypocrisy and superstition. He never worried about a world that might come. He expressed himself here, regardless of religious creeds. Whether it was St. Peter who opened the door for him in the other world or Papa Satan, he was surely written down as one "who loved his fellow men". And his helpmate and wife is with him. We can be sure of another thing. The Fra is either making heaven more lively and interesting, or devising means of making hell comfortably cool.

Elbert Hubbard's untimely death ended Freddie's plans to open a health farm with the Roycroft 'Fra'. Freddie was to take over Emerson Hall on Hubbard's East Aurora farm in Erie County, New York State, where he would establish a health home. Freddie thought the venture would be a way a way of keeping him in touch "with the athletic life of the country". Even as he was contemplating retirement from boxing Freddie was putting contingency plans in place that gave him a route back to the ring. "I will not be altogether out of the rush of life," he said, "and naturally there will be fewer regrets." Following Hubbard's death Freddie almost closed a deal for fifty acres on the north shore of Long Island where he trained for the Charley White fight. The Selby – Brown estate was in Lockport and Freddie had already planned $32,000 of improvements to cater for the best citizenry. And there was now another reason for the longed for house in the country. In June 1915 Freddie's second child, Freddie Jr, was born. Freddie Sr was particularly pleased the boy resembled his father. "I told my wife if this baby didn't have a dimple on his chin that I would chuck him in the ocean," he joked.

On the night of July 7th, the first anniversary of his winning the world championship, Freddie gave a dinner for some friends at the Seabourne on Coney Island. It was attended by some of the most important figures in American boxing and many a Broadway celebrity. After the dinner they all left for a night at the movies. The following day Freddie set off for California to rest for the summer. His wife and two children were already in Venice, Los Angeles along with his pet Welsh terrier Mike. Freddie's sister Kate also travelled to California to recuperate from an illness contracted working as a nurse in the war. While in Los Angeles the family visited Universal City where Freddie consulted with Director-General McRae regarding a career in moving pictures. Freddie told McRae that he harboured the impression that he "could put the punch" into a feature film if given a chance.

The Welsh family basked around the sands at Venice for ten weeks. Freddie bathed in the Pacific Ocean and went goat shooting on Catalina Island. It was quite a precarious pastime, treading along narrow trails up mountainous paths on horseback but Freddie managed to shoot half a dozen goats. When it was time to move back east he looked better than he'd done since winning the championship. The family moved back into their apartments at the St Paul Hotel and Freddie was ready for another fight campaign. It was obvious that Freddie was tiring of the ring and he spoke to Tom Andrews of the *National Police Gazette* about how he was now entering the final phase of his career and intended to retire to settle down to a quiet life. "It's one of the most dependable tales in all of sports," wrote Bert Sugar, "the faded warrior, the fire that once burned in his soul now but a dull ache, believing in the smithy of his heart that he has one 'good' fight left in him."

Freddie felt under a great deal of pressure from the press to defend his title over a twenty-round championship fight. He didn't want to quit before fighting at least one of the legitimate challengers in such a contest, although his own experiences at the hands of former champions had made him reluctant to undertake such a risk without sufficient recompense. Freddie had been forced to give away every penny of his share to get a bout with Willie Ritchie and as champion he was not about to be dictated to in terms of whom he should fight and for how much. "The glamour of the game doesn't allure me in the least," he told one reporter. "I know that, as a rule, the people who applaud a fighter are the people who kick him when he's down. That's why I have never paid any attention to the criticisms fired at me because I haven't taken a chance on my title over a long route for unsatisfactory purses. They can roast me all they choose, but I know that as long as I am champion I can get the money. I see no reason why I should risk my health unless there is a sufficient monetary inducement."

By October 1915 Freddie had made plans for what he declared would be his final year in the ring. His main aim was to fight four championship battles, decision contests of twenty rounds at any venue where such a bout was still legal. He wanted $15,000 per contest, with all four fights to be staged before July 4th 1916 – the day on which he

Elizabeth, Fanny and Freddie Jr.

intended to retire. To generate further publicity for these events Harry Pollok suggested the sporting editors of all the leading newspapers in the United States be polled on the question as to who was entitled to the first crack at the champion. Pollok pledged to abide by the decision of the poll. The *Chicago Herald* had already conducted a vote amongst its own readership and unsurprisingly chose Chicagoan Charley White. Harry Pollok pointed out that each city had its own 'favourite son' candidate for the championship and he called for a nationwide ballot. The *Chicago Herald* responded by mailing out letters to newspaper offices throughout the land urging them to cast their vote in a fistic election. Charley White also won the newspaper poll: Willie Ritchie came second, followed by Joe Welling and Johnny Dundee. Within days Charley White's manager Nate Lewis and Harry Pollok had agreed all the conditions for the fight and it was decided to put the bout out for bidding. The promoter with the highest offer to reach the managers by December 16th would get the fight to be held within six weeks of that date. The major stumbling block was the venue. The only places where such a contest was legal were Colorado, Louisiana, Mexico and Cuba. The most obvious choice was Tia Juana, Mexico, under the auspices of a club recently established by Freddie's old friends Baron Long and Jimmy Coffroth. But their venture soon went out of business. The only other serious offer came from Denver where a number of rich sportsmen joined together to offer Freddie $12,500 to fight White there. It wasn't enough and the whole plan was aborted and Freddie returned to the no decision game. On November 13th Freddie, his sparring partner Eddie Moy and Harry Pollok travelled to Winnipeg. The world champion was matched with Johnny O'Leary, a fighter that Freddie had sparred with while on a previous visit to Canada. While he was preparing at the Deer Lodge in Winnipeg a teenage boy turned up having walked twenty miles from his farm near Saltcoats, Alberta, to get a train just to meet the lightweight champion. Freddie broke off from his training and sparred seven rounds with the boy. For the rest of the afternoon Freddie entertained him with yarns from his boxing career.

Since he last shared a ring with Freddie back in 1913 Johnny O'Leary had come to be recognized as the lightweight champion of Canada. The young boxer now had serious aspirations of relieving Freddie of his title. It was not to be. A few years later, Jack Skelly recalled their fight in a feature for the *Boxing Blade*. Under the headline 'Humane Fistic Gladiators Who Took No Advantage Of Foes', Skelly subtitled his piece 'Magnanimous fighters who might have knocked out inferior opponents, but who showed regard for very helpless boxers whom they had then subdued'. Skelly argued that Freddie's record could have shown a series of knockouts had the Welshman "not been inclined to take a human view of the business". Writing of the O'Leary fight, Skelly recalled:

Welsh always said that he liked to see young fellows entering the boxing game get along. He didn't want to be the fellow who stood in the way of a young fighter's making money in the ring.

One time he fought John O'Leary, one of the classiest lightweights ever turned out of Canada. They met in Winnipeg, and just as they had started scrapping Welsh whispered to O'Leary; "now go along nicely with me and don't try to double cross me, and I'll not do anything to you to hurt you as a box-office fighter. If you make a good showing with me you'll be able to get some good matches and the coin that goes with them."

But O'Leary couldn't see things Welsh's way, and immediately produced to try to knockout the champion. The result was Welsh forgot to be human and handed O'Leary the worst pounding he ever got in the ring. After the bout Welsh met O'Leary and told him he had made a mistake, and he shouldn't have tried to score a knockout. O'Leary's answer was:

"Well I thought I could slip it over on you, and I tried my best."

That demonstrates the difference between a human fighter and one who isn't.

In early December Freddie, Harry and Eddie Moy travelled to Memphis, Tennessee, for a fight with the Mexican Benny Palmer. This was Freddie's first fight in Memphis but Palmer wasn't really in the same class as the champion and he was virtually nursed through it. Several times Freddie started punches at Palmer's kidneys and then pulled them back. "I don't want to beat him to death," Freddie told one reporter after the fight who'd obviously turned up for a knockout. Straight after the bout Freddie was back on the train for a nine hundred mile journey to Philadelphia. His opponent was the local man Jimmy Murphy and because both men were well over the lightweight limit Freddie's title wasn't on the line. Murphy was a convincing winner on points and there were two real moments of concern for Freddie. His lip was badly cut by a hard left as early as the second round and a spray of blood accompanied his every exhalation for the duration of the contest. Then in the fourth Murphy threw a right cross to Freddie's bleeding mouth that sent the champion staggering around the ring before saving himself in a clinch. The injuries to his lips and damage to his teeth forced Freddie to cancel a $1,000 engagement with Johnny Griffiths in Akron, Ohio, a few nights later.

His enforced break from the ring did give Freddie the opportunity to do 'his bit' however. Back in the summer he had promised Tom Flanagan of the Toronto Sportsmen's Association that he would help raise funds for the families of Canadian soldiers fighting in the Great War. The association was playing Santa Claus to the soldiers' children but its funds had been exhausted in helping army recruitment and equipping the Canadian soldiers with sports goods. So Freddie, accompanied by Fanny and Kate, travelled from New York at his own expense to appear at the Sportsmen's Show in Toronto on the night of December 15th. The presence of the world champion ensured that Loew's Winter Garden Theatre was packed to capacity. Freddie was due to box with Eddie Moy, but he became snowbound on the journey north so three local boys were selected instead. Freddie took quite a chance by taking on three young strangers looking to 'land one' on the world champion. His mouth hadn't healed and his teeth hadn't been repaired and one stray punch could have cost the world champion several thousand dollars. But Freddie managed to get through ten rounds unscathed and the Sportsmen's Association raised $3,000 to buy Christmas presents for the soldiers' children. When the boxing was over Freddie was the guest of honour at a dinner in the Walker House in Toronto. He had tendered his services to the cause of Canadian khaki and the city's sportsmen recognized his patriotic spirit by presenting Freddie with a diamond stickpin while Fanny and Kate were given sets of Canadian furs. At first they refused the gifts thinking they'd been paid for out of the gate receipts but they were assured that individuals had donated them. The money raised bought 12,000 Christmas presents for the wives, widows and orphans of Canadian soldiers. Each present was put in a box stamped *Compliments of Freddie Welsh and the Sportsman's Patriotic Fund*.

The following night Freddie, Fanny and Kate travelled to Buffalo for a few days before returning to New York. "Don't ask me about the war," pleaded Kate to one reporter, "it's too horrible to think about. People in America who don't know the conditions can't imagine what it really means. Men who are trying to write of this war can't begin to tell the story. I saw for myself. I'm going back after the holidays. I must report for duty not later than the last week of January." Kate eventually returned to Birmingham to nurse Belgian refugees while Stanley was made a sub-lieutenant in the Royal Navy and was sent to the Dardanelles on the *HMS Sarnia*.

Freddie and the family spent Christmas in New York. It was usually a busy time of year for Freddie with plenty of festive bouts to keep the dollars rolling in, but he spent the 1915 holiday season resting while the wound in his mouth healed. He was out of the ring for three weeks and did very little training. Freddie tried not to waste a single punch anymore and he used the minimum energy required to get through fights. "That's business," he explained, "for those punches and that energy are my stock in trade. I have just brought good business principles into the prize ring." He returned to action on New Year's Day 1916. Harry Pollok had arranged a match for him in Atlanta, Georgia; the first time a world championship had been contested there. A huge crowd turned out to see the local man Frank Whitney try to take the title. Interest in the fight was especially high as Whitney had beaten Ad Wolgast after just five rounds in a recent contest. Freddie and Harry arrived in Atlanta on New Year's Eve and were met by Homer George, a local theatrical impresario. Freddie stunned local boxing writers by partying the night away despite having a fight the following day. The party ate supper at the Piedmont Hotel before dancing the New Year in. Freddie stayed on the dance floor until 2 am. He then spent the more civilised hours of the morning walking the streets of Atlanta and meeting many of the friends he'd made during his last visit in 1914. Four thousand five hundred people turned up to see Frank Whitney try to knock out Freddie Welsh and according to one reporter "four thousand five hundred people came away saying, 'It can't be done'." After the fight Freddie dined with the famous sports writer Fuzzy Woodruff. The champion ordered a "double-barrelled steak" and a bottle of beer. "I feel tonight like I need a bit of stimulant, so I'm taking it. I am enjoying it, and it's bound to be good for me. I'm not a teetotaller, but I am just as far from being a drunkard or a man afflicted with the sin of overeating. Some day when I retire from the ring I will eat and drink what I choose. Right now I must eat and drink and sleep and exercise and rest and do everything else from a pugilistic point of view."

Freddie's next scheduled contest was against Johnny Dundee in New York as the first fight of the 71st Regiment Athletic Association's boxing season. But it was cancelled the night before on the command of the Governor of New York, Charles S. Whitman, who didn't want state armouries used for boxing matches. So Freddie returned to the ring on January 17th against Eddie McAndrews in Philadelphia. According to the *New York Times*, Freddie was "whipped" in the six-round bout by the unheralded McAndrews. Impartial accounts of the fight claimed Freddie won every round. After the contest Freddie wrote a letter to *Boxing*, in Britain:

> I fought last night, Eddie Andrews, and I did not get much sleep, as you know I rarely do after a fight. I won easily, of course, and of course the local papers, as is customary, gave the paper decision to the local boy – at least most of them did. However, that is never the cause of my loss of sleep. On the contrary, I think if they gave me the best of it in the local papers I should be so surprised and excited that I would not sleep for a week. I have not bothered to cable you each fight this season because there has been such contradictory and insane reports that I have entirely lost interest as to whether my opponent or I get the newspaper decision.

Freddie fought again the following week, this time in Akron, Ohio, against a little-known, local fighter called Johnny Griffiths. Although officially a draw, most people at ringside seemed to agree that had there been a decision it would probably have been given to Griffiths. Once again Freddie was content just to stay out of trouble against limited opposition. As if aware of the crowd's displeasure, Freddie put on a flourish in the last round during which he cut open Griffiths' face. Within an hour of the final bell Freddie was on the train back to New York, but reports of another poor performance arrived in the city before he did. He was being hit far more often than he used to and his face was beginning to show the signs of a protracted boxing career. Fanny wanted Freddie to get out of the ring before he was carried out feet first but her husband couldn't do it. He wasn't alone. The fight game then, as it is now, was full of ageing boxers failing to acknowledge the inevitable and Freddie was about to square up to a champion of self-denial. Ad Wolgast had retired several times since losing the world title to Willie Ritchie in November 1912. After one particularly poor performance against a journeyman fighter Wolgast said he'd rather quit than spend his time training and boxing around like a "sideshow man". But back he came again and again. "You just can't quit, that's all," he said after one failed comeback. "They say a criminal is drawn back irresistibly to the scene of his crime. Well, so is a fighter drawn back to the old rings, to the old crowd, and the old excitement. Why not let the ex-champs have their little pipedreams?"

On March 6th 1916 Freddie gave Wolgast another chance to realize his pipedream. The 'Wildcat' was so keen to make the match that when the Milwaukee club did not see fit to meet the guarantee demanded by Freddie, Wolgast stepped up and assured the promoters that he would make up the shortfall if there was a deficit at the gate. He also placed a $200 wager on himself at 2 to 1 against to win. Wolgast needn't have worried about the gate. Over 5,000 people turned up but his $200 was lost for good. Freddie showed once again that when he really needed to put on a show he could still do it. He decided to fight Wolgast at his own game and stood there, toe-to-toe, trading blows with one of the toughest brawlers in boxing history. Not that it was any sort of fair trade, as Freddie did all the hitting and Wolgast did all the receiving. The scribes unanimously awarded the fight to the world champion and when the bout was over Wolgast was left with a slash so deep across his nose that his corner could barely stop the bleeding.

Freddie told the press, his friends, family and himself that he was boxing on to secure his standing in the ranks of the great light-weights. He didn't want an historian to be able to write that he retained the title by engaging in no decision contests. But Freddie knew he was still some way from being financially secure. Again he instructed Harry Pollok to arrange twenty-round matches with three or four of the best lightweights within the next year. Up to this point Freddie had held out for $25,000 for any such fight but by the spring of 1916 he was prepared to settle for considerably less. Time was running out. "If one of them knocks me out, that means the finish for me," said Freddie. "And if they don't, well, I'll quit anyway."

While Pollok was looking for the big fights Freddie took the 'ten rounders' on a weekly basis. Next up was Phil Bloom at the

Broadway Sporting Club in Brooklyn. Freddie pecked and jabbed
away at Bloom and cut his opponent's nose open after just four
rounds. For the rest of the fight Freddie was content to keep his tired
and dispirited opponent away and "impressed on the durable
Brooklynite the futility of trying to gain a reputation at his expense".
Just three nights later he appeared on a bill at the Harlem Sporting
Club that featured two ten-round bouts with two world champions as
the principals. Johnny Kilbane, the featherweight titleholder, was to
fight Harry Donahue and Freddie was to box Frank Whitney.
Freddie was beginning to tire of the criticism in the newspapers and
he took out his frustrations on his opponent. Whitney received such
a sound thrashing that he sat in his corner after the end of five rounds
and refused to come out for the sixth, his left eye so badly cut he was
unable to see. The ferocity of the world champion's performance may
also have had something to do with the presence of a young boxer
named Benny Leonard sitting at ringside. Leonard was only nineteen
years old but he was already being written about as the next lightweight champion. He was born and bred on the dangerous streets of
New York's Lower East Side and had turned professional at just
fifteen. His career got off to an unpromising start when an Irishman
named Mickey Finnegan stopped him in three rounds. But the young
Jewish fighter fought on in illegal fights and bootleg brawls until he
worked his way through the lightweight ranks. He'd knocked out
nearly all the genuine contenders for the title except for Packey
McFarland and Willie Ritchie who were now too heavy to be realistic
challengers. The emergence of a new fighter to carry American hopes
of regaining the title was good news for Freddie. The crowds watching him fight were dwindling as it became increasingly obvious that
none of the existing crop was capable of knocking him out. Jimmy
Johnston of Madison Square Garden was ready to guarantee Freddie
a purse of $12,500 for a match with Leonard, and the prospect
generated real excitement in New York. Leonard was fast becoming a
crowd favourite and Freddie's frequently lacklustre displays did little
to endear him to American boxing fans. This was the first contest in
a long time in which there was a genuine belief the title could finally
change hands. The advance ticket sales exceeded $16,000, the largest
amount for any lightweight bout held at the Garden.

Freddie trained at Joe Wagner's on Bleecker Street. He used the
gymnasium when he was fighting in New York because it was near to
where he used to live as a down-and-out when he first arrived in the
United States. He had never forgotten the people who helped him
then. Whenever he trained at Wagner's he only employed local fight-

ers as sparring partners. But by this time the only preparation Freddie did for a fight was to see that the sponges were soft and the towels were clean before they were carried to ringside for his use. He also made sure that his seconds had smelling salts and collodian in case of an accident. The fight with Benny Leonard was a social event in New York, with the great, the good and the glamorous occupying the arena boxes. At over 9,000 people, it was the biggest crowd for a lightweight fight in New York since the Frawley Law took effect and proof of boxing's new respectability could be seen in the number of women in attendance. Leonard was first into the ring much to the delight of the partisan audience. Freddie kept him waiting several minutes, but for a relative novice, Leonard had the demeanour and poise of an old-timer. When the champion finally entered the ring he looked overweight and unfit.

The pattern was set from the first bell; Leonard always the aggressor, Freddie defending most of the blows but certainly taking more punches than he was used to. When the first round was over many in the crowd stood on their chairs and threw their hats into the air. Maybe their boy would be champion after all. Leonard drew first blood in the fifth round when a quick left flattened itself on Freddie's nose, tearing the skin in a horizontal slash. It was said the cut was deep enough to expose clean, white bone. Another left opened a cut under the champion's left eye in the ninth and by the end of the fight Freddie's face was a better indication of the way the fight went than any scorecard. Leonard had a slight scratch over one eye while Freddie had two deep lacerations that oozed blood; his nose was badly swollen and bleeding. "It was a case of youth charged with fight from his toes to his head pitted against a veteran ring master whose long sojourn in the ring is counting against him," wrote the *New York Times*, "and the old-time skill of Welsh is plainly on the wane."

At least it was a good night financially. Pollok had forced Leonard to accept just 15 per cent of the receipts that eventually amounted to $4,258. Freddie got $13,341 for his end. It was the largest house he had fought before in the United States and the largest percentage he'd earned. It also allowed him to pay a little debt of honour. Freddie gave $4,500 of his share to George Considine, who'd put up part of the fund to lure Willie Ritchie to London for the world title fight. There had been no written agreement that Freddie should repay the money because Considine, like the boxer, agreed to take a risk on the receipts at the Olympia. But after Ritchie had received his enormous guarantee, Freddie and Considine lost $5,000 each. After the Welshman won the title he promised Considine that he would take a

big fight and share the receipts with him. This was it. Freddie had
taken a dreadful beating but he stayed on his feet until the final bell,
and was still champion.

The severity of Freddie's defeat in New York boosted the crowd
for his next defence of the title a week later in Milwaukee against a
local fighter, Ritchie Mitchell. Such was the support for Mitchell that
a parade of 275 cars was staged through the streets of south side
Milwaukee, all of them flying Mitchell banners. A calliope and a brass
band heralded the parade's coming two blocks in advance. Freddie
arrived in the city just as the festivities were starting. He stayed at the
Pfister Hotel and the parade stopped outside his room to serenade
the champion. Freddie went to the window and spoke to some of
them. "This is the first time that I know of that an opponent to the
home boy has been shown such courtesy," said a tired champion. The
disturbance made little difference to the outcome of the fight
however. The margin of Freddie's victory was so great that even local
reporters were forced to admit the champion had won. Freddie left
Milwaukee the following day and headed north to Winnipeg for
another fundraising exhibition for the families of the soldiers fighting
in Europe. The 90th Regiment of the Canadian Army staged the bout
and Freddie was matched with the garrison champion, Joe Thorburn.
The exhibition marked the end of Freddie's dispute with the referee,
Bun Foley. It was Foley who'd signed a letter for Milburn Saylor
stating that the latter had knocked out Freddie but who had been
disqualified for a low blow. Freddie and Foley shook hands in the ring
before the bout started.

While he was in Winnipeg Freddie met with the military authorities to discuss two schemes he'd thought up to help raise funds for
the Canadian Army. The first, and most ambitious, was to start a
cross-Canada campaign for recruits for a battalion of sportsmen for
the British army. "I may not be qualified to command such a body of
men, but I have had more than the usual training of a British subject
outside the regular army, and I feel sure I could qualify," Freddie
explained. "I would like the opportunity for I feel satisfied I could
attract to my standard hundreds who have not felt impelled as yet to
offer themselves. There are plenty of most desirable recruits to be
had for a battalion of this kind, to be got, like the Princess Patricia's
Light Infantry was formed, from all over the dominions." His other,
more attainable, idea was for a series of boxing bouts in various cities
throughout Canada to raise $100,000 for the benefit of the soldiers
and their families. Freddie offered to put his title on the line in
competitive fights over ten, fifteen and twenty rounds with the

proceeds going to patriotic relief funds. He intended to keep expenses low by using army halls or armouries and asking the Canadian railways for free transportation.

Having done his bit for the cause Freddie crossed back to Milwaukee for a bout with another local favourite, Ever Hammer. The night started badly as Freddie and Harry got into an argument with officials of the National Athletic Club. They demanded the $1,500 guarantee in advance and the bout was delayed by twenty-eight minutes until the money was paid. When he reached the ring the booing was deafening but Freddie simply smiled. Hammer had sat in his corner for nearly half an hour. He was a fighter who laid no claim to cleverness or speed and his rise to prominence was due to sheer aggressiveness and a willingness to mix it. He was the kind of fighter Freddie usually enjoyed boxing because he was in little danger of being hit by a man who burrowed away without finesse. Freddie hadn't trained for the contest and as the first round ended it didn't seem to matter. The challenger failed to land a blow and it looked like an easy night. But in the second things changed dramatically. Freddie put up his glove to block a punch just as he had done thousands of times previously. On this occasion he got the angle slightly wrong and the blow broke a bone in his right hand. It was the bone he'd broken before and he was forced to fight eight rounds with one hand. Freddie looked in great distress several times and the frantic Milwaukee fans thought the championship was going to change hands at last. Every time Hammer sent a left hook towards Freddie's head he had the choice of taking it flush on the jaw or putting his broken hand in the way. Time and again Hammer rocked Freddie's head because of the weak guard. At the conclusion of each round a large delegation of Chicago fans who'd journeyed to Milwaukee rocked the building with their cheers for Hammer. But Freddie held on. He could have retired but he wasn't about to let his precious title go this way. Freddie once wrote that the difference between the champion and the other man is a difference in morality – one has the determination to do the impossible: the other merely does his best.

The National Sporting Club in Milwaukee was furious with Freddie's late entry into the ring and his poor performance and it filed charges against him with the Wisconsin Boxing Commission. The club claimed that Freddie had failed to file articles in time, failed to post a forfeit for his appearance and he was also charged for using alcoholic stimulants in his corner. It had been another bad evening for Freddie just weeks after his demoralizing defeat to Benny

Leonard. The following morning Freddie told Chicago pressman Bill
Forman that he now intended to quit on July 7th that year – the
second anniversary of his becoming champion. Forman and Freddie
rode in the same railway car together from Milwaukee back to
Chicago. The two men were friends and Forman tried to persuade
Freddie to retire right away. "Freddie Welsh is about through and he
knows it," wrote Forman in the following day's newspaper. Boxer
and journalist were standing on the platform waiting for the train
when Ever Hammer and his manager Howard Carr walked past
them. Freddie pulled his hat down to cover a badly battered face, put
his hands in his pockets and looked on at the young, unmarked
fighter strutting past him. Later Freddie settled down to a large meal
with a cigar for dessert in the diner car. He was in a talkative mood
for the duration of the two-hour journey with Forman hardly getting
in more than a question or two. Freddie was sore in spirit and body,
his face was badly cut and his right hand was in a heavy bandage.
He'd been fighting continuously for almost two years. He was offered
some 'easy money' doing theatrical work but passed it up because he
preferred fighting to acting. All the money Freddie earned was by
hard work in the ring, meeting all-comers and barring nobody. He
had taken twenty-two fights during his first winter as world
champion at the end of which he went out with his family to the
California coast, laid down on the sand and took a vacation. But
while the champion was resting a fresh crop of hopes – young,
strong, ambitious boys were training to take his title. "I heard about
Jack This and Tommy That and Benny Somebody Else, who were
going to knock my head off the first time we met," Freddie told
Forman. "Well, they all got a chance. I never ducked away from any
of them. You fellows of the press are fond of picturing me as a
runaway champion, taking no chances and playing a safe game
always. That is not true. I have been compelled to go around the
country, meeting any newcomer or old-timer who wants a crack at
me under whatever laws their home place provides. I always was the
one who was taking the chance. To be beaten by a champion is no
disgrace to most of these boys. They have everything to gain and
nothing to lose. So they're always trying to sweep me off my feet, and
I want to tell you that every time I step into the ring I have to fight.
There has been no easy money for me."

In his hotel room the previous evening Freddie calculated that
he'd earned something more than a quarter of a million dollars in the
twelve years he'd been fighting. He'd spent much of it but had also
bought property in California to insure his wife and children "against

the future". But Freddie was aware that his investments were not enough to provide for a retired prizefighter and his family. His biggest asset was the title and his best way to exploit it was in the ring. He knew that his time as champion was coming to an end but he needed to fight just a little longer. Freddie told Forman to print a story that he was going to fight for just another ten weeks and unless he was knocked cold before July 7th, he would walk out of the ring an unbeaten champion. Despite the pain of a broken hand and the extensive bruising it was the damage to his pride that prompted the decision. After every fight Freddie hurried to his room to treat his face with hot and cold towels to reduce any marks or swellings. "It doesn't do to look like a fighter," Freddie once remarked. But after his pounding by Hammer the towels didn't work and for the first time in his career Freddie bore the scars of battle and he wore them like a badge of failure. "I'm taking home the first black eye my kiddies ever saw their old man wear," he told Forman. "I'm not fool enough to consider myself unbeatable. I know the chances I am taking against these young upstarts. Probably it is only a question of time until one of these boys full of pep and with the handicap of youth comes out of the sticks and crumples me up. That is the natural finish of a champion, and I don't see any reason why I should be immune. The only way it can be escaped to a certainty is to retire before it comes. As fighters go, I am getting old. I want to spend the rest of my life quietly, with my wife and children."

A week after his fight with Hammer, Freddie was suspended by the Wisconsin Boxing Commission for four months for causing a delay before the bout and failing to file contracts with the Commission before a fight. The charge that he had used an intoxicant during the bout was dropped. The Wisconsin ban in itself wasn't too serious; the problem was the relationship between the Commission and its counterpart in New York. Although no formal agreement existed there was an unwritten understanding that the two boards would recognize each other's actions. Harry Pollok was already negotiating for a big money fight against Benny Leonard at Madison Square Garden and he persuaded the New York Athletic Commission to appeal the ban. The Wisconsin Boxing Commission declined to rescind Freddie's suspension and the issue severed the agreement between the two boxing authorities. A month or so later the Wisconsin Boxing Commission, with the aim of "placing boxing on a higher plane", introduced a new rule governing the payment of guarantees by clubs to boxers. It called for all guarantees of $150 or more to be lodged at the Commission; boxers were to post a forfeit of at least twenty-five per cent of the guarantees they received to warrant their appearance. No fight would be sanctioned until all the money had been posted with the Commission and all contracts filed. The rule ensured that boxers didn't drop out of a match at the last minute and that clubs couldn't cancel shows because of poor ticket sales. The Wisconsin Commission claimed that the "fabulous guarantees" that had hurt the game in New York would now be eliminated because it would know how much money was being paid. Freddie, meanwhile, was unrepentant about the stand that he'd taken over the money. "Prize fighting is a bad business at best," he claimed. "I went into it for the simple reason that I could make more money as a boxer than I could by putting my brains and energy into any other business."

Freddie's increasing vulnerability in the ring and the punishment he now routinely took ironically increased his appeal at the box office. The fight with Benny Leonard at the Garden in April had resulted in Freddie's biggest defeat during a career that was now in its second decade. But the increased appetite for a re-match meant Freddie's price for title defence increased accordingly. Within a matter of weeks after the first Leonard fight, $25,000 was put up to take the return to Argentina. Billy Gibson, the American representative of the Buenos Aires government, was sanctioned to offer the champion the chance to defend his title in a big boxing carnival planned for the Argentine capital in July 1916. Approaches were made to other leading fighters such as Charley White, Kid Lewis and Jack Britton, but Freddie was the world lightweight champion and Gibson did everything he could to get his man including issuing a public ultimatum to the Welshman that he must box Benny Leonard or Charley White in Buenos Aires or lose his title by default. There was no need to threaten the champion if a $25,000 purse was in the offing and on May 17th, at a press conference at the Hotel Cumberland in New York, Billy Gibson, Harry Pollok and Charley White's manager Nate Lewis announced that a championship match would be held in Argentina in July or August.

Freddie, Fanny and the children had lived at their apartments in New York City for most of the previous winter. The only time the family got to spend at the house they owned in Venice was when the fight game shut down for the summer after Independence Day. But in the spring of 1916 New York was in the grip of a polio epidemic. The outbreak left 27,000 people paralyzed and 6,000 dead. It caused widespread panic and thousands fled to nearby mountain resorts. Movie theatres were closed, meetings were cancelled and public gatherings were almost nonexistent. Children were warned not to drink from water fountains and to avoid amusement parks, pools and beaches. On May 24th Freddie insisted that Fanny and the children spend the summer in Venice while he prepared to go to Buenos Aires. Before he left for Argentina Freddie had his right hand re-broken because it hadn't healed since the fight with Ever Hammer. It was a month's sailing to Buenos Aires and Freddie hoped the bone would knit properly while on board ship. He planned to arrive in Argentina a month before his first bout to get fully acclimatised. But as the day of his departure from New York neared rumours abounded that the proposed boxing carnival in Buenos Aires was in serious financial difficulty. Freddie had been offered two fights: the first against Charley White for $20,000 and the second against Benny Leonard for $25,000. Freddie insisted on the entire guarantee being lodged in his bank before he set sail. The money never arrived and at the last moment the promoters told Harry Pollok that it would be impossible even to meet the first payment of $20,000 for the match with Charley White. Freddie immediately cancelled his passage.

By staying home Freddie made more than $20,000 in a series of short bouts. First up was a routine ten-round victory over Tommy Lowe in Washington DC following which Freddie returned to New York to be at ringside in the Harlem Sporting Club on 135th Street to watch Benny Leonard beat Vic Moran of New Orleans. At the end of the fight, Freddie "cheered his rival out of sight". Since their first meeting back in March Freddie and Benny had grown to like each other; they also knew that their rivalry was good box office fodder. After the Leonard fight Freddie travelled west to Denver, for yet another contest with Ad Wolgast. The match was made over fifteen rounds, the longest Freddie had agreed to box for two years. Wolgast was always a good draw and a match with the Michigan Wildcat ensured a good return, especially as the fight was to be staged on July 4th. Freddie was so confident the fight would be a financial success he agreed to waive a guarantee in return for fifty per cent of the house; Wolgast and the promoters would share the other half. Freddie worked hard to get into shape for the fight. He shed any extra weight he was carrying, working mainly in his hotel room where he would go through a strenuous set of exercises dressed in worn corduroy trousers, shoes torn across the instep, heavy flannels and a sweater coat that bulged with underclothing.

In his prime, when he battered Battling Nelson for the title with a sickening array of gloves, elbows, forehead, knees and teeth, Wolgast was one of the most vicious and uncompromising men to set foot in the ring. He'd won the championship in the dirtiest fight ever staged under Queensbury Rules but within three years had lost it on a foul to Willie Ritchie. Wolgast became champion at a time when boxing in the United States was under constant threat of legislation and could ill-afford the grotesque fights to the finish that were his forte. Boxing was desperately trying to clean up its act but the old act was the only one Wolgast knew. After losing his title he was disqualified in a series of fights against younger opponents. Several years of 'face-first' boxing had taken their toll on Wolgast. Time and thousands of punches had severely eroded his physical powers although the ferocity remained. Wolgast was a broken relic who still managed to draw a crowd for the novelty value of seeing an 'old-time' fighter ply his dark arts again. In Denver on July 4th 1916, he did not disappoint.

This was the third time Freddie had defended his title against Wolgast and the prospect held little fear for him. In the second round Freddie hit Wolgast with a right cross on the chin that drove his opponent up against the ropes. It looked as if he was ready to try to knock out the Wildcat whose only response was to let fly with a low right hand punch. Freddie fell against the ropes with Wolgast, now in a frenzy, chasing him with wild, flailing punches. As Wolgast continued his desperate assault referee Otto Floto tried to hold him off. It took a full minute for Floto to get Wolgast back to his corner and then he called on Freddie's seconds to help their man back to his corner. The referee had missed the low blow and ordered the ringside doctors to examine Freddie. They reported that while there were visible signs of the foul (his metal protector had been dented) they could not determine how badly hurt he was. So the referee called on the fight to continue despite the protests of Freddie and Pollok. After a nineteen-minute delay the champion fought on. In the meantime many fans, thinking the bout was over, left the stadium. Freddie was in excruciating pain for the first round after the restart but recovered to gave Wolgast a terrible beating. The Wildcat's only retort was to continue throwing low blows. Time and again Wolgast tried to turn Freddie to the referee's blind side to avoid detection. In the eleventh round Freddie was hitting Wolgast at will until the former champion swung a wide left below the belt that sent Freddie hurtling towards the ropes. Wolgast followed him and swung another left to exactly the same spot. Freddie reeled against the ropes and clutched them to stay upright. The referee stepped in between the boxers and immediately raised Freddie's right hand. After the fight referee Floto claimed to have cautioned the Wildcat twenty times about hitting low. Several writers called for Wolgast to be banned from the ring. It came to light a few weeks later that there had been a plot to divest Freddie of his title at Denver. Wolgast all but kicked him out of the ring and it was 'framed' to give him a knockout victory but the referee, Otto Floto, thwarted the scheme of the 'sure thing guys' and disqualified the former champion. Freddie vowed after the fight never to enter a ring with Wolgast again. "I would hesitate to say that Wolgast deliberately fouled me, thinking possibly the title would revert to him, but it may be significant that in the three matches I have had with him during the last year he had tried the same tactics," said Freddie. "Possibly he is getting old and desperate, but he certainly is vicious in his style. Wolgast seems to be as strong as ever for four or five rounds, but after that he is through and not a hard chap to beat."

Freddie never did fight Wolgast again. In fact no boxer of note stepped into the ring with the former world champion after his performance in Denver. Just eight months later the heavyweight champion Jess Willard drove Wolgast to St Mary's Hospital in Milwaukee. Wolgast's hospitalization was said to be for a nervous breakdown. On April 4th 1917 a Milwaukee court was told Wolgast was mentally incompetent and without hope of recovery, and control of his financial affairs was given to his estranged wife. Wolgast spent more than a year in various institutions. He was released in April 1918 and drifted to California where he got a couple more fights before being sent to an asylum where he built his own makeshift gymnasium. For many years Wolgast trained to defend the light-weight title that in his mind he'd never lost. When he died on April 14th 1955, Wolgast couldn't even remember being champion. He had lived for more than half of his sixty-seven years in various mental institutions.

Three days after the Wolgast fight Freddie celebrated the second anniversary of being crowned world champion. He spent most of the day on the fast train from Denver to San Francisco in order to say goodbye to his sister Kate who was due to sail from there to the Malay Peninsula to be married. Kate had been staying with Fanny and the children all summer at Venice. This was the day on which Freddie had vowed to retire but like many old fighters he found reason enough to go on. "It has been my wish to close my ring career on this very day," he told reporters on arriving in the city. "But in the meantime I have fought in no championship matches and feel that I want to risk the title in a long bout. In fact, I have in my mind three matches for the lightweight honours." Freddie was still fighting away, looking for another payday, settling another score. Very few boxers ever quit while they're ahead. As one of Freddie's friends in the press wrote on the anniversary, "maybe Champion Welsh, clever and wonderful as he is as a boxer, must stop one with his chin ere he decides that he has had enough". So instead of tossing the gloves aside Freddie was busy negotiating a match over twenty rounds in the heat of a summer's day in Denver. Colorado was one of only two states where boxing over the traditional championship route of twenty rounds to a decision was legal. Freddie was tempted to put his title on the line with an offer of $17,500 from the Colorado Springs Athletic Club, popularly known as the 'Hundred Million Dollar Club'. The backers retained the right to choose the opponent because Freddie was scheduled to meet Charley White in a twelve-round no decision contest at Minneapolis on July 21st and the Colorado syndicate wanted to reserve judgement until they saw how the challenger fared. They didn't get the chance. This match was shrouded in mystery and intrigue from the outset and Freddie and Harry Pollok decided to leave Minneapolis long before the first bell was due to be tolled. Bat Masterson, buffalo hunter, gambler, lawman, gunfighter, friend of Wyatt Earp and in his later years boxing writer, had received information from Minneapolis of a scheme to cheat Freddie out of his title. There had been a spate of incidents that year in which referees had been implicated. When Freddie and Harry arrived in Minneapolis, Pollok named George Barton as his choice to referee the bout. Barton was well known for being an honest referee but the club where the bout was to be staged refused to consider him. Pollok then provided a list of other accept-able referees but this was also declined. The promoter, Harry Sherman, and the State Boxing Commissioner, Robert Seiberlich, insisted that the referee had to be Billy Hoke. Sherman and Seiberlich professed to be offended by the insistence for any referee other than Hoke. Pollok showed the press a set of signed articles that stipulated that the managers of the boxers had to agree to the referee. Seiberlich said the articles did not conform to Minnesota law and that Pollok would have to accept Hoke. At this point the fight was called off. W.S. Forman, in a special dispatch from Minneapolis to the *Chicago Herald* reported that Billy Hoke had been claiming that he would "make the champion fight" or throw him out of the ring. "I won't stand for any ten-round tango stuff," Hoke is quoted as having said. "Welsh will have to do battle or get out."

Harry and Freddie were told of Hoke's behaviour and began their own investigation. They found out that White had been made an overwhelming favourite for the fight because several very large bets had been placed on the challenger in Chicago. "It is nothing but graft and frame-ups everywhere you look," wrote Bat Masterson. "And how could it be otherwise when the very men who are supposed to keep the game clean and protect the public are the prime movers in the corrupt practices which have become so notorious of late? So long as the grafters connected with the sport get their rake-off it matters not to them how the contests are conducted."

The cancellation cost Freddie several thousand dollars but at least he got out of Minneapolis with the championship still in his possession. It also gave him three weeks to prepare for a fight against the biggest legitimate threat to his title, Benny Leonard. The twenty-year-old from Harlem was an exceptionally clever boxer who could also hit with tremendous force. He punched Shamus O'Brien of Yonkers so hard that he was accused of carrying horseshoes in his gloves. Before his bout with Freddie, Leonard was working at Mount Kisco with Jim Coffey and a team of leading lightweight boxers. Living in the open air agreed with the usually pale-faced, anaemic-looking boxer and Leonard finished off his hard training several days before the fight and only took light exercise for the rest of the week to avoid over-exerting himself in the heat. He stayed at Mount Kisco until the morning of the contest. Throughout his training Leonard constantly proclaimed that he would knock out Freddie Welsh and take the title. Indeed, the possibility, even the likelihood, that the title was about to change hands guaranteed a huge crowd for the fight. The Washington Park Sporting Club was based at the former Brooklyn Federal League baseball grounds and the arena held 15,000 people. Freddie's recent performances had led the boxing public to believe that his time had come and the omens were good for the challenger. Leonard was the favourite in the betting and it was a rare thing that a contender should ever be the favourite over a champion. On the morning of the fight the *New York Globe* wrote:

> Boxing fans like to be in at the death of a champion, and there isn't one in a hundred who does not believe that Benny Leonard is just the boy to take Champion Welsh's laurels away.

The reports emanating from Freddie's training camp in a vacated church at Douglaston Inn, Long Island, were of a boxer who knew the grave danger of the undertaking and that he'd prepared himself as seldom before. Stories from training camps always indicated the glowing condition of a boxer, sometimes with more conventionality than truth, but this time Freddie really had prepared well. According to one visitor at the champion's quarters there was a twinkle in his eye as he went through his final gymnasium work and he appeared livelier than for many months. Freddie told the press exactly how he was going to fight Leonard; he was going to take the offensive against his young challenger from the first bell and would not give up until the finish. He intended to carry out an aggressive campaign all the way and show his critics that Leonard could not make him take a backward step. "I'm going to get more personal satisfaction out of this next bout than any I have ever engaged in," Freddie told one reporter. "I've been hounded unjustly ever since I won my title. And why? I have fought oftener in two years' time as a champion than any man in ring history. I fought the best too. Dundee had his chance, so has White, and Leonard is to get a second swing at my chin. It's there to be hit if he can do it. I'll show them tomorrow night the difference between class and mere pretension to class. I've never taken the count, and I don't think I'll break a very same rule this time. Leonard caught me off my feet last time, but Friday night will be – oh, so very, very different!"

Washington Park, Brooklyn was packed to capacity. Not that this was reflected at the box office. Early in the evening several thousand men rushed the fences and a forgotten gateway and broke into the enclosure where they crowded down in front of the grandstand. It was a typical New York boxing crowd. The night was perfect for an open-air fisticuffs carnival, and it seemed as if all Broadway had motored over. Cars filled the streets for several blocks around the venue. The ring had been placed very close to the grandstand and even those in the $1 seats were near the action. It was a stifling, sultry New York summer's evening and the South Brooklyn mosquitoes buzzed around the giant arc lights. There was a fifteen-minute delay in getting the two men into the ring. Leonard insisted on entering second because he'd beaten Freddie in their previous fight. The champion, who came in last according to custom, gave in and marched into the enclosure. Freddie stepped through the ropes looking lean and muscular and obviously feeling pleased with himself. He smiled happily at the crowd that had made him a big underdog in the betting. As the fighters touched gloves before the fight Leonard said to Freddie: "Hello, old man, I hope you're feeling well this evening."

As the first bell sounded Freddie, as promised, went straight at Leonard and hit him with a series of left hands. Instead of boxing cagily as everyone had expected, Freddie forced the challenger backwards across the ring for the full ten rounds. Within a minute of the first round Freddie backed Leonard into his own corner and hit him with a series of rights and lefts. Leonard meanwhile was finding it impossible to land a glove on the champion. By the third round

Freddie was smiling through his defending arms at Leonard's attempts to hit him. The crowd had come to see the young New Yorker knock out the champion but came close to witnessing the opposite. Three times it looked as though Freddie had Leonard at his mercy but the challenger hung on. Surprisingly Freddie was getting stronger as the bout progressed while his opponent, over a decade his junior, was tiring. In one clinch during the sixth round, Freddie was heard to ask Leonard, "old man, eh? Well, what does sonny think of the old man now?" Freddie taunted Leonard by dropping his defence and showing his jaw. The American's supporters screamed for a knockout but Freddie was long gone by the time the punch was thrown. At the final bell Leonard held out his hand and Freddie touched it nonchalantly and grinned his way back to the corner. One of New York's leading boxing writers commented:

> Father Time sat meditatingly at the ringside last night, and marvelled at Welsh's new turn of speed and punching ability. He missed one this time. Benny Leonard escorted the old man to Washington Park to toll the 10 seconds over Welsh's prostrate form, but Father Time's task consisted of 'watchful waiting'.

There was no cheering mob to follow Benny from the ring this time. He hurried to his dressing room through a lane of astonished supporters. According to one newspaper it was the "first time in a decade of moons" that New York's fight experts agreed on a result. Even his staunchest critics agreed that Freddie beat Leonard. Bob Edgren wrote in the *New York Evening World* that "Freddie Welsh 'came back' last night, and long before the ten rounds were over Benny Leonard wished he had stayed away. Fighting in his old style – the fearless and aggressive style he used before he became champion, Welsh took the lead in the first round and never lost it." The great Benny Leonard was outclassed by a superior fighter. It was a beautiful exhibition of boxing and the crowd was on its feet most of the time yelling as Freddie drove the Harlem youth back under a storm of blows. He wasn't as fit or as strong as he'd been in his first fights in Philadelphia, he wasn't as fast or as clinical as he'd been in his definitive contests in Los Angeles in the summer and autumn of 1908. On July 28th 1916, however, Freddie was sublime. If only he had finished that night in Brooklyn. But it's just not the way an old fighter leaves the ring.

> With me fighting is a business, not a game: and, certainly not a pleasure. I have forgotten the days when the glory of the title and the

publicity it brought would have set my head swimming. Every businessman aspires to be the head of his particular business and it is the same in the prize fighting art. I have craved the championship because it is the highest pinnacle of the business in which I was engaged. And now that I am there it is my business to stay there and make as much out of it as possible.

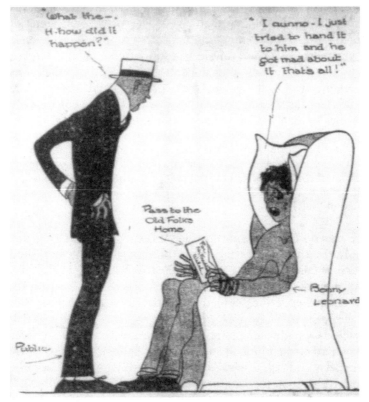

What's the use? Freddie's discovered the Fountain of Youth – *Chicago Evening Telegraph*, 29 July 1916.

Fifteen

No Reign Ends Without Bloodshed

A glorious victory over Benny Leonard at Madison Square Garden just after the second anniversary of becoming world champion would have been the perfect way to finish a career. Freddie could have retired as the undefeated lightweight champion of the world. He'd taken on all-comers and beaten all the best men of his weight in his era. He could have taken his place on the still short list of champions with a capital W as the last letter on their record. But fighters just don't do that. Freddie had made a great deal of money, not a fortune, but enough to set up the health farm and the country life he longed for. He hated training, in fact he hated boxing but he just couldn't walk away. Some great boxers hunger for one more battle because they miss the roar of the crowd while a few genuinely believe they still had 'one good fight left in 'em' and cling on to recapture former glories. The main reason though is simple, as the famous trainer Georgie Benson once said, "I've never seen an old fighter come back without it being for money." By the summer of 1916 Freddie had had his share of glory and the roars of the crowd had mostly turned to jeers but while there were a couple of thousand bucks a week for the taking in the prizering it was impossible for him to walk away. He had spoken of retirement for several years but he always feared that he lacked the strength or the courage to walk away from the game. "Once I had an ambition to become lightweight champion, now I have another one," Freddie told one writer. "All I want is the will to make me retire from the ring an undefeated champion and the power to stay retired. I know it's not going to be an easy matter, but all the same I think that I can make up my mind to do this and do it once and for all."

During his two years as champion Freddie fought over forty times in bouts of six, eight, ten, twelve or fifteen rounds. In each of those 400 plus rounds he was within one punch of losing his title. He realized that the pitcher taken to the well too often is bound to be broken but he also had an instinctive desire to linger a little longer in the spotlight. So while Freddie was preparing to fight Benny Leonard, Harry Pollok was finalizing an agreement for one last big payday. The Hundred Million Dollar Club of Denver, wanted to put on a championship fight to a decision. When the Club was informed that a minimum of $20,000 would be needed, it was fully subscribed in a single day. The fight was set for Labor Day, September 4th 1916, in the shadow of Pike's Peak just outside Colorado Springs. The Hundred Million Dollar Club insisted the opponent be Charley White, following his victory in the poll of challengers conducted by the *Chicago Tribune*. Freddie had been hurt by press reports that he was too cowardly to put his title on the line in a fully-fledged championship match. He put paid to these allegations by agreeing to a match boxing the man nominated by the scribes. It was a fight he believed he could win. "Do you know, I have kind of come to the conclusion that the lightweight bonnet would be very unbecoming to any other but myself, and for that reason I have decided it shall still be numbered among my wardrobe after September 4th," said Freddie. "No use going to the haberdasher for another when this one fits so well."

After his victory over Leonard, Freddie went to Lake Hopateong in New Jersey to rest before taking the train to Colorado. He arranged to have an exercise ring set up in a baggage car. Freddie arrived in Denver almost a month before the fight to get used to the altitude. The contest was to take place at over 6,000 feet above sea level and this was the first twenty-round bout he'd undertaken since beating Ritchie for the title two years previously. Freddie was so concerned about the condition of his hands that he insured each of his fingers for $2,000 until the day of the fight with Lloyd's. He moved into a cottage on Corona Street, Colorado Springs, while Charley White had similar quarters on Yampa Street on the other side of town. Freddie's trainer Charlie Rose and sparring partners Benny Chavez and Jack Braddon joined the camp and a special cook was engaged. Freddie also arranged for his favourite Welsh terrier, 'Pontypridd', to be transported from New York to accompany him on his morning runs. Another welcome arrival at this time was a telegram from his brother Stanley with the news that he'd been promoted to first lieutenant in the Navy. "Cannot keep the Thomas family down," responded Freddie.

Every morning Freddie ran on a different dusty Colorado road having long learned that new sights made roadwork more pleasant. In the afternoons Freddie and Charley White had an allocated time slot at the gymnasium and ring in the Colorado Athletic Club. Freddie's entourage was completed with the arrival of Fanny and Elizabeth in the final week before the fight. When Fanny first saw Freddie in Denver she told friends that without even asking she knew her husband's training had gone well just by looking in his eyes. One afternoon, Freddie broke from his regular training routine to put on a show for an invited audience of nearly three hundred women at the

Antlers Hotel in Denver. Dressed in full-length green silk tights Freddie shadow boxed, lifted dumb-bells and wound up by going ten rounds with his sparring partners. Fanny and Elizabeth were among the spectators.

As soon as the articles were signed telegrams began pouring into the Hundred Million Dollar Club with enquiries for tickets. Every hotel room in Colorado Springs was booked and the local Chamber of Commerce compiled a list of 2,000 rooms in boarding and rooming houses to be made available on the night of the fight which was pinned up on an information board in the middle of town. A 20,000-seat arena was built especially for the contest. It was some sight: a cobweb-shaped structure designed to give everyone a clear view of the ring. Every seat was made wider and longer than usual to give the spectators more room. A hundred carpenters were employed and Bill Farnsworth, who'd built scores of ballpark grandstands throughout the United States, supervised the job.

It was one of the biggest sporting events in America in 1916 but with only a few weeks to go the fight was almost cancelled when news broke that a railroad strike was threatened for the day of the contest. Such a big-money fight in a small town could only succeed by attracting large numbers from surrounding cities. If the trains didn't run the event would be a financial disaster. The Hundred Million Dollar Club, however, prided itself on its reputation for sportsmanship and nothing would be permitted to mar it. When it heard of the strike the club decreed the fight should go on regardless of any financial difficulties: it had given its word to the fighters. Most of the sportsmen and newspapermen from the East Coast decided to travel early, trusting the dispute would be over in time for them to return home. One firm in Denver leased a fleet of 200 motorcars for the event. Word of this arrangement reached other auto rental firms and all roads leading into Colorado Springs were jammed on the day of the fight. The *Denver Post* arranged a special train on which paying customers would be wined and dined, and entertained by former boxing champions on their way to the fight. Jack McAuliffe, the only lightweight champion who had retired undefeated to that point, was one of the guests. The train became known as 'The Champion Special'.

Wagering on the fight, which had been unusually quiet in the weeks preceding the event, picked up in the final few days. A gang of Chicago 'sportsmen' arrived in Denver and Smiley Corbett, the city's well-known Boniface and jazz impresario wired out to ask the odds and said he had several thousands to bet on the champion to win.

Freddie was installed as a 3 to 5 favourite, White was 11 to 10 with 3 to 1 against White winning by knockout. As the Chicago deputation reached Colorado Springs so did rumours that the fight was fixed. It was said that White had promised not to knock out Freddie and had been compelled to post a forfeit of $3,000 to bind his promise. A feeling of corruption pervaded the event. A special corps of plain clothes detectives was drafted in to guard the crowd against possible thefts or disturbance while Freddie decided to arrange his own protection and 'Shoot em up' Bill Lyons was invited to the training camp. 'Wild' Bill Lyons, as he was also known, was an old friend of Freddie's. He was a senator who was never seen without his huge revolver and two remarkable watches. On the face of one was a photograph of Wild Bill with Freddie; on the other the senator was posing with Jack Dempsey and Jack Kearns. Lyons had been in Freddie's corner in his recent fight with Ad Wolgast in Denver armed with his .45 and a sword and was on hand to clear the ring when some people tried to rob Freddie of his title.

As the preparations drew to a close Charley White was reported to be growing irritable, "making it dangerous for anybody to cross

The arena under the shadow of Pikes Peak, Colorado Springs.

him". It was particularly evident in his final sparring session before the fight when he handled his partners roughly whenever they showed a willingness to exchange blows with him. The promoters, meanwhile, spent the day desperately trying to ensure that as many people as possible arrived in Colorado Springs. The railroad strike had been averted at the eleventh hour and a military-style operation was staged to allow the maximum number of trains to reach the venue. More trains were sent from Denver to get people to the fight than had ever left one city for a sporting event in America. Special trains were chartered to bring people from Pueblo, Cripple Creek, Leadville, Trinidad and various other towns throughout the state. A special train came in from Chicago carrying Charley White's supporters. Bob Vernon and a party of sportsmen made the journey from New York in another specially chartered train. Freddie spent the day before the fight playing with Elizabeth.

The following morning the late summer sun appeared once more in a cloudless sky. The mercury was close to ninety as the first of the spectators trickled into the arena just after midday. The heat heightened the tension that had built up around the fight. As the preliminary bouts were being fought, Nate Lewis and Harry Pollok got into an argument over White's use of what was a forerunner of a gum shield – a piece of rubber to cover the upper teeth that prevented cuts inside the mouth. Nate argued that it didn't amount to anything and was just what a lot of fighters used. Harry was furious. "Sure, let him wear anything he likes," Pollok retorted. "I just want to tell you that Fred is going to wear that football head-guard he has been using in his training." Hot words followed but the argument was finally quelled. "It has got to the stage where everybody's nerves are jingling and jumping," wrote one reporter who witnessed the argument. "It doesn't take much to start a fight under such conditions," he added. The build-up to the bout had been ill-tempered. The contest had been threatened by the unions calling strikes and by the 'goodfellas' looking for a sure thing. The rival camps had argued over weight, choice of referee, money, mouthguards and any other issue they could fight over. At many points over the previous six weeks it seemed the whole thing would be cancelled yet the day had arrived and the preliminary bouts had began. But the real drama was about to begin.

Just over an hour and a half before Freddie and Charley White were due to make their way into the ring a deafening crash was heard for miles around. The hot sun of the previous few days had caused the timbers of the new arena to warp and the spikes holding the struc-

Welsh Has Elephant on His Hands;
That's Why He Likes This Picture
Chicago Herald, Aug 26/16

39. Still selling tickets, still a sucker for a circus.

ture together were loosened by the strain. Without warning the upper
tear of the south bleachers collapsed, dropping nearly four hundred
spectators over eighteen feet to the ground. A struggling mob fought
to extricate themselves from the tangle of splintered timbers. Men
and women with blood streaming from their faces staggered from the
pile of broken planks, hysterical with fear and sobbing aloud. One
man was killed and two women suffered broken backs. A further 150
were seriously hurt. Amid great confusion the police and firemen
made their way through the crowd and the injured were laid out on
the ground to the south of the arena. A score of ambulances carried
the most badly hurt through crowded streets to local hospitals. As a
result of the accident over 2,000 people were refused entry. The
management lost $3,000 but insisted that the fight must go on. At
4.45 pm, according to schedule and with the dead and dying barely

out of the arena, Charley White stepped through the ropes. The late summer sun was still blazing down on the ring. Freddie followed immediately and they tossed for corners. White won and chose the west corner with the sun on his back. A woman in the crowd offered her parasol to Freddie who bowed his acknowledgement.

As soon as the opening bell was struck Freddie raced to within a few feet of White's corner, grabbed him around the body and placed his face to the sun. Nate Lewis was screaming at his charge to get out of the sun's rays but White couldn't do it. Freddie fought largely on the retreat always backing into the sun, forcing White to box with the glare in his eyes and the heat on his face. It wasn't long before the sweat on White's brow mixed with blood streaming down his face. In the second round Freddie's left hand scraped off a sore on the challenger's nose and the wound bled throughout the fight. The only moment of concern for Freddie came in the thirteenth round when he was caught with a clean left hook and just for a moment looked weak and tired. But the champion held on, cleared his head and was never troubled again. One reporter wrote that Freddie only hit White five times with his right hand throughout the twenty rounds but that it was impossible to count the number of hundreds of lefts speared into the challenger's face. Charley White could beat almost anybody else but when he faced Freddie something seemed to go wrong. Some believed his heart failed him; others even claimed he was 'yellow'. "If he is against an ordinary man he fights like a world beater," wrote one Chicago journalist, "but when Welsh faces him he throws up his hands."

When the bell sounded for the end of the twentieth round the referee, Billy Roche, waited for several minutes before making any announcement on the result. Most at ringside thought Roche was still undecided as to who had won. After this period of confusion the referee appeared to reach out a hand to each of the boxers as if he was about to signify a draw. Freddie noticed this and rushed over to Roche, placed a glove in the referee's hand and felt his own arm being raised aloft. The referee announced his decision in favour of the champion, having scored the fight ten rounds to Freddie, five to White with five even. There was no doubt about the fairness of the decision. White's camp had wanted the Chicago referee, Ed Smith, to officiate. After the fight Smith, who watched the fight at ringside, supported Roche's decision. The result prompted a shower of cushions to be hurled into the ring, generally in Roche's direction. "Many ladies present were hit and hats ruined," wrote one outraged reporter at ringside. The referee's friends then took to the ring and chaperoned him through the baying crowd to a car, which flanked by a policeman, sped away from the arena to the hotel at which the official was staying. Hundreds of spectators were seen chasing the car until eventually it accelerated away. "The wild and woolly west is not familiar with scientific boxers like Freddie Welsh," commented the *New York Globe*. The famous referee Otto Floto, writing in the *Denver Post*, thought the police should have been more forceful. "Had the policemen of Colorado Springs hit one or two of the ring leaders over the head with their clubs the balance of the herd would have subsided," wrote Floto. "On such occasions there is always a loud-mouthed individual who starts these things. Head him off and the balance are easily handled," he added.

The following day's press attributed the riot to the way in which the bout was fought. There had been prolonged periods when the boxers were locked in a succession of clinches, pushing each other back and forth about the ring. Freddie had instigated most of this and it worked. He barely took a shot through twenty rounds while he hit his partially blinded opponent at will with countless jabs. Freddie left the ring unmarked while White's right eye was closed by swelling and the left one was bruised. But this wasn't what a large faction of the crowd had paid to see. If the contestants didn't beat the life out of each other they made a demonstration and demanded their money back. One newspaperman commented: "The trouble with the fighting game is that it is under the control of roughnecks, who demand their gore. Even the Romans, who liked to see a stack of corpses as the result of a day's pleasure, had a place for the exhibition of skill presented when a man with only net and trident met a heavily armed and armoured gladiator."

A few months later evidence slowly emerged that the unrest following Roche's decision may have had more sinister origins than the disaffection of a few bloodthirsty fight fans. White had a crowd behind him that had a reputation for exerting influence by various means and who were considered to be "a bunch of sure-thing grafters". They had killed boxing in Chicago and had robbed punters of thousands of dollars when Freddie and White fought the first time in Milwaukee. Later in the year Billy Roche returned to Colorado Springs and claimed the riot was part of a plot by a ring of Chicago gamblers who "hoped to rob Welsh of his lightweight title". Roche had an affidavit to attest to his theory and he engaged detectives in Denver and Chicago to collect the evidence to prove the plot existed and to reveal the identity of the ringleaders. Pollok telegrammed Roche to inform him that Freddie was willing to contribute $5,000 to help the investigation and that the champion was determined to "exert every effort to uncover the men who attempted to 'frame' his bout". The *National Police Gazette* supported the investigation:

> It would not be beyond the bounds of possibility that a clique of 'sure thing' gamblers would attempt such a thing. It wouldn't be the first time in history of the sport that such a thing had been attempted. There have been instances where efforts of this kind have succeeded. If Welsh is sincere in his belief that an attempt was made to 'fix' the bout the stand he has taken is a commendable one, and all advocates of clean sport cannot help hoping that his efforts to uncover the 'men behind' will be successful.

Of course Freddie, Billy Roche and their investigators had no more success in proving a case than did the authorities at that time and the newspapers soon dropped the story. Corruption was rarely mentioned because promoters such as Jack Kearns and Tex Rickard normally provided the reporters with a percentage of the gate or bottles of whiskey. But Freddie had made a point, kept his title and earned over $15,000 from the fight. He instructed the stakeholder to turn over all the money derived from his share in the moving pictures to the Red Cross Fund of Great Britain. The donation proved to be in excess of $2,000, and the effort to raise funds for the war effort kept Freddie busy for the remainder of 1916.

After the fight Freddie spent a few days in Venice with Fanny and the children but he was soon travelling again on a tour through Canada to raise money for the patriotic relief fund. On his way north he stopped off at Seattle for a four-round exhibition fight with Harry Anderson and two nights later he was in a Vancouver ring with Jim Clark. The following night it was on to Calgary for a bout with Kid Scaler that raised over $1,000 for the fund. The next beneficiary of Freddie's philanthropic autumn of 1916 was an old friend of his, Hardy Downing. Freddie had agreed to open the winter season at the Manhattan Boxing Club in Salt Lake City where Downing was the manager. The world champion fought a four-round exhibition bout against Mickey O'Brien but Freddie heard that Downing had run out of money paying expenses. He slipped into the box office after the boxing was over and found Downing counting out the guarantee that Freddie had been promised. The money was coming from Downing's own pocket. Freddie waived his own fee and expenses to make sure the club and the other young fighters on the bill were at least able to break even on the venture.

Freddie broke off his fundraising tour in late September to spend

a month with Fanny and the children back at the apartments in the St
Paul Hotel in New York. Freddie spent the days walking through
Central Park with his family or reading in his library. The evenings
were spent promenading down Broadway, taking in a show and dining
at the city's finest restaurants. During his time away from the ring he
gave an interview to a female journalist, Belle McCormick, in which
he explained that he now felt compelled to take time away from the
society in which he'd spent his entire adult life. "Maybe it's because I
see so much of the rough element that I want to get away from men
the minute I leave the ring," Freddie explained. "All men want to talk
about is how many times I've knocked out the other fellow, and I get
sick of talking shop. I get disgusted with the fight atmosphere. When I
get through with a match I am eager to go home to my wife. We read
good books together, we read philosophy and discuss it, or we go to a
good play, or to hear some good music, and those are the things that
I enjoy." But all the while Harry Pollok was negotiating for another
series of fights. Freddie's new plan was to retire in June 1917 and the
world champion was now talking of giving a new generation of lightweights a chance to fight for the title. He just couldn't walk away from
the game he'd come to despise and, Fanny apart, all those around him
were encouraging Freddie to fight on. He was still the lightweight
champion of the world and a valuable asset for the managers and
promoters who were also his closest friends and confidants. Freddie
was not the first, and certainly not the last, fighter whose ring career
was extended on the advice of those entrusted to look after his interests. The former Madison Square Garden publicist Johnny Condon
was once approached by Irving Ungerman, the manager of George
Chuvalo, who wanted to get another match for his charge after he had
just taken a terrible beating. Condon told Ungerman, "Irving, if he's
got one good punch left in him, he ought to throw it at you if you let
him fight again."

Freddie prepared to don the gloves once more. He returned to
Canada for a series of exhibitions to warm up for yet another
campaign against the best young lightweights the American promoters could find. Freddie resumed his "patriotic tour" of Canada at
Sohmers Park, Montreal, on October 25th. His opponent was the
local lightweight Bobby Wilson. The referee had to stop the contest
in the seventh round because Wilson was exhausted. Two nights later
Freddie knocked out Mike Ward in Ottawa and the following night
he out-pointed Ben Allen in ten rounds at Quebec City. He took on
a further three fights in November, all no decision contests against
local fighters – all uninspired, tired displays. Freddie only took the

contests to avoid having to train for what was scheduled to be his first big fight of the winter season against Johnny Dundee on Thanksgiving Night, November 30th at Madison Square Garden. It was to be the first of a series of boxing matches at the venue organized by a new club, the Madison National Show Corporation. Dundee had been one of the most prominent challengers for the lightweight title since Freddie won it in July 1914, and the fight was seen as a spectacular way to launch the club. In the *New York Times* of November 24th, Jim White, the matchmaker, insisted that the venue had been secured and that he would be filing the club's application for a license with Chairman Wenck of the boxing commission that day. But Wenck was unimpressed with the Madison National Show Corporation and refused the application. Freddie took advantage of the cancellation to spend more time with his family in New York. He also wrote for various boxing publications and newspapers. During the next five months, he was only lured back into the ring once, and was badly beaten in a no decision contest by Ritchie Mitchell in Milwaukee in January 1917. His performance was greeted by a roar of disapproval from the crowd and at one stage Chairman Laginger of the state boxing commission warned Freddie to box more aggressively or he'd be disqualified and his title lost. After the fight Harry Pollok told reporters that Freddie was handicapped by a heavy cold. He was briefly tempted back into the ring the following month by an offer from Cuba. The Cuban authorities announced their intention to stage a boxing carnival at the end of February under the guidance of the Havana Agricultural Exposition and Racing Association. The idea was to stage a series of bouts for the championship of Cuba at four different weight classes. A purse of $10,000 was discussed but the venture failed and Freddie stayed with Fanny and the children in New York.

His brief period of semi-retirement ended on April 6th 1917. President Wilson declared war on Germany and Freddie was one of the first boxers to join up. The *National Police Gazette* proclaimed that Freddie's "example may be an incentive to many foreign born exponents of the manly art to show allegiance to the country of their adoption". Freddie had loved America from the moment he first arrived as a sixteen-year-old and when 'his country' went to war he heard the call. "This great country of Uncle Sam's is my home," Freddie wrote. "It has given me my living, my wife and my babies, and I enjoyed the protection of the Stars and Stripes for fifteen years. Why shouldn't I want to fight for everything America stands for? With the grim clouds of war sweeping down on us all, I want to do

my bit with the rest!" Freddie revived his idea of assembling a group
of boxers to fight for the cause. He'd tentatively suggested such a plan
in Canada but now the United States had joined the war Freddie
penned a letter outlining his proposals to Charles S. Whitman, the
Governor of New York.

Dear Sir – I want to offer my services and financial assistance in
recruiting a sportsmen's regiment for 'overseas' service. I am writing
to ask your assistance in securing officers to enroll, train and equip
such a regiment. Since the declaration of war against Germany seemed
assured, I have canvassed the situation among those interested in the
boxing game, and such an undertaking needs but official sanction to
make it a success.

My plan as to finances is to organize boxing shows, at which I will
meet contenders for my title and turn the receipts of such shows over
to a fund to equip the regiment.

If this regiment is organized I am, of course, ready to serve in any
capacity. The United States is my adopted country. I have lived here
for fifteen years; my wife and two children are Americans, and I feel
that the entrance of America into the war is the call to arms of every
man who, like myself, has been given an opportunity to earn a living
in this great country.

If this plan meets with your approval, will you make it possible for
me to have a personal interview with one of your military aids?
Very respectfully,

FREDDIE WELSH,
Lightweight Champion of the World

While he waited for the opportunity to play his part Freddie was
enticed back into the ring for a match in St Louis against the only
leading lightweight of his generation he hadn't fought, Oscar
'Battling' Nelson. Freddie had tracked Nelson around the United
States when the latter held the title in a vain attempt to challenge the
champion. That was back in 1910 and 1911 and by the time they
finally met in St Louis on April 17th 1917 both men were well past
their best. But time had certainly been kinder to Freddie than Nelson
and during the fight it was obvious that the current champion was
feeling sorry for one of his predecessors. Nelson lashed out with
rights and lefts in the same fury that sent many a promising boxer to
the canvas, but Freddie sidestepped, ducked, dodged and back-
stepped until the 'Battler' got weary of trying to land a good blow.
There had been a great deal of bad blood between the two over the
years and Nelson had dismissed Freddie as a "snowflake boxer" who
wasn't worthy to challenge him when he was champion. But that was

the quarrel of young men and Freddie only occasionally cut loose with anything that looked like a solid punch. After the fight Nelson, the man who in his prime proclaimed that "I ain't human" because of the amount of punishment his body could take, decided he could take no more. But Nelson found life out of the ring even tougher. After announcing his retirement, he toured with a circus and then tried, unsuccessfully, to enlist in the US Army as a boxing instructor. He then became an inventor and endeavoured to persuade the military to purchase rights to the 'Nelson Dummy', a punching bag he designed for American soldiers that was fashioned in the likeness of the Kaiser. Just over a year after his fight with Freddie, Nelson was felled by the influenza epidemic that swept around the world, killing thousands. By this time his health and his money had gone. He was hospitalized in Chicago from where he tried to call in a few outstanding debts. Within days of being admitted to the infirmary the Chicago newspapers reported that Nelson had been moved from 'Millionaires' Row' in St Luke's Hospital to a ward for the indigent. "Last night oyster patties for supper; this morning, hash," Nelson wrote to his one-time manager, Teddy Murphy, adding, "just now, old-timer, we had stew that once flirted with a cow". But Nelson was nothing if not resilient and after a seven year struggle he finally rebounded into solvency in 1925 when his father died and left him $150,000. Most of his father's money actually came from ring earnings his son had given him. The money did not last long of course and Nelson spent much of the latter half of his life living in cheap hotel rooms. The destruction of the indestructible Nelson eventually came in February 1954. He was admitted to the charity ward of Chicago State Hospital "a wasted, incoherent little man without a penny to his name". A newspaper report described a 71-year-old fighter babbling nonsensically about fights that had occurred decades before. He died a month later of lung cancer.

Not even the pathetic sight of a dissipated old champion swinging wildly at him in a St Louis ring was enough to persuade Freddie that his time had also arrived. Freddie fought on. He was back in the ring just three nights later to pick up a thousand dollars and a beating at the hands of a local Buffalo fighter, Rocky Kansas. When he started his campaign of defending his title several times a month in ten-round fights Freddie accepted that he would lose the newspaper decision most times but he barely took a blow and cared little about the press or public reaction. By the spring of 1917 he was back fighting with the same frequency but now he was getting badly hurt on a weekly basis. His next painful encounter came just four nights later

against another unheralded boxer, Chick Simler. At the end of the
seventh round Freddie was battered into the ropes and was chased
on the retreat to his corner when the bell saved him. He managed to
stay on his feet for the remaining three rounds and held on to the
title. There were signs of a dramatic decline in Freddie's powers in
the ring and the *New York Times* reported that "local admirers of the
ring sport are sceptical indeed of the Englishman's ability to defend
his laurels as the world's leading lightweight much longer".

From the beginning of his boxing career Freddie had always tried
to learn new techniques, new tricks, that would give him the smallest
of advantages in the ring. As he received one beating after another in
1917 he continued to develop new ideas. By now, however, most of
his thinking was dedicated to self-preservation. "My method is
psychological," Freddie told one boxing writer. "I study my man,
think quickly, and take an advantage of an opening. I never forget
that his mental condition is all-important. If I am hit hard and nearly
knocked out I try to smile. If he has his best at me and yet I smile that
will disadvantage him. I dash at him when at my worst, he will back
up, and I will get ten seconds to recover. Even if my sight leaves me
and I stagger to my feet with my head rolling on my shoulders I will
shout, "Is that all you can punch? By instinct, by second nature, I am
determined to get the best of it. I will get the best of it even if it is
impossible. I will use Christian Science at a crisis."

He got another chance to test out his theories on May 1st 1917 at
Madison Square Garden against the world featherweight champion
Johnny Kilbane. The fight was a match between two of the great
defensive boxers of the time and was certainly not to the liking of a
New York fight crowd and the gate receipts were not as good as
expected for a fight featuring two world champions. Those who did
patronize the Garden that night were sorely disappointed.
Disparaging remarks were heard from the crowd throughout the
fight and some even went so far as to hint that it was not altogether
on the 'up and up'. Once more Freddie was indebted to New York
State law that barred a referee from giving decisions in boxing bouts
for the privilege of still being able to sign himself lightweight
champion of the world.

While Freddie's performances were declining with every fight and
his title was becoming increasingly tarnished, one young boxer re-
established himself as the outstanding challenger. In the same week
that Freddie lost to both Rocky Kansas and Johnny Kilbane, Benny
Leonard had travelled out to Milwaukee and knocked out Ritchie
Mitchell in his hometown to claim what was in essence the American

championship. On his return to New York, Leonard was met at Grand Central Station by a crowd of over 4,000 admirers. From the station a procession of cars headed north to Harlem with Leonard riding in the lead vehicle. Billy Gibson, Leonard's manager, told awaiting reporters that he was going to guide his charge through a campaign that would only end with a fight against Freddie Welsh for the world's championship. After every victory for his fighter, Billy Gibson called on Freddie to defend his title against Leonard. Harry Pollok dismissed the demands by constantly referring to the last ten-round meeting between the two boxers in which Freddie received the unanimous newspaper verdict. But by now large swathes of the boxing press and aficionados regarded Benny Leonard as the world's best lightweight – he just didn't have the title. During the year following his defeat to Freddie, Leonard had fought regularly at local clubs in Harlem and the boxing writers were convinced that the next time the pair met the lightweight title would finally return to an American. Their only reservation was that the Harlem man had never fought a twenty-round contest, while Freddie was a veteran of dozens of such fights. There were various reports of offers of $15,000 for the fight on the west coast which failed to materialize. Such was the hysteria surrounding Leonard's recent performances however, that Freddie was guaranteed a big purse for a ten-round no decision fight in New York and despite his recent showings the champion was still convinced that no-one could knock him out in such a contest. The fight was originally scheduled to take place at the Manhattan Athletic Club on 155th Street and Eighth Avenue on March 28th 1917. The management at the club was reporting a record-breaking demand for tickets, so much so that improvements had to be carried out at the venue to handle the crowd. But with just one day to go the fight was postponed when Leonard contracted a cold that according to his camp would prevent him putting forth his best efforts against Freddie. The match was rescheduled for May 28th. The champion and his challenger shared a ring a few weeks before the contest, when many of the world's leading boxers took part in a series of exhibition fights at Madison Square Garden as part of the United States Navy's recruitment campaign. Over a thousand men from three French warships docked in New York were the guests of honour at the event. The sailors were escorted from the Brooklyn Navy Yard to the Garden by 300 American Bluejackets, 200 marines and an accompanying band for an evening of music, vaudeville and boxing. Freddie and Benny Leonard both took part, each with his own sparring partner.

Benny Leonard was a big favourite with American fight fans

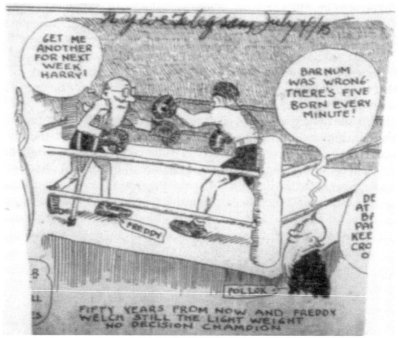

40. *New York Evening Telegram*, 4 July 1915.

because he was a big knockout puncher as well as a clever boxer. In one bout leading up to his title challenge Leonard punched a highly respected local boxer in New York, Packey Hommey, into submission. Hommey was unable to leave his corner to answer the bell for the final round of the contest. Freddie had been unusually careful in his training for the bout because he had seen Leonard fight several times since their last meeting and he knew he was much improved. On the morning of the fight the scribes were divided on the outcome. The local lad had blasted away all his opponents in recent fights; none were left standing. Yet there was a grudging admiration for the skills of Freddie Welsh in the States and this was a no decision contest. All Freddie had to do was to stay on his feet for ten rounds, and the reports were that the champion was in very good condition.

The challenger was the first to enter the ring, though no one could see him at first because he was surrounded by latecomers taking their seats. The cheers were still resounding around the arena when, three minutes later, the world champion took his bow. Referee McPartland announced the weights: Welsh 136 3/4lbs, Leonard 133lbs, then called the boxers to the centre of the ring. Leonard set a fast pace, dancing around the older man, putting him on the defensive. The challenger had taken control from the outset but the crowd and Leonard had seen it all before. In recent fights Freddie was usually out-pointed and he was also taking an increasing number of hard punches. From the third round onwards though, it became apparent that Leonard was trying to do something different. Ten rounds wasn't a long time and most of Freddie's challengers tended to lunge at him from the opening bell, desperately searching an elusive knockout punch. In this fight Leonard appeared to be very calm. There were no frenzied attacks because he believed he had finally found a way in which to take the title from the seemingly indestructible champion. The challenger learned from his two previous fights with Freddie that it was a waste of time and energy to try to hit the Welshman's head or jaw so Leonard shifted his attack to his opponent's stomach. It was soon apparent that this was a vulnerable spot as Freddie weakened noticeably. Leonard threw a series of powerful left uppercuts to the body and whenever they landed Freddie winced perceptibly. Throughout the ordeal Freddie smiled, but grimly.

By the eighth round the champion was carrying his guard much lower to try to defend his battered torso and Leonard got his opening. Freddie's reign as world champion came to a dramatic end in the ninth. Fifteen seconds after the bell sounded for the start of the round an overhand right caught Freddie above the left ear and the blow sent him halfway to the canvas. Suddenly Leonard could see the title was his for the taking. Urged on frantically by his corner the challenger chased the retreating champion into a neutral corner. Freddie settled into the familiar guard that had kept him out of trouble throughout his career. But this was a fight too many. Leonard flailed away until, finally, Freddie dropped his gloves in exhaustion. As he did so, Leonard sent over a right hand blow quickly followed by a left that landed on the proverbial button – the point on the lower jaw that usually signals a visit to the canvas. Freddie reeled away from the punch and landed on one knee in Leonard's corner. Before the referee had a chance to count Freddie was on his feet. He was so dazed he wasn't aware of what was going on. An old campaigner would stay down and take a short count to clear his head. The onslaught continued. Freddie hadn't even made it out of the corner when another flurry of blows knocked him down for a second time. The referee looked over to the champion's corner to ask if his handlers would throw in the towel. There was no response; surely the master of defensive boxing would somehow hold on. The beating continued until Freddie fell to his hands and knees out of sheer

exhaustion rather than as the result of one particular blow. This time
Freddie had to use the ropes in Leonard's corner to help him to his
feet but by now all resistance had gone. His left arm became trapped
around the top rope so he couldn't even put his gloves up. All the
while Leonard was battering Freddie's unprotected head. Freddie
couldn't be knocked down because he was stuck in the ropes. The
referee looked over once more for a towel from Freddie's corner, and
when none was forthcoming he stepped between the two boxers and
tried to release Freddie's entangled arms. He started counting and by
the time he had reached four Freddie had staggered in a half circle
and collapsed over the middle rope of the ring just above the
timekeeper. And that's how Freddie's reign as champion ended,
draped unconscious over the ropes.

He hung there helplessly until the referee hastened his seconds
over to carry Freddie back to the corner. Leonard followed them over
to shake hands with the old champion, but Freddie didn't even
recognize him. He was completely oblivious to the mayhem that
broke out around him as the new title-holder celebrated his victory.
The New York crowd roared its approval. Leonard's friends and
supporters invaded the ring, past the restraining arms of policemen
and club officials. Hats and handkerchiefs were tossed in the air as
the fans in the back seats clambered down from their lofty places and
made their way over the shoulders and heads of those at ringside and
through the ropes where they crowded about the victorious Leonard
in a frenzy of emotion. One of Leonard's wealthier supporters
pressed a cheque for $1,000 dollars into the new champion's gloved
hand. Leonard was eventually taken out of the ring on the shoulders
of the rampaging mob.

For the next few minutes Freddie's seconds attempted to revive
him. He occasionally tried to get up from his stool as if another
round had been called but he sank weakly back down after each
effort. It took fifteen minutes of pretty rough handling by his cornermen to get Freddie back into a state where he could begin to
understand what had happened. When the former champion finally
got to his feet he looked around and asked Harry Pollok, "What's the
matter?" Freddie's first instinct on hearing the news was a feeble
protest to the referee that he was fit to continue but the new
champion was already back in his changing room. When Freddie
finally realized that it was all over he burst into tears. The dream of
retiring as the undefeated champion of the world was gone. He'd
fought one fight too many. To make matters even worse, Harry Pollok
had wagered the entire purse on the champion to beat Leonard.

Freddie returned home without his title or his money. Eventually, at the age of thirty-one, a younger fighter had caught up with Freddie and knocked him out. As Robert Anasi once wrote: "The succession of title-holders is the central story of prizefighting, and no reign ends without bloodshed."

Sixteen

Defeated Partisans Think Up Horror Weapons

The day after the fight Harry Pollok was telling anyone who would listen that Freddie still held the title. The defeated fighter's aides argued that their man was not actually counted out, either standing up or while on the canvas, so he must still be regarded as the champion. They insisted that a count might have given Freddie time to recover and complete the ten rounds. On the three occasions when Freddie was down, he regained his feet before a count could be started. But as he lay over the ropes the referee believed there was no need to count for a man who was clearly unconscious. Pollok cited Rule 5 of the Marquis of Queensbury Rules that reads, "a man hanging on the ropes in a helpless state with his toes off the ground shall be considered down". When a boxer is lying on the canvas, even though he is absolutely insensible when he hits the floor, he has the benefit of nine seconds to get to his feet. Pollok thought it reasonable to suppose that a boxer who was hanging on the ropes was in a better physical and mental condition than one who was prone on the ground, either insensible or partly so. If the man on the ground was allowed to nine seconds to recover, surely one who still "retained the perpendicular" was entitled to as much. When the boxing writers asked the referee to comment, McPartland replied that it was a knockout and that he stopped the bout to protect Freddie from further punishment. The referee also criticized Pollok for not throwing in the towel to save his charge a severe beating. Freddie spent the day after the fight recovering at his recently purchased mansion in New Jersey. In a telephone conversation with a *New York Times* reporter the former champion was philosophical about the defeat:

> I do not wish to make excuses for the outcome of the bout, and I readily concede Leonard's superiority. I think he is a wonderful little fellow in and out of the ring, and I don't mind admitting that the title could not pass into better hands. I could not live on forever, and neither could I hold the championship forever. Then, too, the boxing public has been looking for a change of champions, and will welcome it, and I don't mind saying that I think Leonard will be a very popular title-holder.
>
> I do not believe, though, that my title should go to Leonard, because I was not counted out. Even a preliminary boxer is entitled to the count, and I see no reason why I should not have received it. I might have taken a nine-second count on the first knockdown, but I wanted to show that I was not badly hurt. Arising on the other two

occasions was just instinct. However, it is all over and done now, and I intend in the future to stick to my health farm. I don't think I will seek a return match, and I don't even think I will box again.

When Freddie beat Willie Ritchie to win the title in 1914 he caused a transatlantic boxing row. Three years later, the Welshman's defeat to Benny Leonard started another argument. Writers on many of the leading English sporting papers supported Freddie's contention that he was still champion because the contest was billed as a no decision bout and they didn't consider such an event as an appropriate way for a championship to change hands. Boxing in Europe and the United States was very different at this time. In England and France there was an iron-clad rule that a boxer with a championship was obliged to defend his title at the call of a club or federation, and that failure to do so resulted in the boxer losing his title and belt. The National Sporting Club was the controlling body in England and all other clubs in the country strictly followed its rules. In the United States there was no single organization that compelled boxers to follow rules. The sporting writers recognized the champions until they lost their titles in a contest. So according to American rules, Leonard was the new champion, and he was keen to show his compatriots exactly how he did it. He gave a series of exhibitions; some attended by crowds of 10,000 to 12,000 people, in which his sparring partner took the part of Freddie Welsh. The two fighters re-enacted the fateful round in which Freddie was left flopping between the ropes; much to the amusement of all present.

By the time he lost to Leonard Freddie had bought the 'Pelletreau' property on Long Hill in Chatham Township near the town of Summit, New Jersey. He paid $60,000 for the farm of 162 acres on some of the highest ground in the State and it stretched over a series of hills, valleys, fields and forests. The main house was built on the very peak of Long Hill, overlooking the Passaic Valley, and commanding a view for miles in every direction. The walls of the building were painted white while the roof and the gables were a rich red. Freddie said that he'd searched the country, from New York to California, for a place that would "seem like home to the man who opened the front door". But the lavish house and spectacular estate had brought nothing but bad luck to its two previous occupants. It was built by V.F. Pelletreau, who spared no money in its construction, but who was not privileged to enjoy it for very long. Pelletreau was thrown from his horse in nearby Morristown and killed instantly. The property was then bought by George E. Duncan, a New York merchant, who lived there for a short while before he died in the winter of 1916. Freddie acquired the property from the Duncan Estate, it was rundown and he spent tens of thousands of dollars in improvements. He bought the finest materials and according to one reporter the "appointments were exquisite". There was a lavish parlour, drawing room, dining room, conservatory, library and billiard room and Freddie installed the most modern kitchen money could buy. Many of the bedrooms in the mansion were like "nun's cells" for simplicity and cleanliness; advertised as having all the necessaries but none of the superficials. "These are not supposed to be living rooms," Freddie explained, "I want the guests here to cheer up, be natural, stay downstairs, or outdoors, and keep with the bunch. These are not worry rooms. These are sleeping rooms!" In front of the house, a vast lawn sloped down to the roadway, some distance below. A landscape architect was employed to design sunken gardens. Freddie's idea was that when the flowers were in bloom they would represent a cheerful manifestation of life and health and would be an inspiration to all seeking harmony with "the power that is". The gymnasium was custom built to Freddie's specification and he also installed baths, showers, vapour baths, thermos baths and steam rooms. Outside there were tennis courts, a croquet lawn and even a few golf holes as well as a swimming pool fed by the purest water from a group of springs. Freddie claimed the high altitude made the air pure, clear, refreshing and invigorating. "Your lungs open automatically and every cell fills with air and you feel the thrill of oxygen combining with the iron in the blood," said Freddie. "You feel a part of the great force of the universe." His title may have gone, but the splendour of Long Hill suggested that Freddie, as he had always professed, was different from other fighters. He had used the ring to make the money to buy the health farm to secure his family's future. Within a few months of arriving in New Jersey he had also incorporated the Freddie Welsh Auto Company in partnership with three local businessmen. "Freddie is very far removed indeed from the ranks of the careless calculators," reported *Boxing*. "He may have his faults – who is free from them? – but he has never yet been guilty of an overestimate of his qualities. That is, if we agree to forget about the sad mistake he made in his last meeting with the present champion." The publication's editor was confident that Freddie was going to be as successful in his new ventures as he'd been with the gloves.

> He can make all the money he may want for the future out of the health home he has taken and proposes to open shortly. It will not arrive in chunks, as it does in the ring of course: but if Freddie buckles

down to business he ought to be able to rake in quite as many dollars in weekly increments as he could hope to gather from a contest, and in much about the same time too – when the training period, the loafing around, the diplomatic business, and the subsequent recovery are all taken into consideration. More, in fact, for he would not then be scattering his coin around Broadway and elsewhere as he has been in the habit of doing between fights.

But Freddie had known for several years before his knockout at the Manhattan Athletic Club he'd be unable to turn his back on the ring for good. Even though he hated the training and was sustaining ever more serious injures as his prowess as a fighter declined, boxing held an unending grip over him. He needed to keep the prizering in reach; initially to feel he was still part of it all but also as a psychological and financial safety net. Freddie equipped the farm as much for the needs of a professional boxer as a worn-out businessman, with two regular sized boxing rings, punch bags and exercise rooms.

On August 11th 1917, New York celebrities and dignitaries from all over New Jersey were invited to the opening. One of the guests, Bat Masterson, described the house as a "palatial home sitting high upon a hill, like an acropolis". But Freddie was presiding over the opening ceremony as the former title-holder. When he agreed to those last, fateful fights Freddie was aware of the risk he was taking and the damage that a defeat would have on his farm's prospects. "The public loves a winner, and it doesn't care anything for the man," said Freddie before the Leonard fight. "So long as he is a hero he can start any kind of business and succeed. But let him lose out and the people drop him like a hot cinder. That's why there's nothing in this thing people call fame. And that's why there is everything in having a woman who cares for you. Because you are always a hero with her, whether you win or lose." Had the event been the opening of the world champion's new health farm it would have been big news but now it barely warranted a mention in the major newspapers. The *New York Times* merely reported the occasion as confirmation of Freddie's retirement from the ring. "I have fought the good fight and have now come to the conclusion that I may sit down and enjoy the fruits of my labours," he told the paper's representative.

Freddie's idea was to tailor the Long Hill site to the needs of tired and jaded businessmen in need of rest and relaxation. His magic formula for the health of his distinguished clientele consisted of wholesome food, pure air and water and simple exercises, proportionately prescribed and personally supervised. He wanted to provide these ingredients in an atmosphere of refinement and culture. "You will be surprised how your appetite will return with the hunger of a prodigal son," said Freddie. "A course at my farm is just a playtime with nature; just a wholesome, healthful picnic that will send you back to your work with a joy that you have not felt for many a day and with hope and ambition for future years." In the summer of 1917, the newly renovated Long Hill mansion and the newly retired world champion were able to attract all the "men of refinement" they could cater for. Visitors spoke of the "innumerable automobiles of every make" parked at the back door of the house. They belonged to affluent men who came from as far as Florida to train and spar with the former champion, and to talk over the coming fights. It looked like Freddie had realized all his ambitions. He was the lord of his own manor; he had Fanny, the children, a mansion house, the business he'd always wanted and he was surrounded by the trophies that stood as testament to his status as one of the great boxers. At the height of his fighting career Freddie wrote that he worked zealously "that I and my own may live. The rush and the tread of crowds in the fight clubs; the roars of the throngs, I hope to exchange some day for the still trees darkening overhead; the sweet fern under foot, the white hill mists and the quiet sky where the wide, bright stars are strewn. I want a quiet space, where winter snows fall crisply on the sod, white and unspoiled, just as they came from God." Freddie's dream was so close but it shattered against reality. He found his quiet space, but as soon as he got it he longed for the rush and tread of the crowds once more. After just a few months of life up in the white hill mists Freddie was planning a comeback. "Freddie Welsh and his health farm have had a falling out," reported the *National Police Gazette,* "and the latest scandal in high pugilistic society is that the former champion has soured on the simple life, and wants to get back into the ring." Freddie had consistently written and talked of his utter weariness of the ring and the wild delight with which he would sink into leisured ease and mental toil when it was over. But teaching physical culture was not nearly so interesting or exiting as his old profession and the pitiful state of peers like Battling Nelson, Ad Wolgast and others could not deter him. Freddie's aspirations had been rehearsed, and his tragedy suffered, by generations of boxers before him. As the champion of the world he was, by definition, like no other. Now he had an everyday life Freddie longed to be back in the time of his great deeds. "The imagined cake has once more proved to be dry and stale bread," commented *Boxing,* "for Fred's memory of Leonard's promise to meet him again soon usurped the throne in his thoughts". Freddie's stated ambition was to meet the new champion in a twenty-round bout with the title at stake. "Leonard was always a good fighter, but he learned his boxing in the ring with me," Freddie tried to persuade an increasingly disinterested American press. He was already back in training and Harry Pollok was instructed to make the match as soon as possible. Promoters from two different cities in Connecticut as well as Cincinnati's Queen City Athletic Club expressed an interest in staging the rematch. There was also press speculation about an offer of $10,000 for a ten-round bout to be staged in Ohio. Immediately after the fight at the Manhattan Casino Leonard's manager, Billy Gibson, had promised the old champion a return bout before arranging any further fights for his charge. Harry Pollok reminded the new champion and his manager of their promise by writing to all the leading American newspapers:

> It is about time that Billy Gibson and Benny Leonard had something to say regarding their promise, given voluntarily, that Freddie Welsh should have the first 'championship' match with Leonard for the world's lightweight title. Welsh is champing on the bit for an opportunity to try to win back his old honours. He is confident that he can beat Leonard.
> Five months of country life worked wonders for Welsh. He looks wonderfully fit and says he feels completely recovered from the strains of the three years of hard and continuous fighting he went through after he beat Ritchie.
> Without wishing to interfere with Gibson's plans for Leonard, I think the time has come when he should 'say something.' What about it, Billy?
> Very truly
> Harry Pollok

The indefatigable Pollok made every effort to persuade Billy Gibson there was a "sure and certain prospect of a mammoth gate" for a twenty-round contest with the championship at issue. While his manager was hounding Benny Leonard, Freddie prepared to take a warm-up fight against a journeyman fighter called Jimmy Paul. The six-round bout was scheduled to be part of an all-star programme in New York, but Freddie could only appear with a bandaged hand standing next to the MC as an apology was made for the non-performance of the former champion. Freddie had boxed an exhibition as part of a soldier's benefit performance the previous week and broken his right hand once more. Just a few days earlier Benny Leonard had met with a similar misfortune, having broken a knuckle on the jaw of 'Toughey' Ramsey in Cleveland. With both men injured any prospect of a rematch had gone. In the time it took the broken bones to heal Billy Gibson and Benny Leonard drew up other plans involving younger fighters for bigger purses and Freddie was left to acclimatise to life without the world title. Freddie was now thirty-one-years old and nobody gave him a chance of beating the young new champion. Besides, the crowds that Freddie could attract to a bout had dwindled during the last year of his reign and there were more lucrative opponents for Leonard. Just a few months after the loss of his title Freddie had been consigned to the ranks of the 'old-time' fighter alongside Nelson and Wolgast. Reviving business-men in the New Jersey countryside couldn't replace the excitement of strolling down Broadway as the lightweight champion of the world. He also genuinely believed, like nearly every other deposed champion, that he was capable of regaining all that had been taken away from him. Freddie knew that his powers had waned but as Bert Sugar wrote of old fighters, "the fire that once burned in his soul is now but a dull ache, believing in the smithy of his heart that he has one 'good' fight left in him." The dull ache was certainly not soothed at Long Hill so Freddie looked towards the biggest fight of all – the Great War. He had thought to return to the United Kingdom and fight with the British army but Fanny persuaded him against it. So Freddie enlisted in the United States Army instead. The news of his decision was reported in *Boxing* on September 12th 1917:

Freddie flirted for a while with dreams of martial distinction, and even threatened to prance into our midst as a rough-riding colonel, but he has yielded, it is to be supposed, to the arguments or persuasions of Mrs Welsh and has decided he can serve humanity better by building up the potential fathers of the armies of the future than by exposure of his own person to the undiscriminating bludgeon-work of the Hun.

Freddie is prudent, and we thank him for being so; for although we cannot but doubt that his mental equipment would enviable him not only to shine in lethal war, but might also prove of considerable value to the Allied course, we could only consent, with serious shivers to the imperilling of such a precious life as his. Even if Fred were to ride forth as the greatest military leader in history, we yet have others, possibly less ingenious, but nevertheless, we venture to hope, sufficient for our needs; while it is very certain that, unless we can preserve the Welsh Wizard as a model for at least a generation to come, we shall have to regretfully consent to a sad decay in the science and exposition of defensive pugilism.

Domestic influences and arguments must have been the main factor, of course, for Freddie announced his intention of treading martial paths, and is the last man in the world to go back on a personal announcement – in spite of his susceptibility to pressure – and the pressure to which he would have to submit in his hesitation between

war and peace must have been severe enough to crush a mountain...
Who is there to blame him for remembering that he is the father of a
family when so many single young Britons have sought the safer path
of emigration – before the Conscription law came into force?

During most of his time in the United States Army, Freddie was
consigned to the Walter Reed Hospital in Washington DC where he
helped rehabilitate wounded soldiers. According to one military
report, "he seemed particularly adapted to that kind of work and the
hospital physicians often expressed astonishment at his accomplishments in getting the convalescents on their feet again after they had
been given up as hopeless cripples". In the US Army's monthly
personnel report for March 1919 there's a listing for 1st Lt SC
Thomas Fred H. that describes a professional athlete with "fair
military bearing". Later records report him as a good, hard, consci-
entious worker who did everything well and could be trusted. During
his time in Washington Freddie organized a series of boxing tournaments in which he trained the combatants and also acted as referee
for the bouts. Charles F. O'Connell, general secretary of the Knights
of Columbus committee on war activities in Washington was so
impressed by Freddie's efforts that he started a recruitment
campaign to enlist more boxers to help the Welshman in his work.
While he continued to impress his superiors with his skills as a physical training instructor Freddie was increasingly tormented, though
the war at least offered a temporary relief from a life outside the ring.
He found comfort in a strict daily regime far away from the constant
reminders of his shortcomings as a businessman. The health farm
had been open barely a year when Freddie decided he wanted out.
On October 18th 1918, he placed an advertisement in the *New York
Times* that read:

FOR SALE OR TO LET

Freddie Welsh Health Farm at SUMMIT. N.J.

Freddie Welsh, former lightweight champion, has enlisted in the army,
and will sacrifice at half price the Freddie Welsh Health Farm at
SUMMIT. N.J. about 20 miles from New York; excellent train service.
This is a home of rare beauty, which will make itself self-sustaining
from the land alone. This hilltop estate has 143 acres of productive
land, lawns and woods, which cost $120,000 at pre-war prices.
     Main house, farmer's cottage, barn, &c are surrounded by rolling
fields, orchards, Italian sunken rose gardens and 60 acres of woods.
House of two dozen rooms is beamed and panelled of the finest hard
wood.

Open and screened porches; $25,000 spent this year improving the estate. Hall, Library, billiard Room, dining Room, in and outdoor sleeping rooms, gymnasium, bathing department, concrete icehouse; latest improvement in plumbing, electric lights, telephone; special vapor and steam heat system; large open fireplaces in the living room; purest water, indoor and outdoor concrete spring-fed swimming pool. River flows around estate; fishing, shooting, golf in neighbourhood, ideal for gentleman's estate, country club or health farm. 59 minutes to New York. In and outdoor concrete handball, squash and tennis courts. House, cottage and farm suitably furnished and stocked with farm produce, implements, &c.

Can be bought at low price if taken at once. Twenty thousand dollars cash takes entire estate ready for occupancy; balance on mortgage to reliable party. Apply, ROBERT J. MURPHY, Opp. Station, Summit. N.J.

Freddie had invested $150,000 in the venture. To earn this money he'd trained or boxed nearly every day of his adult life, he'd taken tens of thousands of punches and spilt several pints of blood in the process. Now, just over twelve months later, he was ready to let it all go for just $20,000 – but there were no buyers even at this price. Freddie was in trouble. Throughout his boxing career, he had tried to cultivate an image that he was as shrewd outside the ropes as he was inside and that he could punch above his weight in the business world. Writing in the *All Sports Weekly* Chas Barnett wrote an article entitled 'The Pride of Wales – Freddie Welsh the brainiest Light-weight of his time'. According to Barnett no boxer had ever made such a business of the profession as Freddie who the writer called a "a veritable Minister of Finance". But Freddie's "great business acumen" was all part of the invention and by the time this article was published the health farm was on the verge of collapse and his money had gone.

Freddie dedicated his life to the pursuit of his dream and when it was all over and the grail lost, he found himself in a frightening and unfamiliar world. He had lived too long with a single dream; without it the meticulous creation that was Freddie Welsh disintegrated. When the Welshman was in his prime, Harry Carr of the *Los Angeles Times* wrote, "in the dreary waste of rough necks and low brows who inflict the life of a sporting writer, Freddie Welsh is the one real haven of rest and comfort." But when it was all over the man who Arthur Conan Doyle once described as "the Prestidigitator of Gloves" descended to a level that the majority in the ranks of the "dreary waste of rough necks and low brows" would not dare venture.

On the night of Saturday October 11th 1919, Freddie was dining alone at a restaurant on 50th Street and Broadway. He was the only diner in the restaurant until, by complete coincidence, Harry Pollok showed up. The chance meeting immediately descended into an orgy of gruesome brutality and unspeakable violence. Within minutes the restaurant floor was covered in broken glass, blood and human flesh. Freddie disappeared into the night while Pollok was rushed to the Polyclinic Hospital with half his right ear in an ice bucket. The talk in boxing circles was that the altercation was the result of a feud that dated back to the night Freddie lost his title to Benny Leonard and Pollok's betting the entire purse on his charge to win. After the alleged attack, Pollok swore out a warrant against Freddie and a few days later detectives Fitzgerald and Brady of the West 47th Street Station arrested the Welshman upon complaint that the former champion had bitten his old manager's right ear in half. He was charged on a count of creating mayhem and was arraigned before Magistrate Alexander Brough in the Westside Court the following morning. Freddie's attorney, John C. Dyer, told the court that on the Saturday night in question it was Pollok who followed Freddie into the restaurant and persisted in annoying him. After repeated attempts by the boxer to get his former manager to leave him alone, Freddie admitted to hitting Pollok and that he fell on a broken bottle that cut off his ear. When Freddie asked the judge if he looked like a man who would eat another man's ear the judge replied: "No, you do not. I hold you in $1,000 bail," which, according to one writer in the courtroom, "indicated that the judge does not entirely go on looks". The complainant was unable to attend the proceedings owing to the fact that he was still at the hospital recovering from the lacerated ear. The *Newark Evening News* reporter, one of the few journalists who'd showed in the courtroom, wrote:

> After two years of canned billie, Captain Freddie Welsh of the army was entitled to a bit of desert, and to slip the 'cap' a check for $1,000 for a short order of ear seems to be in the light of treating a soldier rough. Of course the law says an ear for an ear, which is probably why Magistrate Brough in the West Side court of New York asked the captain to separate himself from $1,000 until the alienation of Harry Pollok's ear can be further investigated.
>
> The captain with the alleged cannibalistic tendencies has the most remarkable set of ears outside of those in the Museum of Natural History, and Kid Board's famous ear-ring rocks, and they were remodelled often and not artistically during the long years he worked for Pollok. As the diner and the man who furnished the meal both refuse to divulge what aroused the captain's unexpected depravity of appetite, it is taken that the cap was jealous of the contour and graceful curves of the coral pink Pollok apparatus of audition.

Freddie was back in court a week later. A police officer told the presiding magistrate that Pollok had failed to appear to press the charge for the third time so the judge told Freddie that he had no option but to discharge him. Freddie, in full military uniform, thanked the judge and asserted that Pollok's charge was unfounded. He also said he was through with the fighting game forever. In the New York Municipal Archives, docket number 5990 shows that on October 21st 1919, the case against Freddie was dismissed. After the deterioration of his relationship with Freddie, Harry Pollok moved out to California where he set up wrestling and boxing shows at the Olympic Auditorium in Los Angeles. He later moved to San Diego to promote professional football on the Pacific Coast. On the morning of December 17th 1933, police were called to his home in an exclusive residential district of the city. When they got there they found Pollok's body lying in the driveway with a bullet wound in his head. He had shot himself.

"Biting is a tactic of the overmatched," Jim Murray of the *Los Angles Times* wrote after witnessing the fight between Mike Tyson and Evander Holyfield. "Defeated partisans think up horror weapons. That's what Tyson did. He burst his moorings and began to assault the world in the ring." By the winter of 1919 Freddie Welsh was a defeated partisan. The battles he faced outside the ring were tougher than those he'd faced inside and Freddie had been overmatched for the first time in his life. He was losing control and his life was falling apart. While Freddie was fading from the memories of boxing writers and spectators, the sport was about to enter a period of unprecedented popularity. The key event was the implementation of the Walker Law in New York that essentially legalized boxing in the state. On September 17th 1920 a crowd of 12,000 gathered at Madison Square Garden to watch an old opponent of Freddie's, Johnny Dundee, box Joe Welling in a fifteen-round match. It was the first decision fight in New York in twenty years. Under the promoter Tex Rickard, Madison Square Garden became the focal point of world boxing and the New York State Athletic Commission became, effectively, the sport's governing body. It established and stabilized eight weight classes, and introduced the 10-point system for winning a round instead of the British system of the round's winner getting 5 points, the loser getting 4¾ or 4½. The Commission also implemented the three-judge system, to at least make bribery more difficult. Judges were instructed to sit on different sides of the ring, in order to see the fight from different viewpoints and to prevent a judge who might have been bribed from influencing the others. When Freddie started boxing a fight crowd was typically made up of rowdy blue collar workers in the gallery with the politicians, gangsters, businessmen and 'blue bloods' at ringside. Since his defeat to Leonard boxing had become respectable and the big fights became a place for the 'middle classes' to be seen. Freddie had lost the title just as the golden age of boxing was about to begin. The sport's new found glamour and wealth were too much for him to resist and Freddie became part of the most dependable tale in sport, the old champion making a comeback.

Freddie knew that such ventures were nearly always an attempt by the fighter to contradict a once accepted belief that he was past it. Retirement from the ring and a respite from the Spartan demands of making weight usually ushered in a prolonged bout of easy living, leaving an old boxer less able to fight than the day he retired. But Freddie believed he was different for two reasons. Firstly, he had never put his gloves away. He had spent nearly all his time since the defeat by Leonard on his health farm or at the Walter Reed Hospital. Freddie prescribed boxing for his 'patients', and as he was directing the work he indulged in the sparring on a daily basis. Most fighters having declared themselves through with the game never wanted to see a gymnasium again. But the gym was Freddie's business and the smell of leather, sweat and liniment never left his nostrils. In the three years since he last fought, Freddie hadn't gained a pound in weight and was able to make the lightweight limit with little difficulty. His second reason for believing that he could defy precedent and launch a successful comeback was the manner of his defeat and the calibre of the man who perpetrated the beating. When Freddie lost to Benny Leonard he knew that he'd lost to a great fighter. This was borne out by the new champion's performances since winning the title. Freddie mistakenly believed that he could have gone on and held his own with all the other leading lightweights. But back in 1917 he didn't need the money and with his title gone there was no point fighting on. By the summer of 1920 things were very different.

When his time at the Walter Reed Hospital was over he had no choice but to return to Long Hill. A few jaded businessmen turned up, largely to say that they sparred with a former world champion and one or two novices or old-timers arrived to prepare for an undercard fight somewhere. The rather bleak atmosphere at Freddie's health farm after the war was captured in *Fifty Grand*, Ernest Hemingway's short story based on the welterweight championship bout at the New York Hippodrome on June 26th, 1922. In the thirteenth round of the fight, Benny Leonard, who'd taken the lightweight title from Freddie, deliberately fouled Jack Britton, which gave Jack the fight on a foul. Hemingway's story doubled the double-cross. His character, Jack Brennan had bet $50,000 on his opponent to win. When Brennan was fouled late in the fight, just as Britton had been, Jack knew he had to stay on his feet or he'd 'win' the fight. Through the pain Brennan remained upright long enough to foul his opponent in turn, lose the fight and collect his fifty grand. By the time he takes the fight Brennan is pretty much finished as he goes to Danny Hogan's health farm "up in the hills" in Jersey. Hogan is an old champion who spends most of his time in the barn sparring with a few customers. "They neither one wanted to hit the other, for fear the other would come back and hit him," wrote Hemingway. Danny Hogan, like Freddie Welsh, was a retired fighter playing host to fighters who should have retired. Danny also followed the horses "pretty close". Like many other boxers of his era, Freddie placed big bets on his own fights and he also had a reputation of having more than a passing interest in horseracing. Once the fighting was over his bets got bigger and his horses got slower and Freddie eventually made it onto a list published in the *National Police Gazette* of "noted gambling champions". The health farm and the horses had relieved Freddie of everything he'd earned into the ring and he took the same path as countless other 'hard luck story' fighters and donned the gloves once more.

Joe Louis once said: "They say money talks, but the only thing it ever said to me was 'Goodbye'." Freddie had said farewell to everything he earned through boxing. Reports from Florida in early 1920 claimed the Governor of the Bahamas had given permission for a boxing contest to be held there for the lightweight championship of the world between Freddie and Benny Leonard, who was still champion. During the height of a hot New Jersey summer, Freddie got back to the serious task of preparing himself to fight for a living once more. He started slowly; taking long walks around the Summit hills under the July sun. The autumnal air signalled a return to the gym and hours of hardening his stomach muscles and as the winter chill started to bite, Freddie was boxing five rounds a day with two local boys, Al Thomas and Bennie Cohen. It took six months of training until Freddie was finally ready to return to competitive boxing. His comeback fight was on December 28th 1920 at the Colliseum in Newark, New Jersey. It was the first time he'd ever fought in his adopted state. Freddie's opponent was Willie 'Kid' Green of Boston who was certainly not a kid any more. Green was a veteran New England journeyman and was nothing more than a 'trial horse' for the old champion.

Freddie had many of his friends at ringside and even his old adversary and former world champion Battling Nelson made the journey from New York. When Freddie stepped through the ropes for the first time in three and a half years, he was in much better shape than anyone had dared expect. But while he may have looked like he did when he was in his prime, he certainly didn't fight like he used to. From the opening bell, Freddie discarded the defensive, scientific style that had won him the title, and instead he planted the feet that once danced around the ring firmly on the canvas and launched a series of heavy blows at his opponent. The old champion had become an old brawler. But he was good enough to beat Kid Green. By the end of the fourth round Green's eyes watered and he walked back to his corner almost bent double after a series of unanswered punches to the ribs and stomach. He stayed in his corner. Green called over referee Hymie Kugel complaining of a severe pain in his right arm. Freddie sat in his corner as the doctor examined his opponent. A few minutes later the referee announced that Green had not suffered a dislocation or break but might have sustained a muscle strain, and the fight was over.

Later in the evening Freddie told reporters the bout was just a forerunner to a series of contests he had arranged that would eventually end in a return match with Benny Leonard. His immediate plan was to rest over the Christmas period and to resume training on New Year's Day. But Freddie didn't tell the journalists the real reason for his short festive break from training. The morning after his win over Green, Freddie was back at the farm and ready to welcome the most famous sportsman in the world to his home for a three-week stay. Jack Dempsey was the heavyweight champion of the world, and he'd just completed a two-month tour on the West Coast vaudeville circuit. Apparently exhausted by his exploits on the stage, Jack went to his old friend Freddie's place for some rest. Dempsey's arrival in the small New Jersey town befitted his celebrity status. According to the *Newark Evening News*, he "blew into the Welsh household yesterday afternoon, carrying trunks and grips numerous enough to belong to an entire carnival company". Along with Dempsey's luggage came a little monkey that had been presented to the champion by a New York friend, and while the animal was a great hit with Elizabeth and Freddie Jr, it was far from being welcomed by Fanny. In two hours it destroyed curtains, portieres and picture frames, and as a result spent the night in the gymnasium, and not in bed with Dempsey, as Jack had planned.

Dempsey's visit was the first of several he made to Long Hill in the build up to the 'Battle of the Century', his heavyweight championship fight with Georges Carpentier in July 1921 that was boxing's first million dollar gate. The fight, staged at Boyle's Thirty Acres in Jersey City was an extravaganza which was credited with introducing sport as leisure for the masses at the beginning of the 1920s. The sheer scale of the event was largely down to Dempsey's manager Jack Kearns and the ingenuity of the planning and scheming it took to generate such interest in the match was satirised by Ring Lardner's *The Battle Of The Century* which was first published in the *Saturday Evening Post* on October 29th 1921. Lardner knew Kearns, Dempsey, and, of course Freddie, very well. He also knew the whole enterprise was something of a sham.

Jack Dempsey had become world champion on beating Jess Willard on July 4th 1919. Although there was a great deal of money to be made in boxing in the early 1920s Dempsey was struggling to attract the big purses because the heavyweight division was devoid of credible challengers. Jack Kearns decided to "build something up" to capitalize on the heavyweight title: a contest in which there was at least the perception that the title could change hands. Dempsey was not a popular champion at the time and Kearns knew the public would pay to see him beaten. His idea was to have "some young fella spring up from nowheres and knock out five or six of these 'contenders' for a gool; then we'll have to stall a w'ile and pretend like we're scared of him till we've got the bugs thinking that maybe he has a look in." The young fella chosen by Kearns was Georges Carpentier. The Frenchman was a handsome war hero who was also the champion of Europe. Kearns' task was to convince "some guy with money and a lot of nerve" to back a contest between Dempsey and Carpentier. It took him over a year, but finally Kearns managed to raise a million dollars for a fight he knew his man couldn't lose. As part of the build-up to the big event Carpentier and his manager, Francois Deschamps, were invited to a lunch hosted by the International Sporting Club at the Waldorf Astoria in New York. Freddie was among the guests who listened to the Frenchman announce that he was ready to face Dempsey at any time and also that he would prepare for an upcoming fight with Battling Levinsky at the Long Hill camp.

Dempsey was a much bigger man than Carpentier and Kearns needed to keep his man interested and motivated for a fight for which he would normally have prepared for in a week. Kearns needed to make Dempsey's training camp accessible to the press to show that his man was working hard and it wasn't a farce. So Jack Dempsey was sent to Summit and to Freddie's farm to begin his 'preparations' for the big contest. Kearns knew his charge would be bored and restless with such an extended training programme so he asked Ring Lardner to visit. In *The Battle Of The Century* Lardner writes that Larry Moon, the character he bases on Kearns, tells him that his fighter needed someone to talk to and play rummy with. "It's going to be a lonesome time for him and I don't know if he can stand it or not," said Moon. "But he likes you and having you there once in a while would be a help."

Before arriving in New Jersey, Dempsey had finished two months on the Pantages vaudeville circuit, travelling continually and generally sleeping on the trains. He weighed 202 pounds on reaching Freddie's farm and hoped to gain more poundage before moving on to Atlantic City to complete his training a few weeks before the fight. During his stay at Long Hill Dempsey did little but walk along the country roads, play some golf and loll about in the open air. The champion's visits to Freddie's farm were more to do with public relations than serious training. "It's a safe bet that Dempsey hasn't made any enemies by his affability, which is characteristic also of his host, Freddie Welsh," wrote one visiting reporter. Dempsey certainly wasn't undertaking any strenuous training at Long Hill and the only physical work he undertook that wasn't for the benefit of the photographers was to help Freddie around the estate. One local newspaper reported: "All the times he's performing little helpful stunts about the household, rolling the approaches to the house, cutting the grass or giving a farmhand assistance at odd jobs." The fight with Carpentier was the social as well as sporting event of 1921, and Freddie's two children appeared in photographs in every newspaper in the United States, playing with the heavyweight champion on the long sloping lawns in front of the farmhouse. Freddie's name was being mentioned in boxing circles for the first time in a long while and the publicity even sparked talk of a rematch with Benny Leonard. On April 26th 1921 Wild Bill Lyons, a close friend of both Freddie and Dempsey, announced in New York that the Welshman would finally get his return match with the champion, over four years since the title changed hands. According to Lyons the bout was to be staged at Tex Rickard's Jersey City Arena on July 1st as part of the Dempsey – Carpentier event. The story was 'placed' to generate an appetite for another Welsh – Leonard match but few people regarded Freddie as anything other then a has-been.

On the day before he was due to leave Freddie's farm, Dempsey refereed the main contest at a series of bouts staged by the American Legion at the Elks' Home in Summit. The top-of-the-bill fighter was Freddie, appearing in only his second bout in nearly four years, against Young Willie Jackson of Trenton. 'Young' Willie wasn't much younger than Freddie's previous opponent 'Kid' Green. The old champion outpointed Jackson easily, knocking him down twice in the fifth round. Dempsey showed up like a regular referee in shirtsleeves and he got a bigger ovation than any of the fighters on the bill, Freddie included. The heavyweight champion was due in Atlantic City the following day and a reception had been arranged for Dempsey at the city's Alamac Hotel. All the invited dignitaries had arrived and waited patiently and hungrily for Dempsey to show. Their wait was over when the mayor received a telegram that read: "Missed train", signed Jack Dempsey. The champion had stayed on in New Jersey to referee Freddie's second contest in as many nights. The fight was staged in nearby Morristown and the Welshman's opponent was local fighter Kid Murphy. It was scheduled for ten rounds but a flurry of body shots from the former champion prompted Murphy's seconds to throw in the towel in the second round.

Freddie's brief return to prominence ended with Dempsey's departure and the boxing writers followed the heavyweight champion to Atlantic City. A slow trickle of fighters arrived at Long Hill in Dempsey's wake. Bob Martin, a former soldier-boxer asked Freddie for help and he brought with him sparring partners like Gunboat Smith, Mexican Joe Lawson and a novice fighter called Pete Latzo. But the farm was in a sorry state once more and Freddie looked around for more fights to keep the business afloat. He called on a few old friends in Canada to fix him up with a bout or two. His campaign started in Calgary, where he won every round of a contest against the Canadian Bert Forbes. General Haig sat at ringside as Freddie's guest. Freddie then moved on to Winnipeg to fight the Canadian lightweight champion, Clonnie Tait. The two fought ten rounds to a draw in a bout that was advertised as being for the championship of the British Empire. It was a poor fight with neither man landing any effective punches. Freddie was finding it difficult to get a decent fight in the United States before this performance and the reports that filtered back of his Canadian contests did not help. It took Freddie eight months to convince an American promoter that he still had one good fight left in him. The Rink Sporting Club in Brooklyn decided to take a chance on the old champion and on April 15th 1922, Freddie was matched with Archie Walker, a local favourite. It was the first time Freddie had fought in New York for five years. Much had changed in the meantime and the New York boxing public had had plenty of time to forget him. He created some interest in his return by sparring with Rocky Kansas, as part of the latter's preparation for an unsuccessful challenge to Leonard. Freddie had also impressed reporters at his training camp sufficiently to start another raft of stories about a possible title challenge of his own. In the past a match between Freddie and Leonard would have broken all records for gate receipts for a lightweight fight, but now Freddie had to re-establish himself as a credible opponent for a champion who'd beaten all-comers since relieving the Welshman of his title. In the build-up to the fight, the *Newark Evening News* reported:

> If he wins this bout Welsh will continue to compete. He'll probably win. At any rate there's no good reason for having wasted so much valuable time since surrendering the lightweight championship to Benny Leonard. This is one of the few championship bouts in which the unseated monarch neither clamoured for nor received a return bout. Five years ago it was that Welsh lost to Leonard, just about the time that pretty nearly everybody who wasn't in the service began making more money than he knew what to do with.

But any aspirations Freddie had of fighting Leonard, or anybody else for that matter, disappeared soon after the opening bell of his fight with Walker. Freddie lost seven of the ten rounds and by the end of the tenth he was being chased around the ring, desperately covering up. Freddie was a pitiful shadow of the fighter he once was. As the bell sounded for the end of the contest, a weary old man plodded back to his corner, his eyes staring down at the canvas, his days of glory gone forever. The defeat was too much for Freddie to bear and he never stepped into a professional ring again.

Seventeen

His Dream Must Have Been So Close

The years between 1919 and 1927 were the Golden Age of Boxing. It began when Jack Dempsey beat Jess Willard for the heavyweight championship after which the Manassa Mauler became the most famous athlete in the world. Dempsey's victory also heralded the arrival of sport as big business in a prosperous post-war United States. Just over 20,000 people showed up to watch Dempsey win the title on July 4th 1919. Less than eight years later he drew a crowd of 120,000 for his first bout with Gene Tunney; the largest crowd to attend a fight to this day. But this was just a few years too late for Freddie, who watched from the sidelines as his friend became one of America's four great sports celebrities in the twenties with Knute Rockne, Red Grange and Babe Ruth. This was the dawn of the celebrity era and sports heroes were among the first to be idolized. The adulation and riches now heaped on leading boxers proved too much for Freddie to resist. Even though his last fight had ended in an abject defeat, he convinced himself that he still had a good fight left in him.

Early in 1923 Freddie desperately wanted to go back to how things used to be. He wanted to return to boxing and return to Wales. He spoke of how he'd been smitten with a desire to step between the ropes once more and that he intended to test his ability against the "comparatively inferior boxers of Europe" before undertaking matches with the "leaders in America's lightweight ranks". Freddie's plan was to travel with another boxer long since passed his best fighting days. Jack Sharkey, the veteran West Side Italian bantamweight was also looking for a series of matches against European fighters. Sharkey, who gave world flyweight champion Jimmy Wilde his first contest in America, hired Freddie as his manager in the belief that the former champion could find him profitable fights in Britain. The two boxers, along with Freddie's brother Stanley and the promoter Humbert J. Fugazy sailed from New York on the SS *Baltic* and arrived in Liverpool on Monday February 26th 1923. Just a few years previously Freddie would have been welcomed home by tens of thousands of people as befitting a national hero. This time there was nobody to greet him and his return was reported in terms that his particular American dream was over. "We regret to have to report that Fred Welsh's health home venture has proved a failure and Freddie, ex-lightweight champion of the world is on his way back home to England," reported *Boxing* on February 21st, adding that "America can no longer provide him with a living".

Almost as soon as he stepped off the boat Freddie said he would like a match with anyone in England at his weight, which was about 9st 4lbs, if a "suitable inducement" was forthcoming. "Welsh must be classed with the has beens since he reached his 37th birthday on Monday of last week," commented *Boxing World*, adding that "although the lightweights here do not rank as highly as Freddie did when he was at his best, several of them might prove too good for him today." Freddie stayed in Britain for nearly two months but found that just like in America, the patrons of the ring were no longer interested. He spent much of his time in Wales, visiting relatives in Merthyr and refereeing local boxing tournaments in the area. He went to see a fight at the National Sporting Club in London and met up with Jimmy Wilde, and then promptly disappeared. His departure from Britain was even more low-key than his arrival and no-one outside his immediate circle of friends knew he'd left. Under the title, 'The Mystery Of Fred Welsh', one English boxing publication commented that it had been left with an "ungratified yearning for knowledge" as to the real object of Freddie's visit. "If it was too soon to be done for, what was it begun for?" it asked. The answer was that Freddie was unhappy that the promoters were not interested in him anymore and he'd also fallen out with Jack Sharkey who'd returned to America even sooner than the Welshman.

In December 1923, Freddie was given the job of training some of the leading boxers and wrestlers in the United States Navy for their annual championships. It was quite an event; previously the finals of the Navy's tournament had been confined to rings pitched on the decks of American dreadnoughts. But in 1923 the competition was being held just before Christmas at Madison Square Garden. Freddie supervised the training of the Brooklyn and Philadelphia delegations and he took them to Summit for a week before the finals. From early morning to nightfall Freddie put the sailors through a punishing regime, with time-out for eating and sleeping only. It was a job the old champion relished. Freddie pulled the gloves back on to demonstrate some of the finer points of ringcraft. Indeed, Freddie thought his students were the finest group of physical specimens he'd worked with since going into the conditioning business. "They are trained to the minute," he announced proudly. "It is a pleasure to work with these boys after mingling with the professional boxers. They take such a keen interest in their preparation."

A truly distinguished gathering turned up to watch the tournament at the Garden. Prominent New York businessmen, city officials and dignitaries joined high-ranking Navy and Army officers including Colonel Theodore Roosevelt. Freddie was back in front of a large crowd once again. Not only did he train many of the fighters, he was asked to referee the flyweight and bantamweight fights. It was a good Christmas for Freddie with his farm busier than it had been for many years and there was particular interest in the arrival of one ambitious young fighter from Macon, Georgia. William Lawrence 'Young' Stribling was a prodigious nineteen-year-old boxer written up as the best fighter from the southern states for many a day. Young Stribling was preparing for his first big fight in the east against the experienced Brooklyn middleweight Dave Rosenberg. Thirteen years earlier the Stribling family performed as an acrobatic troupe as part of a vaude-ville review touring in Altoona, Pennsylvania. During their stay they spent every afternoon watching Freddie train for a fight. The Striblings had to leave Altoona for another engagement and missed the bout but the whole family, including six-year-old William Lawrence, were great admirers of Freddie Welsh from that time on. Within minutes of arriving at Freddie's farm the old champion and the young pretender donned the gloves for a few rounds so that the new guest could limber-up after a long and tedious train ride. Accompanying Young Stribling on his journey were Ma and Pa Stribling along with the even younger Herbert Stribling, the sixteen-year-old veteran of twenty professional bouts. Pa Stribling was quick to rather undiplomatically inform reporters that Herbert was a better prospect than his older brother. Not that either of the fighting Stribling siblings were that interested in boxing that afternoon. It had been a white Christmas in Summit and the morning of the family's arrival heralded a fresh fall of snow. The brothers had seen very little snow in the Deep South and they persuaded Fanny to take them into Summit to buy a sled. On the way back to the farm they pleaded with her to hitch the sled onto the back of the car and were towed along for several miles until they hit a dirt road and the snow turned to mud.

The Striblings may have been avid disciples of Freddie's methods in the ring, but they certainly didn't follow his ideas in the culinary department. Ma Stribling took complete charge of the Welsh kitchen during the family's stay at the mansion. "I spend all my time in the kitchen," she told reporters. "The most important thing for an athlete is proper nourishment, and I won't trust anybody else to prepare my boy's food. He is not a heavy eater though. Really, he is more like a girl than a boy in his tastes, being fond of salads and fresh fruit next to ice cream." When reporters asked Young Stribling what his favourite sport was, he answered, "eating ice cream". Freddie, the great nutritionalist, just looked on. Representatives of the National Sportsmen's Club, which was staging Stribling's bout with Rosenberg, had been invited to the farm to look over the fighter before the contest. They were suitably impressed, as was Freddie. A battery of photographers had been sent to the farm along with a moving picture cameraman whose footage was shown in the local theatre to whip up ticket sales for the fight. Even though he was only nineteen Stribling was quite a celebrity and not since Freddie had moved into the Long Hill mansion had the place housed so many visitors. Over a hundred, the majority of whom had travelled up from Newark, were turned away after Freddie had been compelled to put up the 'no more room' sign at three o'clock one afternoon.

The most famous resident of Long Hill in December 1923 was undoubtedly Jack Dempsey. The heavyweight champion left his quarters in New York for a long stay at Freddie's farm. Dempsey had arrived in the city in early December, his first visit since beating Luis Firpo at the Polo Grounds a few months previously. He'd been on a tour through Las Vegas, Salt Lake City, Chicago and St Louis, culminating in a series of Christmas benefit exhibitions in New York. The heavyweight champion now wanted to escape the noise and strife of the city. Since beating Willard for the title Dempsey had preferred a life of semi-seclusion in the country and his manager Jack Kearns said that future developments would determine the length of Dempsey's stay at the farm. These future developments were more to do with vaudeville than the ring. According to Dempsey biographer, Roger Kahn, the heavyweight champion was lured to the farm by the promise of cheap booze because Freddie home-brewed "excellent cider and beer". During the days of bathtub gin and Prohibition a regular supply of alcohol was one of the farm's main attractions. Hemingway was aware of the illicit drinking that occurred at Long Hill when he wrote *Fifty Grand*, his short story set on an old champion's health farm. Danny Hogan, the fictional proprietor, supplies quarts of liquor to help a restless boxer sleep.

Dempsey's regular visits to Long Hill also kept Freddie in contact with many of the sportswriters he'd befriended when he was world champion. The Golden Age of boxing in the twenties was also a golden age of boxing writers, and it can be argued that the age might not have seemed so golden if such men had not been around to record the exploits of Dempsey and his contemporaries. One of the most successful was Ring Lardner who enjoyed both critical acclaim and widespread popularity. Lardner had been a great admirer of

Freddie's boxing and he regularly defended him in the face of scathing criticism from the vast majority of American boxing writers. Lardner also featured Freddie in his short stories, most famously in *Champion*, which in 1949 was made into a film starring Kirk Douglas. The story's central character, Midge Kelly, is an ambitious young fighter who believes he can beat anybody. After one contest the matchmaker tells Kelly: "You looked all right. But you aren't Freddie Welsh yet by a considerable margin." To which the fighter replies, "I ain't scared of Freddie Welsh or none of 'em."

In 1923 Ring Lardner was assigned to cover two fights involving the 'Wild Bull of the Pampas', the Argentine heavyweight Luis Firpo. The first bout was in June against Jess Willard and the second took place in September against Dempsey. Lardner's summer in the training camps of the world's leading heavyweight boxers coincided with his intense friendship with F. Scott Fitzgerald, the most famous chronicler of 1920s America and the man who dubbed the era 'the Jazz Age'. Early in October 1922 Scott and Zelda Fitzgerald rented a house at 6 Gateway Drive on Great Neck Estates, Long Island. Great Neck was only half an hour from Broadway by the Long Island Express and the area was populated by actors, writers and theatre producers with whom the Fitzgeralds embarked on a dissolute period of partying and socializing. Some of Great Neck's famous residents included Lillian Russell, Samuel Goldwyn, Oscar Hammerstein and P.G. Wodehouse, another of Long Island's celebrity boxing aficionados. He had been an enthusiastic schoolboy boxer and was often seen at the big fights in New York. Like Lardner, Wodehouse made reference to Freddie in his work. In *Keeping It From Harold*, a young boy tells how one of his friends has "a snapshot of Freddy Welsh. At least, he says it's Freddy Welsh, but I believe it's just some ordinary fellow. Anyhow, it's jolly blurred, so it might be anyone."

Despite their glittering and glamorous neighbours and the many parties, Scott and Zelda Fitzgerald's only real friends in Great Neck were Ring Lardner and his wife, Ellis Abbott. Lardner and Fitzgerald frequently talked the night away over a case of Canadian ale, but the friendship was not just about drinking and they had an enormous impact on each other's careers. When Fitzgerald admired a writer he had a habit of bringing them to his publisher Charles Scribner's & Sons. Ring Lardner was probably America's most widely read humourist at the time through his columns and stories in newspapers and magazines and Fitzgerald persuaded Scribner's to publish a volume of his friend's work under the title *How to Write Short Stories*.

In return Lardner taught Fitzgerald about sports and its mass consumption and engendered in the novelist a fascination with physical competition and the athlete. It was a critical phase in Fitzgerald's career, when the young writer was assembling the components for one of the landmarks of American literature. Fitzgerald began to think about his third novel in the summer of 1922. He worked on it for the next two years but was generally dissatisfied with the result. By April 1924, as his time in Great Neck was coming to an end, he had reconceived the novel. He wrote to Maxwell Perkins, his editor at Scribner's that his new work would draw on "the substantial imagination of a sincere and yet radiant world".

According to his biographer Andrew Turnbull, during the year Fitzgerald spent formulating his ideas for a novel that would eventually become *The Great Gatsby*, Lardner was "the supreme influence" in Scott's life. He convinced Fitzgerald that sport, especially boxing, illustrated the patterns in people's lives; the rhythms, victories and defeats. In his work *Sport And The Spirit Of Play In Contemporary American Fiction*, Christian Messenger argues that it was authors such as "Ring Lardner and Fitzgerald who proved that modern American society may be imaginatively conceived and explained through its games and players". One such player was Lardner's old acquaintance, Freddie Welsh. Freddie's relative, the author Alun Richards, wrote in his memoir *Days of Absence*, of how the old champion sparred with F. Scott Fitzgerald in his gymnasium. According to Richards, Fitzgerald was "proud to have boxed three rounds with Freddie". It's unlikely the novelist's boxing skills were greatly improved in the encounter but it seems that his time in a Summit ring with the former world lightweight champion was quite inspiring for Fitzgerald. Those three short rounds of boxing may have been a significant step towards the creation of Jay Gatsby, the eponymous 'hero' of one of the great novels of the twentieth century. Fitzgerald found a man who was, as is written in the conclusion of *The Great Gatsby*, "borne back ceaselessly into the past". As a young man Frederick Hall Thomas, like James Gatz, undertook a regimen of fanatical self-improvement through physical exercise and study. He changed his name just before the first bell sounded for his first fight just as James Gatz of North Dakota became Jay Gatsby "at the specific moment that witnessed the beginning of his career". Jay Gatsby and Freddie Welsh assembled themselves "with care". Gatz and Thomas created Gatsby and Welsh respectively as men of both physical and intellectual prowess. Fitzgerald based the novel's 'Owl Eyes' on Lardner, the character who discovers that Gatsby's Gothic library is stocked not with the fake,

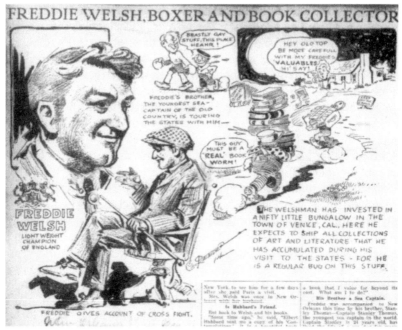

Cartoon above an article headed 'English Champion Buys Home Just to Keep His Books' (*New Orleans Item*, 25 May 1914).

cardboard backs of books, but with the works themselves. He knows that Gatsby has never read the books because the pages have never been cut. One of the central parts of the creation that was Freddie Welsh was the enormous library the fighter transported around with him in trunks to be reassembled wherever he was training for a fight. "This fella's a regular Belasco," Owl Eyes tells Nick and Jordan. "It's a triumph... Knew when to stop, too... didn't cut the pages." David Belasco, the great playwright-producer-director, was a frequent dining companion of Freddie's when he fought in San Francisco and when he later moved to an off-Broadway apartment.

Freddie was also an ardent believer in the rugged individualism espoused by Fitzgerald's creation. The biggest influence in shaping his beliefs was Elbert Hubbard and many of the ideas Freddie held about religion and morality stemmed from his time at East Aurora. Freddie was a regular subject of articles in Hubbard's controversial but successful publication, *The Philistine*.

Freddie found in Hubbard a teacher who confirmed the merits of much that he already believed in, such as the importance of physical fitness and unashamed ambition, and who set out these values as a religion he could believe in. Hubbard's then scandalous personal 'Credo' became an important element in the construct that was 'Freddie Welsh':

I believe in the Motherhood of God.

I believe in the Blessed Trinity of Father, Mother and Child.

I believe that God is here, and that we are as near Him now as ever we shall be.

I do not believe He started this world-a going and went away and left it to run by itself.

I believe in the sacredness of the human body, this transient dwelling place of a living soul,

And so I deem it the duty of every man and every woman to keep his or her body beautiful through right thinking and right living.

I believe that the love of man for woman, and the love of woman for man is holy;

And that this love in all its promptings is as much an emanation of the Divine Spirit as man's love for God, or the most daring hazards of the human mind.

I believe in salvation through economic, social, and spiritual freedom.

I believe John Ruskin, William Morris, Henry Thoreau, Walt Whitman, and Leo Tolstoy to be Prophets of God, who should rank in mental reach and spiritual insight with Elijah, Hosea, Ezekiel, and Isaiah.

I believe that men are inspired to-day as much as ever men were.

I believe we are now living in Eternity as much as ever we shall.

I believe that the best way to prepare for a Future Life is to be kind, live one day at a time, and do the work you can do best, doing it as well as you can.

I believe we should remember the Week-day, to keep it holy.

I believe there is no devil but fear.

I believe that no one can harm you but yourself.

I believe in my own divinity - and yours.

I believe that we are all sons of God, and it doth not yet appear what we shall be.

I believe the only way we can reach the Kingdom of Heaven is to have the Kingdom of Heaven in our hearts.

I believe in every man minding his own business.

I believe in sunshine, fresh air, friendship, calm sleep, beautiful thoughts.

I believe in the paradox of success through failure.

I believe in the purifying process of sorrow, and I believe that death is a manifestation of life.

I believe the Universe is planned for good.

The Great Gatsby is, however, a tale about its hero's ultimately tragic pursuit of his dream and the moral failure of a society obsessed with fame and wealth. One of the novel's central themes, like much of Fitzgerald's other work, is that the American Dream is not an index of aspiration but a function of depravation. These were dishonest times during which a corrupt core ran through what seemed on the surface to be glorious successes. Gatsby's greatness is brought into question by the company he keeps. One of his acquaintances is Meyer Wolfsheim, a character modelled on the real-life figure of Arnold Rothstein, the man who helped fix the 1919 World Series. It shows how far removed Gatsby is from the idyllic world he seeks. Much of his wealth has been made in tandem with the man who turned America's national pastime into a joke. For many years after Freddie's victory over Willie Ritchie in London rumours circulated that the fight had been fixed. The story had such credibility that no American boxer defended a world title in the United Kingdom for nearly thirteen years after that night at the Olympia Theatre in July 1914. The reason the rumour had currency was that Arnold Rothstein was one of the men who put up the massive guarantee to secure the fight. Every leading boxer at this time needed connections with a shady underworld and Freddie certainly 'enjoyed' the friendship of some the most infamous gangsters and racketeers of the day. It was a world in which the American Dream, that romantic notion of a noble quest for the boundless possibilities of life, had withered and died.

Freddie moved from Wales to the United States as a seventeen-year-old and dedicated his life to the pursuit of a single dream; to become lightweight champion of the world. But just like Gatsby, Freddie paid a high price for living too long with a single dream. When he lost the championship, just like the hero of the novel, he became a "Mr. Nobody from Nowhere". Freddie discovered that his adopted home had largely forgotten him and that he'd left his real home too far behind. "He had his critics and his enemies, and nowhere were these so harsh or so fierce as in these Islands," commented one English boxing writer, "for if ever there was living proof of the old proverb that 'no prophet is without, etc' Fred Welsh was that man." The point in the novel that precipitates Jay Gatsby's demise may be the biggest clue as to just how much of a source of inspiration Freddie was for Fitzgerald's creation. The pivotal episode in the story is a motoring accident in which a woman is killed by a car in which Gatsby is riding. At about eight o'clock at night on Saturday October 11th 1924, Freddie was driving his car down the wrong side of Park Street in Summit when he collided with a car at the corner of

Springfield Avenue. Meanwhile in Saint-Raphael on the French Riviera, Fitzgerald was under pressure to keep his promise to deliver the novel to his publisher. On October 27th Fitzgerald dispatched the first draft of *The Great Gatsby* to the office of Scribner's in New York. The proofs name the woman hit by Jay Gatsby's car as Myrtle Wilson. The only person hurt in the accident involving Freddie's car was called Myrtle Wilson.

By the time *The Great Gatsby* was published in April 1925, Freddie was once again teaching enthusiastic amateurs how to throw a left jab. One such guest was Dr Carl Reiland, Rector of St George's Episcopal Church of New York. Dr Reiland was well-known as one of the leaders of the Modernist movement within the church but he agreed to abide by Freddie's strict rule that religion was a taboo subject on the farm. After a strenuous day of exercising and running, Dr Reiland had to content himself with discussions on 'public affairs' with his host and the other guests. By this time Freddie was no longer invited to the big fights in New York and within a few months he sought escape from his dream once more. Just as he had done when he first became disenchanted with the life of a health farm proprietor back in 1918, Freddie found solace in the army. He signed up for a spell in the training camp at the Plattsburg Barracks in upstate New York. Officially known as the Business Men's Camp, it was branded early and irrevocably by the press as the 'Tired Businessmen's Camp'. The objective of these camps was to improve the calibre of the trained military reserve of the United States. Major General Robert Lee Bullard issued Captain Fred H. Thomas 'orders to duty' as a boxing instructor. Freddie held daily classes and organized championships in ten weight divisions. As soon as he was back in uniform Freddie placed a small advertisement in the classified section of the *New York Times* offering reduced rates of "$40 up" for summer borders to stay at the Fred Welsh Health Farm. The advertisement announced that new management had taken over in the absence of Captain Freddie Welsh who had been called up for active service. Fanny and the children moved out to Long Island while Freddie was stationed at Plattsburg and with no takers for the farm, the former world champion turned to his friends and neighbours to keep his business afloat.

Sidky Bey and his wife Hranoush, known to all as Madame Bey, became close friends with Freddie and Fanny after they moved into a thirty acre estate at 516 River Road in Chatham Township, about a mile from the Long Hill mansion. Hranoush Agaganian was born in Turkey in 1881 to French and Armenian parents. She was sent to the

American College in Constantinople where she met her future husband Mehmed Sidky. When Sidky was offered the position of Secretary of the Imperial Ottoman Embassy in Washington DC they left for America together, where they later married and settled into the life of a diplomat's family. Hranoush became well-known in the Capital and she developed a friendship with President and Mrs William McKinley. She was a trained opera singer and the McKinleys asked her to sing 'The Star Spangled Banner' at the opening ceremony of the Pan-American Exposition in Buffalo, New York on September 5th 1901. She was standing just yards away from President McKinley when he was shot by an assassin's bullet that afternoon. Sidky Bey resigned from the diplomatic service after Turkey entered the First World War on the side of Germany and he and his wife became American citizens. They moved to New York and set up a successful business importing oriental rugs. As the business grew the Beys moved out to New Jersey but heavy fighting between Russia and Turkey resulted in a lost rug shipment worth $200,000. It put them out of business. Their salvation came one afternoon in a telephone call from their neighbour. Freddie told them he was being commissioned as a captain in the United States Army and that Fanny, Elizabeth and Freddie Jr were moving to Long Island while he was in the service. He asked the Beys to move into his mansion and run the health farm while he was away. Freddie wanted no money from the Beys; all they had to do was look after his home while he was in the army. When Freddie's telephone call came in the Beys were entertaining another close friend, the boxing writer Willie Ratner. "I says 'Do it, take it over'," Ratner recalled saying. "You'll get a million dollars worth of publicity as the first and only woman in the country with a training camp." The journalist advised the Beys to accept only if Freddie would permit them to take in fighters instead of restricting the farm to business and professional men as the Welshman had done. Sidky said no but his wife said yes and she got her way. They moved from their home to Freddie's Long Hill mansion and Madame took over the business.

Madame Bey transformed the fortunes of the farm in a very short period of time. Boxing was booming again in New York and prize-fighters flocked to Madame Bey's to train for upcoming fights. Freddie's hunch that such an enterprise could work was correct; he simply didn't have the skills to make it happen. During his brief period in charge Freddie spent most of his time sparring in the gymnasium whereas Madame Bey knew how to run a business. She ruled with a firm, motherly hand, forbade 'guests' and alcohol and was never afraid to reprimand any of "her boys". She never saw any of them fight because it would pain her to watch them getting hurt. Madame Bey saved Long Hill from bankruptcy and it looked as though Freddie would have a going concern to which to return when his time in the army was over. But her tenure at the farm and her relationship with Freddie ended very acrimoniously over the arrival of a black boxer at the training camp. Battling Siki was a Senegalese light-heavyweight with a reputation to rival Jack Johnson's. He was often seen walking around Paris with a white lady on his arm and a tiger on a leash. "He was a wild guy, not a bad guy but wild," recalled Ratner. Freddie read about Siki's arrival in a newspaper and he called Madame Bey from the Plattsburg to say that the new guest was a "bad element" who would ruin his reputation. He issued an ultimatum to Madame Bey demanding that Siki be told to leave or she should vacate the farm. Madame quickly conferred with several of her regular clients such as middleweight champ Johnny Wilson, light-heavyweight title-holder Paul Berlenbach and bantamweight champion Joe Lynch. They all pledged to support Madame Bey if she set up her own training camp and they even lent the Beys the money to build a new a gymnasium and other training facilities. The Beys had kept their own house on the other side of the hill so they returned to 516 River Road. Training was suspended for the day and a troupe of champion boxers marched into Summit to buy timber, bricks and building supplies. Johnny Wilson's manager, Jim Buckley, was a former carpenter and with the help of the fighters he transformed the garage into a gymnasium in one night. Willie Ratner believed that Freddie was less upset about Siki's presence at his farm than he was about the fact that Madame Bey was clearly succeeding where he'd clearly failed. Many years later Madame Bey recalled Freddie fondly, as a man who enjoyed having a good time but who was a terrible businessman. With Madame Bey and her fighters gone and Freddie still in the army, Long Hill fell into disrepair. Its very size made it imperative that a capable executive be at hand to keep it flourishing and Freddie realized that the task was beyond him.

Over the next few years Freddie struggled on at the health farm but by now his own health was beginning to fail. He was diagnosed with 'athlete's heart', a common term for an enlarged heart caused by repeated exercise. Freddie's years of strenuous training had increased the workload required of his heart causing the chambers to become enlarged and the muscle mass to increase. When Freddie first noticed palpitations he was put in the care of Dr Cavello at the Overlook Hospital in New Jersey. The condition was not pathological and there was generally no problem with any cardiac disability arising from athlete's heart. But if the condition itself wasn't inherently dangerous Freddie was certainly risking further damage to his heart by the way his alcohol consumption increased dramatically. During his fighting career Freddie had always been careful to present an image of being a teetotaler. This wasn't entirely true as his four-day drinking binge after winning the world title testified, but compared to the dissolute lifestyles of many of the old-time fighters Freddie was a very moderate drinker when he was boxing. When his ring career was over, however, Freddie increasingly turned to alcohol to fill the void. He became an expert brewer and developed a taste for his own produce. The promoter Humbert Fugazy tried to help Freddie reverse his failing fortunes by setting up the former champion as a manager. Fugazy had handled a promising young lightweight, Jimmy Goodrich, and now turned over his protégé to Freddie. But the man who managed himself to a world title found his methods were too idiosyncratic to be applied to anyone other than himself and his attempts at guiding others to success in the ring failed miserably.

As Freddie's health began to deteriorate his public appearances grew more infrequent. He was seen at the quayside in New York in July 1925 welcoming back Jack Dempsey from a trip to England, but for the most part his only other appearances in print during this time followed various court appearances. As he became increasingly desperate for money, Freddie sued his old friend Jack Sharkey for a couple of hundred dollars. The former bantamweight champion had trained at Freddie's farm before his title fight with Johnny Buff four years earlier and according to Freddie's attorney, Leon E. Cone of Morristown, Sharkey left with $225.27 of his bill unpaid. On September 23rd 1925 Freddie was embroiled in another legal battle; only this time the future of Long Hill was at stake. The farm was sold in a foreclosure proceeding for a mortgage of $15,237. But under the headline, FREDDY WELSH SAVES HEALTH FARM IN HURRY, the *New York Times* reported that Freddie had been away and had forgotten that the mortgage was due. When he was notified of the proceedings he hurried to Chatham and retrieved his property. Freddie told the reporter, "like a lot of men in my profession, I can condition men and restore health, but I can't remember the details of business. I went away two weeks ago and forgot all about the mortgage and left no instructions about it." Freddie told the reporter at the Hotel Astor in New York where he was staying at the time that he had received word it was sold and he "hustled out" to clear things up. "The farm is a great place, though there are so many healthy folks nowadays and golf has made such inroads that we health farmers have to keep on our toes," said Freddie. "Anyway, the farm won't close. But it certainly was in danger for a time." The desperate state of his finances mirrored the desperate state of his physical and mental well-being.

Freddie was back in court on February 26th 1926 when he appeared in front of Judge W.F. Mountain in the Circuit Court, Newark, on a charge of reckless driving. Myrtle Wilson and her father Williams Wilson of 462 Valley Road in West Orange, New Jersey, were suing him for damages after the motoring accident. Miss Wilson told the court she was travelling with seven other people in a sedan along Springfield Avenue in Summit. Freddie was driving his car south along Park Street and according to Miss Wilson he was on the wrong side of the street when he collided with the vehicle she was in at the junction. She showed the court a permanent scar on her forehead, apparently caused when she hit the windshield in the accident. Myrtle Wilson's suit of $20,000 was for compensation for her injuries and permanent disfigurement, while her father's claim of $1,000 was for loss of earnings during the time needed for his daughter's recuperation. Freddie sat alertly by his counsel throughout the first day's proceedings during which a number of witnesses testified for the plaintiffs. Freddie took the stand the following Monday. On March 21st the jury awarded Miss Wilson $300 for her injuries, and her father, William, $100 for his inconvenience. The following day's edition of the *Newark Evening News* reported that "the former lightweight champion of the world, lost a decision yesterday, but it was not in the ring".

Freddie's slide towards ill-health and depression temporarily abated in the summer of 1926 with the arrival of a world champion at Long Hill. Back in the spring of 1921 a young fighter arrived at Summit railway station with a small kit bag and the reputation of being the brother of a pretty good fighter. There was nobody to meet Pete Latzo, so he walked the four miles to Long Hill in search of the former lightweight champion of the world. Latzo stayed several months at the farm learning what he could from Freddie and also having the chance to spar with Jack Dempsey. When his time came to leave, Freddie bid the young fighter farewell with a wise word. "Pete, my boy, you're going out to fight in the battle rings of the world. My advice to you is to pitch your aspirations high and always pin your chin low on your chest. Stand on your own two feet and good luck to you." Five years later Pete Latzo returned to Long Hill mansion but he didn't walk from the railway station this time. He arrived in a brand new car, with a new bride of a few months and the world welterweight championship belt in the trunk. Latzo repaid his debt to Freddie by coming to Long Hill to prepare for his first defence of the title against Willie Harmon. Apart from Latzo's trainer Al Thoma, Freddie was the only one who thought the young fighter would ever amount to anything. Freddie publicly predicted that Latzo would go on to be a great fighter and according to the *Newark Evening News* "the greeting he received from Welsh would have led one to believe that Latzo had brought back to Freddie his old championship; that's how pleased the former world lightweight king was to see Pete". When reporters found out there was a world champion in town, Latzo told them of the debt he owed Freddie Welsh:

> You can tell the world I am glad to be back at my old pal's home. It was here I got my start, and I owe a great deal to Welsh, both as a friend and as a teacher. Welsh stood by me when I could not get a match, and he boosted and boosted me. I will always train here when possible. Welsh always was and always will be my friend and adviser.

But by the winter of 1926 it was Freddie who was in critical need of good friends and advisors as he was in danger of losing his property once more. Freddie was unable to make the necessary payments and George T. Browne, a Florida-based real estate operator who held the mortgage, instituted foreclosure proceedings at the Chancery court. The foreclosure was actually signed but Freddie persuaded Vice Chancellor Backes to re-open the case and he was given thirty days to redeem his property. Freddie won his reprieve after he explained that the subpoenas foreclosing the mortgage were served on a "Negro servant", the lone occupant of the place while he was away training as an officer in the army reserve corps. He told Vice Chancellor Backes that he intended to pay off the mortgage by selling part of the estate. Freddie failed to raise the money but was given a succession of new deadlines. Now desperate, he spent Christmas 1926 in a frenzied search for financial backing. Even his championship belt was pawned for $100. The only thing that he would never consider selling was the property in Long Island which had remained in Fanny's name and which Freddie vowed not to sell however dire his financial position became. The estate at 220th Street, Bayside was eventually sold by Fanny in November 1932 to the Skillman Building Corporation who built nine houses on the land.

He was in the Chancery court again on March 2nd 1927 and once more his solicitor, Mr Greene, managed to secure a thirty-day stay of execution. Greene told the court that his client had obtained a loan of

$45,000 but the lender had withdrawn "because of litigation". Freddie then persuaded a local man, William C. Armstrong of Chatham, to advance the money. But before the transaction was completed Armstrong was killed in a motoring accident. This was enough to persuade the judge to give Freddie yet another thirty days to find the funds. When the case was resumed on April 1st Freddie said that he'd turned down offers of $35,000 and $50,000 for his farm because they were from persons "seeking to take advantage of his predicament". The judge was also told how heavy snowfall had prevented potential investors from visiting Long Hill. His solicitor eventually secured yet another respite for Freddie by announcing that Mr Albert Birkenmeier and a syndicate of Newark businessmen had stepped into the breach to loan the money to cover the mortgage. He managed to get the sale set aside by the Chancery Court and was given until April 29th to repurchase the farm for $32,500. It seemed that this time Freddie had finally managed to save Long Hill. The local *Chatham Press* reported "the long fight between Freddie Welsh and Adversity, with the former's health farm at Chatham Township as the prize, seems about to be won by Welsh". But it was not to be. There was a hitch in the negotiations and the farm was lost forever. Long Hill was sold to satisfy a mortgage of $30,000 even though it was valued at $150,000. The money went directly to Freddie's creditors. Freddie filed a suit for $150,000 in the Supreme Court in Newark against the nine men he charged with failing to fulfil a promise to back him in retrieving his health farm. They were Albert G. Birkenmeier, Harry Sellner Jr, Harry and Fred Herpers, Ernest Minier, Rutland Lee, Benjamin Oppenheim, Charles Baker and Ottamar Venino. According to Freddie these men had entered into an agreement to advance him $45,000 to redeem the farm. With Long Hill mansion lost, Freddie and Fanny, who'd been married for over twenty years, separated. Freddie took a cheap room in New York at 333 West 35th Street and Fanny took a live-in job as housekeeper at the St Paul Hotel at 60th Street, the same hotel where she and Freddie had lived in a suite of apartments in the heady days of the world title. The strain of losing his business and his wife was too great for Freddie to bear. It took a toll on his health and he complained of severe chest pains. In the spring of 1927 he was put under the care of Dr Bagley who reported that Freddie was down and drinking heavily.

In early June Freddie left his room on West 35th Street for an equally cheap one in the Hotel Sidney at 59 West 65th Street. From his small window Freddie could just catch a glimpse of Broadway, the street once described by the famous boxing writer A.J. Liebling as being "fraught with temptations for fighters to spend money". Freddie could certainly testify to this. But he hadn't moved there for a view of his old stomping ground. Hotel Sidney was in the vicinity of the St Paul Hotel where Fanny worked, and he was hoping for a reconciliation. It was the worst possible place for an old boxer with a weakness for backing slow horses to be staying. Hotel Sidney was a gambling den and in December it was raided by the police and by agents of the Society for the Suppression of Vice. The raid created considerable excitement as the officers hurried to a second floor room where they found seven well-dressed men at work on green-covered tables aided by adding machines and gambling slips. There were several five-gallon cans of whiskey in the room. One of the men arrested was Benjamin Dworett, the proprietor of Hotel Sidney. They were running a 'policy game'; a lottery in which players bet on a series of three numbers from 0 to 999. The object was to 'predict' the last three digits of a pre-selected index in the following day's newspaper. This could be the New York Stock Exchange total, the United States' Treasury Balance or the total bets taken at a given racetrack. The policy game seldom favoured the players and the results were often fixed. 'Numbers runners' collected the money for bets daily giving each punter a receipt from what was called the 'policy book'. The cash and policy book were then returned to the clearing-house, also known as a 'policy bank'. The Hotel Sidney was one such policy bank.

Freddie was keeping dangerous company during the long, hot summer of 1927. It had been a bleak, cold spring in the city but the seasons finally changed on June 9th when the mercury suddenly hit 81 degrees. For weeks afterwards New York baked under a deadly sun. Every day the newspapers carried lists of deaths and prostrations. Those who could make it out of the city did. The so-called heat refugees made for the coast: to Rockways, Coney Island, Staten Island and the seashore resorts of New Jersey. Freddie's only sanctuary from the sunshine was a series of illicit drinking dens. After one neighbourhood speakeasy tour he got embroiled in a street brawl and it was clear that he certainly wasn't the fighter he once was. It was only the intervention of a policeman that saved the former world champion from a battering. On the morning of July 17th 1927 Freddie appeared in front of Magistrate Francis X. McQuade at the West Side Court in New York City. He was a sorry sight. Long gone were the days of the immaculately dressed world boxing champion. Freddie was a mess and sporting a blackened right eye as he faced a charge of disorderly conduct. Patrolman George Meyers had been called to a fracas at Ninth Avenue and 44th Street at 2.30 am.

Freddie was arrested along with his opponent, Edward Delaney of 410 West 50th Street. As soon as the patrolman got him back to the station, an ambulance surgeon from nearby Bellevue hospital was called to examine Freddie and patch up a deep gash above his eye. The old champion, prompted by professional pride and unwillingness to admit Delaney had inflicted the injuries single-handed, insisted a gang beat him up. The two protagonists spent the night in separate cells at the station house before appearing in front of the magistrate later that morning. Freddie gave his real name, Frederick Hall Thomas, to the court, and sadly stated his business as that of boxing instructor. Patrolman Meyers assured Magistrate McQuade that it was just a friendly fight and the defendants were warned to "express their friendship in a different way" before the charges against them were dismissed. According to one reporter in the courtroom it was not the arrest that irked Freddie so much as the black eye he received. The truth is that the injury probably saved Freddie from a few more nights in a cell. The magistrate told the court he was being lenient since this was "probably the first time Freddie Welsh ever had a black eye". In his questioning of Freddie, Magistrate McQuade had asked, "This comes pretty late in life. What was the trouble?" Little did anyone in the courtroom realise just how late in life it was for Freddie Welsh. Freddie had sustained far greater injuries than he let on to the court. Those who visited him at his room in the Hotel Sidney later told how he was recovering from the effects of the beating he took at the hands of Delaney.

Just ten days later it was all over. At 1pm on the afternoon of July 28th the maid knocked on Freddie's hotel room door. There was no reply so she tried the handle and discovered that it was unlocked. She pushed the door open and found Freddie, dressed in a pair of pyjamas and a bathrobe, stretched face downward on the floor between a chair and a writing table. On the bed was an open copy of *Elbert Hubbard of East Aurora* by Felix Shay. The upward facing page carried just one sentence, "Get your happiness out of your work, or you will never know what happiness is." Freddie had died in the night. A life of action and adventure, adulation and acclaim ended in a low-rent New York hotel room. Freddie's old friend at the *Newark Evening News* wrote:

> That indefinable something lying within all men who become eminent in anything – the 'genius' which sometimes is madness – is only one element in what may be summed up in a 'successful career.' There must be something more to achieve the final success. One must hold as well as gain.

The particular failings that brought about Welsh's pitiable end are not essential to the general thesis. He simply was one of the great company of slippery-fingered. His heart was soft; so, to his sorrow, was his head. He owned a goldmine, but he did not know how to operate it as a businessman. Not the first Bonanza king, by any means, to end so.

Only those who stay up reach independent old age. The Freddie Welshes of the world never find out about that until they are among the downs.

A doctor was called and he opined that Freddie had suffered a heart attack. When Stanley was informed of his brother's death he insisted the Medical Examiner be instructed to perform an autopsy to determine the exact cause of death. Fanny objected and said that she was satisfied her husband had died a natural death. But Stanley got his way and accordingly case number 4158 in the office of the Chief Medical Examiner of the City of New York, Borough of Manhattan, is 'Fred Welsh, Occupation: Prizefighter'. The cause of death is given as "classic cardio-vascular disease". The report also drew attention to the beating Freddie received the previous week. As well as the black eye reported in the press Freddie had sustained a broken rib and had deep abrasions on the left side of his head and on his right leg. Arthur Mefford of the *New York Daily News* wrote:

> While heart disease was given by the medical examiner as the cause, old timers along the gay White Way shook their heads and muttered:
> "He died of a broken heart. Freddie Welsh has been dying on his feet for the last six months. Yes, sir! Dying on his feet because the friends he aided when he was rich wouldn't look at him when he became poor."

On October 13th 1927, three months after his death, Freddie's old health farm was destroyed by fire. Firefighters were summoned from New Providence and other surrounding towns in the early hours of the morning but their efforts were hampered by low water pressure and in less than an hour Long Hill was burned to the ground. "This is a valley of ashes," wrote Fitzgerald in *The Great Gatsby*, "a fantastic farm where ashes grow like wheat into ridges and hills and grotesque gardens." In the novel, to live and work in this valley is to be constantly reminded of the things that are possible to others but beyond your reach. It is a site in which happiness and inner peace are unattainable. Freddie had worked for his dream for over twenty years but when he finally got what he yearned for he found, just like Jay Gatsby, that it wasn't enough. Yet even as the end was near Freddie seemed content that at least he had the courage to fight for his dream, even if it was ultimately a futile quest:

> You see I have done a good deal of wondering and have turned my
> hands to a whole lot of trades. People – really interesting people – have
> come into my life and gone out of it. I have washed up dishes in eating
> houses, slung hash (been a waiter, that is) in restaurants, cleaned
> boots, jumped freight trains as a 'hobo', worked in engineering shops,
> been a salesman in an outfitting store, worked my passage on a cattle-
> boat (and that was really the stiffest and hardest job I ever had), and
> oh, I've done any number of other things. I don't regret any of them,
> and wouldn't mind having to live my life all over again, every minute
> of it.

Bibliography

To the boxing writers on the following publications, many thanks:

All Sports Weekly, Akron Journal, Akron Times, Allentown Chronicle & News, Allentown Evening Item, The Atlanta Constitution, Atlanta Georgian, The Atlanta Journal, Billings Daily Gazette, Birmingham Daily Post, Boston American, Boston Evening Record, Boston Evening Times, Boston Globe, Boston Herald, Boston Journal, Boston Poet, Boston Post, Boston Record, Boston Sun, Boston Traveller, Boxing, Boxing and Sporting Gazette, The Boxing Blade, Boxing News, Boxing Record, Boxing World, Bridgeport Evening Post, Bridgeport Telegram, Brooklyn Citizen, Brooklyn Eagle, Brooklyn News, Buffalo Commercial, Buffalo Courier, Buffalo Evening News, Buffalo Evening Times, Buffalo Enquirer, Buffalo Express, Butte Miner, Butte Post, Calgary Daily Herald, Canadian Courier, Chatham Press, Chicago American, Chicago Daily News, Chicago Daily Tribune, Chicago Bulletin, Chicago Evening American, Chicago Evening Post, Chicago Examiner, Chicago Herald, Chicago Journal, Chicago Post, Chicago Sunday Record-Herald, Chicago Tribune, Cincinnati Enquirer, Cincinnati Post, Cincinnati Times, Cleveland Leader, Cleveland News, Cleveland Plain Dealer, Colorado Springs Gazette, Colorado Springs Telegraph, Columbus Citizen, Columbus Dispatch, Cork Free Press, The Daily Chronicle, The Daily Mail, The Daily Express, The Daily Mirror, The Daily News and Leader, The Daily Sketch, The Daily Star, The Daily Telegraph, Denver Daily News, Denver Post, Denver Republican, Denver Times, Detroit Free Press, Detroit News, Edmonton Bulletin, Edmonton Journal, Edmonton Daily Capital, The Evening Express, The Evening Wisconsin, The Evening World, Fort Wayne Daily News, Fort Wayne Gazette, Fort Wayne Sentinel, Glamorgan Free Press, Grand Rapids Herald, Grand Rapids News, Grand Rapids Press, Grand Rapids Times, Hamilton Spectator, Harrisburg Patriot, Health And Strength, Hearst's Sunday American, Hudson Observer, The Illustrated Police Budget, John Bull's Magazine, Kansas City Journal, Kansas City Post, Kansas City Star, Liverpool Express, Lloyd's Weekly News, London Evening News, London Morning Advertiser, London Morning Leader, The London Star, The London Sun, Los Angeles Evening Journal, Los Angeles Examiner, Los Angeles Herald, Los Angeles News, Los Angeles Pink, Los Angeles Record, Los Angeles Telegraph, Los Angeles Times, Los Angeles Tribune, Louisville Times, Mail Pouch Tobacco Co News Service, Manchester Daily Dispatch, Manitoba Free Press, Memphis Commercial Appeal, Memphis News Sentinel, Memphis Press, Merthyr Express And Advertiser, Merthyr Guardian And Dowlais Advertiser, Milwaukee Evening Wisconsin, Milwaukee Free Press, Milwaukee Free Sentinel, Milwaukee News, Minneapolis Journal, Minneapolis Tribune, Mirror Of Life, Montreal Daily Herald, Montreal Daily Star, Montreal Daily Telegraph, Montreal Evening News, Montreal Gazette, Montreal Standard, Moose Jaw Evening News, Moose Jaw Times, The Morning Post, The National Police Gazette, New Haven Evening Register, New Orleans American, New Orleans Daily States, New Orleans Democrat , New Orleans Item, New Orleans Picayune, New Orleans Star, New Orleans States, New Orleans Times, New York American, New York Daily News, New York Evening Herald, New York Evening Mail, New York Evening News, New York Evening Post, New York Evening Telegram, New York Evening Telegraph, New York Evening World, New York Globe, New York Herald Tribune, New York Journal, New York Morning Sun, New York Post, New York

Times, Newark Evening News, News Of The World, Oakland Enquirer, Oakland Tribune, Ohio State Journal, Oregon Journal, Pall Mall Gazette, Passaic Daily News, The People, Philadelphia American, Philadelphia Bulletin, Philadelphia Evening Star, Philadelphia Evening Times, Philadelphia Inquirer, Philadelphia Ledger, Philadelphia North American, Philadelphia Press, Philadelphia Public Ledger, Philadelphia Record, Philadelphia Telegraph, Pontypridd Observer, Porthcawl News, Portland Oregonian, Quebec Chronicle, Quebec Telegraph, The Referee, The Ring, Rocky Mountain News, Salt Lake Telegram, Salt Lake Tribune, San Diego Sun, San Diego Tribune, San Francisco Bulletin, San Francisco Call, San Francisco Chronicle, San Francisco Evening Post, San Francisco Examiner, St. Louis Globe & Democrat, St. Louis Post & Dispatch, St. Louis Republic, St. Louis Star, St. Louis Times, St. Paul Dispatch, St. Paul News, St. Paul Pioneer Press, St. Paul Times, Seattle Daily News, Seattle Post Intelligencer, Seattle Sunday Times, Sheffield Daily Telegraph, South Wales Daily News, South Wales Daily Post, South Wales Echo, South Wales Football Echo, South Wales Football Express, The Sporting Budget, The Sporting Chronicle, The Sporting Life, The Sporting World, The Sportsman, The Strand Magazine, The Summit Herald, The Summit Record, The Sunday Sun, The Sunday World, Syracuse Herald, Syracuse Journal, Syracuse Post Standard News, The Times, The Times Democrat, Toledo Daily Blade, Toledo News, Toledo Times, Toronto Daily News, Toronto Daily Star, Toronto Evening Telegram, Toronto United Empire, Toronto World , Vancouver Daily Province, Vancouver News Advertiser, Vancouver Province, Vancouver Sun, Vancouver World, Venice Vanguard, Washington Post, The Weekly Dispatch, The Western Mail, Winnipeg Tribunal, Winnipeg Free Press, Winnipeg Late Post, Winnipeg Saturday Post, Winnipeg Telegram, Winnipeg Tribunal, The World Magazine, Yonkers Herald.

Balch, David Arnold: *Elbert Hubbard, Genius of Roycroft* (Stokes, 1940)

Bettinson, Arthur Frederick: *The Home Of Boxing* (Odhams Press,1922)

Corri, Eugene: *Gloves And The Man* (Hutchinson, 1927)

Corri, Eugene: *Fifty Years In The Ring* (Hutchinson, 1933)

Dartnell, Fred: *Second's Out* (T. Werner Caurie, 1924)

Dempsey, Jack: *Dempsey* (Harper Collins, 1977)

Dempsey, Jack: *Round By Round* (McGraw Hill, 1940)

Elder, Donald: *Ring Lardner; A Biography* (Doubleday, 1956)

Erns, Robert: *Weakness Is A Crime: the life of Bernarr Macfadden* (Syracuse University Press, 1991)

Fitzgerald, F. Scott: *Afternoon Of An Author* (Princeton University Library, 1957)

Fitzgerald, F. Scott: *As Ever, letters between F. Scott Fitzgerald and his literary agent Harold Ober*, 1919-1940. (Edited by Matthew J. Bruccoli, with the assistance of Jennifer McCabe Atkinson. Lippincott, 1972)

Fitzgerald, F. Scott: *Conversations With F. Scott Fitzgerald* (edited by Matthew J. Bruccoli and Judith S. Baughman. University Press of Mississippi, 2004)

Fitzgerald, F. Scott: *Correspondence Of F. Scott Fitzgerald* (edited by Matthew J. Bruccoli and Margaret M. Duggan, with the assistance of Susan Walker. Random House, 1980)

Fitzgerald, F. Scott: *Dear Scott / Dear Max; the Fitzgerald-Perkins correspondence.* (Edited by John Kuehl and Jackson R. Bryer. Scribner, 1971)

Fitzgerald, F. Scott: *The Great Gatsby* (C. Scribner's sons, 1926)

Fitzgerald, F. Scott: *The Letters Of F. Scott Fitzgerald* (Edited by Andrew Turnbull. Scribner, 1963)

Fitzgerald, F. Scott: *The Notebooks Of F. Scott Fitzgerald* (Edited by Matthew J. Bruccoli. Harcourt Brace Jovanovich, 1978)

Fitzgerald, F. Scott: *Thoughtbook Of Francis Scott Key Fitzgerald* (Princeton University Library, 1965)

Fitzgerald, F. Scott: *Trimalchio: an early version of The Great Gatsby* (Edited by James L.W. West III. Cambridge University Press, 2000)

Fleischer, Nat: *Jack Dempsey* (Arlington House, 1972)

Geismar, Maxwell David: *Ring Lardner And The Portrait Of Folly* (Crowell, 1972)

Goldstein, Ruby: *Third Man In The Ring* (Funk & Wagnalls, 1959)

Hemingway, Ernest: *Men Without Women* (C. Scribner's sons, 1927)

Hunt, William R.: *Body Love: the amazing career of Bernarr Macfadden* (Bowling Green State University Popular Press, 1989)

Johnston, Alexander: *Ten – And Out! The story of the prize ring in America* (L. Washburn, 1943)

Kahn, Roger: *A Flame Of Pure Fire* (Harcourt Brace International, 1999)

Lardner, Ring: *First And Last* (C. Scribner's sons, 1934)

Lardner, Ring: *How To Write Short Stories* (C. Scribner's sons, 1924)

Lardner, Ring: *Letters From Ring* (edited by Clifford M. Caruthers, 1979)

Lardner, Ring: *Ring Around Max: the correspondence of Ring Lardner & Max Perkins* (Northern Illinois University Press, 1973)

Lardner, Ring: *Round Up, the stories of Ring Lardner* (The Literary Guild, 1929)

Lardner, Ring: *Some Champions: Sketches & Fiction* (edited by Matthew J. Bruccoli & Richard Layman, 1976)

Lardner Jr., Ring: *The Lardners: my family remembered* (Harper & Row, 1976)

Macfadden, Mary Williamson: *Dumbbells And Carrot Strips: the story of Bernarr Macfadden* (Holt, 1953)

Messenger, Christian K.: *Sport And The Spirit Of Play In Contemporary American Fiction* (Columbia University Press, 1990)

O'Brien, Philadelphia Jack: *Boxing* (C. Scribner's sons, 1928)

O' Connor, Richard: *Hell's Kitchen; the roaring days of New York's wild West Side* (Lippincott, 1993)

Rice, Harold: *Within The Ropes; champions in action* (Stephen-Paul, 1946)

Richards, Alun: *Days of Absence* (Michael Joseph, 1986)

Roberts, Randy: *Jack Dempsey, The Manassa Mauler* (Louisiana State University Press, 1979)

Shay, Felix: *Elbert Hubbard Of East Aurora* (W.H. Wise & co, 1926)

Spivey, Donald: *Sport In America: new historical perspectives* (Greenwood, 1985)

Suster, Gerald: *Lightning Strikes: Lives and Times of Boxing's Lightweight Champions* (Robson Books, 1998)

Turnbull, Andrew: *Scott Fitzgerald* (Scribner, 1962)

Turpin, Guy: *Forgotten Men Of The Prizering, a reference book of old time boxers* (Naylor Co, 1963)

Wignall, Trevor: *The Sweet Science* (Chapman and Hall, 1926)

Wignall, Trevor: *The Story Of Boxing* (Hutchinson & Co, 1923)

Yardley, Jonathan: *Ring: A Biography Of Ring Lardner* (Random House, 1977)

Index